Tunneling to the Future

Peter Derrick

Tunneling to the Future

The Story of the Great Subway Expansion That Saved New York

New York University Press • New York and London

NEW YORK UNIVERSITY PRESS
New York and London

Dr. Gary Hermalyn, Project Editor

First published in paperback in 2002.

Library of Congress Cataloging-in-Publication Data
Derrick, Peter, 1944–
Tunneling to the future : the story of the great subway expansion that saved New York / Peter Derrick.
p. cm.
"History of New York City Project"—T.p. verso.
Includes bibliographical references (p.) and index.
ISBN 0-8147-1910-4 (cloth : acid-free paper)
ISBN 0-8147-1954-6 (pbk. : acid-free paper)
1. Subways—New York (State)—New York—History. I. History of New York City Project. II. Title.
HE4491.N7 D47 2001
388.4'28'097471—dc21 00-012174

New York University Press books are printed on acid-free paper, and their binding materials are chosen for strength and durability.

Manufactured in the United States of America
10 9 8 7 6 5 4 3 2 1

To the people who made this book possible: Edward and Margie Derrick, Bayrd Still, Gary Hermalyn, and Janice Molnar

Contents

List of Maps and Tables ix

Acknowledgments xi

Introduction 1

1 Never Enough: The Beginnings of Rapid Transit in New York 9
2 The Deadlock over More Subways, 1902–1909 47
3 Rapid Transit to Save New York 90
4 Stumbling toward a Solution 123
5 The Dual System of Rapid Transit 153
6 The Battle over Financing the Dual System 186
7 Impact of the Dual System 231

Conclusion 263

Appendix 1: Summary of the Dual System Contracts and Related Certificates 269

Appendix 2: Opening Dates of the Dual System Lines 284

Notes 287

Bibliography 401

Index 423

About the Author 442

Illustrations appear as a group following p. 154.

Maps and Tables

Maps

1. New York City's Rapid Transit Network in 1910 31
2. The Proposed Triborough System 66
3. Proposed Expansion of the IRT System, March and July 1910 128
4. Proposed Expansion of the IRT System, December 1910 144
5. Proposed Expansion of the BRT System, March 1911 162
6a. The Dual System of Rapid Transit, IRT Lines 175
6b. The Dual System of Rapid Transit, BRT Lines 176
6c. The Dual System of Rapid Transit, All Lines 177

Tables

1. Population of Greater New York by Borough, 1790–1997 10
2. Annual Rapid Transit Ridership, 1901–1998 44
3. Population Change in New York City by Districts, 1910 and 1940 247

Acknowledgments

Many people provided help and advice during the preparation of this book. The support of the staff of The Bronx County Historical Society was superb. The executive director of the Society, Dr. Gary Hermalyn, encouraged this book from the beginning and was steadfast throughout all its permutations. Librarian Laura Tosi and curator Kathleen A. McAuley provided research assistance. I would like to thank Ivette Arroyo, Madeline Cook, Jeffrey Davis, Daniel Eisenstein, Katherine Gleeson, Teresa Moran, Debra Nickolson, Catherine Pellicano, and Lorie Vitanza for their help and support.

Thanks also go to the staffs of the Bobst Library at New York University, the Avery and Butler libraries at Columbia University, the Seely G. Mudd Manuscript Library at Princeton University, the New York Public Library, the New York Municipal Reference Library, the New-York Historical Society Library, The Bronx County Historical Society Library, the New York Transit Museum Archives, and the Library of Congress.

Individuals who provided help and advice include Andy Bata, Juliette Bergman, Ray Bromley, Fredericka Cuenca, Ximena de la Barra, Beth Diefendorf, Larry Hirsch, the late Walter Green, Clifton Hood, Douglas Lazarus, Joseph Leiper, Robert A. Olmsted, Sue-Ann Pascucci, and John Tauranac. A special thank you goes to Tim Cooper, Proteus Design, who prepared the maps. While I was a graduate student at New York University, the late Professor Bayrd Still provided a model for scholarly research. He also spent hours of time on an earlier version of this work. I can still hear him insisting that historical writing must be clearly written and have a narrative flow.

My deepest gratitude goes to the individuals who read drafts of this book and made extensive comments and corrections: Gary Hermalyn, Rob Hess, Janice Molnar, Aleksandrs Rozens,

Emanuel Tobier, and D. Leslie Winter. The many hours put in by these stalwart readers not only resulted in a better product, but sustained me through many long nights. I am also especially grateful to Niko Pfund, former director and editor in chief of New York University Press, for his encouragement and insightful advice. Thanks also to editor David Updike and the staff of NYU Press, including Asha Curran, Despina Papazoglou Gimbel, Stacy Hague, and Rachel Weiss.

My family has always been a prime support. My parents, Edward and Margie Derrick, encouraged me during my research for this book. They now are deceased, but their spirits will always be with me. My sisters, Ann Martin, Irene Germain, and Liz Derrick, have always been a strength. My wife, Janice Molnar, has been a bedrock in making sure that this book was completed. All along the way, she gave her love and support without measure.

Thank you all for your assistance.

Tunneling to the Future

Introduction

In March 1913, the City of New York decided to build the largest subway system in the world. Called the Dual System of Rapid Transit, it was the largest single public works project in American history up to this time. Using both municipal funds and private funds from two transit companies, the project doubled the size of New York's subway network and tripled its capacity, at a cost of $366 million (in current dollars, about $22 billion).[1] The result was a publicly owned rapid transit system that was largely in operation by 1920.[2] The Dual System had a huge impact on the development of New York City, more than any other project ever built. As the new subway lines opened, millions of New Yorkers moved to new homes and apartments in the subway suburbs of the Bronx, Brooklyn, and Queens. At the same time, new underground tunnels in Midtown Manhattan helped lay the foundation for its growth as one of the largest business districts in the world.[3]

The Dual System saved New York from many of the problems caused by rapid urban growth. In 1898, the city took on its present boundaries, with Brooklyn, Queens, and Staten Island joining Manhattan and the Bronx to form what was called Greater New York. The newly expanded metropolis was booming, with its population growing by more than a million each decade. For

Manhattan alone, the population rose from 516,000 in 1850 to 1,441,000 in 1890 and 2,332,000 in 1910. For Greater New York as a whole, the population was 3,437,000 in 1900 and 4,767,000 in 1910. By 1910, the older parts of New York had become the most congested places in the world.[4] In the Wall Street district, many tall skyscrapers were crowded together, blocking out sunlight on the streets. Traffic could barely move on narrow streets that had once been cow paths.[5] On the new subway, opened in 1904, passengers were packed like sardines.

Much of the increase in residential population up to 1910 was in tenement-house districts, most of which had been built up along the elevated lines and the first subway. Such districts included Manhattan's Lower East Side, Hell's Kitchen on the West Side, East Harlem, the South Bronx, and Brooklyn's Williamsburg, Bushwick, and East New York.[6] In overcrowded working-class neighborhoods such as these, hundreds of thousands of people, many of them new immigrants from southern and eastern Europe, were jammed into a limited supply of tenement buildings.

Despite severe overcrowding in the older tenement neighborhoods, vast areas of Greater New York were still relatively undeveloped. They included the West, East, and North Bronx, all of southern Brooklyn, and most of Queens, as well as the distant borough of Staten Island. Together, they constituted more than three-quarters of the city's land area. These sparsely populated districts were beyond commuting distance from the center of employment in Manhattan. Until the Dual System plan was devised, no one had been able to figure out how to build enough new rapid transit lines to the outlying districts simultaneously, so that congested conditions would not repeat themselves again.[7] By 1910, the Greater City had a large rapid transit system serving the built-up areas, but the amount of land opened for development at any given time had never been enough to allow for the construction of decent, uncongested housing for working New Yorkers.[8]

As waves of immigrants continued to pour into New York, the result was "bestial overcrowding" in the tenement districts.[9] In 1903, the Tenement House Department reported that there were over 82,000 crowded tenement buildings in Greater New York.[10] In 1910, over two-thirds of the population lived in such tenements.[11] The Lower East Side had the highest population density in the world; its less than two square miles contained 592,541 inhabitants.[12] The congestion of population in the tenement districts was of great concern to New York's business leaders as well as to social reformers working in these neighborhoods. The new immigrants did not seem to be adapting well to life in America's largest and most crowded metropolis. Family life among the Jews, Italians, and other newly arrived groups was said to be breaking down because of the overcrowding. The average three-room apartment often had as many as ten people, including boarders. Juvenile crime was on the rise. There was also the ever present possibility of arson in the tenements, which were firetraps.[13] These problems, played up in newspaper and magazine articles, seemed to middle- and upper-class New Yorkers to be threatening the very social order.[14]

Even more disturbing, and more threatening, was the prevalence of disease in the slums. By the turn of the century, better-off residents were well aware of how diseases spread. The poor sanitation in tenement apartments and the streets and alleyways of the immigrant districts was linked to high rates of tuberculosis, known then as the "Captain of Death" and the "Great White Plague."[15] Among other diseases found among the new immigrant population were cholera, typhus, and typhoid fever. Conditions in the tenement areas, one commentator noted, "might well earn for New York City the title of the City of Living Death."[16] The threat of infectious diseases, which could easily spread to the general population, heightened the unease of many New Yorkers with the new immigrants and led them to seek solutions to the problem of the overcrowded conditions in the slums.

From the 1880s on, many efforts had been made by settlement house workers and reformers to improve living conditions in the tenement districts. By 1910, however, conditions had not improved. Many believed that traditional relief efforts, such as housing reform, child labor reform, and settlement houses, would be of little help unless the density of population in slum areas was reduced.[17] As a result, the focus of reform efforts changed from trying to alleviate conditions within the tenement neighborhoods themselves to dispersing the population to new homes in less crowded areas. Businessmen and reformers concluded that the government needed to take the lead in this effort.

Between 1906 and 1913, a group of reformers came to hold high political office at both the state and city levels. They were led by Manhattan Borough President George McAneny, who in his previous capacity as president of the City Club had sponsored efforts to relieve population congestion in the slums. This group labored to transform New York's physical infrastructure and social conditions by implementing a program of planned development aimed at controlling the city's growth. At the heart of their efforts was a vast expansion of the subway and elevated network, which became the Dual System of Rapid Transit.

The 1906 state elections had brought Republican reform governor Charles Evans Hughes to power. In 1907, Hughes created the New York State Public Service Commission (PSC), which, among other things, was given the mandate of planning new rapid transit lines for New York City. In the 1909 municipal elections, other reformers took control of the City's Board of Estimate and Apportionment, which had the power of deciding on subway funding.

Members of the PSC and the Board of Estimate had been active in the development of a new set of ideas about how to relieve overcrowding in the tenement areas through a program of city planning. As part of this new paradigm, the City of New York, in cooperation with the PSC, developed a plan to build a large number of new rapid transit lines to the outlying areas of the Bronx, Brooklyn, and Queens at the same time. These new lines were intended to open up a great deal of land at one time for the construction of new homes and apartments for working families.[18]

In trying to get many new subway lines constructed simultaneously, however, the reformers were confronted with both financial and political obstacles. Under the City's debt limit, only about $200 million was available for new subways.[19] But building enough new lines to meet the needs of the growing population was estimated to cost well over $300 million.[20] Clearly, if a way could be found to get the private transit companies to contribute part of the cost of construction, a larger system would result.

The private rapid transit companies, however, were reluctant to use their funds for the construction of many new lines all at once, because the new routes would not be profitable for many years.[21] The Interborough Rapid Transit Company (IRT), in particular, was extremely reluctant to see more than a modest expansion of the rapid transit system. The company operated the first subway, opened in 1904, and regarded the high population densities that had developed in areas along the route of the first subway, such as the new tenement district of the South Bronx, as a good thing. More people meant more fares, and more profits.[22]

Until the end of 1910, various attempts were made by city and state officials to devise a method whereby a large number of new transit lines could be put under construction simultaneously.

This involved discussions with the IRT as well as a scheme to build a brand new rapid transit system, called the Triborough System. Little progress was made, however, because public officials were split over which plan was best and over the proposed financial arrangements necessary to build the new lines. Finally, in January 1911, George McAneny was asked to head a new Transit Committee of the Board of Estimate to deal with transit expansion.

The creation of this new committee marked a turning point in the history of rapid transit in New York. For over a decade, expanding the transit system had been debated extensively, with no practical result. McAneny aimed to break this deadlock. His main goal was to put a large number of new subway lines under construction at one time. By June 1911, McAneny, working closely with members of the PSC, had devised a plan called the Dual System of Rapid Transit, whereby the IRT and the Brooklyn Rapid Transit Company (BRT, later BMT)[23] were to participate with the City of New York in a comprehensive scheme of rapid transit that would embrace their existing lines as well as the newly planned lines.

To induce the private transit companies to participate, the City would assume most of the financial risk of building the new lines. Under the Dual System plan, the construction costs were to be shared by the companies and the City, and almost all of the lines were to be owned by the City. The City was to provide over $200 million of the $366 million required for construction and equipment of the Dual System lines and related improvements. The IRT and BRT were to provide the balance.

The financial aspects of the proposed Dual System contracts between the companies and the City, which would carry out the plan, were attacked in the Hearst press as a sell-out to the transit companies and the Wall Street interests that financed them. The struggle over the contracts became the biggest and most hotly debated political issue in New York.[24] Throughout this debate, McAneny, PSC chairman William R. Willcox, and other public officials argued that the proposed subway lines would relieve congestion of population and foster rational city growth, and that the financial arrangements with the private transit companies were secondary to the primary goals of opening up the outlying boroughs for new homes and providing the transportation lines needed for the development of Midtown as a major business center.[25] In the end, this argument won the day, and the Dual System contracts were formally approved by the PSC on March 19, 1913.[26]

The Dual System encompassed a vast network of rapid transit lines serving Manhattan, the Bronx, Brooklyn, and Queens. Over 325 new miles of track were built, more than doubling New York's rapid transit mileage to 621 miles.[27] Most of the new lines were opened for operation between 1915 and 1920.[28] The number of passengers using rapid transit rose from 810 million riders a year in 1913 to over two billion riders annually by 1930.[29]

The Dual System lines had precisely the effect that was predicted by advocates of the plan. The vast amounts of new land that the new lines made accessible were quickly built up with a mixture of housing types.[30] This new and better quality housing was available for about the same price that people had been paying for small, unsanitary apartments in Manhattan and the older areas of Brooklyn.[31] New York's population, in the years following 1913, did disperse to the outlying areas, which had significantly lower population densities. And, at a time when the city's population as a whole continued to grow rapidly, the older congested areas significantly declined in population.[32] By the middle of the twentieth century, a large portion of the workers in the Manhattan Central Business District commuted to work each day from the new subway suburbs, built up in the districts along the Dual System lines.[33]

The Dual System had a greater impact on the development of the outer boroughs than any other single addition to New York's basic infrastructure, including more acclaimed projects such as the Brooklyn Bridge and the highway system built by Robert Moses from the 1930s on. The Dual System lines also reinforced the continued growth of Midtown Manhattan as a business district and sustained the vitality of the skyscrapers in Manhattan's financial district. More than any other single activity ever undertaken by the municipal government, the Dual System subway lines helped to improve the lives of the average New Yorker. It saved the city for its people. This book tells the complete story of the Dual System—why it was needed, how it was planned, and the impact it had on New York.

1. Never Enough

The Beginnings of Rapid Transit in New York

The first serious proposals for rapid transit in New York were made in the 1860s, in response to the city's rapid population growth. From the 1830s on, New York's economy had boomed and large numbers of people had migrated to the "New Metropolis."[1] Between 1840 and 1870, the number of people living in Manhattan tripled, from 313,000 to 942,000. (Until 1874, New York City consisted solely of Manhattan.)[2] (See Table 1 for the population growth of New York City.)

As more people moved to the city, the limited space available for residential and commercial purposes became more and more congested. Manhattan's roads were packed with pedestrians, horses, wagons, omnibuses, and the most common form of public transit, horsecars moving over rails in streets. Movement on the streets and sidewalks was difficult and getting worse each year.[3] By the 1860s, there was also severe overcrowding in New York's tenement neighborhoods, home to hundreds of thousands of recent immigrants from Europe.

Conditions in the tenement districts quickly became a concern to businessmen and reformers in New York. During the 1860s, the problems caused by forcing people to live in small apartments in buildings five to seven stories high were seen as a threat to public health and safety. The disease, crime,

Table 1

Population of Greater New York by Borough, 1790–1997 (in Thousands)

	Manhattan	*Bronx*	*Brooklyn*	*Queens*	*Staten Island*	*Total*[a]
1790[b]	33	2	5	6	4	49
1800	61	2	6	7	5	79
1810	96	2	8	7	5	120
1820	124	3	11	8	6	152
1830	203	3	21	9	7	242
1840	331	5	48	14	11	391
1850	516	8	139	19	15	696
1860	814	24	279	33	25	1,175
1870	942	37	420	45	33	1,478
1880	1,165	52	599	57	39	1,912
1890	1,441	89	839	87	52	2,507
1900	1,850	201	1,167	153	67	3,437
1910	2,332	431	1,634	284	86	4,767
1920	2,284	732	2,018	469	117	5,620
1930	1,867	1,265	2,560	1,079	158	6,930
1940	1,890	1,395	2,698	1,298	174	7,455
1950	1,960	1,451	2,738	1,551	192	7,892
1960	1,698	1,424	2,627	1,810	222	7,782
1970	1,539	1,472	2,602	1,987	295	7,896
1980	1,428	1,169	2,231	1,891	352	7,071
1990	1,488	1,204	2,301	1,952	379	7,323
1997[c]	1,536	1,188	2,240	1,976	402	7,343

[a] Totals may not add due to rounding.
[b] Greater New York was not formed until 1898.
[c] 1997 U.S. Census Estimate.
SOURCE: U.S. Census and Emanuel Tobier.

alcoholism, and perceived general lack of morality in the poor districts could, it was feared, spill over into the "decent" neighborhoods if something was not done to reduce overcrowding in the slums.[4]

From the 1860s on, the construction of rapid transit lines seemed to be a way out of this problem.[5] Reformers hoped that, by reducing travel times, new subways or elevated lines would open up large amounts of land in outlying areas for residential development. In these areas, new homes would be built for both middle-class and working-class families. If enough rapid transit lines were built at the same time, the slums would empty out. By choice, working-class families would move to new, affordable, uncrowded homes in the outlying districts, homes with proper light, air, and sanitation. In doing so, they would alleviate the threats to affluent New Yorkers posed by the increasing overcrowding in poor and working-class neighborhoods.[6]

This vision of rapid transit as a means to improve the daily lives of working-class families and protect public health and safety was not to be achieved for more than fifty years. In the late nineteenth century, New York, followed by the independent city of Brooklyn, approved the construction of several elevated lines. At the turn of the century, a subway was finally approved and soon placed in operation. These rapid transit lines allowed many middle-class families, and even some working-class residents, to disperse to better housing in less crowded neighborhoods. But the number of rapid transit lines put in operation was never enough to reduce congestion of population in older residential areas, especially in the tenement districts where the city's "other half" was consigned.[7] By 1910, the "intractable" problem of overcrowding in the tenement districts was worse than it had ever been.[8]

The root of the problem lay in the belief that the private sector could, and would, build enough rapid transit lines to outpace New York's steady population growth. This belief foundered on the fact that it was in the interest of existing private transit companies to promote congestion.[9] More riders meant more profits. Private companies were not interested in building a large number of new lines to undeveloped areas at one time because the risks were high and the expected return on investment was low.[10] Only when government leaders recognized that public transportation was primarily a public responsibility could New York's transit problems finally be resolved.[11]

Development of New York to 1860

The high density of New York's commercial and residential buildings had much to do with the city's geography, which limited the amount of land within easy access of the business center in Lower Manhattan.[12] Manhattan is a narrow island, an average of about two miles wide from east to west along the thirteen miles from the Battery to its northern tip, where it is less than one mile wide. Lower Manhattan is surrounded by wide bodies of water—the Hudson River to the west, the East River (actually a strait of the ocean) to the east, and Upper New York Bay to the south. Until the opening of the Brooklyn Bridge in 1883, the only land connections to Manhattan were bridges over the Harlem River, at the northern end of the island, to what is now the Bronx.

Manhattan was the economic center of the New York region from the earliest European settlement. The Dutch settled New Amsterdam in 1625, building a small group of houses at the island's southern tip.[13] In 1653, a defensive barrier a few blocks to the north was built along what is now Wall Street to protect against a possible attack from New England.[14] In 1664, the English took over the city, renaming it New York, but retaining the urban center in the area that is today the financial district.

From the beginning, residential choices for New Yorkers were constrained by geography and the main thrust of development was to the north, the only direction not impeded by large bodies of water. During the colonial era and through the early national period, however, population growth was slow. In 1790, when New York was the capital of the United States, Manhattan had only 33,000 inhabitants.[15] The built-up area extended to about Canal Street.[16] President George Washington lived on suburban Cherry Street, near the East River, in what is now the Lower East Side.[17]

The Manhattan street system of the colonial period had developed without any overall plan, resulting in narrow and sometimes curved streets in the Wall Street area. Lot sizes varied, depending on the configuration of each block. During the 1790s and the first decade of the nineteenth century, more streets were laid out, with one grid of streets on the East Side to Houston Street and another in Greenwich Village on the West Side. The lack of an official street system north of these areas, however, hindered real estate development. To remedy this situation, a grid plan of streets and avenues was approved in 1811. Modeled on the grid systems of other American cities such as Philadelphia, the plan laid out the largely unsettled area north of Houston Street in a system of numbered east–west streets and north–south avenues.[18]

Starting from Houston Street, the new streets ran from 1st to 155th, the latter being the northern border of what is now Harlem.[19] Except for major cross streets such as 14th, 23rd, 34th, 42nd, and so on, which were a hundred feet wide, the streets were fifty or sixty feet wide. Twelve avenues were laid out to run the length of the island; each was a hundred feet wide.[20] The only major thoroughfare north of Houston Street that did not conform to this grid was Broadway, the main existing north–south road, which intersected with the avenues as it sloped northward.[21] Within the grid, the standard block size was two hundred by eight hundred feet, and within each block, each lot had a uniform size of twenty-five by one hundred feet. This made it very easy to divide the land up for real estate development.[22]

As Manhattan's population grew, and as buildings increased in height, movement on the street system became difficult, especially for north–south travel. In addition, the twenty-five-by-one-hundred-foot lot size fixed in the plan was to have unintended consequences later in the century, when real estate speculators discovered they could make huge profits by building five- and six-story walk-up tenement buildings to house the poor on these small parcels of land.[23]

The opening of the Erie Canal in 1825, together with several other local initiatives, boosted New York's economy. As a result, the population began to grow rapidly. During this initial period of rapid growth, New York cemented its position as the nation's largest city and premier business center. It was the linchpin of trade between Europe and the rest of the United States. Because of the Erie Canal, many of the goods passing to and from the Midwest moved through the port. New York also dominated the coastal trade with the southern states. As trade expanded, merchants established numerous banks and insurance companies, as well as what became the New York Stock Exchange (which took its current name in 1863). From this period on, the power of the city's financial institutions grew, extending out to the region, the nation, and later the world. By 1860, in addition to being the nation's center of commerce, New York was also the nation's largest manufacturing center.[24]

The First Public Transit

The growth in the economy and in population transformed New York. Until the 1830s, it was still largely a "walking city," that is, an urban place with a relatively small developed area not yet segregated fully into districts by function (such as offices, factories, warehouses, and homes). Businesses and residences were concentrated well below 14th Street. Within Lower Manhattan, most people could walk to work easily, hence the term "walking city."[25]

Public transit, however, already had begun to assist in the breakup of the walking city. After the establishment of regular steam-ferry service between Manhattan and Brooklyn in 1814, well-to-do businessmen created the nation's first commuter suburb in Brooklyn Heights. By the 1830s, thousands of passengers were traveling across the East River each day to and from work.[26]

Transit lines also developed within Manhattan. By the 1830s, some of the more affluent families had decided to move from their old neighborhood west of City Hall to less congested residential districts to the north. The well-drained, high ground in the center of the island from Washington Square north along Fifth Avenue, for example, became an affluent upper-class neighborhood.[27] This neighborhood, and others like it north of Bleecker Street, was beyond convenient walking distance from Manhattan's business center south of Chambers Street. Starting in 1827, omnibus service provided a means of commutation for these Manhattan suburbanites.[28]

Omnibuses—horse-drawn, stagecoach-like vehicles—operated along a fixed route according to an established schedule and passengers paid a single fare, usually six cents by the 1850s. During the 1830s and 1840s, these omnibuses were the primary form of public transit for Manhattan residents; by 1853, 683 were operating over the streets. Their slow speeds and bumpy rides, however, limited the expansion of omnibus services, as did their relatively high fares.[29]

After 1840, rising demand for commercial space in the Wall Street area quickly drove remaining residents out.[30] Affluent businessmen, office managers, and better-paid skilled workers sought new housing as far away from Lower Manhattan as possible, in order to escape from noise, street congestion, factories, and port activities, as well as the rising number of poor immigrants.[31] The Brooklyn suburbs attracted many of these people, as ferry service expanded. By 1860, the East River ferries were carrying about 100,000 daily passengers.[32] Ferry services also transported thousands of passengers each day from Hoboken and Jersey City to Lower Manhattan.[33]

Seeing this move to the suburbs across the rivers as a threat to New York's prosperity, city leaders raised a cry that Brooklyn and New Jersey towns were growing at the expense of New York City. The development of an extensive network of horsecar lines during the 1850s helped sustain Manhattan's attractiveness for the middle and upper classes by allowing them to move further up the island.[34]

A horsecar was a vehicle that operated on rails on local streets, pulled by a horse. The first horsecar line had opened in 1832, but expansion was stymied by political opposition from the omnibus companies and the fact that the rails interfered with traffic. In the early 1850s, the technology was improved so that the tops of the rails were level with the streets, rather than above the surface, and service was greatly expanded. Riding on rails that were level with the street surface, the horsecar did not interfere with traffic and provided a smoother ride than the omnibus, with speeds of up to six to eight miles per hour.[35]

In Manhattan during the 1850s, horsecars filled the transit needs of middle- and upper-income commuters. By 1860, the area between 14th Street and 42nd Street had been almost completely developed, largely with brownstone or brick single-family attached row houses for the middle and upper classes.[36] The ride by horsecar from this area to City Hall took thirty to forty-five minutes. During the 1850s, the normal fare on the horsecar lines was five cents. As with the omnibuses, the chief benefits of the horsecars were for middle- and upper-income commuters. The low wages and long hours of unskilled workers kept them largely out of the market for these services.[37] In 1860, the horse-railway companies in Manhattan were carrying about 38 million riders annually, or about 125,000 a day.[38]

The Threat from the Slums

While the upper and middle classes moved uptown to new areas segregated from the homes of the poor, the quality of housing for working-class families declined. Under the new system of dividing up the city's residential neighborhoods by class, income, and ethnicity, poorer working people were forced to live in the worst housing in the worst neighborhoods. Seeking housing within walking distance of their places of employment, they moved in large numbers to areas contiguous to the downtown business district, such as the Lower East Side. Beginning in the 1830s, this area became increasingly overcrowded, as landlords sought to pack as many families as possible into the former homes of the wealthy, now converted to small apartments.[39] George Washington's residence on Cherry Street, for example, was turned into a squalid multiple dwelling.[40] As this hand-me-down housing ran out, a new form of housing, the tenement, was invented for low-income families.

The tenement was the cheapest form of housing that could be built, on a per apartment basis, filling each small twenty-five-by-one-hundred-foot lot as much as possible. Until 1867, there were no laws regulating the type of building that could be constructed. At its worst, a pre-1867 tenement was a brick building five to seven stories high occupying 90 percent of the lot, with four apartments to a floor. Each apartment usually had three or four rooms. Since there was no space between buildings, only the one room of each apartment facing the street or backyard had windows to the outside; the interior rooms got sunlight and air only through the outer rooms.[41] There were no toilets within the building; such needs were accommodated by privies in the backyards. The yards also contained the water taps. The worst apartments were in the cellars; these often received the overflow from the privies, or were flooded during storms. The overcrowding in the poor districts, together with poor sewerage and sanitation, resulted in poor health. By the middle of the century, "epidemics of typhus, yellow fever, cholera and other diseases swept through the tenements and slums of the city with fearsome impact."[42]

Most of the inhabitants of the poorest neighborhoods were immigrants from Europe. The largest group were the Irish, followed by the Germans.[43] Most moved into the tenement districts, which took on the aura of "foreignness" that they would retain until well into the twentieth century.[44] Many upper- and middle-class New Yorkers perceived the newcomers as a threat to their health and safety.

These fears seemed to be confirmed by riots that took place at the height of the Civil War. On July 13, 1863, the working-class districts of New York exploded in the largest outburst of violence the city had ever seen. The immediate cause of the mayhem was the drafting of immigrant workers as soldiers in the Union Army. The rioters, many of whom were Irish, first burned federal offices and destroyed railroad tracks and telegraph lines. But soon they turned their attention on African-Americans, whom they blamed for the war and the fact that they were being drafted. The Colored Orphan Asylum on Fifth Avenue was burned to the ground and mobs began to lynch and mutilate black men on the streets.[45] By July 17, when the riot was finally crushed by troops who had recently fought at Gettysburg, 105 people were dead.[46]

The murder and pillage that occurred during the draft riots were catalysts for the first systematic survey of living conditions on Manhattan island. The survey was conducted by the Citizen's

Association of New York, directed by the city's business elite. Manhattan was divided into twenty-nine districts and a physician was assigned to each district to survey conditions and prepare a report. The summary report quoted a reporter who had written about the riots:

> The high blocks of closely-packed houses where the mobs originated seemed to be literally hives of sickness and vice. . . . It was difficult to believe that so much misery, disease and wretchedness can be huddled together and hidden by high walls, unvisited and unthought of, so near our own abodes. . . .
>
> The elements of popular discord are gathered in those wretchedly-constructed tenant-houses, where poverty, disease, and crime find an abode. Here disease in its most loathsome form propagates itself. Unholy passions rule in the domestic circle. Every thing, within and without, tends to physical and moral degradation.[47]

According to the report, a large portion—"always the majority of the whole"—of New York's population was composed of "the laboring or poor classes" which had been "more and more concentrated upon given areas . . . until a degree of crowding has been attained which by itself has become a subject of sanitary inquiry and public concern." There were 15,309 "tenant houses" in New York, inhabited by 495,592 residents, packed in at 240,000 persons per square mile.[48]

Visions of Rapid Transit

The Citizen's Association's 1865 report recommended a number of public health measures aimed at improving sanitation and sewerage, many of which were implemented. The report also led to the creation of the New York City Health Department, which became a crusader against disease in the tenement districts. In addition, the report was influential in the passage of the first building regulations, approved by the State Legislature in 1867.[49]

The 1865 report did not make any proposals to help move people out of the congested areas of Manhattan. Other concerned citizens, however, began to advocate the construction of rapid transit lines as the means to save New York. The requirements of economic growth had led to the concentration of business and industry in a relatively small area of land in Lower Manhattan. At this time, 85 percent of Manhattan's population lived within two miles of 14th Street, and almost all the jobs were located in this area.[50] Since workers had to live within reasonable commuting time from their jobs, the type, extent, and cost of the transportation services in place helped determine residential locations. The question was how to enable workers to move to new residential areas in northern Manhattan and beyond.

Plenty of open land was available in the region for residential development. In the 1860s, almost all of Manhattan north of 42nd Street was still largely undeveloped. Other parts of the region, including the outlying districts that would become part of New York City by 1898, also had lots of vacant land.[51] If these outlying areas were to be developed for residential purposes for middle- and working-class families, workers needed transportation to and from these sections and the main employment center in Manhattan. It was clear that even an expansion of the already-overcrowded horsecars could not fill this role, since their slow speeds along the congested streets limited their range to neighborhoods three to four miles from the center.[52] To reach districts beyond this limit, other forms of transportation were required.

One possibility was commuter rail service. In the 1830s, steam railroad lines began connecting central Manhattan with what is now the Bronx, as well as communities further north.[53] Railroad lines also appeared on Long Island, some of which could be reached by ferry from Manhattan.[54] There were also railroad lines in New Jersey that connected to ferry service to the metropolis.[55] Although the steam railroads did encourage a limited amount of residential development within what is now New York City, their role as a provider of mass transportation was limited.[56] One reason was the relatively high cost, which ranged from $35 to $150 a year.[57] In addition, trips on commuter rail services could take over an hour or more.[58] Commuter railroad service was thus too expensive and time-consuming to move masses of workers to and from Manhattan's business district.[59]

Opening up land for new housing geared to middle- and working-class residents required a fast and reasonably priced form of transportation. Rapid transit seemed to offer this possibility. Trains operating with frequent service and low fares either above or below the streets could, it was hoped, provide access to areas four miles and more away from the business center in forty-five minutes or less.

The vision of rapid transit as a means of alleviating population congestion in Lower Manhattan was played up by promoters of various schemes for elevated and subway lines in New York. In 1866, for example, the literature of one company proposing an elevated line contained photographs showing "the social evils and disorders which must follow from the fearful overcrowding" in the tenement districts, together with statistics on the prevalence of disease.[60] According to these promoters, if their plan was approved:

> The boon to the working class would then be obtained, which the merchants, the physicians and the clergy so anxiously crave, but confess themselves unable to devise. . . . If the above hope [that is, the proposed elevated line] is realized, there will

> be nothing to deter the working man from having his family comfortably housed at the northerly end of the island, or in Westchester County [in what is now the Bronx], and with the lapse of half an hour be placed in his workshop door before the labors of the day commence, and at night find a comfortable seat in a car . . . to take him back to the pure air of the country, in the same time it formerly took him to walk to his comfortless perch in some lofty tenement-house. The shop-girl will, in like manner, be accommodated, and need no longer know the temptation to spend her evenings in the excitement of the theatre or the glare of the pavement to escape from a suffocating domicile.[61]

To some reformers, such as physician Rufus Gilbert, rapid transit quickly became a moral crusade. Dr. Gilbert had visited European hospitals in the late 1850s and came home convinced that population dispersal could solve health problems caused by congestion. After the Civil War, Gilbert gave up the practice of medicine to promote mass transit. According to historian Clifton Hood, Gilbert believed that the building of rapid transit lines would empty hospital beds "by allowing the poor to move from overcrowded disease-ridden slums to the green hills of the surrounding country side."[62]

These hopes were not soon to be realized. During the next fifty years, New York never built enough transit lines to halt increasing congestion of population in the tenement districts.[63] Every year from 1860 on, more and more people moved into Manhattan, resulting in housing conditions that were barely tolerable for the middle class and became even more wretched for the poor and working class.[64] The difficulty in reducing congestion lay in overcoming the many obstacles to the building of an adequate network of rapid transit lines.

Obstacles to Rapid Transit Development

All proposals for building rapid transit in New York faced a series of obstacles that fell into three categories: technological, financial, and political. These obstacles were interrelated and all had to be dealt with successfully before any subway or elevated lines could be built. This proved to be an extremely difficult and complicated task.

The technological problems were the most straightforward. The core problem was the question of motive power to run the trains. Electric traction was not yet a possibility. The first electric motor for transit was invented in Europe in 1879 and perfected for trains in the 1890s.[65] London's subway, which was steam powered, ran in a series of short, well-ventilated tunnels. If steam locomotives were used in New York, where longer tunnels were anticipated, the smoke would cause major problems. Steam engines, however, could be used on elevated railroads, as the smoke could dissipate into the air. But since no elevated lines had ever been built, engineers were uncertain of their practicality.

The financial issues centered around who would take the risk of investment and under what terms. Who would pay for the new lines and railcars? What fare would be charged? Finally, what ridership, revenues, and profits were likely to result? Technological uncertainty also caused difficulties in raising the financing to build, equip, and operate proposed rapid transit lines. Many of the proposed subway and elevated plans may have been feasible, but businessmen were reluctant to invest in them without any examples of previous successes. As a result of the high risk, from early on many felt that the city government should finance the construction of rapid transit lines.

Political infighting, however, was usually the major impediment to progress. Because rapid transit lines would use public streets, nothing could be built without the approval of one or more government agencies of the State or City of New York. There was never a "free market" with respect to new companies entering the transit market. New transit services always had to be approved by one or another level of government, since they involved the use of public streets. This meant that entry was contingent in large part upon political influence.

Government agencies were also the final arbiter of the financing and ownership of rapid transit lines. Who would pay to have the lines constructed? Who would own them? If a franchise was given to a private company to build, own, and operate rapid transit lines, what would be the terms of this franchise? If the City of New York used its money to build transit lines, under what terms would a private company be allowed to operate them?[66] Many of these questions were related to the most essential finance issue: Who would assume the risk of investing in new rapid transit lines?

Most critical to the public was what the fare would be. At first, there were discussions of variable fares, as high as ten or fifteen cents depending on distance. Starting in the 1880s, however, the fare came to be fixed by the companies at five cents for a single ride on any given system.[67] In 1894, the New York State Legislature set the fare at five cents a ride.[68] From this time on, the five-cent fare became one of the most important parameters in discussions of the financing of new rapid transit lines.

The First Rapid Transit Lines

The first proposal for a subway in New York was made by Hugh B. Willson, a Michigan railroad man.[69] Willson had been in London during the construction of the first underground railroad in the world and was present at its opening in January 1863.[70] When he returned to America in June 1863, he set out to secure the aid of prominent New York businessmen in the financing of a subway in Manhattan. By the beginning of 1864, Willson's Metropolitan Railway Company had $5 million in subscribed capital stock. In March of that year, Willson petitioned the New York State Legislature to give his company the right to build a subway under Broadway.[71]

Willson's idea was to operate underground trains by steam locomotives, just as the London railroad was doing. His proposal was not received with enthusiasm in the State Legislature. Existing street railway companies and others lobbied against it and his bill was not even brought up for a vote.[72] This first subway scheme had received a good deal of public attention and its defeat was attacked in the press. The *New York Times*, for example, cited the "enormous power over our property and comfort which is now wielded by omnibus proprietors, railroad corporations and political jobbers."[73] Willson refused to be dismayed by his defeat and made preparations to petition the Legislature again in 1865.

In the meantime, he directed A. P. Robinson to draw up a detailed plan for the subway. Robinson's plan showed that a subway was possible as early as the late 1860s. With proper ventilation, even the smoke from the steam engines would not pose a great hindrance. Robinson contrasted New York with London, where the underground railroad was designed to connect existing railroad terminals. In New York, he said, conditions were different. Traffic on the streets increased every year, "in a far greater ratio than the population." What was needed in New York was a "Great Trunk Line," extending up Broadway and Fifth Avenue to 59th Street, with branches to the East and West sides above 59th Street.[74]

In 1865 the Legislature approved the plan for Willson's subway, as drawn up by Robinson, but Governor Reuben Fenton vetoed it. Again, opposition had come primarily from the existing street railway companies. The veto gave opponents of Willson's plan time to organize rival projects, which ultimately defeated this first proposal for a New York subway.[75]

In 1866, Willson's bill was reintroduced and a number of other subway proposals were submitted to the Legislature, but none passed. The Legislature did pass a bill in 1866 that eventually resulted in the building of New York's first rapid transit line. This bill got in through the back door at a time when most attention was focused upon subway proposals. The bill was passed in the interest of Charles T. Harvey, who had invented plans for the propulsion of trains on an elevated railroad by means of cables operated by steam power furnished by stationary engines along the route. The bill authorized the formation of a company to build this experimental line.[76]

In 1867, the Legislature authorized construction by Harvey and his West Side and Yonkers Patent Railway Company of a line one-half mile long extending from the Battery north along Greenwich Street and up Ninth Avenue to 30th Street. Harvey built the line from Battery Place to Cortlandt Street. When this cable-powered line opened to passengers on July 3, 1868, it was New York's first rapid transit line.[77] Harvey's company, however, soon ran into financial difficulties and Harvey himself was forced out. The bankers who took over the company did nothing with the line until 1870, when they completed it along Ninth Avenue to 30th Street.[78] Cable power did not work well on the elevated line and in 1871, the company switched to operation with steam locomotives. Having solved the motive problem, the company opened its elevated line to the public on April 20, 1871. At the end of 1871, the operating company was reorganized, changing its name to the New York Elevated Railroad Company.[79]

While the Ninth Avenue elevated line was being built, the scramble for rapid transit charters continued in Albany. The only segment of an underground line that was actually constructed before 1900 also came in through the back door. Alfred Ely Beach received a charter from the Legislature in 1868 for a "pneumatic dispatch" line fifty-four inches wide, intended to carry letters and parcels. Beach had not requested permission to build a passenger subway for fear of opposition from Tammany Hall boss William Marcy Tweed, head of the Democratic political machine.[80] Under the cover of constructing a mail system, he nonetheless went ahead and instead constructed a tunnel nine feet in diameter and 312 feet long under Broadway between Murray Street and Warren Street. Beach's intention was to prove the feasibility of passenger subway operation by a pneumatic system. In 1870, the tunnel was opened to the public and thousands of people took rides on a tubular car that was blown forward, and sucked backwards, by a large fan.[81] Once proving its success, he hoped to obtain a charter for a five-mile subway. Beach's plans, however, were speculative and failed to obtain the necessary financial backing, in part due to opposition from Boss Tweed.[82]

Other rapid transit schemes approved by the State Legislature between 1868 and 1871 also encountered both political and financial trouble. The New York City Central Underground Railroad Company, for example, was given the right to build a subway up Fourth Avenue and Madison Avenue in 1868, but the company had problems raising the necessary capital. As with Beach's scheme, the Central Underground was opposed by Tweed.[83]

During the early 1860s, Boss Tweed had successfully extracted tribute from the existing horsecar companies in New York City. Once rapid transit proposals began to proliferate, he began to think of constructing a rapid transit line over which he would have control.[84] Tweed's machinations in the rapid transit field were significant because, in the end, they convinced many conservative New Yorkers that the city government should have nothing to do with the financing, construction, or operation of rapid transit.

Tweed's rapid transit proposal was, according to one historian, a stupendous "scheme of plunder," whose estimated cost was $60 million.[85] His plan called for the construction of a viaduct with a foundation of solid masonry through the middle of blocks from Lower Manhattan up the East Side to the Harlem River and up the West Side to Spuyten Duyvil, over which steam railroads would operate. Because of Tweed's political power, this fantastic scheme had the support of respected businessmen such as A. T. Stewart, August Belmont, Horace Greeley, and John Jacob Astor, who took subscriptions of stock in the company Tweed organized to build this railroad.[86] A bill authorizing Tweed's scheme was approved by the Legislature in 1871 and was signed by Governor John Hoffman. The bill was unique in that it did not specify on or through which streets the viaduct was to go, thus allowing Tweed to block any other transit proposal.[87] Once his bill was passed, Tweed proceeded to try to eliminate all possible competition. He also persuaded Governor Hoffman to veto a bill passed by the Legislature in 1871 allowing Beach to construct a subway.[88]

Tweed even tried to destroy Harvey's existing elevated line on Greenwich Street and Ninth Avenue. On March 28, 1871, Tweed introduced a bill in the Legislature providing for the removal of the elevated structure on the allegation that it was a safety hazard. Harvey was able to save the elevated road only through the intervention in the Legislature of Erastus Corning, an Albany merchant and financier, for whom he had once worked. If Corning had not intervened, New York's first rapid transit line would have been destroyed before it opened.[89]

The demise of the Tweed ring after its corrupt practices were exposed in the summer of 1871 discredited the viaduct plan. For a while, the plans of the Central Underground were revived, but the depression of the early 1870s made it difficult to raise the necessary capital for this as well as for other subway proposals.[90] In addition, the conservative businessmen in control of New York's government after Tweed's downfall eventually decided that the cheapest and most certain way of obtaining new rapid transit lines was through the construction of elevated railroads by private companies. This limited the extent of any network that was built to whatever private capital was comfortable with.

Before the decision to build elevated lines was made, however, one further proposal was put forth for a subway for New York. In 1873, a Rapid Transit Association was formed at a meeting attended by a large number of civic leaders, including Abram S. Hewitt. This association approved the idea of municipal construction of a subway, which would be leased to a private company for operation.[91] This did not happen in 1873, but this concept was revived fifteen years later during Hewitt's term as mayor. For the years immediately following 1873, however, elevated railroad schemes dominated the discussion of rapid transit in New York City.

To accomplish their goals, business leaders lobbied for passage of a general law, the Rapid Transit Act of 1875, which established a procedure for the planning and implementation of rapid transit lines without the direct involvement of the State Legislature. Under the act, taxpayers could petition the mayor of the City of New York (or the mayor of Brooklyn) for the creation of temporary rapid transit commissions, which would then solicit proposals from private companies. The commissions would decide on the plans they thought should be implemented and grant perpetual franchises to the companies selected. Once the lines were constructed and in operation, the temporary commissions would cease to exist.[92]

Under the 1875 Act, networks of elevated lines, without any

underground segments, were constructed in Manhattan, the Bronx, and Brooklyn and placed in operation in the last quarter of the nineteenth century (see Map 1). The trains on these lines were powered by steam locomotives. In Manhattan, elevated lines, called "els," were opened between 1878 and 1880 on Second, Third, and Sixth avenues, and the Ninth Avenue line was extended north. Branches on 34th and 42nd streets connected the East Side lines to ferries crossing the East River to the Long Island Rail Road and to Grand Central Station, respectively. The Sixth Avenue line connected with the Ninth Avenue el at 53rd Street.[93] The els proceeded from Lower Manhattan to the northern boundary of the island at the Harlem River. The cost of these lines was $18 million.[94] By 1880, the Manhattan Railway Company had achieved a monopoly over all these elevated lines.[95]

In 1886, an elevated line built by the Suburban Rapid Transit Company was opened that ran from a station in northern Manhattan across the Harlem River into the southern Bronx. This line was extended north up Third Avenue to 177th Street by 1891, and to Fordham Road in 1901.[96] The Third Avenue el in the Bronx was soon incorporated into the Manhattan Railway Company system, with direct through service via its East Side lines to Downtown Manhattan starting in 1896. In 1902 and 1903, the Manhattan and Bronx elevated lines, which had been operated using small steam locomotives to pull the trains, were converted to electric power from a third rail.[97]

As in Manhattan, battles over financing and political infighting delayed early efforts to build rapid transit lines in Brooklyn. Eventually, under a number of temporary rapid transit commissions appointed by the mayor of Brooklyn, a network of elevated lines was constructed and put in operation between 1885 and the mid-1890s. These lines extended within Brooklyn east from Downtown Brooklyn along Fulton Street, Myrtle Avenue, and Lexington Avenue. In addition, one elevated line proceeded

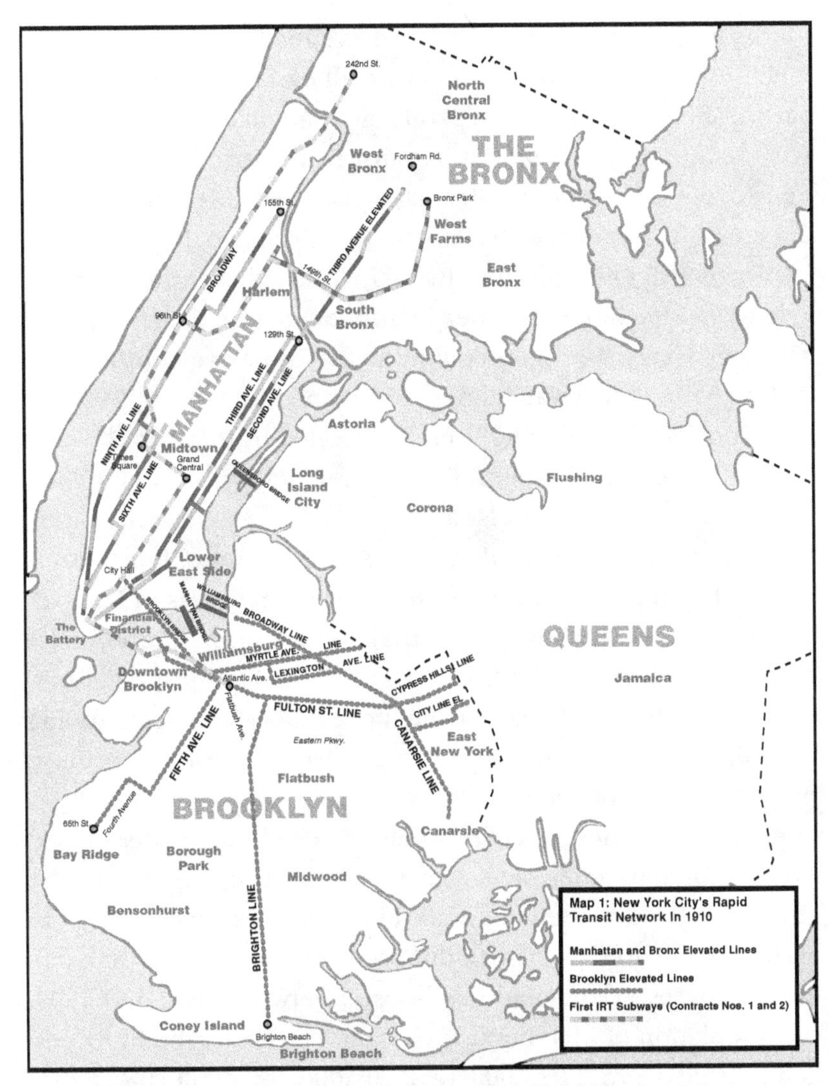

Map 1. New York City's Rapid Transit Network in 1910

south along Fifth Avenue and Third Avenue to 65th Street. From Williamsburg, an elevated line was built east on Broadway to Canarsie. (Brooklyn, being a separate city, had many streets with the same names as streets in Manhattan.) By the turn of the century, trains from several of the Brooklyn els, as well as from some of the steam railroads controlled by the Brooklyn Rapid Transit Company (BRT) in southern Brooklyn, passed over the Brooklyn Bridge to a terminal in Lower Manhattan across the street from City Hall. Here passengers could transfer, by paying another fare, to the Manhattan elevated lines serving the East Side. By 1900, all the Brooklyn elevated lines were controlled by the BRT.[98]

In 1900, the Manhattan Railway Company carried 184 million riders annually; the BRT els carried another 58 million. This represented about 850,000 riders a day.[99] The elevated lines were a catalyst for the development of new residential areas in Manhattan, the Bronx, and Brooklyn that were beyond the effective reach of the streetcar network.[100] This included most neighborhoods four to eight miles from Lower Manhattan, including Yorkville, East Harlem, the southern Bronx, most of northern Brooklyn, and Brownsville.[101]

Although the network of privately owned elevated lines helped to accommodate some of New York's burgeoning population, the amount of land opened up for development was never enough to allow these new areas to be built up with anything other than tenement houses or attached row houses. Between 1880 and 1890, the population of what became Greater New York grew by 31 percent, rising from 1,912,000 to 2,507,000; by 1900, the figure would rise another 37 percent to 3,437,000. (See Table 1.) Even though the els helped some residents to move out of the tenements to less congested districts, the density of population in most older neighborhoods continued to increase. Moreover, some of the tenement districts built up along the el lines, such as East Harlem, also became very overcrowded.[102]

The First Subway

By the mid-1880s, it was obvious that the elevated railroads had not solved New York's transit problems. Overcrowding and traffic congestion were worse than ever. Meanwhile, the elevated lines were jammed to capacity. Once again, demands were made by business and civic leaders for the construction of a subway to relieve this situation.[103]

Technological advances during the 1880s and the 1890s made the building of an extensive underground railroad network possible. The key development was the electric traction motor, which permitted safer and more efficient operation of subway trains. In 1879, Dr. Werner Von Siemens demonstrated the first electric railway in the world at an exposition in Berlin. The development of electric street railways gave impetus to the idea of subway trains powered by electricity. On December 18, 1890, the first subway train using electric power was put in operation in London. Meanwhile, Frank J. Sprague designed electric cars, which were operated on Chicago's elevated loop railroad in 1897.[104] Sprague also developed multiple-unit control of trains under which a motorman at the head of the train controlled the power motors in each railcar.[105] There were related improvements in signaling, door controls, and brakes. Electric traction held promise of speeds up to thirty miles per hour. Even with stops, a subway train would be able to transport people living eight to twelve miles from the Manhattan business districts to work in forty-five minutes or less.

Despite these technological advances, however, financial barriers remained. The estimated cost of constructing a subway was four to five times greater than that of an elevated line. This meant that, at a five-cent fare, there might not be enough profit to justify the investment.[106] Jacob H. Schiff, a senior partner at the investment banking house Kuhn, Loeb, and Company, warned that, given the high costs, private capital would be reluctant to tackle building a subway, which could cost as much as $100 million.[107]

From the late 1880s though the close of the century, political battles persisted over the best way to proceed with the expansion of the rapid transit network in Manhattan and the Bronx. (Only after consolidation in 1898 did the debate encompass Greater New York as a whole.) In 1891, the State Legislature passed a new Rapid Transit Act, establishing New York's first permanent governing agency for public transit, the Board of Rapid Transit Commissioners. This Board was empowered to lay out new routes and make detailed engineering plans for subway construction.[108] The Board was authorized to grant a private company the right to build, own, and operate a subway at the company's own expense. The commissioners laid out a route plan, but they were unable to obtain a satisfactory bid for a franchise.[109] Their failure was due largely to the opposition of Jay Gould and Russell Sage, who controlled the Manhattan Railway Company, and the Metropolitan Street Railway Company, which controlled most of the street railway system in Manhattan. The opposition of these powerful interests frightened away private capital.[110]

The Manhattan Railway Company's leaders hoped to force the Board into accepting their own plans for an extension of their elevated network. They almost succeeded; the Board, despairing of hopes for obtaining a subway, soon began to negotiate with the company for thirty-eight miles of proposed extensions of its lines. These negotiations proved unsuccessful, however, because the Board refused to accept the company's demands concerning financial arrangements.[111] Had the negotiations been successful and the Manhattan Railway Company received rights to build the proposed extensions, all plans for a subway might have been delayed for many years.

By the beginning of 1894, it had become obvious that the

Board of Rapid Transit Commissioners had no options left. Private companies would not pay for a subway and the Board did not have the power to construct one with municipal funds. In order to explore the best means by which New York could obtain new rapid transit lines, the New York Chamber of Commerce appointed a rapid transit committee to study the problem.[112]

The report of this committee, issued on February 15, 1894, indicates the conservative, business-oriented approach of the Chamber of Commerce. It argued that the future greatness of New York, as "the commercial metropolis of the United States," required that the municipality obtain the very best rapid transit system possible.[113] Since private capital was unwilling to risk investment in a subway, the report urged making a "single exception" to the provision in the New York State Constitution forbidding the loan of municipal credit to private corporations. It recommended that the City of New York lend a private company two-thirds of the costs of constructing a subway. The company would provide the other one-third of the cost plus the cost of equipment and would own the subway.[114]

At a meeting of the Chamber of Commerce to consider this report, a number of prominent men, including Schiff, urged that the Chamber approve the report of its committee. At this same meeting, Abram S. Hewitt, who had been mayor in 1887–1888, argued against the use of City credit to back a private corporation. Hewitt, who had proposed in 1873 and again in 1888 that the municipality build subways with its own funds, insisted that if the City of New York were to invest its own money it ought to own the subway. Hewitt was aware of the deep distrust most members of the Chamber had for the local government, citing "the danger and abuse that might come from the construction of the work by city officials and the operation of the railroad afterwards by public officials."[115]

The way around this problem was to use municipal funds to

finance the building of the subway, but to have a private corporation build and operate it. This way, the company would have every interest in building the subway as quickly as possible.[116] The company would employ "competent men . . . no politicians—because the lessee will find that his profits depend upon the economy with which the work is operated."[117]

The Chamber of Commerce approved Hewitt's proposal and prepared a bill for the State Legislature to carry it out. This bill passed and was signed by the governor on May 22, 1894. The new law amended the Rapid Transit Act of 1891 to allow the use of City money for the construction of rapid transit lines. The maximum amount of money that the City could borrow to pay for a subway, however, was set at $50 million. The amendment also provided that a public referendum was to be held on the question of whether rapid transit lines should be constructed at government expense. On election day in 1894, the voters overwhelmingly approved municipal ownership of the future subway.[118]

The new law also created an agency, the Board of Rapid Transit Railroad Commissioners, to replace the 1891 Board. The new Rapid Transit Board (RTB) was to consist of the mayor, the comptroller, the president of the Chamber of Commerce, and five other men named in the law. The Board itself could fill any vacancies, thereby insulating it from the City government. The new Board received all the records, plans, and property of the 1891 Board.[119]

The RTB was authorized to devise a general plan for new rapid transit lines. Once these lines had been approved by the New York City Board of Aldermen, the RTB's engineering staff was to draw up detailed plans for the routes. The Board was then to advertise for bids for the construction and operation of the lines. The successful bidder was required to enter into a contract with the City for building the subway, and also would agree to equip the lines at its own expense. The fare was to be five cents for the life of the contract. The private company would lease the lines for a term of thirty-five to fifty years. For this privilege, the company was to pay the City an amount not less than the interest on the bonds the municipality would issue to pay for construction.[120]

The fact that the Rapid Transit Act specifically limited New York's borrowing capacity for new rapid transit lines to $50 million indicates the conservative nature of the whole endeavor. Given the high cost of subway construction, this level of funding would allow only a limited underground network to be built, which would open only a few new residential areas for development. At the rate the metropolis was growing, any subway network the City could build would not be large enough to stem the spread of overcrowded tenement districts.

The limitation on transit financing was aimed at guaranteeing that the bonds sold by the municipality to cover construction costs would produce enough revenues from a five-cent fare to cover operating expenses as well as the principal and interest on the City's bonds. The underlying issue was to what extent the City would be allowed to risk its own funds in new rapid transit lines. In no event was there to be the possibility that operating revenues would not be enough to pay off the bonds since, if this happened, the bond payments would have to be paid for by tax revenues.[121]

The limits to transit expansion caused by the $50 million cap on spending soon became obvious. The RTB initially laid out a subway system with a line extending from Lower Manhattan up Broadway to 14th Street. From this point, one branch would proceed up the East Side and under the Harlem River to the southern Bronx. Another branch would follow Broadway north to the vicinity of 181st Street on the West Side.[122] This first route plan, however, was successfully contested in the courts on the grounds that the proposed lines did not extend from one end of the city to the other, as required by the Rapid Transit Act. In addition, property owners on Broadway protested against a subway from 14th Street to 42nd Street.[123] As a result, the commissioners adopted a modified version of their original plan, which became the oddly shaped zig-zag route of the first subway. The aim was to reach close to the northern borders of New York on both the east and the west. (See Map 1 for the route of the first subway.)

To comply with the law, and to stay within the spending cap, the north-south trunk line on the East Side of Manhattan north of 42nd Street was eliminated. Instead, the subway was to extend up the East Side from City Hall to the Grand Central Terminal area at 42nd Street, where it would turn left and proceed to Times Square, on the West Side. From here the line was to pass up Broadway to 96th Street, where it would split. One branch would continue up Broadway and other streets to the northwestern Bronx. (This line now terminates at 242nd Street.) The other branch would proceed up Lenox Avenue in Harlem, go under the Harlem River, and then pass through the southern Bronx to a point just south of Bronx Park, in a neighborhood called West Farms. To further reduce construction costs, the line to West Farms was to be elevated north of 149th Street; the northern portion of the Broadway line also was to be elevated.[124] By 1898, the RTB had prepared detailed plans and proposed contract documents for the revised subway network and was prepared to go out for bids from private companies.[125]

At this juncture, something happened that was to delay the approval of the first subway contract for another two years. In the fall 1897 elections, Tammany Hall candidates took control of the municipal government. This meant that Democrats controlled not just Manhattan and the Bronx but the Greater City that came into existence on January 1, 1898, which included Brooklyn, Queens, and Staten Island.

The Tammany Hall platform of 1897 had been favorable to the RTB's plan for a subway, but by the time the Democrats came into office they had done an about face. On January 1, 1898, Mayor Robert A. Van Wyck declared that there would be no solution to New York's rapid transit problem that involved spending City money. Van Wyck claimed that the City was very close to its constitutional debt limit because of its assumption of the debts of the towns and municipalities in Brooklyn, Queens, and Staten Island. He called instead for the extension of the existing elevated systems.[126]

Tammany boss Richard Croker attacked the RTB in February, saying that its plans were a waste of time and money. Croker went so far as to have a bill introduced in the Legislature calling for the abolition of the Board and its replacement by an agency to be appointed by the mayor. This bill failed largely because of opposition from New York civic groups.[127] In an interview given in 1900, Democratic comptroller Bird S. Coler said that, in early 1898, Tammany officials were ordered to have nothing to do with the RTB because of a deal that had been made between Tammany leaders and the Manhattan Railway Company.[128]

The Manhattan Railway Company now saw its opportunity and made yet another offer to the RTB for the extension of its lines. The Board responded by offering seven franchises on its own terms.[129] George Gould, president of the Manhattan Railway Company, rejected this proposal, insisting that he be able to dictate the terms of any new franchises for his company.[130]

The situation, by the summer of 1898, was a stalemate. Tammany could neither abolish the RTB nor force it to approve elevated extensions. The Board, on the other hand, could not further its plan for a municipally owned subway until the Tammany-dominated City administration cooperated with it. The Board sent letters to both the mayor and the Board of Estimate, citing the fact that the debt limit problems seemed to have been overcome and requesting that the City approve the contract. No replies were received.[131]

Hope for a City-owned subway, however, now returned in an unexpected way. In the spring of 1899, Tammany officials began to attack the Manhattan Railway Company. By April, every department of the government began to harass the company in every way possible.[132] It is unknown exactly why this happened. There were rumors that certain Tammany politicians had been shut out of buying Manhattan Railway Company stock at the beginning of a spectacular rise in its value in January 1899. Other rumors had it that Croker had a large interest in a company that sold compressed air motors. Croker had tried unsuccessfully to get the Manhattan Railway Company to buy these motors to run its trains.[133] It is also possible that Tammany leaders had seen that there were great profits to be made from controlling subcontracts for various aspects of construction of the subway. John B. McDonald, the contractor who was eventually to begin constructing the first subway in 1900, had close ties to Tammany Hall. Whatever the reason, this dispute between former allies cleared the way for New York to build its first subway.[134]

In September 1899, the City sent the RTB a letter recommending minor changes in the form of the proposed subway contract. The changes were made and the contract received final approval on October 11, 1899.[135] From this point everything went smoothly and the Board began advertising for bids. At the end of 1899, the only doubt that remained was whether anyone would bid on the contract.

It was made clear to the Board even before the bids were opened that none of the existing transportation companies in New York was going to try to get the contract.[136] Indeed, what August Belmont's secretary called the "Whitney-Ryan" group (William C. Whitney, Thomas Fortune Ryan, Stephen Elkins, and

P. A. B. Widener), which controlled the street railways in Manhattan and the Bronx, issued warnings to the banks that construction of a subway was financially risky. The group argued that a subway should not be built unless a perpetual franchise was offered. This opposition, together with that of the Manhattan Railway Company, made most New York bankers hesitant to finance companies willing to bid on the subway.[137]

On January 15, 1900, the RTB received two bids. One was from Andrew Onderdonk, who offered to build the lines for $39.3 million. Onderdonk also offered to share some of the profits from the operation with the City. The other bid was from John B. McDonald, who was willing to undertake the task for $35 million. For the moment, no one had guaranteed him this amount, but he had hoped to find bankers willing to do so, once he had the support of the Board. On January 16, the Board accepted McDonald's bid.[138]

McDonald was a contractor who had recently completed a five-mile-long railroad tunnel under Baltimore. Not only was he a close friend of Croker, but he had access to Belmont through his friend, the banker Andrew Freedman.[139] Belmont was interested in the subway. He recently had been squeezed out of several financial deals by Wall Street opponents and now had idle money and a grievance.[140] Belmont was, at this time, unconnected to either the Sage-Gould interests that controlled the Manhattan Railway Company or to the Whitney-Ryan group. He had, however, been involved in the affairs of various Brooklyn elevated railroad companies.[141]

With Belmont's financial backing, McDonald was able to sign Contract No. 1 with the RTB on February 21, 1900. McDonald and Belmont then organized the Rapid Transit Subway Construction Company to undertake the actual construction. Ground was broken for the subway on March 24, 1900.[142] During the spring of 1902, the Interborough Rapid Transit Company

(IRT) was organized to operate the first subway and took over the contract rights of the construction company.[143]

Even before the first contract had been awarded, people in Brooklyn had been demanding a subway. Soon after the contract with McDonald was signed, the RTB asked the State Legislature for an amendment to the Rapid Transit Act, extending its power to all of Greater New York. This power was granted in April 1900.[144] In May, public hearings on a route to Brooklyn were held. On January 21, 1901, the RTB adopted a route extending from the end of the first subway near City Hall down Broadway to the Battery, then under the East River to Joralemon Street in Brooklyn. The route then passed under Fulton Street to Flatbush Avenue and down Flatbush Avenue to the Long Island Rail Road station at Atlantic Avenue.[145] (See Map 1.)

This route received the approval of the mayor and aldermen in 1901, and the Rapid Transit Board proceeded to draw up Contract No. 2. This contract was similar in its provisions to the first contract, except that the lease was to run for only thirty-five years, with a twenty-five-year renewal option. The actual cost of constructing the route was estimated at between $8 million and $10 million.[146]

On July 21, 1902, three bids were received on this contract. The first was from the Brooklyn Rapid Transit Company, which controlled all of the existing elevated lines in Brooklyn. The BRT offered to build the subway for $8 million. The two other bids were from John B. McDonald, representing the IRT. The first of these, which included an offer to construct an extension of the first subway under Broadway from 14th Street to 42nd Street for only $100,000, would construct the Broadway extension for $4 million. The second bid was for $3 million. Under both of McDonald's bids, the Brooklyn route was to be completely integrated with the route of the Manhattan-Bronx subway and a single five-cent fare was to be charged. In September 1902, the Board decided to accept the $3 million bid.[147]

This low bid, well below the actual cost of construction, reflected the IRT's expectation that operation of this line would be extremely profitable since it would provide a new crossing of the East River between Downtown Brooklyn and Lower Manhattan, would pass through dense business and residential areas, and would provide a fast connection between the Long Island Rail Road's Brooklyn terminal at Atlantic and Flatbush Avenues and Lower Manhattan.[148] In 1902, the IRT also entered into a long-term lease (999 years) with the Manhattan Railway Company for all of the elevated lines in Manhattan and the Bronx.[149]

All of the lines called for in the two subway contracts opened between 1904 and 1908, with the initial segment—from City Hall to 145th Street and Broadway—going into service on October 27, 1904.[150]

Impact of the First Subway

The first subway was a huge success, proving beyond a doubt that an underground railroad powered by electricity could safely carry hundreds of thousands of daily riders. The first IRT subway attracted large numbers of short-haul passengers within Manhattan and between Manhattan and Downtown Brooklyn, which resulted in the high profits that Belmont had expected.[151] In 1910, the IRT subway carried 269 million riders. From the start, the trains were overcrowded, especially during the morning and evening peak periods. Meanwhile, the Manhattan and Bronx elevated lines, now controlled by the IRT, were carrying more passengers than ever, with 294 million riders annually. The BRT's

Table 2

Annual Rapid Transit Ridership, 1901–1998 (in Millions)

Year	*Ridership*	*Year*	*Ridership*	*Year*	*Ridership*
1901	253	1934	1,799	1967	1,298
1902	285	1935	1,817	1968	1,303
1903	327	1936	1,877	1969	1,330
1904	384	1937	1,891	1970	1,258
1905	448	1938	1,864	1971	1,197
1906	521	1939	1,853	1972	1,145
1907	595	1940	1,857	1973	1,101
1908	631	1941	1,838	1974	1,099
1909	663	1942	1,870	1975	1,054
1910	725	1943	1,940	1976	1,010
1911	746	1944	1,926	1977	998
1912	779	1945	1,941	1978	1,042
1913	810	1946	2,002	1979	1,077
1914	837	1947	2,051	1980	1,009
1915	830	1948	2,031	1981	1,011
1916	891	1949	1,764	1982	989
1917	990	1950	1,681	1983	1,005
1918	1,029	1951	1,636	1984	1,003
1919	1,118	1952	1,574	1985	1,010
1920	1,332	1953	1,552	1986	1,030
1921	1,419	1954	1,416	1987	1,058
1922	1,438	1955	1,378	1988	1,074
1923	1,506	1956	1,363	1989	1,073
1924	1,612	1957	1,355	1990	1,028
1925	1,681	1958	1,319	1991	995
1926	1,752	1959	1,324	1992	997
1927	1,830	1960	1,345	1993	1,030
1928	1,919	1961	1,363	1994	1,081
1929	1,972	1962	1,370	1995	1,093
1930	2,049	1963	1,362	1996	1,110
1931	1,996	1964	1,375	1997	1,132
1932	1,867	1965	1,363	1998	1,203
1933	1,756	1966	1,296		

SOURCE: Metropolitan Transportation Authority.

elevated lines carried 162 million passengers in 1910.[152] (See Table 2 for annual rapid transit ridership, 1901–1998.)

What the first subway did not do was to open up much land for residential development. The route mileage of the first subway was a modest 21.4 miles; the extension to Brooklyn added another 3.8 miles. In comparison, the existing solely elevated lines in New York had 66.1 route miles.[153] Only in northern Manhattan and a relatively small portion of the Bronx did the routes of the first subway pass through districts that were sparsely inhabited. Because of the great demand for housing, these districts were quickly built up to very high densities.

In northern Manhattan, block after block of dense five- and six-story apartment buildings were constructed. In the South Bronx, along the route of the line to West Farms, real estate speculators built hundreds of "New Law" tenements catering largely to a lower-middle-class and working-class population.[154] Many of these families were fleeing older areas such as the Lower East Side.[155] Seeing the scale and density of this housing, reformers soon began to warn that the overcrowded conditions in the old tenement districts were being repeated.[156]

On the West Side of Manhattan north of 59th Street, the subway sparked the development of luxury apartment houses for the rich and upper-middle classes, adding to the stock of housing for these groups that had begun with the building of row houses on the side streets along the route of the Ninth Avenue el.[157] Luxury apartment buildings were also constructed in Harlem along the Lenox Avenue line of the first subway. Because too many apartment houses were built in a short period of time, however, there were many vacancies. Some of the apartments began to be rented to blacks and many were subdivided. As a result, Harlem soon became a major center of African-American life and culture.[158]

Manhattan, the southern Bronx, and northern Brooklyn could not have developed as they did during the late nineteenth century and the first decade of the twentieth century without the elevated lines and the first subway. Yet, up to 1902, the business elite and government officials who had the power to decide on new rapid transit services had never been able to build enough new lines at one time to make a serious dent in the problem of overcrowded housing.

This inability on the part of decision makers to provide New York with the transportation system it needed would continue as the new century began. Transit expansion became the biggest and hottest issue in New York politics. But despite much rhetoric, for more than ten years after the decision to extend the first subway to Brooklyn, almost nothing was done in the way of actually building more subways.

Meanwhile, the number of people living in New York City was growing by about 100,000 each year, in large measure because of heavy immigration from southern and eastern Europe. Many of the newcomers were poor. They moved into the old tenement districts of Manhattan and Brooklyn, which became more crowded each year. But it was only after fears were once again raised about threats to the city's health and safety from worsening conditions in the tenement districts that action was finally taken to build enough new lines to allow the population to disperse to less crowded neighborhoods.

2. The Deadlock over More Subways, 1902–1909

The beginning of construction of New York's first subway in 1900, and the quick approval of its expansion to Brooklyn in 1902, led to optimistic predictions of many more subway lines in the near future. Both the Board of Rapid Transit Railroad Commissioners (Rapid Transit Board, or RTB) and the public regarded the initial subway lines as only the first steps toward the development of a comprehensive subway network covering large areas of the city.[1] The RTB made extensive plans for further lines beginning in 1902. By the spring of 1905, it had laid out nineteen separate new routes and expected that contracts would soon be signed with private companies to construct many of these lines.[2]

The Board's optimism proved to be misplaced. By the end of 1909, construction work had begun on only two of these routes.[3] This lack of progress was the result of ongoing political controversy over how the City should develop its rapid transit network. This controversy involved old questions of how large a system should be built, where new rapid transit lines should be located, who was to assume the financial risk of investing in new lines, who was to operate them, and which governmental agencies were to be responsible for planning any new lines.

All public officials agreed that new subway lines were needed to meet New York's rapid population growth and to relieve overcrowding on existing transit services. They could not decide, however, how best to accomplish this goal. One faction believed that the best policy was to expand the City-owned subway leased to the Interborough Rapid Transit Company (IRT). Others argued that the best way to proceed was to build a brand-new subway system, independent of the lines leased by the IRT. Adding to the controversy, many officials wanted to do both.

Much of the political squabbling was about financing. Conservative members of New York's business elite favored modest expansion of the rapid transit network using private capital as much as possible. The leaders of Tammany Hall, the Democratic political machine, had close connections to the IRT and wanted to use all available public funds to expand the first subway network. Others, most importantly publisher William Randolph Hearst, argued that all available City funds should go to the construction of an independent subway to be owned and operated by the City. Directly related to the debate over financing was the question of the profitability of new subway lines, especially those extending to undeveloped areas.

The most striking aspect of the lack of progress was that there were no technical obstacles. The successful operation of the first subway from 1904 on proved that an underground multiple-unit train powered by electricity from a third rail was both fast and practical. The use of the first all-steel subway cars was another technological innovation.[4] Subway tunnels had been built successfully below the streets and under the East and Harlem rivers, as engineers dealt effectively with the numerous construction problems that were encountered.[5]

How to proceed with expanding the rapid transit network became the biggest political issue in New York during the 1905 and 1909 municipal elections.[6] The deadlock was broken only after a group of Progressive reformers took control of much of the municipal government in the 1909 election and joined forces with other reformers on the New York State Public Service Commission.

Modest Plans

The RTB had been under continuous pressure for more subways from numerous civic and real estate groups ever since the signing of Contract No. 1 in February 1900.[7] As a result of this pressure, on May 3, 1902, the Board instructed its chief engineer, William Barclay Parsons, to prepare "a comprehensive scheme or plan of rapid transit for the whole city."[8] The RTB did not intend for this plan to be executed immediately. What it wanted was a general scheme of routes that could be built as rapidly as City funds and private capital ready for investment in rapid transit would permit.[9]

Parsons recognized that two distinct and unconnected systems of rapid transit existed in New York City. These separate networks had their origins in the fact that, until 1898, New York and Brooklyn had been competing cities, and each had designed its rapid transit facilities to meet its own goals. In Manhattan and the Bronx, most transportation lines ran along a north-south axis from the Battery to the Bronx. None of the Manhattan elevated lines had any direct connections to Brooklyn or Queens. The subway being constructed under Contract No. 1 also was limited to Manhattan and the Bronx. The only step taken toward unification of the disparate parts of Greater New York by means of an integrated rapid transit system would be the approval of the subway extension to Brooklyn under Contract No. 2.

In Manhattan, the obvious need was for two direct north-south lines, one on the West Side and one on the East Side, connected by a shuttle at 42nd Street, and thereby forming an "H." The zig-zag route of the first subway being constructed under Contract No. 1, which ran up the East Side to 42nd Street, across 42nd Street to Times Square and then up the West Side, was regarded as illogical.[10] This zigzag route could easily be converted into an "H" by extending the existing subway north of 42nd Street on the East Side and south of 42nd Street on the West Side. Specifically, Parsons called for a new subway to be built under Lexington Avenue north of 42nd Street and another under Seventh Avenue south of 42nd Street.[11]

Parsons also proposed a number of new lines for the Bronx, to connect either with the "H" lines or with lines of the Manhattan Railway Company, now controlled by the IRT. The first subway, which was actually on an elevated structure in most of the Bronx, was to be extended north along White Plains Road to the Westchester County border. In addition, the Third Avenue el was to be extended north from Fordham Road to a connection with the White Plains Road line at Gun Hill Road. For the East Bronx, there would be a new subway/elevated line to Pelham Bay Park, in the far northeast, connecting to the Lexington Avenue subway. For the West Bronx, Parsons proposed that the Ninth Avenue el be extended across the Harlem River to Jerome Avenue, and along this street up to Woodlawn Cemetery, near the northern border of the borough. Except for the southern portion of the Pelham route, these lines would pass through districts that were then lightly developed.[12]

In Brooklyn, all of the elevated lines then controlled by the Brooklyn Rapid Transit Company (BRT) connected Downtown Brooklyn and Williamsburg with outlying residential districts. The Brooklyn Bridge had rail tracks connected to the BRT network that carried trains from Downtown Brooklyn across the East River to a terminal building on Park Row in Lower Manhattan, but the capacity of these tracks was limited and could not meet growing passenger demand. The extension of the first subway to

Brooklyn via tunnel promised to meet some of this demand temporarily, but additional service was clearly needed.[13]

Parsons's plan for Brooklyn and Queens was aimed at taking maximum advantage of the new bridges that the City was building across the East River, as well as of the capacity of the IRT subway extension to Brooklyn.[14] From north to south, the new crossings were the Queensboro Bridge (opened 1909), connecting Midtown Manhattan to Queens; the Williamsburg Bridge (1903), connecting the Lower East Side to Brooklyn; and the Manhattan Bridge (1905), extending from Canal Street to Downtown Brooklyn. The Brooklyn Bridge (1883) is south of the Manhattan Bridge.

At this time, no rapid transit service existed to any part of Queens, across the East River from Midtown Manhattan.[15] Parsons did not believe that Queens needed much rapid transit, but he did propose that a branch of the Second Avenue el be extended over the Queensboro Bridge to Long Island City. He also called for the extension of two existing BRT elevated lines in Brooklyn into Queens.[16]

To better connect the built-up areas of Brooklyn with Lower Manhattan, and relieve overcrowding on East River crossings, Parsons called for construction of a loop subway running from the Williamsburg Bridge through Delancey Street to Centre Street and then down Centre Street to the Brooklyn Bridge. Trains from the BRT's Broadway elevated line in Brooklyn would cross over the Williamsburg Bridge and into the loop.[17] The loop also could be linked in the future with a line running over the Manhattan Bridge, which lay between the other two bridges. The loop was to alleviate congestion at the Brooklyn Bridge by taking advantage of the larger capacity of the new Williamsburg Bridge.[18]

Parsons also looked to expand subway service farther out in Brooklyn. The IRT extension to Brooklyn being constructed under Contract No. 2 would terminate at the intersection of Atlantic Avenue and Flatbush Avenue, in Downtown Brooklyn. Parsons's plan proposed a subway route extending south on Flatbush Avenue to Prospect Park and then going eastward along Eastern Parkway.[19]

In addition to having its engineer lay out new subway routes, the Rapid Transit Board moved to increase its ability to finance new lines. Under existing law, the Board could only incur City debt for new transit lines up to $50 million. The RTB, realizing that this was not enough to construct all the lines Parsons had proposed, asked the State Legislature to abolish the cap. In early 1904, the Legislature complied, but included a proviso that all future expenditures had to be approved by the City's Board of Estimate and Apportionment.[20] This was a small body composed of three officials elected on a citywide basis—the mayor, the comptroller and the president of the Board of Aldermen—along with the five borough presidents.[21] The Board of Estimate had full power over City capital expenditures, and from this time on the RTB's authority to incur debt was subject to its concurrence. The RTB was also subject to the provision of the State Constitution that limited New York City's debt, for all public purposes, to 10 percent of the assessed value of real estate within the five boroughs.[22] In May 1905, the State Legislature also transferred all powers to grant municipal approval of subway routes away from the Board of Aldermen to the Board of Estimate.[23]

As of 1903, the Rapid Transit Board was composed of Mayor Seth Low, Comptroller Edward M. Grout, and Morris K. Jesup, president of the Chamber of Commerce, all ex officio members, and five appointed members. All of the appointed members were wealthy and respected men, with long experience in business and the law.[24] The policy followed by the Board in 1902 and 1903 was conservative both in the number of routes it proposed to build at one time and in its encouragement of the extension of existing rapid transit systems controlled by the IRT and the BRT. One of its main concerns was to protect the City's credit. If the Board had proceeded with Parsons's modest plans of 1903, it is possible that a limited number of new lines would quickly have been constructed under contracts similar to the ones for the first subway and its extension to Brooklyn. The IRT, for its part, had indicated its willingness to carry out the Board's plans. The BRT would have cooperated at least to the extent of making the proposed extensions of its elevated lines.[25]

False Hopes

The Rapid Transit Board, however, did not proceed immediately to carry out Parsons's plans. A new chimera arose, offering the hope that competition among rival rapid transit companies would make it possible to build a large number of new subway lines at little cost, or risk, to the City of New York. In December 1903, the Metropolitan Street Railway Company (the Metropolitan, for short), which controlled most of the streetcar (trolley) lines in Manhattan and the Bronx, indicated to the RTB its intention to compete with the IRT for the construction and operation of new subway routes. This changed the picture entirely. For the next two years, much of the discussion of rapid transit in New York dealt with the supposed benefits the city would receive from active competition among transportation companies.

Many now thought that private companies, which could make large profits from subway operation, would offer to construct subway lines, to be owned by the municipality, in competitive bidding for amounts well below the actual costs.[26] The RTB hoped to extend subway lines to many outlying areas that had not been provided for under Parsons's plans of 1903, and to do this at small expense to the City.[27]

The Board requested that the Metropolitan put its verbal offer into written form. The company did so, submitting a formal proposal on February 24, 1904. It proposed to build a subway line southward from 138th Street and Third Avenue in the Bronx, which was a focal point of the company's network of streetcar lines in the borough. From there the line would proceed south under the Harlem River and down Lexington Avenue and other streets to the Battery. The line would then go up the West Side to 34th Street and across 34th Street to a junction with the East Side branch at Lexington Avenue. To sweeten the pot, the company said that it would give free transfers between this proposed subway and all of its streetcar lines. Passengers would thus be able to travel between most areas in Manhattan and the South Bronx for a single five-cent fare.[28]

The Metropolitan's proposal covered only Manhattan and a small section of the Bronx. But the publicity that it received encouraged an outburst of proposals for new subways from neighborhoods all over Greater New York. Numerous citizens' groups and real estate promoters now besieged the RTB with requests to approve subways to their particular areas.[29]

In addition, both the IRT and the Metropolitan began public relations campaigns in order to win the public to their respective positions. The Metropolitan hired Lemuel C. Quigg as a lobbyist. Quigg was a politician who had been the chief lieutenant in New York City of state Republican boss Thomas Platt. He helped to organize citizens' groups in Manhattan and the Bronx, which appeared before the RTB praising the merits of the Metropolitan's proposal.[30] In the summer of 1904, Quigg obtained over one million signatures on a petition to the RTB asking that no subway contracts be awarded that did not include free transfers to streetcar lines as one of the ingredients.[31]

The demand for new rapid transit lines soon got even more heated. The first subway from City Hall to 145th Street and

Broadway opened on October 27, 1904, in a burst of public enthusiasm.[32] After this, the RTB felt compelled to hold public hearings on new subway routes. At these hearings, held in January 1905, "representatives of all parts of the city, especially those most distant from the centre, very fully presented their views."[33] At one of the hearings, for example, a delegation of more than three hundred people headed by Brooklyn Borough President Bird S. Coler came before the Board advocating the construction of a subway under Fourth Avenue in Brooklyn. Inhabitants of this area, extending from Downtown Brooklyn south to Bay Ridge in the southwest corner of the borough, already had limited rapid transit service via a BRT elevated line, but wished to have more direct service to Manhattan. Based on this outburst of public enthusiasm, the RTB's Committee on Plans proceeded to lay out a great number of routes to almost every section of the city.[34]

On May 13, 1905, the Board proposed nineteen separate new lines, estimated to cost up to $250 million.[35] (In comparison, the actual cost of the subways being constructed under Contracts No. 1 and No. 2 was about $52 million).[36] Unlike Parsons's modest but easily implementable plans, the 1905 plan was a confusing document. It contained a jumble of individual routes, and it was not at all clear how the different lines would be pieced together into logical systems that could be operated together.

The RTB's plan for Manhattan included the lines previously proposed by Parsons as well as a number of other routes, including lines on First, Third, Fifth, and Eighth avenues, in addition to a crosstown route on 34th Street passing under the East River to Queens.[37] The intent was to allow the IRT to complete the "H," but also to open up other north-south streets for competitive lines. All of Parsons's 1905 lines for the Bronx were included, plus a subway for Jerome Avenue in the West Bronx.[38]

For Brooklyn, the 1905 plan included an expanded version of Parsons's Brooklyn and Manhattan loop, which now became a circular rapid transit line connecting the Lower East Side, the financial district, Downtown Brooklyn, Bedford-Stuyvesant, Bushwick, and Williamsburg. Also proposed were a subway running across 14th Street, under the East River and through numerous streets in Brooklyn to a connection with the loop line; a line to Jamaica, Queens, via northern Brooklyn; and a Brooklyn-Queens crosstown line. The major new proposal, however, was a subway to run from Canal Street over the Manhattan Bridge, through Downtown Brooklyn, and then down Fourth Avenue to Bay Ridge.[39]

In June 1905, the RTB formally approved the nineteen proposed routes; the Board of Estimate gave its approval to the routes in July.[40] During the final months of 1905, the RTB's engineers proceeded to make detailed plans for many of the routes, with an eye to inviting bids in early 1906. There were high hopes that 1906 would be a banner year for new transit.

The Interborough-Metropolitan Merger

These hopes were soon dashed. On December 22, 1905, the IRT and the Metropolitan Street Railway Company announced that they were about to merge.[41] This negated the hope that competition between private companies would result in the construction of many new subways. The merger also put a stop to the plans about which the RTB had been so optimistic.

The IRT-Metropolitan merger had its roots in the competition between the streetcar lines in Manhattan and the Bronx and the IRT's rapid transit network. During the 1890s, the Metropolitan had opposed the building of a subway out of fear that it would lose much of its streetcar business.[42] By 1902, the Metropolitan was almost insolvent. One muckraker, Burton J. Hendrick, later alleged that this had been the result of manipulations of Metropolitan stock by the company's top officers. The Metropolitan was overcapitalized, and company officers knew it. Some of them secretly sold their stock for large profits between 1900 and 1902.[43] But Thomas Fortune Ryan, who, together with William C. Whitney, had been most influential in the consolidation of Manhattan and Bronx streetcar lines, did not sell out. Instead, Ryan devised a scheme whereby he could make even more money.[44]

Ryan was well aware of the popularity of IRT stock on Wall Street in 1902 and 1903, as people had rushed to purchase it once subway construction had begun. Ryan's scheme was to force August Belmont's IRT into a merger with the Metropolitan. Despite the fact that during 1904 and 1905 the Metropolitan had said that it was anxious to compete for lines, it never had intended actually to engage in subway construction or operation. Its proposal to compete with the IRT had been made only as a threat to force a merger. Such a merger would increase the value of stock in the Metropolitan Securities Company, the holding company that controlled the Metropolitan Street Railway Company.[45]

The Metropolitan Securities Company had been organized in 1902. Soon after it was organized, Ryan began to conduct an expensive public relations campaign against the IRT. Quigg's activities as lobbyist were part of this campaign.[46] Ryan even obtained the funds he needed to build a subway in order to make competition seem a reality. He did this by acquiring control of the Equitable Life Assurance Society, an insurance company that had been racked by internal dissension. His control over this company provided him with an ostensible source of funds to invest in new subway lines.[47]

By late 1905, Ryan felt confident enough to negotiate with the IRT on the terms of a merger. Belmont was initially opposed to the idea of a merger but soon began to believe that the IRT could not stand the kind of competition threatened by Ryan.[48] Belmont eventually felt that he had no choice. Terms were agreed upon in December 1905, and in January 1906 a holding company, the Interborough-Metropolitan Company, was formed. Both the IRT and the Metropolitan Securities Company continued their respective corporate existences, but were now controlled by the new corporation.[49]

Under the terms of the merger agreement, the new Interborough-Metropolitan Company would offer to purchase all the capital stock of the IRT, the Metropolitan Securities Company, and the Metropolitan Street Railway Company. In exchange, IRT stockholders would receive bonds and common stock of the new Interborough-Metropolitan Company; owners of Metropolitan Securities Company stock would receive common stock; and Metropolitan Street Railway Company stockholders would receive common stock and preferred stock.[50]

After the merger, Ryan watched the price of Interborough-Metropolitan common stock. At the appropriate moment, he sold his interests in the Interborough-Metropolitan for a large profit.[51] Ryan knew the true condition of the Metropolitan's street railway system. He got out of the transit field before the New York City Railway Company, the company controlled by the Metropolitan Securities Company, which actually operated the streetcars, went into receivership. Belmont and other investors were left to pick up the pieces. Belmont later testified that the merger had cost the IRT owners about $40 million.[52]

The announcement of the IRT-Metropolitan merger shocked civic leaders and the general public. It made it clear that the small group of capitalists who controlled the existing transit companies had no intention of financing massive expansion of the subway network. It also injured the reputation of the IRT, which until this time had been seen as a responsible company. Even the conservative *New York Post* felt obliged to attack the Interborough-Metropolitan merger as a stock-watering plan of no public benefit, saying that "we are not likely to hear again very soon the assertion which the subway's financial managers have been wont to make with pride, that here at least is a railway enterprise in which capital inflation has played no part."[53]

The RTB now faced the problem of trying to work out another method for creating a sufficient number of new rapid transit lines. The chief problem was financial. Without the competition that would have resulted in offers from private companies to build lines at below cost, the City could not hope for extensive additions to its transit network in the near future.[54]

The Board now returned to a conservative approach to subway expansion, basically revisiting Parsons's original plans. It focused first on new subway lines that would expand the existing subway network controlled by the IRT. In an editorial, the *New York Times* hailed this decision as a return to a proper businesslike approach to the expansion of the rapid transit network.[55] On January 17, the *Times* reported that bids would soon be sought on the routes in Manhattan that would allow the IRT to complete the "H."[56]

These plans, however, were now obstructed by rising popular resentment against transit monopoly. The revelation of the Interborough-Metropolitan merger had helped fuel hostility toward public utility companies. This hostility had been growing steadily since 1900. It now came to a head in a demand for changes in the New York State Rapid Transit Act. Largely because of the changes to the law that resulted from this public outcry, private companies refused to participate in transit expansion and very few new transit lines were put under construction during the next few years. Meanwhile, the public authorities responsible for transit could neither cooperate with each other nor obtain sufficient public funds for large-scale subway expansion.

The Politics of Public Utilities

While the Rapid Transit Board had been making its plans for new subways, the press and various civic groups had been exposing the activities of the public utility companies. All public utility services in New York City, including gas, electricity, and streetcar and elevated railroad service, were provided by private companies that had received government franchises. These franchises often had been granted on generous terms. The street railway franchises, for example, were granted in perpetuity and the streetcar companies were allowed to operate their lines with only token government supervision.

In 1904 and 1905, numerous magazines and newspapers ran stories about how public utility companies operated in New York. It was alleged that utility companies were able to charge excessively high prices while rendering poor service, thereby reaping large profits, because of a corrupt alliance between company leaders and politicians in both the Democratic and the Republican parties. Politicians "bought" by the companies had granted generous franchise privileges and had refused to insist on proper safeguards to the public for their operation.[57]

Public criticism of the utilities was topped off in 1905 by a legislative investigation of New York's gas and electric companies. This investigation was conducted by Charles Evans Hughes, a successful young lawyer with a reputation for honesty, who in 1904 had conducted a similar examination of the insurance business in New York State. Hughes's investigation of the utilities showed that both Republican and Democratic legislators had been bribed by the gas and electric companies.[58] Before 1904, Hughes had been unknown outside the legal profession; these two investigations helped launch his political career.[59]

Given the public's heightened concern over utilities, the first subway contract of 1900 came under attack for being overly generous to the private contractor. As early as 1901, State Supreme Court Justice William J. Gaynor (who would be elected mayor of New York in 1909) had attacked Contract No. 1 for not providing that the City receive a share of the subway profits.[60] In 1902, while Contract No. 2 was being drawn up by the Rapid Transit Board, the Citizens Union launched a campaign demanding that the Rapid Transit Act be amended to mandate a maximum twenty-year lease for new subway contracts. In 1903, the Citizens Union and allied civic organizations persuaded State Senator Nathaniel Elsberg, from Manhattan, to introduce a bill to this effect in the Legislature. The proposed bill also allowed separate contracts to be made for construction and operation of new transit lines, rather than tying construction and operation into one contract; and for the municipality to operate its own transit facilities. The Elsberg bill was defeated because of Tammany opposition in 1903, 1904, and 1905.[61]

Meanwhile, the attack on the private transportation companies intensified. Gustavus Myers, in a March 1905 article in the *New York World* entitled "The Gold Mines of the New York Subway," alleged that there were tremendous profits to be made in operating the first subway, but that these profits had been given away to the IRT.[62] In the same month, another article, "The Subway Deal," written by muckraker Roy Stannard Baker, appeared in *McClure's*, attacking the Rapid Transit Board for its failure to guard the public interest with respect to the IRT. As a result, the new subway was "nourishing a new private monopoly, more piratical than any of its predecessors." Despite these harsh words, Baker was modest in his suggestions for remedying the situation. He believed that the changes in the Rapid Transit Act sought by the Citizens Union would, if passed, provide the City of New York with proper protection against the IRT.[63]

Another force was not so restrained in its approach. William Randolph Hearst published two local newspapers, the *New York*

American and the *New York Journal.* These mass circulation newspapers had wide appeal among workers and small shopkeepers, and they were frankly and unabashedly sensational. The Hearst papers made little attempt to be objective, opting instead for what one historian has described as "incomplete news articles which often misrepresented the facts."[64] Hearst focused his attacks on the public utility companies and their alleged ties to politicians.[65]

Hearst's motivations are the subject of conjecture. Some historians have regarded him as a demagogue out to sell his newspapers, others as a sincere democrat with a deep concern for the condition of the masses.[66] From 1901 on, Hearst had ambitions of running for president of the United States and saw the attacks on the public utility companies as a way of winning popular support.[67] Hearst's championship of the little man against the "interests" was thus good politics.[68] Indeed, according to one account at the time, it was so effective that the movement called Hearstism "became fiercer and stronger than any similar movement in our recent politics—perhaps than any movement in any period of politics—because of the unscrupulous methods by which it has been organized and fomented."[69]

Hearst used New York City as his political base. In 1902, he was elected to Congress from a Manhattan district.[70] In 1904, he unsuccessfully sought the Democratic nomination for president at the party's national convention. After his defeat, he realized that he needed to broaden his base if he was to campaign successfully at the national level.[71] To this end, he founded a movement called the Municipal Ownership League, which attacked the terms of the subway contracts with the IRT and called for municipal ownership and operation of all public utilities. Hearst played up the alleged alliance between politicians and leading corporate executives. He created an enemy of all working New Yorkers in what he called the "Traction Trust," a cabal of unscrupulous capitalists out to maximize profits at the expense of the little people.[72]

In 1905, Hearst decided to run for mayor. The political landscape in New York was changing rapidly as a result of the activities of Progressive reformers such as Charles Evans Hughes, as well as Hearst's increasing power. Previously, the political line-up had been the Tammany Democrats versus business-oriented "good government" organizations such as the Chamber of Commerce, often allied with the Republicans. The Rapid Transit Board itself was a reform product of the old mercantile elite.[73] Neither Tammany nor its usual opposition saw the municipality as having a major role in solving social problems or in regulating public utility companies. Now, however, the focus of debate had become how to best use government to control public utilities in the interest of the people.

The issue of municipal ownership and operation of new subways dominated the mayoral election of 1905. Hearst ran on a Municipal Ownership League platform that advocated, among other things, City ownership and operation of all new subways. The other major candidates were incumbent Democrat George B. McClellan and Republican William M. Ivins. McClellan was a staunch supporter of the Rapid Transit Board and the private transportation companies and had opposed the Elsberg bill. Ivins was a Progressive-type Republican, but stood little chance of being elected.[74] The race thus evolved into a contest between a supporter of the status quo, with respect to rapid transit, and Hearst.

It was not a gentle campaign. Former state senator John Ford, the Municipal Ownership League's candidate for president of the Board of Aldermen, accused the Republican and Democratic parties of conspiring to sell out the city to the private transportation companies. The Hearst press, in a cartoon, portrayed Tammany chief Charles Francis Murphy wearing a striped prison uniform over the caption "Look out, Murphy! It's a short lockstep from Delmonico's to Sing Sing."[75]

Hearst's opponents painted him as a radical. The *New York Times,* which normally supported the Republican candidate, was so concerned that Hearst might be elected that it urged Republicans to vote for McClellan as the lesser of two evils.[76] Tammany supporters, fearing a loss, were out in full force on election day. By registering nonexistent voters, destroying ballot boxes, and other tactics, they were able to win the election for McClellan. The vote was close, with McClellan ahead of Hearst by a few thousand votes and Ivins running a distant third.[77]

The closeness of the election was a clear indication of public concern over how utilities operated in New York. The election also showed that many citizens were dissatisfied with the way the Rapid Transit Board was dealing with the problem of providing new transit lines for New York City. The vote sparked major changes in New York State law regarding new subways, since public opinion was now heavily in favor of the proposed Elsberg Act.

In 1906, Senator Elsberg again introduced a bill in the State Legislature allowing for separate contracts for construction and operation of subways as well as for municipal operation. One aim of the bill was to give the Rapid Transit Board more flexibility in obtaining new transit facilities. Using municipal funds, the RTB could plan and construct a transit system without having to worry about finding an operator beforehand. If, after the new lines were constructed, an operator could not be found, then the City could operate the new system with municipal employees. The Elsberg bill also limited the length of leases to private operators to twenty years, with a possible twenty-year renewal. In April 1906, the Elsberg Act was approved by the Legislature and signed by the governor.[78]

The RTB had opposed the Elsberg bill, believing that it would discourage private capital from participating in rapid transit expansion.[79] Despite the bill's passage, however, the Board went ahead with its plans for constructing the IRT's "H" lines in Manhattan. It also directed its staff to make detailed plans for the proposed loop subway in Lower Manhattan connecting the East River bridges.[80]

Under pressure from Brooklyn Borough President Bird S. Coler, the RTB also began work on the development of a subway system that could be operated independently of the networks already controlled by the IRT and the BRT. Many reformers in New York's civic groups still thought that competition among rapid transit operators was the key to achieving an extensive rapid transit network. The passage of the Elsberg bill was premised on this notion. The fact that the IRT was making large profits from the operation of the first subway led these people to believe that private companies would be willing to construct a large independent system under a short-term lease, at low cost to the City.[81]

A new subway system that would compete with the IRT was thus a compelling idea. The result was the proposed Triborough System. This plan pieced together a number of routes that had previously been proposed as separate lines into one network that could be operated as a unity. The initial RTB plan combined the proposed Pelham and Jerome Avenue lines in the Bronx with a trunk line on the East Side of Manhattan to the Battery. The Fourth Avenue subway from Brooklyn, passing over the Manhattan Bridge, would connect to this line at Canal Street. In southern Brooklyn, a branch of the Fourth Avenue subway, the New Utrecht Avenue line, would pass through Bensonhurst, terminating at Coney Island.[82] (See Map 2.)

At the beginning of 1907, the RTB was thus proceeding on plans for the Manhattan "H," the Triborough System, and a subway loop in Lower Manhattan. The key question became how these lines would be financed and in what order. In January, Mayor McClellan reported that the City's estimated new

Map 2. The Proposed Triborough System

borrowing capacity was about $66 million, much of which was already committed to projects other than subways.[83] Clearly, the Board could not hope to begin construction immediately on all of the routes. The estimated cost of the "H" lines alone, for example, was over $66 million.[84]

The RTB therefore decided that its first step would be to accept bids on sections of the Manhattan loop lines, which it felt the City could afford to build under a contract providing for construction alone. After this, bids would be accepted on the "H" lines. Even under the provisions of the Elsberg Act, it was thought that the IRT would bid on these routes because they ran through areas that were already densely settled, as well as through the main business and commercial centers. If the IRT made bids to build these routes below actual cost, then the Board might proceed to contract for construction of future lines.[85]

On April 11, 1907, bids were received for construction alone of five sections of the Lower Manhattan loop subway between the Williamsburg Bridge and the Brooklyn Bridge. The Board accepted the lowest bids. At the end of June, contracts were signed with private companies for construction of these five sections.[86]

Bids were to be received for the Manhattan "H" lines on April 25. It had been expected that the IRT would be the only bidder. Even before this date, however, there were ominous indications that the IRT might not be willing to participate in the building of new subways, but would wait until it could get a more favorable deal from the City. On April 11, Comptroller Herman Metz, a Democrat, and August Belmont appeared on the same platform at a meeting of the Queens Borough Real Estate Exchange. Metz strongly defended the IRT at this meeting. There had been too much talk, he said, about how much the private transportation companies had gained from the public and too little appreciation of what they had accomplished. "The time has come," said Metz, "when we will cease to hound the corporation. Instead we are going to knock at their gates to beg them for God's sake to lay some tracks for us." Metz was followed by Belmont, who warned that the hostile spirit against the private companies "frightens the investors, and the moment hostility started, the corporations found it difficult to get capital with which to make improvements." The corporations were now threatened with increased government regulation. If the City wanted new transit lines, threats of increased regulation had to cease and the law requiring short-term franchises had to be changed.[87] Two weeks later the IRT refused to make any bids on the completion of the "H."[88]

The Public Service Commission Takes Over

Soon after the IRT's refusal to cooperate in building new transit lines, the Rapid Transit Board itself was abolished, to be replaced by the New York State Public Service Commission for the First District (PSC). The new commission, which came to power on July 7, 1907, was a triumph of progressivism, a key tenet of which was public regulation of private utility companies.[89] Its creation was a direct result of the New York State gubernatorial election of 1906, which had offered the voters a choice between Charles Evans Hughes and William Randolph Hearst.

After his defeat in the 1905 mayoral election, Hearst formed the statewide Independence League, a political organization he used to launch his bid for governor. The Independence League advocated municipal ownership and operation of public utilities, as had the Municipal Ownership League. Hearst also won the Democratic gubernatorial nomination with the help of Tammany boss Charles Francis Murphy. Murphy, whom Hearst had portrayed in prison stripes a year before, realized that the Democrats would lose many state government positions in a three-way race between Republican, Democratic, and Independence League candidates. Allied with the Independence League, Murphy hoped to be able to carry the lesser state offices, whether or not Hearst was elected governor.[90]

The Republican candidate, Hughes, was a champion of public regulation of public utilities, an idea that by late 1906 had the support of many New York's progressive reformers. Advocates of this idea believed that public utility monopolies were inevitable, and that the best way to deal with these monopolies was through continuous government regulation by an independent commission with power to supervise all aspects of public utility operation. Such a commission also would be responsible for planning and authorizing extensions of utility systems. Proponents of regulation argued that private public utility monopolies were not inherently wrong. They believed that although private utility companies had abused their power in the past, they were still the best type of organization to operate public utilities since they would do so more efficiently in the interest of making a profit.[91]

The 1906 election was thus, in part, a struggle between the different approaches to the problem of public utilities. The race was even more bitter than the 1905 mayoral election. Hughes was portrayed as a tool of corporate moguls and Republican bosses out to line their own pockets at the expense of "the people." For their part, Hearst's Republican opponents portrayed him as a hypocrite and a demagogue.[92]

Five days before the election, President Theodore Roosevelt sent his secretary of state, Elihu Root, to give a speech in upstate New York. Root charged that the person who had assassinated President William McKinley in 1901 had been influenced to do so by attacks on the president in Hearst newspapers. Root noted that in his first presidential message, Roosevelt, who succeeded McKinley, had denounced "the reckless utterances of those who, on the stump and in the public press, appeal to the dark and evil spirits of malice and greed, envy and sullen hatred." Root concluded by saying that Roosevelt had authorized him to say that in writing these lines, the president had Hearst specifically in mind. Two million copies of Root's speech were distributed before the election.[93] Hughes won the election with a 76,000 vote plurality out of a total of more than 1.5 million votes.[94]

Hughes's first annual message to the State Legislature, in January 1907, called for stricter and more comprehensive public utility regulation through the creation of a new commission that would centralize regulatory authority over subways, elevated railroads, streetcar lines, and gas and electric companies.[95] Acting together with leaders of New York civic groups, Hughes's supporters drafted a public service commissions bill.[96] It had the active support of only a small group of Republicans, most of whom were from urban areas, who shared Hughes's ideas about regulation.[97] The Old Guard Republicans in the Legislature, allied with the Democrats, had the power to ensure the bill's defeat. In May, however, President Theodore Roosevelt called upon New York Republicans to support the PSC bill as a party measure. Soon after this, the bill was passed and signed by Governor Hughes.[98]

Two public service commissions were created by the act. The Public Service Commission for the First District (PSC) had jurisdiction over New York City; the Second District commission had jurisdiction for the rest of the state. All of the powers of the Rapid Transit Board, the State Railroad Commission, and the State Gas and Electric Commission pertaining to New York City were granted to the First District Commission. In addition, the PSC assumed powers never before vested in any governmental agency in New York: to give or withhold permission for the issuance of corporate securities of public utility companies; to establish uniform accounting systems; to compel the production of all records, documents, and papers of utility companies; to supervise mergers and consolidations; to fix rates and services on its own initiative; and otherwise to enforce its orders.[99] The Commission also was given the power to oversee the operation of the existing subway and elevated lines. All of these were powers that had not been given to the Rapid Transit Board.[100]

The PSC consisted of five men appointed by the governor. The chairman was William R. Willcox, former Parks Commissioner of Manhattan, who at the time of his appointment was Postmaster of New York City. Willcox, a friend of Hughes, was devoted to the idea of public utility regulation.[101] Milo R. Maltbie, of Manhattan, was the secretary of the Municipal Art Commission and had written a number of articles about rapid transit in New York.[102] Edward M. Bassett, of Brooklyn, a lawyer and former congressman who had assisted in the drafting of the Page-Merritt bill, had a reputation as a transit expert.[103] William McCarroll, also from Brooklyn, was a businessman who had taken an interest in rapid transit development.[104] John E. Eustis, a lawyer, had been Bronx Parks Commissioner under Mayor Low.[105] Willcox, McCarroll, and Eustis were Republicans; Maltbie and Bassett were Democrats.[106] All of Hughes's appointments were men whose integrity was above suspicion and, although all had been active in politics at one time or another, none was tied to any political machine. The commissioners were removable only on cause, to keep them free of political interference. Their terms of office were arranged so that each year one man's term would expire. Their $15,000 annual salary, a huge amount at the time, was aimed at insuring their independence.[107]

Upon entering office, three of the Public Service Commissioners, Willcox, Bassett, and Maltbie, had written letters to George McAneny, who had become president of the City Club of New York in January 1907. New York civic groups often took it upon themselves to become experts in certain fields. By building up expertise they gained access to government officials, who increasingly saw the need to base policy decisions on careful studies of distinct problems.[108] The City Club fit this pattern. It hired transit experts, and the executive staff of the club, headed by McAneny, gave its chief attention to rapid transit matters from 1907 on.[109]

In May 1907, the City Club's transit committee had been authorized to prepare and submit a memorandum to the PSC about improvements in transit service, completion of present transit projects, and ideas for new lines. In order to prepare this memorandum, the club's transit experts had conducted exhaustive studies of passenger mileage, traffic flow, and overcrowding on the city's transit facilities. They also had studied previous plans for new rapid transit lines.[110]

With respect to new lines, the City Club recommended that the PSC should first act on proposals on which extensive public discussion had already taken place, and for which detailed plans had been drawn up by the RTB. Relief of the crush of passengers on the Brooklyn Bridge was to have top priority. The difficulties experienced daily by Brooklyn residents traveling to and from work, and the inability of the RTB to solve this problem, were said to have been one of the main reasons for the creation of the PSC. The City Club believed that the PSC should proceed with the construction of the Lower Manhattan loop subway as quickly as possible. It also suggested that a quick decision should be made about the Fourth Avenue and Bensonhurst subway routes. The City Club also recommended the immediate extension of the IRT subway to Prospect Park. For Manhattan, the City Club advised the PSC to complete the IRT's "H" as soon as possible.[111]

After making these necessary additions, the PSC could then turn to making long-range plans for further transit lines. The first step would be a comprehensive assessment of the city's needs. According to the City Club's memorandum, no thorough and exhaustive study of the city's rapid transit requirements had yet been made. In addition, the financial feasibility of subways was still up in the air. Did the failure to receive bids from the IRT for the "H" lines indicate that most underground construction was too expensive? How far could subway lines be extended into the Bronx, Brooklyn and Queens and still pay for themselves?[112]

The City Club also pointed out that subway planners were as yet unaware of the actual effect of the first subway on the movement of population within the city, or about the effect of the subway on relative rent costs. No one knew for certain what unoccupied land remained in New York City or what the relationship of unoccupied land should be to new subway lines. In short, much further study had to be done before new transit lines could be planned intelligently.[113]

The Public Service Commission Discovers That Subways Are Not "Gold Mines"

From its inception, the Public Service Commission followed a two-fold policy toward rapid transit development. It made clear its willingness to negotiate with the IRT for the extension of its network, especially the "H" lines, but it also saw the need for a new system that could operate independently of the IRT.[114] With regard to the latter, the proposed Triborough System initially put forward by the old Rapid Transit Board quickly became the favorite. The Commission conducted detailed studies and determined that the East Side route of this system should run from the Battery up local streets and Broadway to 14th Street, and then up Lexington Avenue to the Bronx. Here the route would branch, one line going to the West Bronx (Jerome Avenue), the other to the East Bronx (Pelham line). This combination of routes was called the Broadway–Lexington Avenue subsystem.[115]

The PSC also modified the Triborough System plan to include a circular loop subway connecting Lower Manhattan with the built-up areas of Brooklyn via the new East River bridges (the

Williamsburg and Manhattan bridges). In Manhattan, the plan used the Centre Street loop subway, then under construction. This loop was called the Broadway–Lafayette Avenue subsystem, after the two major streets it was to use in Brooklyn. In Downtown Brooklyn, this subsystem would connect with the Fourth Avenue subsystem, consisting of the Fourth Avenue subway from Canal Street to Bay Ridge and the branch line through Bensonhurst to Coney Island.[116] (See Map 2.)

The Triborough System, as refined by the PSC, was intended to be a unified network that could operate independently, that is, without any connections to any of the existing rapid transit lines of the IRT or the BRT. The system was designed to provide service to many areas of Greater New York that had not yet been heavily developed, such as the western and eastern Bronx and southern Brooklyn. It also was intended to relieve overcrowding on existing elevated lines in northern Brooklyn and the East Side of Manhattan and to provide many more direct services from Brooklyn to Manhattan.

For the PSC, the main issue with the Triborough System was how to pay for it, given the unquestioned assumption that the fare would be five cents. To assess the economics of the plan, the Commission conducted detailed financial studies of capital and operating costs and projected operating revenues of portions of the Triborough System. Its 1907 study of the costs and revenues of the Fourth Avenue subsystem proved to have ramifications that extended far beyond the economics of these particular routes. For in studying the probable passenger traffic on the proposed subsystem, Commissioner Bassett discovered that it would not pay for itself for several years. In southern Brooklyn, the Fourth Avenue subway and the Bensonhurst line would run through areas that were then thinly populated. As a result, passenger fares would barely cover fixed charges on the construction costs, much less the line's operating expenses, interest on capital invested in equipment, and a fair profit to the operator. According to predictions, it would be fifteen years before the area had enough population to support a subway line.[117]

This discovery had a great impact on the PSC. It led the Commission to the conclusion, reinforced by subsequent PSC studies of the IRT's finances, that subway lines to outlying areas of the city would be generally unprofitable for the first decade or more after operation began. The only subway lines that could make a quick profit were lines, such as the existing IRT subway, that traversed overcrowded sections. One PSC study of the IRT network determined that the company lost money on long-haul trips north of 96th Street, although it made up this loss by large profits on short-haul trips south of 96th Street.[118]

Another study concluded that "the fundamental problem of rapid transit in New York City at the present time is how to provide additional rapid transit facilities and maintain the present five-cent fare."[119] For a subway route to pay for itself, income from passenger traffic had to average one cent per mile per passenger. This meant that if a route were longer than five miles, it could not pay for itself. There were ways to get around this problem, such as lowering the costs of building rapid transit lines (for example, by building elevated lines rather than underground ones) and/or subsidizing new transit lines. Another alternative was to have lines in built-up areas cross-subsidize the long-haul lines. Surplus revenues from profitable short-haul trips could be used to cover the losses on the trips to distant outlying areas.[120]

The studies done by the PSC reversed previously held notions that subway lines were extremely profitable. In its 1908 *Annual Report*, the PSC now stated: "All know now that both sides were deluded as to the profits of subway railroads. . . . Subway operation does not prove so profitable or attractive as it appeared to be in 1904."[121] It was now clear to private operators and public officials alike that building a large number of new lines at one time was a risky proposition. In order to attract private companies to bid on subway construction and operation, lease terms had to be more generous. If this were the case, then the Elsberg Act could be said to have been based on a false premise and might have to be repealed.[122]

There was also the issue of the City's borrowing capacity, which under the New York State Constitution was limited to 10 percent of the assessed value of real estate. This limitation was intended to preserve the City's credit, but it constrained the amount of municipal funds available for subway construction at any one time.[123] The City's limited borrowing capacity made it clear to the PSC that there was little hope of soon building an extensive subway network solely using City funds.

This problem was made worse by the unrelenting hostility of the City administration to the Public Service Commission. Mayor McClellan and Comptroller Metz had both served on the old Rapid Transit Board. They resented the fact that much of the power of deciding on new transit lines had now been transferred to a new Republican-dominated and -created PSC. Both Metz and McClellan were partisans of the IRT, believing that arrangements should be made with the company for the completion of the Manhattan "H" lines before anything else was done.[124] Metz later commented that the PSC's plans for the Triborough System were not fair to the private companies. "There was no justice," said Metz, "in requiring a railroad company to haul a passenger from Woodlawn Cemetery [at the northern end of the Jerome Avenue line in the Bronx] to Coney Island [in southernmost Brooklyn] for five cents." Instead, according to the *New York Times,* Metz "declared that subways should be built in congested districts, where they are needed."[125]

The PSC's independence threatened the cozy relationships that existed between the City and the private transit companies. The answer to this threat was to do everything possible to discredit the Commission by making it seem incapable of action. The hope was that, in the end, the PSC would be abolished or, if this were not possible, have its members replaced with more malleable commissioners. Once the PSC came into office, Comptroller Metz began to warn that the City did not have the necessary borrowing capacity to build any new subway lines and would not have this ability in the near future.[126]

Faced with this situation, and now well aware of the realities of subway economics, throughout 1908 and 1909 the PSC made proposals to the governor and the State Legislature aimed at increasing the City's borrowing capacity and increasing its own flexibility in negotiating arrangements with private companies. These included proposals to exempt self-supporting projects, such as docks and subways, from the calculation of the debt limit; extending the length of subway franchises; allowing private capital to participate directly in constructing new subways; and constructing new rapid transit lines by raising the real estate assessments for the properties that would benefit from increases in value along the routes.[127]

One thing that the PSC did not attempt was to lift the overall limitation on the City's borrowing capacity. Such a move would have been politically impossible. During the nineteenth century, several states had risked their credit on schemes for building railroads and other transportation facilities and had gone bankrupt. The result was that many state constitutions, including that of New York, were amended to limit the ability of states and cities to borrow to a fixed revenue stream. In order to preserve the City's credit, business interests in New York were adamant that the borrowing limit in the State Constitution not be changed.[128]

In 1908 and 1909, the State Legislature adopted a constitutional amendment that exempted self-supporting subway and dock bonds from the calculation of the City's debt limit. It was projected that this would free up $120 million in borrowing capacity in 1910.[129] In 1909, the Legislature repealed the requirement that subway leases be limited to twenty years, giving the PSC the discretion to decide the length of leases.[130]

The PSC also convinced the Legislature to approve what was called "the indeterminate franchise plan," under which private companies would receive long-term leases in return for their willingness to provide capital for new subway lines. The City, however, would have the right to take over any lines built with private capital after ten years, by paying the companies the amount they had invested plus 15 percent. The aim was to increase the ability of the PSC to put many new lines under construction at one time. The hope was that the IRT "H" lines and new IRT lines in the Bronx, Brooklyn, and Queens, as well as all or part of the Triborough System, could be built under such a financial arrangement.[131] The plan was controversial among reformers because it seemed to go against established policy that all future subway lines would be owned by the municipality. This was taken care of in the final legislation in 1909, which specified that ownership of all new subway lines would be vested in the City.[132]

The PSC's last proposal was a plan for building new rapid transit lines by reassessing property along the new routes, on the assumption that new lines would result in increased real estate values. These properties would be assessed at a higher value, and an increment of the increase would be used to pay off the bonds sold to cover the construction costs of the subways.[133] One merit of this plan was that it "would largely solve the problem that confronts the Public Service Commission in attempting to decide between factions, each contending for a line to its own particular section. The sincerity of speculators and real estate speculators would quickly be tested by the requirement that their petition be accompanied by an assurance of a willingness to be assessed for the cost of the line."[134] At the request of the PSC, the State Legislature approved the assessment plan in 1909.[135]

While new legislation was being sought in Albany, the PSC set its policy for future dealings with private transit operators. The Commission's primary goal was to build as many new rapid transit lines as possible to undeveloped districts, based on the need to reduce overcrowding in the older neighborhoods. Now that it was clear that, at a five-cent fare, such lines would not produce profits over the short term, the PSC decided that any franchise grants to private companies would have to include a combination of short-haul lines and long-haul "development" routes. The short-haul "cash cows" would produce a surplus from operating revenues that would cross-subsidize the long-haul lines, when operated as one system with a uniform fare. Ideally, the end result would be a greatly expanded IRT System as well as the construction of the complete Triborough System. The IRT's "H" lines would cross-subsidize its new long-haul lines, and surplus revenues from the Broadway–Lexington Avenue trunk line of the Triborough plan would help to cover the costs of lines to sparsely developed areas.[136]

In order to achieve this goal, the PSC believed that it had to be able to threaten existing transit operators with competition. This made the proposed Triborough System even more appealing, since it could be run by an operator independent of the existing transit companies. In testifying before the Legislature regarding funding proposals, Chairman Willcox claimed that without the threat of real competition, the City "will be victimized by gentlemen's agreements such as have been made in the past." Willcox said that there was a gentlemen's agreement under which the BRT was precluded from constructing rapid transit lines in Manhattan, so as to leave the IRT with a transit monopoly in Manhattan and the Bronx. Under this agreement, the companies could insist upon terms for participating in the development of new lines that would enable them "to take the fat and leave the lean."[137] The only way to force the companies to come to proper terms was to threaten to build a new subway system independent of the IRT or the BRT.

Partly with this in mind, the PSC continued to move forward with the Triborough System.[138] To back up its threat of competition with action, the Commission announced that it planned to let contracts for construction of individual sections of the Broadway–Lexington Avenue line and the Fourth Avenue line, using whatever municipal funds were available; an operator would be found later. In the spring of 1908, it solicited bids for construction of portions of the Fourth Avenue line. The PSC accepted the lowest bids, amounting to less than $16 million, and requested that the Board of Estimate appropriate funds for less than $3 million to begin construction of the first section.[139]

Comptroller Metz, however, had other ideas. He claimed that the City did not have the borrowing capacity to pay for construction of any new lines.[140] Just before the Board of Estimate was about to vote on the money for the Fourth Avenue subway, its members were served with an injunction barring the Board from appropriating any funds on the grounds that the City's borrowing capacity was too small to pay for this subway.[141] Upon hearing of the injunction, Willcox said that the "transit combination," meaning the IRT and the BRT, would rejoice in the delay.[142] The result of this injunction was to block any appropriations for new rapid transit lines until the court could determine exactly what the City's borrowing capacity actually was. This process took over a year to complete. The referee appointed by the court eventually decided, in 1909, that the City's credit margin on June 30, 1908, had been over $100 million, but Metz's goal had been accomplished.[143] He had successfully halted construction of any lines that could be operated independently of the IRT.

From the time the PSC came into office in July 1907 until the middle of 1909, the IRT continued to play a waiting game. The company was making high profits from the operation of the first subway.[144] Each year, the number of passengers on the IRT subway increased, climbing from 137 million in 1905 to 200 million in 1908, when the Brooklyn extension was opened. In 1910, annual ridership was 269 million.[145] With all these passengers on what was a relatively small system, the subway was overcrowded from the day it opened.

Since it was making a good profit from the operation of the existing subway network, the IRT saw no immediate need to participate in transit expansion. This conclusion had been reinforced by the company's own studies of the financing of new subways. On the cost side, prices for construction and equipment had increased and interest rates had gone up, further reducing the possibility of long-term profits. On the revenue side, the company's own financial estimates indicated that even if the City were to pay the full cost of the subway extensions to the IRT system then under consideration, passenger traffic would not be enough to provide a decent rate of return to the company. Many of the reasons for these dim financial prospects had to do with the terms of any subway contract for subway expansion that could be made under the restrictive requirements of the Elsberg amendments to the State Rapid Transit Act.[146] Lifting these restrictions would allow profitable operation on an expanded IRT system since, in various ways, it would lower the rate of return required to attract private capital to invest in new subways.[147] As a result, the IRT believed that the best thing to do was to wait for these restrictions to be removed. In the meantime, it would use all of its political clout to make sure that no competitive lines were built in Manhattan that might reduce the company's profits. As part of this effort, the IRT attacked the proposed Triborough System as being financially irresponsible.[148]

Chairman Willcox of the PSC was well aware of the IRT's strong position. He wrote that the IRT had no fear "that its business will not remain stable or that it will decrease." This had resulted in "a reluctance or refusal to increase facilities until the point is reached where the public necessities are so great that franchises would be offered to the company on a silver platter."[149]

Hopes for a New Beginning

The PSC's success in obtaining the State Legislature's approval of its package of bills in the spring of 1909 resulted in a burst of activity. Private companies, in part fearing that the PSC would soon have the ability to build transit lines with City money, and in part attracted by the lifting of the restrictive requirements of the Elsberg bill, began to make proposals for new transit lines.[150]

The most interesting proposal, and the only one seriously considered by the PSC other than one made by the IRT, was made on May 26, 1909, by the Bradley-Gaffney-Steers Company. Bradley was a contractor who had constructed much of the first subway. Gaffney was a former alderman allied to Tammany boss Murphy.[151] The company proposed to construct the Manhattan and Bronx sections of the Triborough System with its own funds. The Broadway–Lafayette Avenue and Fourth Avenue–Bensonhurst subsystems were to be constructed with City money. The company also offered to equip and operate the entire system except the Fourth Avenue–Bensonhurst routes.[152]

The IRT made an offer in a letter to the PSC dated June 30, 1909. The company proposed to complete the Manhattan "H" by constructing a four-track subway down Seventh Avenue, south of 42nd Street, and two two-track subways north of 42nd Street. One of these was to go up Third Avenue, the other up Lexington Avenue.[153] The Seventh Avenue line was to split at Canal Street, with two tracks proceeding south to the Battery and two tracks going across Canal Street and into Brooklyn to a junction with the first subway. The Lexington and Third Avenue lines were to connect in the Bronx with the existing subway running across 149th Street. The IRT also proposed to add a third track to its Second Avenue, Third Avenue, and Ninth Avenue elevated lines to allow for express service. In addition, the IRT proposed to build an elevated extension of the Ninth Avenue line up Jerome Avenue in the Bronx, and to extend the Second Avenue el across the Queensboro Bridge. The company further offered to operate a subway in the Steinway Tunnel, which it then controlled, between 42nd Street and Long Island City in Queens.[154]

The IRT wished to do this work as "extras" under the existing subway contracts or under contracts similar to the existing contacts. That is, the money for subway construction was to be provided by the City. The company would equip and operate the lines under a lease similar to the existing leases under which it was operating the first subway. The company would operate all of the lines, old and new, for a single five-cent fare, with free transfers between all lines.[155]

Under the Rapid Transit Act as amended in 1909, the IRT could build minor extensions to its present system under terms similar to Contracts No. 1 and No. 2.[156] What the IRT was proposing, however, included more than just minor extensions to its system and was, therefore, of doubtful legality. Over and above this fact, the IRT proposal did not include any major extensions into outlying areas.

In July, after considering these two offers, the PSC decided to proceed along the lines of the Bradley-Gaffney-Steers proposal.[157] It applied to the Board of Estimate for permission to prepare contracts for different sections of the Triborough System, either for separate construction by the City with an operator to be found later, or by a private company under the indeterminate franchise plan. During the summer, PSC engineers and lawyers continued to work on detailed plans and contracts for the Broadway–Lexington Avenue and Bronx lines of the Triborough System.[158]

The PSC formally rejected the IRT's offer on August 27. In a letter to IRT president Theodore P. Shonts, Chairman Willcox said that the IRT's proposals were not acceptable. The PSC was looking to the future and believed that "the development of all rapid transit lines shall proceed in a logical, practical and systematical form, and not in a haphazard, disjointed and temporizing manner." The IRT's proposals did not meet the PSC's standards. Allowing the IRT new lines on Lexington and Third Avenues would render improbable an independent through route to the Bronx. The Commission suggested that the IRT consider a line up Madison Avenue as an alternative.[159]

The IRT's proposals for Bronx lines were also inadequate. The company was even unwilling to build an extension of its present subway from West Farms up White Plains Road to Mt. Vernon. The one line that the company did propose for the Bronx, on Jerome Avenue, interfered with the Commission's Triborough plan. The Triborough plan, by contrast, tapped several new areas in the Bronx. In conclusion, the PSC pointed out that the Triborough System in no way interfered with the logical extension of the IRT's system, whereas the IRT's proposals seemed designed to hinder development of the Triborough System in the Bronx, Manhattan, and Brooklyn.[160]

After this letter, conferences were held between the PSC and the IRT, resulting in another proposal by the IRT on September 22. Shonts now proposed that the IRT build a four-track subway under Madison Avenue, but he also proposed that this subway be connected to a Jerome Avenue line. The IRT also offered to construct the northern section of the Pelham line, connecting it to its present subway in the southern Bronx.[161]

Willcox's response to this proposal was harsh. He told Shonts that "the fundamental objection to your proposition is that it does not deal with the rapid transit problem in a broad, metropolitan way." The IRT, for example, had, in its discussions with the PSC, refused even to consider extending its lines in Brooklyn. Willcox believed that this was an obligation the company had assumed when it "took upon itself the construction and operation of the spur to Brooklyn" and "preempted one of the principal approaches to lower Manhattan and one of the principal streets of Brooklyn." If the IRT could offer to build the Pelham line, which would carry passengers for a five-cent fare between the North Bronx and Lower Manhattan, then it could also afford to operate an extension to Brooklyn, running a much shorter distance east or south. The only conclusion that Willcox could come to about the IRT's policy with respect to Brooklyn was that it was "plainly a blocking policy." Willcox ended his letter with an attack on the IRT's financial plan for the proposed subways, saying that they could not be built as "extras."[162]

The 1909 Municipal Elections Alter the Playing Board

While the PSC had been considering the offers of the Bradley-Gaffney-Steers Company and the IRT, New York was going through a municipal election campaign. The outcome of this campaign proved crucial to subway development during the next four years, because it brought a new Board of Estimate into office, a majority of which was committed to working closely with the PSC. The harshness of Willcox's response to Shonts was no doubt due to the outcome of this election.

The mayoral election of 1909 was a three-sided race between Republican-Fusion candidate Otto T. Bannard, Democrat

William J. Gaynor, and William Randolph Hearst, running on the Civic Alliance ticket.[163] Contests for the other offices represented on the Board of Estimate were two-sided races between Democrats and candidates jointly endorsed by the Republican-Fusion movement and the Civic Alliance. The key issue during the election campaign was rapid transit development.[164]

The 1909 Fusion movement—so named because it fused together elements from different parties—consisted of Republicans, dissident Democrats, Hearstites, representatives of various civic organizations, and labor union representatives, among others. Preliminary steps toward a Fusion movement had been taken in the early part of 1909 with discussions between leaders of different civic groups.[165] On May 11, City Club president George McAneny chaired a mass meeting to organize the Fusion campaign. The *New York Press* hailed this meeting with the headline "Subways Is Slogan of Newest Party."[166] The final Fusion platform asserted, with reference to subways: "Immediate steps should be taken to give the whole city proper transit facilities. Not only must the present disgraceful condition of transportation be relieved; but a comprehensive and adequate system of transit development which will meet the needs of every section of the city must be adopted and built without further delay." Future subway lines were to be constructed with municipal funds, "construction by private capital being permitted only when the city is financially unable to keep up with the demands for transit extension, and then upon terms that will preserve strict and continuous municipal control."[167]

The Fusion movement was unable to agree on a slate of candidates. As a result, the Republican Party, many of whose leaders had been active in the Fusion movement, selected its own slate, which the Fusionists proceeded to endorse.[168] At the head of the ticket was New York Trust Company president Otto T. Bannard, who had long interested himself in social work.[169] For president of the Board of Aldermen, the Republicans had chosen John Purroy Mitchel, a young lawyer who was a Democrat.[170] For Comptroller, the Republicans picked Republican William A. Prendergast, a self-made businessman from Brooklyn, who was the registrar of Kings County.[171] Democrat George McAneny received the nomination for borough president of Manhattan; like nominations went to Cyrus L. Miller of the Bronx and Alfred Steers of Brooklyn. Republican George Cromwell was nominated for the borough presidency of Richmond.[172]

Unlike the Fusionists, Hearst could not accept Bannard as a candidate, so he decided to run for mayor himself on his Civic Alliance ticket. All the other Fusion candidates received the nomination of the Civic Alliance.[173]

The Democratic mayoral candidate, William J. Gaynor, was from Brooklyn and had served as a judge on the New York State Supreme Court for sixteen years.[174] Although he was independent-minded, Gaynor won the Democratic nomination with the support of Tammany boss Charles F. Murphy, who knew that no ordinary Democratic candidate stood a chance against the Fusionists.[175]

Gaynor had helped set himself up for the nomination by attacking the IRT. In the spring of 1909, Gaynor had written an article called "The Looting of New York," in which he alleged that enormous profits had been made from transit lines by grasping and clever men. This article deliberately linked the IRT with the Metropolitan Street Railway Company in a manner which implied that IRT officials had somehow been responsible for the financial chicanery of Metropolitan officials prior to the merger. The time had now come, said Gaynor, to elect public officials who would be free of the influence of such men.[176] The Democratic platform, much of it written by Gaynor himself, blamed the RTB and the PSC for the failure to provide adequate transit facilities.[177]

The 1909 campaign began with a rational discussion of subways and other major issues, but it quickly degenerated into a clash of personalities. During the last weeks of the campaign, Gaynor became bitterly hostile toward Hearst because of the intensity of the publisher's personal attacks on him and began to attack Hearst.[178] In the November election, Gaynor won the mayoralty, but the Republican–Fusion–Civic Alliance candidates carried every other position on the Board of Estimate except the borough presidency of Queens.[179]

The election swept into office men whose positions on rapid transit development closely paralleled that of the PSC. The only doubtful person was Gaynor, and even he was personally committed to using the maximum amount of City money possible for subway development. At the very least, once the new Board of Estimate came into office, the PSC would be able to proceed with its plans for the Triborough System.

Even before the 1909 election, some progress had been made. The Court of Appeals had ruled in October that the City had sufficient credit to begin construction of the Fourth Avenue line in Brooklyn up to 40th Street, as the PSC had proposed in May 1908.[180] In a reversal of policy, Mayor McClellan and Comptroller Metz and other members of the Board of Estimate on October 29 voted in favor of appropriating funds for such construction.[181]

Meanwhile, the PSC had proceeded to advertise new contracts, both for construction and operation of the Triborough System under the indeterminate franchise plan and for construction alone of additional portions of the system, using City funds. The only sour note came from the Bradley-Gaffney-Steers Company. After examining the details of the proposed contract for construction and operation of the Triborough System, the company informed the PSC that it would not make a bid because the financial risks were too great. The PSC therefore began to consider the bids for construction alone, which totaled $85 million.[182] Chairman Willcox stated that the PSC intended to proceed with further construction of the Triborough System with City money as quickly as possible.[183]

With the outcome of the 1909 election, the beginning of construction of portions of the Fourth Avenue line, and the new transit laws passed by the State Legislature, the prospects for extensive subway development seemed better than they had been in years.[184] The year 1910 began with optimistic hopes that New York's transit problems would be solved in a matter of months.[185] This proved not to be the case, however, as months turned into years. Before we begin this story, however, we must retrace our steps in order to show the development of a new way of thinking about rapid transit expansion and its role in society that began in the 1890s and peaked about 1910. This new paradigm had a great impact on the final decision in 1913 to build a vast expansion of the rapid transit network.

3. Rapid Transit to Save New York

In 1910, New York was the most crowded city in the world.[1] Several residential districts in Manhattan had already been overcrowded in the 1860s, when the first serious discussions of building rapid transit lines began. Throughout the nineteenth century and the first decade of the new century, population densities had steadily increased in many of Manhattan's tenement neighborhoods. Moreover, what was called "congestion of population" had begun to spread to residential areas of Brooklyn and the Bronx.[2]

The business districts of New York also had become more congested. In the Wall Street area in Lower Manhattan, new skyscrapers crowded together, some towering hundreds of feet above sidewalks on which pedestrians jostled for space.[3] A bird's-eye view of Lower Manhattan in 1911 shows a dense concentration of tall buildings, many of them more than twenty stories high. The Woolworth Building, opened in 1913, towered fifty-five stories, or 792 feet.[4]

North of the financial district, hundreds of loft buildings stretched across Manhattan, some of them ten or more stories high. These lofts housed the largest concentration of manufacturing in the United States.[5] Many of the city's streets were filled with traffic of all kinds. Above the streets, the elevated railroads carried capacity crowds. Below ground, the first subway had been severely overcrowded from the day it opened in 1904.[6]

In New York's residential districts, three-quarters of the population was jammed ever more tightly into tenements, with block after block of solid masonry four- to seven-stories high, going on for miles.[7] Housing overcrowding was especially acute in the poorest neighborhoods. Each year, tens of thousands of immigrants moved into the oldest tenement districts, resulting in intolerable living conditions.[8] By 1910, progressive reformers in New York believed that conditions in the slums had reached a breaking point and that immediate action was needed to relieve overcrowding.[9]

Until this time, most reform efforts to improve the lives of working families living in tenement districts had focused on public health measures, public education, settlement houses, and housing reform.[10] Policymakers now believed that such efforts were not enough. To solve the problems resulting from overcrowding in the tenement districts, and to save New York for its citizens, they had to provide people with the means to disperse to better environments in the outer boroughs. To accomplish this, many rapid transit lines had to be constructed simultaneously to the Bronx, Brooklyn, and Queens, in the context of an overall plan for urban development.[11]

The belief that expanding rapid transit could help alleviate social problems was not new—it had been espoused from the 1860s on. What was new was the concept that government, not the private sector, should be primarily responsible for making sure that many new subway lines were financed and built.

Many of the progressive reformers who had helped develop this new way of thinking were in positions of political power by 1910. They controlled the two public agencies authorized to make final decisions on new rapid transit lines—the New York State Public Service Commission and the New York City Board of

Estimate, which had the power to fund rapid transit lines. They were now ready to mesh their knowledge of the costs and financing of new subways with their assessment of the metropolis's social and economic needs.[12]

The (Congested) Greater City

On January 1, 1898, the City of New York took on its present boundaries, which stretch in an arc extending more that twenty miles from City Hall to the far reaches of the Bronx, Queens, and Staten Island. The formerly independent City of Brooklyn, with the third-largest population in the United States in 1890, was now a borough of Greater New York. In population, the expanded city was the world's second largest, after London.[13] The Greater City also was much larger geographically. The five boroughs together cover 322 square miles; in contrast, Manhattan is only 24 square miles.[14]

Greater New York's population was growing rapidly. In 1890, the area had 2,507,000 inhabitants; in 1900, the number was 3,437,000. By 1910, there were 4,767,000 residents. (See Table 1 for New York's population by borough from 1790 to 1997.) The growth from 1900 to 1910 alone exceeded the total population of the city in 1860. More than 100,000 new residents were being added each year. Most of this population increase was the result of immigration from Europe. In 1910, 41 percent of New York's residents were foreign born, the vast majority from Europe. Most of the rest of the population were second- and third-generation descendants of European immigrants.[15]

Prior to 1890, most of the "old immigrants" had been from northern Europe, predominantly from Ireland and Germany. From then on, the majority of the increase was the result of what has been called the "new immigration" from southern and eastern Europe.[16] The largest group among the "new immigrants" were Jews from eastern Europe. The next largest group was from Italy.[17] Most of the new immigrants were poor, and many were relatively unskilled. They were forced by circumstance to take the lowest-level jobs and to live in the worst housing.[18]

From the late 1870s on, New York's economy boomed, despite periodic short-term downturns. The rising number of jobs, at relatively better wages, was the attraction for New York's immigrants, as well as for migrants from other parts of the United States. The city continued to serve as the nation's premier port, with docks, warehouses, and other port-related activities, such as stores, bars, restaurants, and lodging houses, crowding the shores of the East River in Lower Manhattan and Brooklyn and the Hudson River on the West Side of Manhattan to 59th Street.[19]

New York also had retained its dominance as the nation's leading financial center, although the emphasis had shifted from mercantile banking to investment banking. Large New York firms such as J. P. Morgan and Company and Kuhn, Loeb, and Company dominated American finance.[20] New York investment banks, with strong connections to financial resources in Europe, had led the effort to rationalize the country's rail network by consolidating numerous small railroads into a few large systems. They also had led the great merger movement of the 1890s and early 1900s, which had resulted in the creation of large national companies in several industries.[21]

To be close to their sources of finance, many of the new national companies had established their headquarters in the city. Several large insurance companies were also headquartered in Manhattan. The banks, corporations, and insurance companies helped support many firms and individuals providing business services, including those in law, accounting, architecture and engineering, advertising, publishing and printing.[22] The tall skyscrapers and other office buildings that dominated Lower

Manhattan and were beginning to be built uptown were filled with white-collar workers.[23] In 1910, approximately one-third of the jobs in the city were white collar.[24]

Despite the prominence of Wall Street and its related activities, however, the largest employment sector in New York at the turn of the century was manufacturing. During the late nineteenth century, New York had become the largest manufacturing center in the country. Surprisingly, most of the production work done in the city had no connection with the Wall Street banking houses or the large national corporations. Instead, industry in New York was dominated by a large number of small entrepreneurs, many of whom were immigrants. New York's factories and sweatshops were where most of the people living in the tenements worked.[25]

In 1905, of New York's 593,000 factory jobs, 321,000 were located in Manhattan south of 14th Street, one of the densest concentrations of factory jobs in the world.[26] Most of the manufacturing here was done in what were called "lofts." The loft district stretched across Manhattan just north of the skyscrapers in the Wall Street area. Lofts occupied almost all of each lot, with little space between the structures.[27] South of 14th Street, many of the factories were close to, and in many cases mixed in with, the tenement homes of the working class.[28] The largest industry in 1910 was clothing manufacture, with over 10,000 firms employing 236,000 workers.[29]

Congestion of Population

In 1910, the great majority of New Yorkers lived jammed together in densely populated corridors extending out up to eight miles from City Hall. These neighborhoods were either within walking distance of job centers or were commuter suburbs built up along the streetcar and elevated lines or the first subway.[30] In most of these districts, there were almost no detached single-family houses surrounded by yards and trees. Whether rich, poor, or middle class, most residents lived in attached houses lined up against each other, block after block, mile after mile.[31] Population densities in many of these neighborhoods had increased steadily from the 1860s on.[32]

The poorest districts had the highest population densities. In Manhattan, these included East Harlem and Central Harlem, inhabited largely by Jewish and Italian immigrants; portions of Greenwich Village, which was mostly Italian; and Hell's Kitchen, a predominantly Irish area near the Hudson River docks that extended on streets from the 30s to the 50s.[33] In Brooklyn, Williamsburg and Bushwick had neighborhoods with very high population densities, as did distant Brownsville, at the end of the elevated lines.[34] The most famous slum was the Lower East Side, where population densities in several wards exceeded six hundred persons per acre and many blocks had more than a thousand per acre.[35] These were the highest population densities in the world at the time.[36] In fact, though by one contemporary definition it occupied only two square miles, less than one-half of 1 percent of the city's total area, in 1905 it was home to 593,000 people, or 15 percent of the city's population.[37] This neighborhood alone contained more people than every other American city save Chicago and Philadelphia.[38] By the turn of the century, most of the inhabitants of this area were Jewish and Italian immigrants and their families.

The Lower East Side was becoming more and more crowded every day, as was Manhattan as a whole, which added almost a half a million new residents between 1900 and 1910, for a total population of 2,332,000. Brooklyn also added half a million people during the decade, with most of the growth in the most congested neighborhoods.[39]

Despite the overcrowding in many New York neighborhoods,

the city still had plenty of relatively open land. A broad band of lightly developed (at least for New York) and sparsely populated districts existed eight miles or more from City Hall.[40] With densities below ten people per acre, these districts had 73 percent of the city's land but only 18 percent of its population.[41] Most of Manhattan's workers couldn't commute to their jobs from these bucolic regions because trips took too long and cost too much.[42]

Housing

High population densities in New York were exacerbated by the poor quality of housing available to most working families. The division of the residential areas of New York City by income level, begun in the 1820s, accelerated in the late nineteenth century. By the turn of the century, rich and poor were sharply segregated from one another, with a broad middle class usually occupying the space in between.[43]

Until the 1880s, most upper- and middle-class families lived in attached single-family row houses, three or four stories high, made of brownstone or brick. From 1869 on, however, a new type of multiple dwelling was developed for the more affluent, the "French Flat," or luxury apartment house. These modern structures, many twelve or more stories high, took advantage of improvements in housing technology, such as steel frame construction, elevators, modern plumbing and heating, fireproof materials, and new fire safety systems. In addition, doormen were posted at entrances to keep out undesirables.[44]

By 1900, many of Manhattan's more affluent families had moved uptown from their former bastion on lower Fifth Avenue and adjacent streets. They now lived on the East Side between Fifth and Lexington Avenues from 34th Street to 96th Street, along Central Park South and Central Park West, and along Broadway, West End Avenue, Riverside Drive, and the streets in between. These areas contained a mix of luxury apartment houses and row houses, as did upscale districts in Brooklyn such as Brooklyn Heights and Park Slope.[45] Many of these districts were densely populated, but the high quality of the housing and lack of overcrowding within buildings meant that there was no public concern about "congestion of population."

This was not the case with respect to most working- and lower-middle-class neighborhoods, where most families lived in tenement buildings.[46] More than two-thirds of the inhabitants of Greater New York in 1900 lived in tenement houses.[47] By 1910, even more were crowded into tenement buildings.[48] Although some of New York's tenements were decent habitations, most were of low quality.[49] Thousands of such tenement buildings blanketed neighborhoods such as the Lower East Side, Hell's Kitchen, and East Harlem, as well as many other neighborhoods.[50]

Jacob Riis's definition of a tenement in *How the Other Half Lives* was the common one:

> It is generally a brick building from four to six stories high on the street . . . four families occupy each floor, and a set of rooms consists of one or two dark closets, used as bedrooms with a living room twelve feet by ten. The staircase is too often a dark well in the centre of the house, and no direct through ventilation is possible, each family being separated from the other by partitions. Frequently the rear of the lot is occupied by another building of three stories high with two families on a floor.[51]

In 1879, the State Legislature passed a law intended to improve housing conditions in New York City. (This was called the "Old Law" Tenement House Act after it was replaced by a "New Law" in 1901.) The 1879 law required that all new tenements have a window for each room, and that an indoor toilet (just a toilet, not a bath) be supplied for every twenty residents. The latter requirement was usually met by having two common water closets on each floor, off the hallway. The ventilation requirement was met by inserting an air shaft along each interior side of the building, giving the structure a "dumbbell" shape. These air shafts were narrow, the distance between the wall of each tenement and the next tenement being about five feet. Interior rooms had windows opening onto this air shaft. Cold water was supplied to sinks in the kitchens, hence the term "cold-water flat." Heating was by coal stoves in each apartment.[52]

It was the "Old Law" dumbbell-shaped buildings that housing reformer Lawrence Veiller called "the typical New York tenement." This type of building usually had a hundred to a hundred and fifty residents. Veiller thought that the air shaft, which had originally been regarded as a great improvement, had been a big mistake. The narrowness of the opening meant that the air shaft provided "instead of fresh air and sunshine, foul air and semi-darkness."[53]

Daily Life in the Tenements

The tenement neighborhoods were bleak. Yiddish writer Leon Kobrin described the Lower East Side as "a gray stone wall of tall tenements, where even on the loveliest day there was not a blade of grass."[54] The near total absence of local parks also meant that there were almost no trees to be seen. There were also few public playgrounds for children, so they played in the crowded streets.[55]

If the external appearance of the tenements was bleak, it was, as Emanuel Tobier has noted, even worse when you went inside.[56] Hallways were dark and each of the small rooms in each apartment was crowded with people. Families tended to be large, yet many took in boarders to help pay the rent.[57] Half of all apartments in tenement buildings citywide contained less than two rooms for every three persons.[58] In most apartments, each room (including the kitchen) was used for sleeping, with beds folded up or used as sofas during the day.[59] Apartments were stifling during hot New York summers, so much so that tenants took to sleeping on the fire escapes and the roofs. In 1900, Veiller claimed that working people in New York were housed worse than anywhere else in the world, despite the high rents they paid.[60]

According to Irving Howe, the dominant impression of the Jewish neighborhoods on the Lower East Side, shared by immigrants and visitors alike, "was of fierce congestion, a place where the bodily pressures of other people, their smells and noises, always seemed to be assaulting one. Of space for solitude and privacy there was none."[61] In the tenements, residents were exposed to the threat of death by fire (the older buildings were fire traps and the fire escapes were often filled with household goods); to all sorts of contagious disease; and to a variety of criminal activities, from petty thievery to prostitution.[62] Nearby factories spewed fumes into many apartments, and the bar or restaurant on the first floor of one's building could be the source of many smells and noises.[63]

At the turn of the century, many of the tenants themselves thought that the "greatest evil" was the lack of light and air. Others thought that the toilets, many of which often backed up, flooding the hallways, were the worst problem. One mother reported: "I have the children go to the toilet at school, for I am afraid of sickness. It is so horrid for my daughter, that she waits to use the toilet where she works." The common sinks in the halls were another source of complaint. They were used by people to wash themselves, to "wash their meat," and to wash their dishes. Many of the common sinks and toilets were not cleaned properly; the remaining backyard privies were cleaned infrequently and often backed up into cellar apartments. The lack of bathtubs meant that "many tenants do not bathe more than six times a year, and often less," at public bathhouses.[64]

The most frequent source of complaints among tenants, however, were the narrow air shafts between buildings. Twenty or more apartments opened out on each air shaft, which had no outlet on the ground floor from the front or rear. Into these air shafts, some tenants threw out "garbage and dirty papers and the insides of chickens and other unmentionable filth." The resulting smells made residents sick to their stomachs. The garbage also attracted cockroaches, flies, rats, and mice. Because of the stench and the vermin, many tenants kept the windows to the air shafts shut, even in the middle of the summer.[65]

To make matters worse, many tenement apartments themselves were workshops, appropriately called "sweatshops." Most of the workers in the sweatshops did piece work for the garment industry, but tobacco products and other goods were also made in the tenements. Many of these workers were women and children. Often, teams of eight to twenty workers pored over worktables or sewing machines in unventilated rooms with poor lighting. Most of the sweatshop workers were Jewish, although many were Italian; almost all were recent immigrants from Europe. As late as 1911, there were thirteen thousand tenement buildings licensed for work in the home.[66]

The Perceived Threat to the City

Living conditions in the poorer tenement districts were terrible in and of themselves. They were made worse by high rates of disease, crime, and social dislocation that were seen at the time as the "indirect consequences of congestion."[67] These problems, moreover, did not just make the lives of working people more difficult; they also were regarded as a threat to the wider society. In particular, the fear that contagious diseases would spread to the general population became a spur to action to break up the congestion of population in the worst tenement districts.

On March 8, 1908, for example, the Reverend Dr. Joseph Silverman, Rabbi of Temple Emanu-El, addressed his congregation on "The Congestion of Our People."[68] Rabbi Silverman's talk reflected the concern of the uptown German Jewish elite about what was happening in the poorest residential neighborhoods of New York.[69] After summarizing the high densities of population below 14th Street, Silverman went on to say that the problem was spreading to the Bronx, which "now has new five- and six-story tenements." Health conditions were terrible in the congested districts, and the death rate was high. Infant mortality rates among Italian children had grown to "710 out of every 1,000." Silverman concluded: "We find ourselves confronted by a great problem. Grave dangers are imminent from disease, contagion and the spread of uncontrollable conflagrations. Then there is the effect of these conditions on the morals, the social conditions, the religion and the education of the people and in time of financial stringency the possibility of misery, of starvation, and of death are greatly increased." Unless the overcrowding in the tenements was reduced, matters could only get worse.[70]

Academic commentators who had carefully analyzed the effects of congestion of population were no less concerned. Edward Ewing Pratt said that the lack of proper light, ventilation, and sanitation in the tenement neighborhoods led to "prevalence of disease, high rates of mortality, [and] high death rates among children." Lack of privacy led to "moral deterioration," as revealed in the "gradual breaking down of family ties, in the increase and prevalence of crime and delinquency in the congested districts, and, not least, in the extensive moral looseness and the virulence of prostitution in densely populated districts."[71]

Poor housing conditions had to be solved not just for the benefit of slum dwellers but also for the health and safety of the city as a whole. In an otherwise upbeat book, *The City: The Hope of Democracy*, Frederic C. Howe told Americans that the housing problem was "the problem of the city, just as the city is the problem of our civilization." Bad housing, itself the result of congestion of population, was the greatest threat to the civic order; it "not only affects the physical stamina of men, it destroys womanhood, invites to prostitution, and encourages vice. From it crime emerges, filling our jails, reformatories and prisons. Here the saloon and the low resort thrive, while disease spawns its frightful record of mortality."[72] Historian Charles A. Beard and others saw the overcrowding in great cites such as New York as "a menace to our civilization."[73]

Disease

Disease was indeed taking its toll. Although public health measures in New York City had been successful over several decades in reducing the death rates from most contagious diseases, the rates were still high in the congested areas.[74] Moreover, although the discovery in the late nineteenth century that diseases were caused by germs had contributed to a decline in overall death rates in New York, germ theory, paradoxically, had increased people's fears about some contagious diseases.[75] This was particularly the case with tuberculosis. There was no known cure for tuberculosis, but it was now clear that anyone could catch the disease through close contact with an infected person.[76]

Tuberculosis was the single most important disease in New York in the late nineteenth and early twentieth centuries, despite the attention paid to other epidemics such as cholera, typhoid fever, typhus, smallpox, and diphtheria.[77] In 1901, about twelve thousand new cases of tuberculosis occurred in New York City, and the disease was responsible for one out of every four deaths in people ages fifteen to sixty-five.[78] Rates of tuberculosis in Manhattan were rising rapidly and were a special concern in the tenement districts.[79] Once contracted, it was generally held to be incurable.[80]

The great concern at this time was that tuberculosis could easily be spread from one person to another. This could happen by being in close quarters with a person who had the disease and breathing the same air, such as on a train or in a tenement apartment. It was also believed that the germ could be transmitted through an infected person's sputum via objects he or she had handled.[81] Since the tuberculosis sputum was regarded as infectious, public health campaigns emphasized cleanliness and mounted massive anti-spitting efforts.[82] Everything an infected person touched, including clothing, tooth brushes, doorknobs, papers, and bedding, was thought to be a possible source of transmission.[83]

The tenement buildings themselves, with their lack of proper ventilation and sunlight and severe overcrowding, were breeding grounds for tuberculosis.[84] One authority on child labor claimed that infected garments being produced in overcrowded tenement sweatshops were transmitting the disease nationwide.[85] Indeed, a fictional account in a labor journal described an immigrant wife toiling in a sweatshop, who infected the skirt she sewed, which in turn infected the buyer. The twist to the story was that the person who bought the skirt was the daughter of the owner of the tenement building where the seamstress worked.[86]

Tuberculosis was the most feared disease in New York's tenement districts.[87] Unlike many other contagious diseases, death came slowly once a person was infected, as patients "wasted away" over a period of years.[88] Since most poorer families could not afford to send infected family members to sanitariums in the country, where light and air were thought to stem the process of the disease, the tenement houses were filled with people infected with the disease.[89] As a result, few children and adults in the tenement districts were free from the threat of tuberculosis infection.[90] Moreover, those in more affluent neighborhoods feared that the disease would not remain confined largely to the poorer districts. Rabbi Silverman's sermon to his congregation about conditions in the tenement districts reflected the concern of many New Yorkers that tuberculosis and other diseases might spread out to the rest of the city.[91]

Many of the contagious diseases of the time were linked to specific ethnic groups, resulting in increased fear of these groups among the general population.[92] Around 1900, tuberculosis was known as the "Jewish disease" and the "tailor's disease."[93] With polio, which became prevalent from 1907 on, the stigma was put on the Italians.[94] In 1910, many feared that immigrants coming to New York from Italy and eastern Europe would bring with them Asiatic cholera, then widespread in these areas.[95]

The public reactions against the new immigrants because of tuberculosis and other diseases were similar in many ways to reactions against gay men during the AIDS epidemic of the late twentieth century. Many people believed that contact with an infected person, or even with an object they touched, could result in infection, starting a slow process of bodily deterioration that ended in death.[96] As with AIDS in the 1980s, exactly how tuberculosis was transmitted was not known, leading to grave concern that the general populace might be exposed in one way or another.[97]

In addition to the public health threat from contagious diseases, many reformers were concerned about high mortality and poor health among children in the tenement districts. The rates of infant and childhood mortality among the children of Italian immigrants were especially high and were blamed on the conditions in the tenement districts.[98] Many of the children's diseases were stomach ailments caused by bad food and spoiled, sometimes tubercular, milk.[99] Besides stomach ailments, the large number of people packed into the tenement districts meant that poor children were likely to be exposed early in life to a great variety of contagious diseases, including diphtheria, smallpox, and polio.[100] The summer heat in the tenement buildings was also believed to cause the death of many infants.[101]

Crime

In addition to causing disease, many commentators at the time believed that conditions in the tenement districts led to crime. For example, the City's chief magistrate said in 1911:

> There can be no question but what the connection between congestion of population, especially in that form which it takes in tenement houses, particularly the old style tenements, crime and delinquency are very marked. The crowded conditions in these small rooms, lack of personal privacy and separation of the sexes must, in the very nature of things beget conditions which conduce to immorality and the lack of self respect.[102]

Whatever the precise relationship, there is no doubt that crime rates in the poorest tenement districts were high, and that they were regarded as a threat to civic order.[103] Crime among the new immigrants, particularly the Jews and the Italians, was a major focus of attention.[104] Among Jews, violent crimes were uncommon, but "other forms of illegal activity, among them arson, gambling, fencing stolen goods, picking pockets, and juvenile hooliganism, victimized the neighborhoods and attracted wide attention."[105] Prostitution was also widespread on the Lower East Side, as was the numbers racket.[106]

The image of Jews as criminals was a shock, since up to the end of the nineteenth century, Americans believed that crime among Jews was rare.[107] Of greatest concern was the high crime rates among children and teenagers, which sparked an effort on the part of New York's Jewish elite to found a reformatory for Jewish children upstate. The founders of this institution were convinced that the high rates of crime were the result of conditions in the tenements.[108]

Rapid Transit as a Solution

From the 1890s on, many proposals were offered aimed at solving the problems resulting from congestion of population in New York.[109] These proposals were sparked by an increasing awareness of the terrible conditions in the tenement districts, as exemplified in Jacob Riis's famous book, *How the Other Half Lives,* published in 1890. The settlement house movement was focused primarily on improving conditions in the tenement districts, in part by changing the mores of the immigrants, and especially their children. Many of the efforts to improve public education were aimed at enabling children growing up in the immigrant areas to eventually move out of the slums.[110] In addition, various public health campaigns led by Dr. Hermann Biggs were aimed mainly at the poorer tenement districts.[111]

One of the more successful efforts at alleviating New York's worst living conditions was housing reform. The State Tenement House Act of 1901 was the result of a sustained effort by a group of reformers, led by Lawrence Veiller and Robert W. DeForest and supported by Governor Theodore Roosevelt, to substantially raise the minimum standards for multiple dwellings.[112] Although the "New Law" did require some modifications to existing buildings, it was mainly intended to assure that the worse aspects of the older tenement buildings would not be repeated in the future.[113]

Public health measures, education, and housing reform, however, could not stop the many immigrants coming to the city from moving into the existing tenements. Nor would these measures relieve existing housing overcrowding. There was nowhere else for the new arrivals to find affordable housing that was also within reasonable travel time from their places of employment. Progressive reformers recognized this, and by 1910 the most popular of their solutions to New York's congestion problem was massive expansion of the rapid transit system, in the context of an overall effort to control urban development. The social function of transportation, as opposed to economic returns to private companies, now became the primary concern.

The theoretical basis for this new outlook on the role of transportation in society had been developed from the 1890s on. In an 1894 article entitled "The Theory of Transportation," economist Charles Cooley had put forth the idea that transportation underlies social development and is at the same time determined by that development.[114] Cooley noted that in the new industrial society of the late nineteenth century, manufacturing had concentrated within dense urban areas. Concentration was a natural accompaniment of industrial progress, which was good for society as a whole.[115] In large cities, however, such concentration caused social problems. The conditions of industrial life were such that residential districts for working-class families became more and more congested. Industry's tendency to concentrate in small geographic areas was thus in conflict with the needs of humanity, since it was not healthy for people to live in dense aggregations. The main function of urban transportation was to reconcile these conflicting requirements of the social organism.[116]

According to Cooley, in large cities the main function of transportation was to spread out the population. Proper transportation could mitigate, or even do away with, those aspects of concentration that were socially undesirable. The rise of the railroads had made extreme congestion possible within large cities; now it was in the interest of the cities themselves to eliminate the evils that had resulted, by providing adequate systems of mass transit. This had to be done because humanity demanded access to sunlight, fresh air, grass, and trees. Rapid transit could make it possible for people to work in the crowded business centers, yet reside in "decent isolation." If industrial concentration and adequate transportation did not go hand in hand, then grave social problems would result.[117]

What people needed was cheap, efficient, and rapid transit that would enable them to move to suburban areas but continue to work in the central city. It was clear to Cooley that competition, both among transit companies and among different parts of the metropolitan area, would no longer work as a guiding principle for achieving the best transit system. Transportation was a highly organic activity that had to be conducted according to a comprehensive plan and by unified methods. Transit planning had to be done by a public body for the good of society as a whole. What's more, this public body had to be as large, powerful, and well organized as the private transit companies.[118]

According to Cooley, it could no longer be expected, as had been the case in the 1860s, that private companies would build the transit lines that were needed. Private companies would not act for the good of the people because their main interest was in maximizing profits. The issue was how actually to go about getting the government more involved in transportation. Public operation of transit facilities would not work because public employees lacked "those simple and comprehensible motives of personal advancement that control private business" and therefore could not be expected to operate a transit system efficiently on a day-to-day basis.[119]

Instead, Cooley called for government regulation of the private transportation companies. A government body could be created to gather together facts and figures about population movement, plan new rapid transit lines, coordinate the activities of the private transit companies, and require the building of whatever transit lines it thought necessary. This government agency would assure that the people had rapid transit facilities adequate to their needs.[120] An urban area's transit system had to be extensive. The more extensive the system, the more rapid transit would contribute to a reduction in rents by distributing population and business over a wider area. The more land available for development, the cheaper the land would be.[121]

Cooley asserted that in order to be effective, mass transit had to be affordable for working people, and a number of other observers repeated this point. Adna Ferrin Weber cited the fact that in Belgium the government provided state-owned transit at a low fare.[122] In England, the Cheap Trains Act of 1883 had compelled London railroad companies to offer low workers' fares, which were meant to encourage migration to the suburbs and to relieve congestion of population in central London.[123] In the United States, the main emphasis was upon the establishment of a flat five-cent fare, regardless of distance traveled.[124]

In 1901, Weber commented on the change in attitude toward the function of rapid transit that had occurred during the 1890s. He said that American cities had awakened to a sense of danger posed by congestion of population. Government leaders and reformers alike saw that the most effective solution to this problem was rapid transit expansion to outlying areas, directed by the government; other remedies were "mere palliatives."[125]

Between 1900 and 1910, reform-minded New Yorkers, who were aware of what had been written about the social function of rapid transit, applied these ideas in their efforts to solve the congestion problem in America's largest city.[126] For example, in 1905, Calvin Tomkins noted that New York was "rapidly assuming the position of the metropolis of the world." New York was a great city, in part, because of its location. Just as Rome had once been the center of the Mediterranean basin, after which power had shifted to Venice and Genoa and later to Amsterdam and London, now New York City would be the metropolis of an area stretching from the Rockies to the Urals. Within this basin, New York was the central point of exchange. Rail and sea connections tied it to the cities of America's vast hinterland.[127]

There was, however, one problem—the same problem Cooley and Weber had analyzed in general terms—the City of New York had not yet arranged its own internal plan "so that it shall be commensurate with the destiny which is awaiting us as a result of our situation." Up to the present, geographic barriers such as the East River had hindered healthy growth. Now, however, with new technology—with railroads, subways, bridges, and tunnels—the entire metropolitan area, including Greater New York, northern New Jersey, Long Island, and Westchester, would be linked together in a common plan of development. Parks, streets, sewers, and the like could be planned in advance of development. So could the "most important of all" aspect of urban development, rapid transit. New subway lines had to be built "to provide for expansion without congestion," in the context of an overall plan for urban development.[128]

The Congestion Committee

By 1907, much had been written about congestion of population in New York, but little had been accomplished in the way of alleviating the problem. In order to educate the public about the extent of the problem and the threat it posed to urban life, and in the hope that increased public awareness would result in a speedy solution, New York reformers of every persuasion banded together in 1907 to form the Committee on Congestion of Population in New York.

The Congestion Committee was initially formed by a group of people active in the settlement house movement.[129] These individuals had close ties with members of New York's many charitable organizations and civic groups, who also joined the Congestion Committee. They also were supported by several businessmen and bankers. The committee thereby united a broad spectrum of New Yorkers, all of whom were concerned with alleviating existing conditions in overcrowded areas.[130]

The motives of the members of the Congestion Committee varied. Many of the settlement house workers who sparked its creation had labored in the tenement districts for many years and were sincerely concerned about improving living conditions for working families simply because it was the right thing to do. Others, such as financier Henry Morgenthau, who was for a time the "honorary chairman" of the Committee, believed that the congestion problem needed to be attacked because it bred "physical disease, moral depravity, discontent and socialism."[131] Whatever the motivation, according to Mary Simkhovitch, the official chairman, the individuals and groups on the Committee had come together "in their conviction that back of all the evils of city life lay the dominant evil of congestion of population."[132]

Florence Kelley was the person most responsible for the formation of the Congestion Committee. She had worked at Hull House in Chicago from 1891 to 1899 before moving to New York. She lived at Henry Street Settlement on the Lower East Side for the next twenty-seven years. In 1899, she was appointed general secretary of the National Consumers' League, which strove to improve working conditions for women and to end sweatshop labor. Kelley drew connections between housing and working conditions and public health. She also pointed out the side effects of congestion—the rise in the death rate from tuberculosis and the relatively high overall death rate in New York compared to other large cities.[133]

Speaking at an event commemorating the twenty-fifth anniversary of the Charity Organization Society in 1908, Kelley said that after a quarter century of effort by social workers, conditions in New York had not improved, that there was more overcrowding, and that the congested area of the city was growing. Under such circumstances, relief work in the tenements was like "turning water into a rat hole," or "stemming the tide with a broom." Housing reform, child labor reform, settlement houses, and the like would be of little help unless the density of population was reduced.[134]

In order to arouse public concern, the Congestion Committee planned an exhibit showing the dangers and results of congestion of population and suggesting solutions.[135] The organizers were particularly interested in promoting the idea of planning as a means of achieving good housing and public health.[136] They invited civic groups and charitable organizations to participate by making displays for the exhibit. The result was the Exhibit of Congestion of Population in New York, popularly called the "Congestion Show," which showed at the American Museum of Natural History March 9–22, 1908, and at the Brooklyn Institute April 6–19 of the same year.[137]

There were twenty-four exhibits at the Museum of Natural History. One of them, "Tenement Houses and Tuberculosis," used photographs and models of tenement buildings, together with statistics, to show how tuberculosis bred in the dark and poorly ventilated tenement buildings, and the relationship of the disease to congestion. It also showed the ways infection could be spread through "tenement manufactured clothing." In addition, there were exhibits on infant mortality, the home conditions of Italian immigrants, children in congested districts, the concentration of factories in Lower Manhattan, town planning, model tenements, and the need for more parks, among others. There were several exhibits on better housing for working families.[138]

The exhibit by the City Club of New York focused on the need for rapid transit expansion in the context of an overall plan for city development. Primary consideration in all subway plans was to be given to the social effects of the new lines. The City Club exhibit had photographs, maps, diagrams, charts, and other illustrations showing which outlying parts of the city needed to be provided with rapid transit lines. This exhibit also demonstrated how zoning and land use regulations could be used to help control the development of these new neighborhoods, so as to avoid repetition of congestion of population.[139]

At the opening ceremonies for the Congestion Show in Manhattan, Governor Charles Evans Hughes gave the main address. Hughes said he had toured the exhibits and had found them "the most instructive commentary upon conditions in the City of New York that I have ever seen." He had come away "feeling oppressed and depressed by the facts that are there made so clear and the models that are so eloquent of the wretchedness and misery which are incident to our progress." Hughes complimented the voluntary organizations that prepared the exhibits for "applying training and skill, knowledge and force to the betterment of conditions that are right around us." The exhibits showed conditions that were intolerable, and could not last. For, said Hughes, what did congestion mean, with so many people in a "great mound" in the lower part of Manhattan, while there was lots of "free territory . . . virtually unoccupied" on the outskirts?[140]

Hughes commented that it was a common view that many people were bound to be unfortunate and that it was easy to "shrug our shoulders and go about our own business as though it did not concern us." But this was not the way to look at it. The Governor then noted:

> Who pays the bills? The City and the State are paying for the crime, for the disease, for the wretchedness that comes from these congested conditions. . . . No man, however he might pride himself upon his success, can get away from his brethren altogether; and he cannot afford to have plague spots in the city.
>
> You have got to pay for hospitals. What is the use of putting people in hospitals and feeding them and paying the expenses of these great establishments, imprisoning them for crime, carrying the large loads of our prison bills, if, to a great degree, you can prevent that outlay, save human beings from disease and from crime and in the same time provide an increase in the efficiency of our people and of the output of their productive effort?[141]

As to solutions, what had to be done was to find the means to better distribute both the people and their places of work. To bring about this "greater distribution," said Hughes, "the facts" needed to be marshalled and patiently examined to produce concrete solutions, including more transit. In short, "what we have to do is to go on learning the exact facts and presenting them, and, wherever we see a chance, to do a practical thing."[142]

A few days after Hughes's address, four of the five members of the New York State Public Service Commission, created by Hughes, toured the Congestion Show. Henry Wright of the City Club gave the commissioners a special tour of the club's exhibit. He showed them maps of the Bronx which indicated that areas laying along the route of the first subway would soon be densely populated. Wright pointed out that tenements were being built in great numbers in the South Bronx and that conditions there would soon be equal to those on the Lower East Side. In order that this situation not repeat itself in other areas, Wright urged the building of many more subway lines simultaneously. In this way, many new residential areas would be opened for development at the same time, thereby allowing for the construction of low-density housing.[143]

In both Manhattan and Brooklyn, conferences were held in conjunction with the Congestion Show. These included a forum on "Suburban Development," that is, development of the outer boroughs, chaired by City Club president George McAneny, and one panel on "Congestion and Transportation," chaired by PSC commissioner William McCarroll.[144] At the latter, PSC commissioner Edward M. Bassett gave a talk on "Brooklyn's Needs in Transportation," arguing that Greater New York needed to be made a "round city" in fact through its rapid transit system, rather than the north-south linear city of Manhattan and the Bronx.[145] This argument got right at one of the main issues facing rapid transit decision makers—making sure that Brooklyn and Queens were treated equally with Manhattan and the Bronx in the provision of new subway lines. Bassett also argued that, in order to encourage low residential densities, many new rapid transit lines had to be built at one time.[146]

In addition to organizing the Exhibit on Congestion of Population and its related lecture series, the Congestion Committee was responsible for the appearance of three major books: Benjamin C. Marsh's *An Introduction to City Planning: Democracy's Challenge to the American City*; John Martin's *Rapid Transit: Its Effects on Rents and Living Conditions, and How to Get It*; and Edward Ewing Pratt's *Industrial Causes of Congestion of Population in New York City*.[147]

The purpose of Marsh's book was to stimulate New York, as well as other American cities, "to action and to the adoption of city planning in order to prevent the direful conditions of congestion, maladjustment and preeminately land speculation which have reached their horrible limit in Manhattan."[148] Marsh urged that New York and other American cities solve their congestion problems basically by adopting the German system of city planning.[149] Above all, city planning had to be aimed at improving the conditions of daily life for working people, helping them to escape from the current "ugly, demoralizing and devitalizing conditions" in congested areas.[150]

John Martin believed that the major element in any city plan was a comprehensive scheme of rapid transit development. The question of extending rapid transit lines to undeveloped areas had to be approached primarily as a social problem. Rents in tenement areas were rising rapidly because the supply of apartments was not keeping up with the demand. Without new rapid transit lines, the tenement districts would be increasingly crowded, rents would keep rising, and the fight for decent living conditions for the average worker would be lost. Similar statements had been made before. What was new in Martin's book was his proposal that rapid transit be subsidized "out of the annual tax budget." According to Martin, it was more humane and sensible to subsidize transit expansion out of the tax budget than to let rents in congested areas rise and then relieve destitute families by paying their rent and giving them food. The best way to lower rents and improve family life was "by rapid transit in all directions."[151]

Of the three volumes that emerged from the activities of the Congestion Committee, Pratt's *Industrial Causes of Congestion of Population in New York City*[152] was the most comprehensive in dealing with the congestion problem in New York City. Pratt demonstrated how congestion of population was the natural result of the workings of an unregulated economic system. Supply and demand determined the use and price of land in New York.[153] This did not mean, however, that the City could not take action to influence land values and land use within the city. First of all, the City could build many new rapid transit lines to undeveloped areas of the outlying boroughs. This would open a great deal of vacant land for the construction of new housing, at reasonable prices.[154] The government could regulate the use of land through zoning, keeping factories out of new residential areas. It could also require that new factories be located according to a comprehensive plan. In addition, a drastic and efficient building code for all of New York could limit building heights and restrict buildings according to the proportion of lot area covered. Moreover, the City could set aside large areas for parks, playgrounds, and public buildings in advance of development.[155]

According to Pratt, no single proposal would end congestion; what had to be organized was a "general, broad, inclusive program," the first objective of which would be to prevent the recurrence of crowded conditions. The second objective would be to ameliorate existing conditions; the third to root out the evils of the worst sections. City planning meant, "in its full significance, . . . the provision of low-rent homes for workmen, and the improvement of transit facilities."[156]

The Congestion Committee and its activities were successful in raising public awareness of the problems resulting from overcrowding in the tenement districts.[157] Its publications added substantially to the body of knowledge about congestion of population. The greatest impact, however, was on the shifting of the efforts to alleviate the problem from improving conditions in the slums themselves to breaking up the slums by helping the population to move to outlying areas. It was no longer enough simply to try to ameliorate living conditions in the tenement districts.

Efforts to reduce disease rates in the tenements had to continue, and new housing had to be built to higher standards. Unless the overcrowding in the tenements was reduced, however, the threats posed by the resulting social problems would continue. If the lives of the people in the tenement districts were to be substantially improved, and if the city was to be saved from the threats posed by these people to the wider society, the population had to be dispersed. It was now agreed that one of the best ways to accomplish this task was for the City of New York to build many new subway lines simultaneously.[158]

George McAneny and His Allies

The view that the population had to be dispersed in order to save the city came at a critical moment. It gave impetus to the efforts of men such as George McAneny, who took office as borough president of Manhattan in 1910, and William R. Willcox, Edward M. Bassett, and Milo Maltbie on the Public Service Commission to put a large number of new subway lines under construction as fast as possible. This would be the ultimate solution to the "intractable" problem of the tenement house.[159]

Of these men, McAneny was the most important, because he soon became the leader in putting together a comprehensive plan for subway expansion and was chiefly responsible for getting it financed. McAneny believed that new subways were the first step in a larger effort to control future city development.[160] City planning would improve "the social and living conditions of the people who live in the cities" by a proper distribution of population throughout the city that would end congestion.[161] After his election as borough president of Manhattan in November 1909, McAneny said that the most vital thing for the new Board of Estimate during the next four years would be to solve the city's rapid transit problem in order to allow for residential growth in all areas of the city.[162]

Historians who have examined McAneny's career have been impressed with his vision of city planning as a means of improving daily life for average New Yorkers, and with his ability to make certain that plans were actually implemented.[163] Less attention has been paid to his motivations.[164] An examination of his personal background, however, tells us much about why he was so deeply committed to relieving congestion of population in New York.

McAneny was born in Greenville, New Jersey, in 1869 and graduated from high school in Jersey City in 1885.[165] Gregory Gilmartin has noted that he "was an unusual figure in the reform camp," having been born poor, with no family fortune and little formal education, and having begun his working life "as a barefoot boy selling newspapers."[166] He worked as a reporter for a Jersey City newspaper and then moved to New York, where he was a reporter for various newspapers, including the *New York World*.[167]

McAneny soon became connected to a circle of reformers who were against the corruption of the Tammany Democrats and committed to the creation of a professional civil service.[168] The leader of this group was Carl Schurz, who had been a revolutionary in his native Germany in 1848 and later fled to the United States. Schurz became a supporter of Abraham Lincoln, was commissioned a general during the Civil War, and later became a U.S. senator from Missouri and served in the cabinet as secretary of state. In the 1890s, he was living in New York as the head of the Civil Service Reform Association.[169] It was Schurz who "discovered" McAneny, appointing him as secretary of the association in 1892.[170]

In 1902, Republican mayor Seth Low appointed McAneny executive officer of the New York City Civil Service Commission, where he helped draft the City's civil service rules.[171] In 1903, McAneny, a Democrat, began studying law in the office of Edward M. Shepard, who had been Low's opponent in the mayoral race of 1901.[172] Shepard was a legal counsel to the Pennsylvania Railroad, which was then planning the construction of a massive network of rail improvements in the New York region that included Pennsylvania Station, tunnels under the Hudson and East Rivers, the Hell Gate Bridge, and a number of related rail lines. McAneny was directly involved in these efforts. According to McAneny, he developed his ideas about city planning in his conversations with Shepard, who had been a counsel to the Rapid Transit Board in the 1890s.[173] In 1907, McAneny became president of the City Club and made transportation his prime concern.

McAneny's awareness of the problems of the tenement districts came in part from his in-laws. In 1900, he married Marjorie Jacobi, the only surviving child of Abraham Jacobi and his wife, Mary Putnam Jacobi.[174] The couple had met at the Jacobi's summer home at Lake George, New York, while McAneny was staying at Schurz's nearby vacation home, which was on Jacobi's property.[175] Born in 1830 of Jewish parents, Jacobi had been involved in the failed Revolution of 1848 in Germany while completing his medical studies. Imprisoned for eighteen months, he later fled to the United States, where he first established a medical practice on the Lower East Side. He was one of the pioneers in children's medicine and taught at medical schools in New York. He soon became the most famous pediatrician in the United States.[176]

One of Jacobi's main goals as a physician was to reduce infant mortality rates through improved nutrition, especially among the poor.[177] He was one of the most active leaders in the fight against tuberculosis and was an ally of Dr. Hermann Biggs in his campaign against the disease.[178] Since tuberculosis frequently attacked the young, Dr. Jacobi "battled against crowding, poor air and poor sanitary conditions" in the schools and tenements.[179] He was a member of the Congestion Committee and, at its 1908 conference, spoke on "Congestion and Preventable Disease." He also participated in its forum on tuberculosis and other diseases.[180] In 1911, Dr. Jacobi was elected president of the American Medical Association.[181]

Dr. Mary Putnam Jacobi was the daughter of book publisher George P. Putnam. She was one of the first female physicians in the United States, receiving much of her training in France. She met Abraham Jacobi at a medical meeting in New York, and they were married in 1873.[182] The Jacobis had two children, Marjorie and Ernst. Abraham Jacobi had hopes that his son would become a physician, but in 1883, tragedy struck. At age seven, Ernst contracted diphtheria, probably from a seamstress visiting the Jacobi home. He died soon after.[183] According to his biographer, Jacobi never recovered from his son's death, although he continued to work hard as a doctor and teacher.[184]

Dr. Mary Jacobi was a medical educator and writer who focused on the welfare of children and the status of women.[185] She was also one of the founders of the National Consumers' League and later served as its vice-chairman.[186] Mary also worked with Felix Adler on the education of young children. She died in 1906 of meningitis. At a memorial service, Florence Kelley spoke, outlining Mary Jacobi's efforts on behalf of working women, not merely to cure them of diseases from which they suffered but to help make conditions of work such that disease and death were not forced on them.[187]

After their marriage, George and Marjorie McAneny lived in the same building as her parents occupied, a row house at 19 East 47th Street.[188] They had six children, two daughters and four sons.[189]

With this family background, it comes as no surprise that George McAneny should have devoted much of his own efforts to improve the lives of working people and their children. Both of his in-laws were professionals who had worked to improve the conditions of daily life among poor people. Their methods were to get the facts and then devise a remedy.[190] According to McAneny himself, he was "bent on reducing the volume of misery and dependency in the city through the correction, so far as possible, of the conditions that breed misery."[191] McAneny brought together the concerns of New York's progressive reformers regarding population congestion with a fact-based approach to solving this problem.

By the beginning of 1910, several members of the PSC and Board of Estimate were looking at the building of new subway lines, not just from the point of view of financial return to the City or of relief of transit overcrowding, but also as one tool to be used to regulate urban growth and to alleviate congestion of population and its related social ills. Louis E. Van Norman, commenting on this change of attitude, remarked that a group of public officials in the Board of Estimate and PSC had formulated a "new, coherent conception of the transportation problem," in which new rapid transit lines were to be part of an effort to develop the city in a rational manner. The new rapid transit lines would serve as the skeleton of the city plan, and future development would be planned along them. Looking at transit expansion from a sociological point of view, these men were primarily concerned not with whether new subway lines would be successful as business propositions, but rather how they would affect the city's future growth and how they might alleviate existing social problems such as congestion of population.[192] Now that most of the decision makers in New York was in agreement, it appeared that new rapid transit lines would soon be approved.

4. Stumbling toward a Solution

At the beginning of 1910, public officials in New York were optimistic that many new subway lines would soon be under construction.[1] For two and a half years, the New York State Public Service Commission (PSC) had feuded with members of New York City's Board of Estimate and Apportionment over building new subways. Members of the Board of Estimate had successfully thwarted almost all of the PSC's efforts to begin new construction from the time the Commission came into office in July 1907 until November 1909.

On January 1, 1910, however, a new Board of Estimate came into office. Six of the eight members of the new Board, controlling twelve of the sixteen votes, were Fusionists who had defeated their Democratic opponents in the November 1909 municipal elections.[2] The Fusion members had been elected on a platform that called for the beginning of subway construction as soon as possible. All of the Fusionists were eager to cooperate with the PSC.

From January 1910 on, however, only a few of the members of the Board of Estimate and PSC would play an active role in decision making for new subways. On the Board, Manhattan Borough President George McAneny had the most detailed knowledge of transit financing and of the reasons why new subways were needed. McAneny was convinced that a large number of new rapid transit lines had to be built at one time in order to help break up congestion of population in the tenement quarters and to promote the lateral development of the city's commercial districts.[3]

The other Fusion members of the Board of Estimate actively involved in subway decision making were Comptroller William A. Prendergast and John Purroy Mitchel, president of the Board of Aldermen. Aside from the mayor, the two held the only citywide positions on the Board.[4] Comptroller Prendergast was a Republican from Brooklyn who was determined that any subway expansion plan not slight his home borough.[5] Mitchel was a reform Democrat from the Bronx who had his eye on the mayoralty. He became a consistent opponent of proposals by the Interborough Rapid Transit Company (IRT) to expand the original subway.[6] Both Prendergast and Mitchel received strong support from William Randolph Hearst in 1910 and early 1911 for their advocacy of the Triborough System plan for subway expansion.[7]

The new mayor, William J. Gaynor, also seemed disposed to cooperate with the PSC, despite the fact that he had been elected as the candidate of the Democratic machine. He had been elected in part because of his virulent attacks on the IRT during the campaign.[8] Once in office, Gaynor was quick to establish his independence from Tammany boss Charles F. Murphy and to cooperate with the Fusionists in the reform of City government.[9]

On the PSC, the men most involved in subway expansion plans in 1910 and 1911 were Chairman William R. Willcox and Commissioners Edward M. Bassett and Milo R. Maltbie. These men wanted to build as many subway lines as possible, for the same reasons as McAneny.[10] Maltbie later testified that in 1910 he, Willcox, and Bassett had felt that many new rapid transit lines were needed for the symmetrical development of the entire city, for the relief of overcrowded areas, for the distribution of population into suburban areas in the outlying boroughs, as well as for the elimination of indecent conditions on rapid transit lines during rush hours.[11]

The seeming unanimity over the need to build many new subways as fast as possible led to the expectation that there would be quick agreement on how to proceed. Despite the optimism that the deadlock over subway expansion could soon be broken, however, 1910 proved to be yet another year of bickering and indecision. Threatened by the possibility of an independent Triborough System that could compete for riders on profitable short-haul trips in Manhattan, the IRT made a determined attempt to win Mayor Gaynor to its side. By the summer of 1910, the company had largely succeeded, with Gaynor advocating expansion of the IRT system, using funds provided by the City, and opposing the Triborough plan.

Meanwhile, proponents of the Triborough System plan were stymied by the fact that the City did not have enough money to build the entire system at one time because of limits on its ability to borrow funds. Efforts to attract private capital to invest in the Triborough System, moreover, were unsuccessful. For most of 1910, the PSC failed in its attempt to put more lines of the Triborough System under construction. Frustrated in its efforts, by the end of the year the Commission was willing to accept a new plan put forward by the IRT for the construction of several new lines.

In January 1911, after another year of stumbling toward an answer to New York's biggest problem, McAneny took control over subway decision making. The Manhattan borough president was determined to find a solution to New York's transit problem and to start construction of new rapid transit lines.

First Attempts to Find a Solution

At its first meeting, on January 7, 1910, the new Board of Estimate passed a resolution stating that New York was in need of an immediate solution to its rapid transit problem.[12] To this end, the Board created a Transit Committee consisting of Mayor Gaynor, Comptroller Prendergast, and President Mitchel, which was to confer with the PSC and chart a course of action to put more subways under construction quickly. The *New York Times* reported that Mayor Gaynor had agreed to work with Mitchel and Prendergast under an arrangement with Fusionist leader McAneny.[13]

In early 1910, the PSC and its new allies on the Board of Estimate were intent on finding a way to build a completely new Triborough System while simultaneously expanding the existing subway system operated by the IRT. The estimated cost of the proposed new lines was huge. The Triborough System was now expected to cost between $120 million and $150 million. The figure for the new IRT subways then under consideration was $60 million to $70 million. The IRT also wanted to construct about $30 million in improvements, such as extensions and additional tracks, to the lines of the Manhattan Railway Company.[14] By way of comparison, by 1910 the City of New York had invested about $52 million in subway construction under Contracts No. 1 and No. 2 with the IRT.[15]

As described in Chapter 2, the Triborough System plan had originally been developed in 1907. It called for several new lines to relatively undeveloped districts of the Bronx and Brooklyn. These feeder lines would connect to a north-south trunk line on the East Side of Manhattan. The PSC had vigorously sought to implement the plan since its creation in 1907. Contracts for construction of a portion of one line of the system, under Fourth Avenue in Brooklyn, had been awarded by the PSC at the end of

1909, and the work was underway.[16] (See Map 2 of the Triborough System.)

In early 1910, the PSC hoped to attract the private sector to pay for all or part of the construction costs of the rest of the Triborough System in return for a long-term lease for operation under the indeterminate franchise plan.[17] The PSC and Board of Estimate were aware, however, that attracting a private company to build and operate the Triborough System would be difficult.[18] If no private company was willing to invest in the Triborough System, the Commission and its new reform allies on the Board of Estimate planned to use all available public funds of the City of New York to build it. The system would then be leased to a private operator.

The PSC also still hoped that the IRT would use its own funds, under the indeterminate franchise plan approved by the State Legislature in 1909, to expand the subway it was operating under Contracts No. 1 and No. 2. This expansion would include completing the "H" in Manhattan by extending the network north of 42nd Street on the East Side and south of 42nd Street on the West Side. In addition, the PSC wanted the IRT to build several new lines, or extensions of existing lines, in the Bronx, Brooklyn, and Queens. These feeder lines would connect to the "H" trunk lines in Manhattan.[19] However, the PSC had no way of compelling the IRT to invest in new subways or to operate any service on any new lines. (See Map 3 for the IRT proposals of March and July 1910.)

Financing the Triborough System

One of the first tasks of the Board of Estimate's Transit Committee was to determine how much funding might be available to the City if private companies continued to refuse to participate in constructing the Triborough System, as had been the case

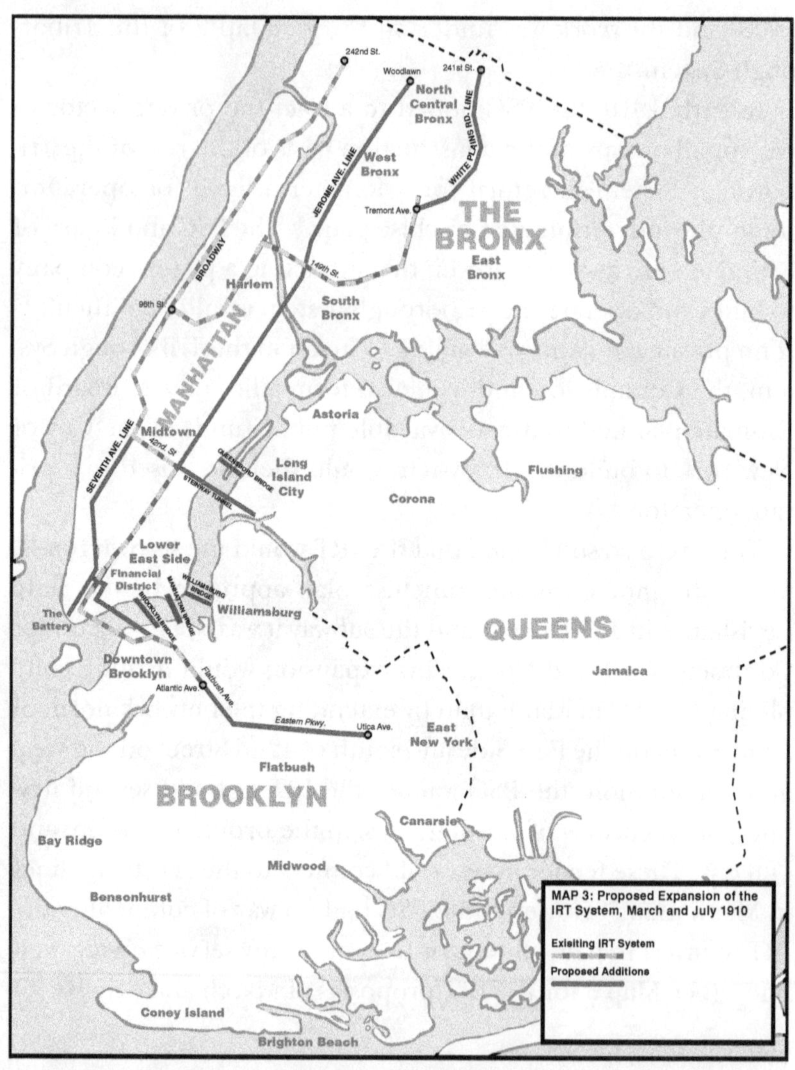

Map 3. Proposed Expansion of the IRT System, March and July 1910

from 1907 to 1909. In March, Comptroller Prendergast reported that the City's total constitutional borrowing power was about $681 million.[20] Most of this sum already had been used for capital projects. Prendergast computed the margin of credit available for all purposes, subway and non-subway, as of January 1, 1910, to have been $59 million. Another $27 million was to be added by July 1, 1910, as a result of increased real estate assessments.[21] In addition, another $24 million more was expected to be available in July from the cancellation of projects that had been approved by the McClellan administration but had not yet gone to contract.[22] This would bring the total available for all capital projects to $110 million. Given New York's needs for other capital improvements, it was clear that the City could not start construction of the entire Triborough System at one time with its own funds.

One hope of raising new funds was by taking advantage of the new state law exempting self-supporting subway and dock bonds from the calculation of the City's debt limit. There was extensive debate within the City government over the amount that would be available for subways in early 1910, but in the end it was decided to use funds from the dock bonds for new dock improvements; this left only $47 million for subways.[23]

Hoping to raise more money for subways, the reformers took a hard look at whether it would be possible to construct new lines under the assessment plan.[24] Under this scheme, approved by the State Legislature in 1909, new subways would be financed with bonds backed by revenues derived from increased tax assessments of property along the new rapid transit lines.

On April 4, 1910, the Board of Estimate held a public hearing on how to build new subways. At the hearing, officials who strongly backed the assessment plan, such as McAneny and Mitchel, learned to their dismay that public support was not as widespread as they had imagined. Most speakers from outlying areas strongly opposed the plan. Property owners in Brooklyn and Queens, for example, felt that northern Manhattan and the Bronx had already benefited from the existing IRT subway, which had been constructed with City money. They did not think it was fair that they should now be asked to pay for new lines to their areas. Mayor Gaynor asked nearly all the speakers what they thought of the plan. He found that property owners were generally "not too anxious" to help pay for the subways, preferring that the City assume the responsibility.[25] After this meeting, the assessment plan still was discussed as a possible way of building lines to outlying areas, but because of strong public opposition nothing ever came of this novel idea.[26]

Faced with the inability to put the entire Triborough System under construction at one time, the Board of Estimate decided to proceed with the funds that were available. On April 6, 1910, the Board allocated $60 million to build additional portions of this network.[27]

Negotiations with the IRT

While the PSC had assessed the possibilities of financing the Triborough System, in early 1910 its members also had been talking to the IRT about building new lines. The company, however, remained unwilling to build an extensive network of new lines with its own funds. IRT President Theodore P. Shonts, who had been authorized by the company's board of directors to conduct all of the company's negotiations with the PSC, was limited by two factors as to what offers he could make. The first was that any plan had to be approved by the IRT's board of directors, which was reluctant to enter into any plan that might reduce the 9 percent annual dividend on the IRT's stock.[28]

The second factor had to do with the House of Morgan, one of the largest and most powerful investment banking firms in

New York.[29] In 1909, the Morgan bank had made an agreement with the IRT to provide needed financial backing for proposed expansions of the existing subway and for improvements to the Manhattan Railway Company lines. President Shonts sought this arrangement because he wanted to have financing in hand before negotiating with the PSC for new IRT lines.[30] Before providing the funds for any final deal the IRT made with the PSC for new lines, of course, J. P. Morgan and Company would have to be convinced that any proposition would ensure the payment of interest on any bonds that were issued for such improvements.[31]

In early 1910, Chairman Willcox had extensive discussions with President Shonts about expanding the IRT system.[32] By March, the two men were close to an agreement, which included most of the new lines the PSC wanted the company to build with its own funds.[33] The proposed agreement was rejected by the executive committee of the IRT Board out of a fear that if the company built new subway lines with its own funds, the City would be able to use its own capital to build the competing Triborough System.[34] One of the main sticking points in the discussions between Willcox and Shonts had been the former's refusal to guarantee that if the IRT paid for new subways on the East Side of Manhattan and in the Bronx, the PSC would drop its plans for the portions of the Triborough System in these areas. The plan that Shonts and Willcox had worked out was rejected, in part, because of advice from the Morgan bank. J. P. Morgan, Jr., expressed it most succinctly: the IRT and his bank, he said, decided not to enter into a proposition that "the city authorities . . . could ruin."[35] (See Map 3.)

The IRT Courts Mayor Gaynor

Unable to negotiate the construction of new subway lines with the IRT, in April 1910 the PSC, together with Comptroller

Prendergast and President Mitchel, continued to try to find ways to implement the complete Triborough System plan.[36] Meanwhile, the IRT turned its full attention to winning the support and good will of Mayor Gaynor. This was a logical move since Gaynor, despite his attacks on the IRT during the 1909 election campaign, was a fiscal conservative in the nineteenth-century Democratic mold. In 1910, he did not agree with the efforts of the Progressive reformers to risk City funds to build what the *New York Times* had labeled "philanthropic subways."[37] Gaynor was essentially looking for a solution to the rapid transit problem that involved the least possible expenditure of City money and the least threat to the City's long-term credit.

Even while Gaynor was making campaign speeches in 1909 attacking the IRT, he had been discussing the IRT's plans to build new lines with his friend Mirabeau Towns, who lived next door to him in Brooklyn. Once it became obvious that Gaynor might be a candidate for mayor, Towns, a lawyer, had been hired by the IRT in May 1909 to help win him over to the IRT's point of view.[38] Towns's task was to convince Gaynor that it was not in the best interest of the City to build an independent system that could compete with the IRT. He argued for the merits of a unified and expanded subway system, to be operated by the IRT, with a single five-cent fare.

Between October 1909 and April 1910, Towns saw Gaynor at his home three or four times per week for a total of about fifty times. For his services, Towns was paid $5,000 by the IRT.[39] This money was well spent, because by the beginning of 1910, Gaynor had ceased to be hostile to the IRT and had become receptive to the company's arguments. On January 26, 1910, Gaynor issued a press release stating that IRT President Shonts had visited him at City Hall and that the two had "talked about subways in Manhattan, the Bronx and Brooklyn as a system." Shonts seemed to him a man "of large and fair views and a man with whom it would be easy to do business."[40]

By the end of April 1910, the IRT had won the mayor to its side. Gaynor stated that he believed the best plan for new subway construction would be to have the IRT build most of the lines it had agreed to in the draft plan discussed with Willcox in March—that is, the Seventh Avenue line south of 42nd Street, the Steinway Tunnel line to Queens, and the Eastern Parkway line—with the company's own money, but that the City should construct the Broadway–Lexington Avenue line and the Jerome and White Plains Road lines in the Bronx. The mayor proposed that these lines would be leased to the IRT for operation, and that connections be made to the existing IRT subway system.[41] Gaynor's plan would have effectively destroyed the possibility of an independent Triborough System, since these routes were a major part of it, and Willcox refused to even consider this proposal.[42]

Nonetheless, the IRT kept wooing Gaynor, since his support was now critical to the company's efforts to block the progress of the Triborough plan.[43] On April 24, Shonts visited Gaynor at his country home on Long Island. Shonts told the mayor that he thought that the Board of Estimate would soon approve construction of additional portions of the Triborough System, but warned Gaynor that this system would mean "financial disaster" for the City of New York. According to Shonts, the Triborough System could not be supported solely out of the fare box. The Triborough lines to outlying areas would be unprofitable for many years, if a five-cent fare were in effect, and would have to be subsidized from the City treasury at the rate of $10 million to $12 million a year. In short, the Triborough System involved "extravagant use of City money with meager results." Shonts also informed Gaynor that if the municipality built the Triborough System, the IRT would withdraw from any participation in new lines.[44]

In order to convince Gaynor that the IRT's position was reasonable, Shonts offered to let Gaynor come to the IRT's offices and look at all of its financial records and cost projections for new subway lines. The mayor's chief concern was whether the IRT's cost estimates for constructing and equipping extensions to the existing subway system were accurate and that its estimates of future revenues and profits, to be derived from a single five-cent fare on the expanded system, were reasonable. He also wanted information on the IRT's overall financial status. Gaynor accepted the IRT's offer and sent two of his senior officials to examine the company's records.[45] By June, these officials had concluded that the IRT was essentially correct, both as to how much new subway lines would cost and the income they would produce from passenger revenues over a period of years.[46]

By June 1910, Gaynor had turned into what McAneny later called a "rabid Interborough man."[47] The mayor had now come to the conclusion that all proposed extensions to the IRT subway should be built with City money. In large measure, Gaynor had arrived at this position because he was now certain that construction of the Triborough System would be a mistake. If the IRT could offer better service at less cost, and certainly less risk, then the City was justified in extending the existing subway system.

On July 5, 1910, the IRT made a subway offer to Gaynor and the PSC that reflected the discussions between the company and the mayor.[48] This proposal was nothing more than a rehash of the plan Shonts and Willcox had discussed in March, except that now it was proposed that the City, not the IRT, should pay to construct all the new lines.[49] The subway routes outlined in this new offer included the "H" trunk lines in Manhattan, except that on the East Side north of 42nd Street the IRT now proposed to build on Lexington Avenue instead of Madison Avenue, as had been proposed in March.[50] (See Map 3.)

The PSC did not formally respond to the IRT, but Willcox did write a letter to Gaynor, pointing out that in all previous negotiations with the IRT, it had been understood that "the cost of constructing and equipping" was "to be borne by the Interborough without the use of the City's credit." Willcox concluded by reiterating his belief that "extensions to the Interborough system should not be allowed to interfere with the completion of the Triborough route."[51]

Gaynor now publicly stated his views in a magazine article in which he argued that the IRT's financial circumstances forced the company to be adverse to the risk of constructing many new subway lines with its own credit. The mayor alleged that "a chief and persistent difficulty" in negotiating with the IRT was that its directors were not free agents. He said that $35 million of IRT capital stock was held by the Interborough-Metropolitan Securities Company, a holding company that also held stock of the New York City Railway Company. (This was the company that operated the lines of the bankrupt Metropolitan Street Railway Company, which had gone into receivership in 1907.) As a result, the stock of the IRT was "the only live asset this holding company has." The holding company used the IRT stock's 9 percent dividend to pay interest on its $70 million in outstanding bonds and debentures. The directors of the holding company feared that if the IRT participated in new extensions, then the 9 percent dividend might decrease or cease, temporarily, and bring about a default of the interest on its debt.[52]

Gaynor's support of the IRT was reinforced by his running verbal battle with publisher William Randolph Hearst. By the late spring of 1910, Gaynor and Hearst had become bitter enemies and would remain so until the mayor's death in 1913. Gaynor was a strong-willed man of blunt opinions who could not put up with the lies and half-truths leveled against him by the Hearst press during the 1909 campaign. By election day, he and Hearst were barely on speaking terms. Then, in April 1910, the Hearst newspapers had started alleging that Gaynor had bought his nomination by paying a large legal fee to a friend of Tammany boss Charles Francis Murphy.[53]

Gaynor reacted to these allegations by sharply attacking Hearst before a joint banquet of the Associated Press and the American Newspaper Publishers' Association on April 28. Gaynor accused Hearst of two felonies, forgery and falsification of public documents, then added: "It is high time that these forgers and libellers were in State's prison, and the time is not far distant when some of them will be there. And just think of a man who is capable of doing things like this being possessed of the notion that he is fit to any office from Mayor to President of the United States. Morally speaking, his mind must be a howling wilderness."[54]

The battle between Hearst and Gaynor spilled over into the subway issue. Hearst was one of the leading supporters of the independent Triborough System; he even went so far as to advocate municipal operation of this system. He also frequently used the power of his newspapers to threaten politicians.[55] Gaynor had now become one of the leading advocates of extension of the IRT's system. From this point on, Gaynor was viciously attacked in the Hearst press for his support of the IRT.[56]

Meanwhile, Prendergast and Mitchel, who together with Gaynor comprised the Board of Estimate's Transit Committee, opposed the new IRT offer. Prendergast commented: "I see nothing to it but a plan to block the already well-considered and now accepted Triborough routes." He also said that he had been aware for weeks that conferences had been going on between Gaynor and the IRT, but that neither he nor President Mitchel nor the PSC had been invited to attend these discussions.[57]

Obscured in the debate over whether the City should invest all of the money it could currently borrow in either the IRT System or the Triborough System was the key question of whether or not the participation of private capital in subway construction was necessary. As we have seen, McAneny, Willcox, and others on the Board of Estimate and PSC had hoped at the beginning of 1910 that the IRT would extend its lines using its own money under the indeterminate franchise plan, while the City would use its limited credit to construct portions of the Triborough System.[58]

According to J. P. Morgan, Jr., the issue public officials had to come to terms with at this time was whether the City had "enough money to build its own subways, all that it wants, without using private capital." If the municipality did not have enough money to do so, then some arrangement would have to be made with a private company upon terms acceptable to the company. Using only its own money, the City could build whatever lines it wanted, but, said Morgan, "you have to induce private capital to come in . . . private capital has to be bought."[59]

On August 9, an assassination attempt by a disgruntled former municipal employee left Mayor Gaynor incapacitated, and he was replaced on the Transit Committee by McAneny.[60] Morgan and IRT President Shonts visited McAneny shortly thereafter to discuss subway financing. McAneny told his visitors that he was of the opinion that the City government could not construct enough new subways to meet the needs of the population, owing to its limited borrowing capacity.[61]

During the course of the meeting, a new possibility for financing subway construction was suggested. Perhaps the City could come to an agreement with the IRT whereby an extensive network of new lines to outlying areas could be built using a combination of municipal funds and private capital. Instead of putting the City's money into the competing Triborough System, the City and the IRT, in cooperation, might be able to construct a greatly enlarged system, to be operated by the IRT. This expanded IRT system would contain enough new lines to satisfy Greater New York's transit needs.[62] This idea was not explored in depth during the summer of 1910, but by the beginning of 1911 it came to dominate discussion of new subway lines.

The Last Gasp of the Triborough System

From April 1910 on, the PSC had moved ahead with its plans to construct as much of the Triborough System as possible with the funding that was available. On September 1, 1910, the PSC advertised a contract for the construction, equipment, and operation of the Triborough System by private capital. It also advertised contracts for the construction of individual sections of the system with City money. Under the proposed contract for private construction under the indeterminate franchise plan, the successful bidder was to pay the construction costs of those parts of the Triborough System not already under construction with City funds (the Fourth Avenue line to 40th Street, Brooklyn, was under construction). This company would also be responsible for equipping the system.[63]

If there were no bidders for private construction and operation, then the PSC planned to accept bids on the contracts for construction only, with City money, of sections of the Triborough System. The entire Broadway–Lexington Avenue line in Manhattan was to be put under construction, but, due to the debt limit restrictions, only small sections of the Jerome Avenue line and the Pelham line would be started. Work was also to begin on the Lafayette Avenue line in Brooklyn. Most of the lines not included for immediate construction were those to outlying areas in the Bronx and southern Brooklyn. These lines would be built when further City credit became available.[64]

Bids for private construction and operation were due on October 20, 1910. None were received. The risk in building such an extensive system was so great that private capital was not interested.[65] On October 27, bids were received for the construction of twenty-one sections (a section was a portion of an individual line) of the Triborough System with City money. The total of the lowest bids came to $85 million.[66]

The receipt of these bids set off another extended public debate of the "What is to be done?" variety. Those who were against the Triborough System leveled new attacks at it for being too expensive and unprofitable.[67] Its defenders pointed out that the Triborough plan had been under consideration for years and that the PSC was committed to it. They argued that with the $60 million the City now had available to borrow, construction could begin immediately on a number of sections for which bids had been received in October. As more money became available, the system could gradually be extended.[68]

According to Hearst's *New York American*, the enemies of the Triborough System were: (1) the IRT, which wished to continue making excessive profits from the existing subway; (2) the Brooklyn Rapid Transit Company (BRT), which did not want competition in Brooklyn; (3) the banks, which controlled certain newspapers and politicians; (4) Mayor Gaynor, a controlled politician; (5) the Chamber of Commerce and owners of Manhattan real estate—the latter of whom did not wish to experience any decrease in the value of their land; (6) the Pennsylvania Railroad, which wanted a line constructed on Seventh Avenue to serve Pennsylvania Station; and (7) a "solid phalanx of lawyers, controlled by the great interests."[69] Rhetoric aside, this critique had a good deal of truth to it.

Caught between the two sides in this debate were those members of the PSC and the Board of Estimate who were neither absolutely committed to immediate municipal construction of the

Triborough System nor adamantly in favor of simply extending the IRT system. Chairman Willcox, as well as the other members of the Commission, wanted to build the Triborough, but also wished to extend the IRT system. Willcox pointed out that it should not be an either/or question. New York needed a great number of new lines, without which "we must go on for another generation with the frightful congestion of population." It did not matter how the City extended its transit network so long as the work got done.[70]

McAneny also occupied the middle ground in the debate. By the middle of November, he had come to represent the balance of power in the Board of Estimate between those who favored and those who opposed immediate construction of portions of the Triborough System.[71] He was the man to whom most of the other borough presidents now turned for advice.[72] What McAneny wanted most was more time to study the subway situation. He believed that it was questionable for the City to sink all of its money into the construction of portions of the Triborough System before it explored all other possibilities.[73]

In November, the PSC requested that the Board of Estimate consider immediate construction of sections of the Broadway–Lexington Avenue line, at a cost of $49 million, and sections of the Lafayette Avenue line, at a cost of $11 million.[74] The Board, however, was still undecided as to the best policy to follow and voted to postpone consideration of the matter. On November 14, Willcox decided to hold back the award of bids on the initial construction contracts for portions of the Triborough System until the Board of Estimate made up its mind.[75]

By that time, Gaynor had recovered from the assassination attempt and was once again fulminating against the proposed Triborough System and arguing the merits of City support for extending the IRT system. On November 17, he delivered a speech to the Chamber of Commerce implying that many who favored the Triborough were "as entirely ignorant of all of the facts as are the sensational newspapers which are instigating them." Because the City only had a limited amount of money to put into subways, and a need to construct many other public works, Gaynor argued that it could not afford to throw millions of dollars, year after year, into the Triborough System. He appealed to his audience, which represented "intelligent public sentiment," to "instruct the city officials and determine what they shall do."[76]

One business group had already taken the mayor's advice. The Chamber of Commerce came out with a report on November 3 concluding that the Triborough System was "fraught with grave dangers to the success of the undertaking and the credit of the City of New York." Moreover, an extended IRT system would provide better service to the people. In Manhattan, for example, the Triborough System would needlessly parallel and duplicate service already provided by the IRT on the East Side, while providing no service for the West Side.[77]

On November 18, William G. McAdoo, president of the Hudson and Manhattan Railroad Company, made an unexpected offer to the PSC. This company operated a rapid transit system between New Jersey and Manhattan, which had opened in 1909.[78] McAdoo now proposed that, if it was constructed with City money, his company would equip and operate the portion of the Triborough System running between 138th Street in the southern Bronx and Wall Street. McAdoo also proposed that the City construct a line running from Lower Manhattan through Wall Street and across the East River to Montague Street in Brooklyn, which would connect to the proposed Lafayette Avenue line. McAdoo did not offer to operate the Triborough System lines in the Bronx or in southern Brooklyn.[79] His offer was thus essentially a plan to equip and operate only those portions of the Triborough System that ran through areas that were already built up. In this respect, McAdoo seems to have missed the main point of the Triborough System. The PSC had consciously designed the system so that it would have a lucrative trunk line in Manhattan, the profits from which could be used to cover the deficits arising from the operation of branch lines to outlying areas. McAdoo was proposing that he be given the profitable sections, without dealing with the fundamental issue of how new lines could be built to the outlying districts.[80]

Nonetheless, Willcox was glad that McAdoo had made a proposal, commenting that "this offer ought to be sufficient answer to the pessimistic arguments which have been recently used against the Triborough."[81] Willcox realized that McAdoo's offer was limited in scope, but he hoped that he and McAdoo could negotiate an agreement for the operation of the outlying portions of the Triborough System.[82] After meeting with Willcox about this possibility, McAdoo instructed one of his engineers to study the possible financial results from operation of the Fourth Avenue line south of 40th Street in Brooklyn.

This engineer, however, came to the same conclusion reached by Commissioner Bassett in 1907, namely, that neither the Fourth Avenue line south of 40th Street nor its New Utrecht Avenue branch could operate in the black for several years until traffic was built up. The City could build these lines, but, at a five-cent fare, a private company would have to be subsidized to operate them.[83] On this issue, McAdoo and the PSC could not reach agreement. On December 4, McAdoo said that he and the PSC had not settled the matter of operation of the southern Brooklyn and Bronx lines of the Triborough System. He also said that if he did not receive an answer from the PSC to his offer of November 18, then he would withdraw this offer on December 15.[84]

The IRT Tries to Forestall Competition

While discussions were going on between the PSC and McAdoo, the IRT put forth an offer on December 5, 1910, that the company hoped would bury the Triborough System forever. Before making this offer, the IRT had made arrangements with J. P. Morgan and Company relative to the financing of proposals it might make to the PSC for new subway lines and elevated line improvements.[85] The latest IRT offer sought to correct deficiencies, noted by the PSC, of previous company offers. The PSC had consistently informed the IRT that it could not expect to get "the tenderloin of the thing" without making adequate provision for extension to outlying areas.[86] As a result, the IRT now added certain lines to outlying areas of the Bronx and Brooklyn. (See Map 4.) It also offered to put up enough money, beyond what the City then had available under the debt limit, to make sure that all the new lines could be constructed at one time.[87] As with all previous offers, however, the IRT first stated its primary desire to complete the Manhattan "H."

In Brooklyn, the IRT offered to build a new line from the existing terminus of the subway at Atlantic Avenue down Flatbush Avenue and then out Eastern Parkway to Brownsville. The IRT also offered to build the Lafayette Avenue line of the proposed Triborough System from Flatbush Avenue to Broadway, in Brooklyn. The IRT also said that it would equip and operate the Fourth Avenue and New Utrecht Avenue lines to southern Brooklyn if the City built these lines with its own funds, and if the City would cover any deficit from operations.[88]

In the Bronx, the Jerome and Pelham lines, as well as the existing subway in the southern Bronx, would be connected to the Lexington Avenue line. In addition, to provide direct service to the West Side of Manhattan for West Bronx residents, the Ninth

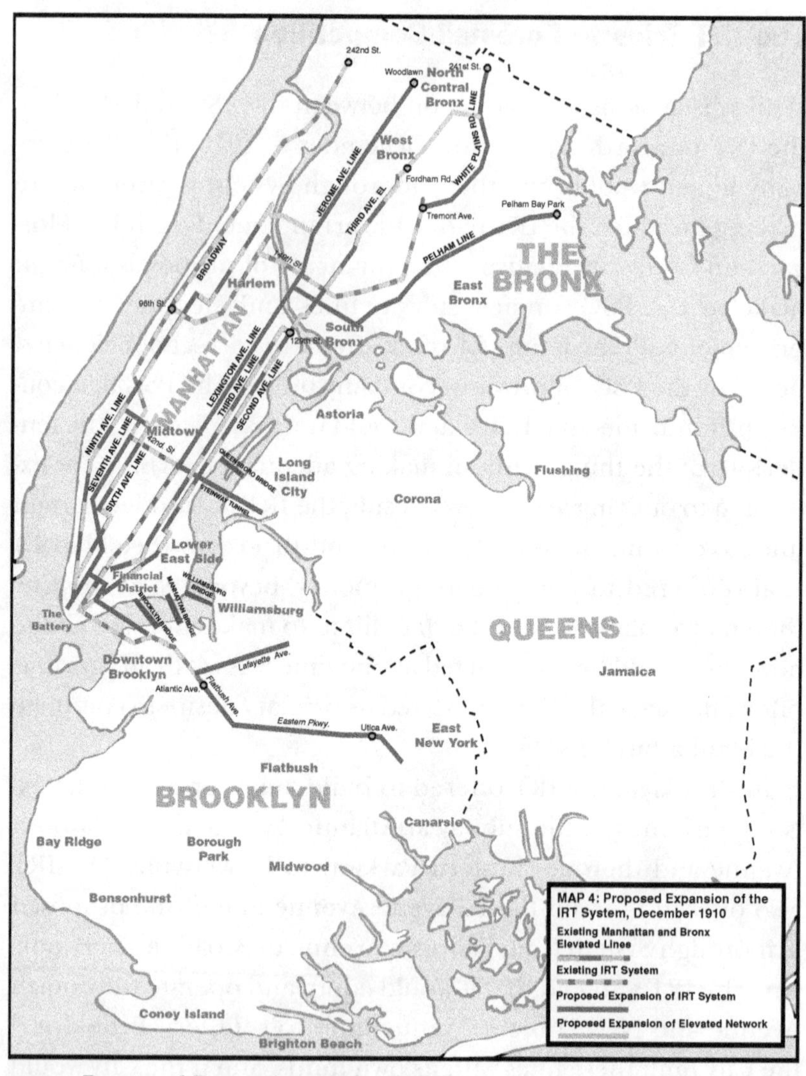

Map 4. Proposed Expansion of the IRT System, December 1910

Avenue el would be extended across the Harlem River to a connection with the Jerome Avenue el. The IRT would also extend the first subway line up White Plains Road. In addition, the Third Avenue el in the Bronx would be extended north from Fordham Road to Gun Hill Road to a connection with this line.[89] All of the Bronx lines would extend almost to the northern border of the city, into areas of low population density in the western, north-central, and eastern portions of the borough.[90]

Although Queens was not part of the formal proposal, the IRT indicated its willingness to convert its existing Steinway Tunnel from Long Island City to 42nd Street in Manhattan into a subway line connecting to the "H" lines. Since Long Island City was just inside the Queens border, however, this would leave most of the borough without any direct rapid transit to the Manhattan Central Business District.[91]

The IRT estimated the cost of constructing and equipping the proposed subway lines at $128 million. (This did not include the Fourth Avenue and New Utrecht Avenue lines.) The company would furnish $75 million of this amount, provided that the City contribute the other $53 million.[92]

The IRT had structured the proposal so that it would retain its profits from the existing subway lines it operated while putting the risk of investment in the new lines on the City.[93] According to Comptroller Prendergast, it was calculated that the future income from these old lines would be such that the IRT would probably continue to earn all its current profits. Earnings from the new lines, on the other hand, would barely cover the interest and sinking fund requirements of the new money invested by both the IRT and the City. It was not expected that the City would ever profit from the operation of the new lines.[94]

The IRT was willing to make such a new investment because this would enable the company to retain its existing profits from its old lines. Moreover, acceptance of the offer would block City construction of a competing independent system. In addition, this offer was contingent upon the PSC allowing the IRT to extend and add third tracks to the elevated lines of the Manhattan Elevated Railway Company, improvements that were expected to be quite profitable.

The December 5 offer was the most extensive one ever made by one company, but it required that the City contribute $53 million toward the cost of construction of new subway lines. If the PSC and Board of Estimate accepted this offer, it would tie up most of the money the City then had available for new subways, making it impossible for the City to construct an independent subway system at any time in the near future.

The PSC was especially unhappy over the possibility that it would have to abandon its plans for that portion of the proposed Broadway–Lexington Avenue line of the Triborough System south of 42nd Street because it believed that Manhattan needed other north-south trunk lines in addition to the "H."[95] Nonetheless, the Commission believed that, for the moment at least, the City's limited amount of credit available for new subways would best be spent by first completing the "H" together with the other proposed extensions to the IRT.[96]

The PSC let the McAdoo offer expire without comment on December 15, since the IRT offer of December 5 was so obviously superior.[97] Then on December 20, the Commission indicated its willingness to accept the new IRT subway proposal with certain modifications. The PSC also informed the Board of Estimate that it was prepared to negotiate the details of a subway contract based on the IRT's offer. It wished to know, however, whether the Board had any objections to the IRT offer that would make its consent to a contract with the IRT impossible. If the Board of Estimate disapproved of the IRT offer, then the PSC was willing to award contracts for the construction of sections of the Triborough System based on the bids received on October 27.[98] The entire question was thus thrown into the lap of the Board of Estimate for a final decision. The Board, however, was still divided, with some members continuing to prefer construction of the Triborough System while others preferred accepting the new IRT offer.

Mayor Gaynor was strongly in favor of accepting the IRT offer. On December 20, 1910, he wrote a letter to former Brooklyn Borough President J. Edward Swanstrom, outlining his views on the matter. Gaynor first cleared up the confusing issue of who owned the present subway and who would own future subways. The Hearst papers had muddled the scene with their constant calls for public ownership of any new lines. This was misleading, because "all subways now built or to be hereafter built under the statute" would be owned by the City of New York, whatever the source of the capital used to build them. Gaynor went on to say that because of the limited credit available to the municipality, he was anxious to have new subways built at least in part by private capital, so that they could be built simultaneously, instead of being strung out over many years as additional funds became available.[99]

Once private operation was accepted, the question was whether there should be one operator or many. Gaynor favored one operating company, the IRT, which would operate a unified subway system, under government regulation, at a single five-cent fare. He contended that the City would do best to settle with the IRT right away, especially since the company was offering to put $75 million of its own money in subways and $30 million in elevated improvements. The City could not hope to have anywhere near this amount available for subways, since "future borrowing margins . . . have to be chiefly devoted to the City's ordinary needs, excluding subways."[100]

The IRT offer was opposed, however, by Comptroller Prendergast and President Mitchel, who continued to advocate immediate construction of sections of the Triborough System. Occupying the middle ground were the five borough presidents, only one of whom, machine Democrat Lawrence Gresser from Queens, was publicly committed to the IRT offer.[101] Of these, McAneny had the most influence. He continued to insist that the Board be given enough time to study the entire transit situation carefully. He also steadfastly refused to commit himself to any one plan.[102]

Together with Prendergast and Mitchel, McAneny already had investigated how much City money might be available for subways from annual increases in tax assessments and had determined that the City would have approximately $116 million for new construction by 1915. This included what was available at the end of 1910, together with a portion of the increases in assessments.[103]

On December 22, McAneny moved that the Board of Estimate consider both the IRT's December 5 offer and the Triborough System plan as a committee of the whole. This meant that the Board could conduct its deliberations in secret since, when the Board was operating as a committee, the public could be barred from the meetings. (In committee, of course, the Board could not formally vote on any proposition.) McAneny pointed out that the members could not now make a decision on the IRT offer because they did not have enough information about it and because the PSC had said that it took exception to certain provisions in the offer. How could the Board make a decision without knowing what these provisions were? In addition, the PSC had not said whether or not it was now giving up the Triborough System plan as impractical.[104]

McAneny's motion to refer this matter to the Board as a committee of the whole was defeated.[105] For the moment, the power to make formal recommendations to the Board of Estimate still lay with its Transit Committee. On January 5, 1911, Prendergast and Mitchel, as a majority of the Committee, issued a report that was severely critical of the IRT proposal and urged its rejection. They also said that accepting the proposal would mean abandoning all hope for an independent subway system. On the same day, Prendergast and Mitchel moved to have the Board adopt the following resolutions:

> First—That the available credit of the City be devoted to the construction of an independent, municipally owned and controlled subway system, whose integrity as a unit can be forever maintained.
> Second—That the present or future available credit of the City shall not be lent in whole or in part to any existing corporation or individual for the extension of any existing system until such independent system shall be completed and in operation.[106]

The choice before the Board of Estimate seemed clear. Prendergast and Mitchel had submitted a report and proposed two resolutions against the IRT and in favor of the Triborough System. Gaynor was expected to submit a minority report favoring acceptance of the IRT offer. It would have been easy for the Board to accept the IRT offer, because there seemed to be strong public support for it.[107]

The decision lay in the hands of the borough presidents. With the exception of McAneny, they had been ignored in the consideration of the subway problem during 1910. They were thus willing to follow McAneny's advice that they be provided with more information before any final action was taken with respect to any subway proposal.[108]

At the Board of Estimate meeting on January 5, McAneny led the fight against accepting the Mitchel-Prendergast report. The resolutions introduced by Prendergast and Mitchel were rejected by a vote of ten to six, with Mayor Gaynor and all five borough presidents voting against them. McAneny then proceeded to introduce his own resolution, which referred consideration of the IRT offer as well as any other rapid transit proposal to the entire Board, sitting as a committee of the whole. According to McAneny, this did not mean that the Board was now willing to accept the IRT offer. What it meant was that before taking action, the Board would carefully examine all subway proposals presented to it, in conjunction with the PSC. McAneny's resolution passed unanimously.[109]

One of the matters the Board of Estimate wished to examine was the question of routes. The IRT offer of December 5 was extensive, but it did not present a complete solution to the subway problem. The IRT had always been oriented toward the routes along the north-south, Manhattan-Bronx spine and had never really shown much interest in operating lines to outlying areas of Brooklyn and Queens. The December 5 offer and the related agreement on elevated extensions had continued this preference for the Bronx, where three new lines were to be constructed extending to the northern limits of the city. In Queens, however, the 42nd Street–Steinway Tunnel line was to extend only a few blocks past the East River. In Brooklyn, the proposed IRT lines also did not reach far into the borough. The proposed Lafayette Avenue line was only to be two miles long. The Eastern Parkway line, from Atlantic Avenue and Flatbush Avenue to its terminus at Buffalo Avenue, would be about three miles long. Neither of these lines extended into areas that had not yet been heavily developed.[110]

Moreover, in its December 5 offer, the IRT had agreed to operate the Fourth Avenue line and the New Utrecht Avenue line, which extended to the southern border of Brooklyn, only if it was guaranteed against loss. Construction of the Fourth Avenue line was underway to 40th Street, a distance of two miles from Atlantic Avenue. This section of the line would certainly be completed;

but given that the City would have to complete the Fourth Avenue line and the New Utrecht Avenue line with its own money, it was uncertain whether any extensions would be made beyond 40th Street in the near future. This left in serious doubt whether the three-mile extension of the Fourth Avenue line between 40th Street and 86th Street and the five-mile New Utrecht Avenue extension to Coney Island would ever be constructed, a doubt that would be increased by the knowledge that the City would have to subsidize any operating losses on these extensions under the IRT plan.[111]

The same was true for two lines that had been under consideration by the PSC in 1910 to serve northern Brooklyn. One of these lines was the proposed subway under Broadway in Brooklyn, which was part of the Triborough System plan. The other was a proposed subway running across 14th Street in Manhattan, under the East River, and then through a number of local streets in northern Brooklyn.[112] The future of both of these lines was in doubt if the IRT offer of December 5 was accepted, since the City would not have the money to put them under construction quickly.

On January 10, 1911, five days after the Board of Estimate referred consideration of all subway matters to itself as a committee of the whole, E. W. Winter, president of the Brooklyn Rapid Transit Company, made a formal proposal to the PSC that contained a possible solution to southern Brooklyn's rapid transit problems. In 1910, Winter had several discussions with Willcox regarding transit extensions. These discussions had dealt primarily with use of the Centre Street loop, construction of which was almost complete, by BRT elevated trains.[113] His January 10 proposal basically consisted of a plan to connect the Fourth Avenue subway in Brooklyn to existing railroads then controlled by the BRT, which would be converted into rapid transit lines. Winter noted that this comprehensive plan would meet the transportation needs of vast undeveloped areas in southern Brooklyn.[114] McAneny, who shared this concern, said that he was glad that Winter had made an offer.[115]

Meanwhile, the Board of Estimate's decision to postpone any immediate approval of new subway lines was being attacked by the Hearst press. McAneny now became the prime target, since his actions seemed to doom the Triborough System. Regarding the Board's January 5 decision, the *New York American* charged that, "Under the leadership of George McAneny . . . a substantial advantage for the Traction Trust was won yesterday by Charles F. Murphy, boss of Tammany, and Mayor Gaynor."[116]

In actuality, what had happened was that the power over subway decision making in New York had shifted to an elected leader determined to end the deadlock over rapid transit expansion. During the next six months, McAneny and his allies would work to produce a subway expansion plan that would more than double the size of the existing rapid transit network and, just as important, would have the public and private financing needed to put all the new lines under construction at the same time.

5. The Dual System of Rapid Transit

In January 1911, Manhattan Borough President George McAneny saw his opportunity to break the deadlock over subway expansion in New York City. From this point on, McAneny was the acknowledged leader in making decisions about new subway lines. The importance of this transfer of power cannot be overemphasized. McAneny had helped to develop a new way of thinking about the role of transportation in urban development. He had been actively involved in the work of the Committee on Congestion of Population in 1908 and had directed studies of rapid transit needs and finances as president of the City Club. Moreover, his ideas on transit expansion were shared by several members of the Public Service Commission, including Chairman William R. Willcox and Commissioner Edward M. Bassett.

McAneny and his allies on the Public Service Commission (PSC) believed that the provision of new subway lines was too important to be left primarily to the private sector.[1] The main purposes of new subways were to relieve social problems, assure proper development of the outlying districts, and strengthen New York's economy. In January 1911, these reformers believed that what needed to be done was to get many new lines in the ground as fast as possible. How new subways would be financed—

whether by the City or by private companies, or both—was of secondary concern.[2]

In their efforts to break the transit deadlock, McAneny and his allies were supported by the recommendations of the Mayor's Commission on Congestion of Population, appointed by Mayor William J. Gaynor in April 1910. The Commission had fully documented the problems resulting from congestion of population and overcrowding in the tenement districts. To alleviate these problems, it had recommended the program of city planning that McAneny had advanced, including the development of a long-range plan for rapid transit expansion, zoning and land use restrictions, and the regulation of building heights and volumes.[3]

The draft of the Commission's final report was under review in December 1910 and January 1911,[4] and its statements about rapid transit expressed McAneny's own views on the matter. The report noted: "The awful congestion of population in the Borough of Manhattan has attracted the attention of lawmakers and reformers for about fifty years, but no adequate system of transit that would decrease, or even prevent its extension northward and spreading over a greater area, has yet been devised or seriously attempted." The reason for this, the report observed, "appears to be due to the fact that the City and State have gone all these years upon the assumption that the provision of rapid transit facilities for a great city was, in the main, a function for private gain, rather than a public function to be initiated and controlled by a strong central public authority with the power to plan a scientific system of transit and carry such a plan through to practical fruition."[5]

In January 1911, McAneny believed that neither the Triborough System plan nor the latest Interborough Rapid Transit Company (IRT) proposal alone would meet the rapid transit needs of the city. He therefore proceeded, along with his allies on the PSC, to find a way to break the deadlock. The result was

The signing of the Dual System contracts at the offices of the New York State Public Service Commission in the New York Tribune Building, March 19, 1913. Seated in the center of the photograph, in the row nearest the map, are PSC Chairman Edward E. McCall *(left)* and Manhattan Borough President George McAneny *(right)*. To McCall's right is former PSC chairman William R. Willcox. (Courtesy of the Museum of the City of New York. The J. Clarence Davies Collection. 29.100.650)

Tenement buildings and stores on Orchard Street, 1898. During the first decade of the twentieth century, the Lower East Side was the most congested district in the world. (Courtesy of the Byron Collection, the Museum of the City of New York)

Sweatshop in a tenement on Ludlow Street on the Lower East Side, circa 1898. At the turn of the twentieth century, many consumer goods, particularly clothing, were manufactured in small tenement apartments. The overcrowding, lack of sunlight, and poor ventilation of these apartments fostered contagious diseases such as tuberculosis. (Courtesy of the Jacob A. Riis Collection, the Museum of the City of New York)

Construction of the Lexington Avenue subway between 61st and 62nd Streets, February 20, 1914. The Lexington Avenue line completed the eastern leg of the IRT's two north-south trunk lines in Manhattan, distributing passengers from the Bronx, Brooklyn, and Queens throughout Midtown and Downtown. Service began on July 17, 1918. In the 1990s, this line carried over 275,000 passengers each way on an average business day. (Courtesy of the New York Transit Museum Archives, Brooklyn)

Construction of the IRT Lexington Avenue subway between 54th and 55th Streets, June 7, 1914. This East Side trunk line opened for service on July 17, 1918. (Courtesy of the New York Transit Museum Archives, Brooklyn)

Lexington Avenue looking north from 51st Street, August 13, 1914. At this time, what is now the East Midtown skyscraper district was largely a residential area, with a mix of brownstones and apartment houses. On the right is the original St. Peter's Lutheran Church, later replaced by a new structure as part of the construction of Citicorp Center in the 1970s. The spires of the 1872 Central Synagogue, still standing, are up the street on the left. (Courtesy of the New York Transit Museum Archives, Brooklyn)

Construction of Seventh Avenue South, looking north from Morton Street, May 20, 1915. The new street, which connected Seventh Avenue with Varick Street, allowed direct north-south subway service on the West Side. It also cut a huge slash through Greenwich Village that destroyed many old buildings. Until this time, Seventh Avenue ended at 12th Street, where the older West Village grid blocked access further south. Service on the new Seventh Avenue subway began on July 1, 1918. (Courtesy of the New York Transit Museum Archives, Brooklyn)

The Ninth Avenue el on Greenwich Street at Fulton Street in Lower Manhattan, August 2, 1914. Opened for passenger service on July 3, 1868, this was New York's first rapid transit line and the world's first elevated railroad. The line was extended to the Harlem River by 1879 and sparked development of the West Side of Manhattan. Service was terminated in 1940. (Courtesy of the New York Transit Museum Archives, Brooklyn)

View up Broadway from John Street, July 18, 1914. The fifty-five-story Woolworth Building, opened in 1913, was the world's tallest building. Called the "Cathedral of Commerce," it rose 792 feet from the sidewalk. The only practical way to transport the tens of thousands of office workers to and from their jobs in the skyscrapers of the Wall Street financial district was by rapid transit. (Courtesy of the New York Transit Museum Archives, Brooklyn)

Looking up Broadway from just south of Spring Street, July 14, 1912. North of the Wall Street area was New York's largest manufacturing district. In the loft buildings of what is now SoHo, many types of consumer goods were made, including, as the signs indicate, brushes, ladies hats, and embroideries. Many of the factory workers lived in nearby tenement districts. (Courtesy of the New York Transit Museum Archives, Brooklyn)

Pennsylvania Station, facing Seventh Avenue between 31st and 33rd Streets, August 11, 1916. This station, opened in 1910, served both intercity travelers and commuters from Long Island and New Jersey. The Seventh Avenue subway, under construction below the street, would bring direct rapid transit service to the station for the first time, permitting easy access to Midtown and the Wall Street area. (Courtesy of the New York Transit Museum Archives, Brooklyn)

Times Square, September 11, 1914. The IRT's West Side trunk subway was being constructed under Seventh Avenue from 43rd Street south to connect to the first IRT subway running down Broadway to 42nd Street. The subways helped transform this area into the nation's premier theater district. (Courtesy of the New York Transit Museum Archives, Brooklyn)

Looking up Westchester Avenue, at Soundview Avenue, November 17, 1916. The elevated structure of the IRT's Pelham line would soon be built on Westchester Avenue, serving as a catalyst for the residential development of the East Bronx. Hundreds of thousands of New York families would move from overcrowded tenements to new homes in the subway suburbs built up along the Dual System lines. Service to the Pelham Bay Park station began on December 20, 1920. (Courtesy of the New York Transit Museum Archives, Brooklyn)

Looking north from the Mosholu Parkway station at the elevated structure of the IRT Jerome Avenue line in the West Bronx, December 3, 1915. Passenger service to the East Side of Manhattan began on July 17, 1918, spurring residential development of the Norwood/Mosholu Parkway neighborhood. (Courtesy of the New York Transit Museum Archives, Brooklyn)

The elegant Mosholu Parkway station of the Jerome Avenue line in the Northwest Bronx, 1924. Opened in 1918, the Jerome Avenue line, connecting to the Lexington Avenue subway in Manhattan, sparked the development of the Norwood/Mosholu Parkway neighborhood. The boyhood home of Ralph Lauren and Calvin Klein, Norwood now has a mix of residents from all over the world. (Courtesy of the New York Transit Museum Archives, Brooklyn)

View of the Norwood neighborhood, November 23, 1998. This area developed as a subway suburb in the 1920s, with a mix of five- and six-story apartment houses and single- and two-family homes. The open space is Williamsbridge Oval Park, once a reservoir. (From the author's collection)

The end of the White Plains Road line at 241st Street in the North Central Bronx, August 18, 1924. The streets around subway stations were designated as retail districts under the 1916 zoning law and had a mix of stores catering to local residents. Ubiquitous were the candy stores, serving the famous egg cream, a drink made of seltzer, milk, and chocolate syrup. (Courtesy of the New York Transit Museum Archives, Brooklyn)

Looking east at the 33rd Street (Rawson Street) station of the nearly completed IRT elevated line to Corona (later Flushing), Queens, January 12, 1917. Most of this area was soon built up as an industrial district. In the 1920s the land up the line to the left was developed as a planned residential community called Sunnyside Gardens. (Courtesy of the New York Transit Museum Archives, Brooklyn)

The Corona-Flushing line, looking west toward Manhattan from about 32nd Street, with the 59th Street–Queensboro Bridge on the left, December 6, 1916. Long Island City, across the East River from Manhattan, was already built up as a factory and warehouse district. The Dual System plan brought three rapid transit lines to this district and sparked the development of large areas of open land to the east. (Courtesy of the New York Transit Museum Archives, Brooklyn)

View down Fourth Avenue, Brooklyn, at 64th Street, October 17, 1912. The Fourth Avenue trunk line subway and three feeder lines connecting to it sparked the residential development of southern Brooklyn. Fourth Avenue itself had several fine apartment houses, and many of the side streets were filled with single- and two-family homes. This portion of the Fourth Avenue subway opened on June 22, 1915. (Courtesy of the New York Transit Museum Archives, Brooklyn)

The old West End Railroad on New Utrecht Avenue at 76th Street in Bensonhurst, in southern Brooklyn, May 18, 1914. This surface railroad would soon be replaced by the BRT's West End elevated line, providing direct service to the Manhattan Central Business District via the Fourth Avenue subway. The West End line opened on July 29, 1916. (Courtesy of the New York Transit Museum Archives, Brooklyn)

Above: Bird's-eye view of the Claflin Estate from the north, part of the auction brochure. (Courtesy of The Bronx County Historical Society) *Opposite, above:* Auction notice for the Claflin Estate, 1919, showing rapid transit services to the area. (Courtesy of The Bronx County Historical Society) *Opposite, below:* View across Kingsbridge Road of David Clarke's Sons greenhouses and the southeast corner of the Claflin Estate in 1918 (the Estate begins where the trees are). The recently built Kingsbridge Armory is to the right. (Courtesy of the Museum of the City of New York. Gift of Mrs. W. G. Hassler)

The Claflin Estate, a large tract north of Kingsbridge Road in the Northwest Bronx, had been the country home of the Claflin family in the nineteenth century. This district was made easily accessible to Manhattan by the opening of the IRT Jerome Avenue line in July 1918. In 1919, the land was divided into building lots and sold at a public auction. Subsequently, the neighborhood developed as a subway suburb, with a mix of apartment houses and single- and two-family homes.

Real Estate is Merchandise 

Absolute Auction Sale

OF THE PROPERTY KNOWN AS THE

CLAFLIN ESTATE

CONSISTING OF

471 University Heights Lots

LOCATED ON

West Kingsbridge Road, University, Sedgwick, Webb Aves. 195th and 197th Sts. and Adjacent Avenues and Streets

TO BE SOLD SEPARATELY

Tuesday, Sept. 23, 1919

at 12 o'clock noon, Exchange Salesroom, 14 Vesey St., New York City

50% / 60% / 70% OF THE PURCHASE PRICE MAY REMAIN ON MORTGAGE FOR THREE YEARS AT 4½% / 5% / 5½%

Title Policies of the TITLE GUARANTEE & TRUST CO. Free

31 Nassau Street
New York City

Joseph P. Day
Auctioneer

Telephone
Rector 6500

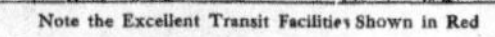
Note the Excellent Transit Facilities Shown in Red

Advertisement at an elevated line station for the Claflin Estate auction, 1919. (Courtesy of the Museum of the City of New York. Gift of Mrs. W. G. Hassler)

the largest subway expansion plan ever proposed in New York. By the summer of 1911, this plan, called the Dual System of Rapid Transit, had become the center of debate over how to build new subways.

A New Transit Committee Is Appointed

In early January 1911, McAneny consulted with a number of people about the transit needs of different areas of the city. Then, on January 18, he issued a public statement summarizing his views on the rapid transit situation as he had presented them to a closed meeting of the Board of Estimate on January 17.[6] McAneny first said that he believed that the proper development of the city, as well as the comfort and convenience of the traveling public, could best be served through the establishment of a single comprehensive system of subways, with the present City-owned lines as a nucleus. According to McAneny, by the beginning of January, a voting majority of the Board of Estimate had come to hold the same view. The question that now had to be answered was whether the IRT, if it wished to participate in transit expansion, was prepared to meet the City's terms. If it were not, then the City was prepared to find alternative solutions.[7]

McAneny pointed out that the PSC was the "natural negotiator" for the City in the provision of new transit lines. Yet the Board of Estimate had the final responsibility for deciding on new lines, since it had to approve all routes and all City appropriations for subway construction. For the moment, however, the Board did not have enough information "as to the cost and detail of several routes . . . embraced in either of the plans that have been proposed. It has no information with relation to population, either present or prospective, that particular routes would serve, prospective traffic, cost of either equipment, operation, or any other essentials of the sort. . . . These are a few of the reasons I have been urging for proceeding with moderate caution."[8]

McAneny said that the IRT would have to add several routes to those in its offer of December 5, 1910, before he could accept granting the company new lines. He also pointed out that the financial terms proposed by the IRT were inequitable. The City wished to have many rapid transit lines built to outlying areas but was aware that these lines would not be self-supporting for a number of years. The principal consideration for the City was the operation of these extensions and "the bearing of the incidental losses to the point where each of these branches becomes profitable in itself." One way of bearing such losses was to have them supported by the profitable short-haul trips in Manhattan. The problem, however, was that the IRT was unwilling to use any of its current profits from short-haul trips to support new lines in outlying areas.[9]

On January 18, at a joint meeting of the Board of Estimate and the PSC, convened at McAneny's suggestion, it was agreed that new terms would have to be developed as a basis for any future subway contract or contracts before any agreement with a private company could be approved. Members of the Board of Estimate were asked to submit their individual views concerning proper terms and to state what routes they deemed most important.[10] The *Post* noted that this decision was "in large measure a personal victory for McAneny."[11] The *Times* approved McAneny's call for a plan that would result in putting a large number of new subways under construction at the same time, saying that "relief of congestion of population can only be had by redistribution of population."[12]

McAneny put all of the suggestions he received into a memorandum, dated January 23, 1911, in which he attempted to present a composite view of the opinions of Board of Estimate members.[13] McAneny asserted that the minimum route requirements of any subway plan were to include all of the lines mentioned in the December 5 offer of the IRT plus the Fourth Avenue line and its New Utrecht Avenue branch to Coney Island. In addition, he listed other lines that had to be included. These were the lines to Jamaica, Woodside, and Astoria in Queens; the 14th Street–northern Brooklyn subway; an adequate transit outlet for the Brownsville section of Brooklyn (which could be accomplished by extending the proposed IRT line on Eastern Parkway to this area); and a Staten Island branch line, which would connect to the Fourth Avenue subway in Brooklyn.[14]

With respect to financing, McAneny argued that the IRT should agree to operate all of the above lines, and any other extensions, provided that this did not reduce the company's net return on its actual investment, old and new, below a percentage to be fixed in the contract. He wished to assure the company that it would receive a minimum profit on its entire investment. In order to receive this guarantee, the IRT had to agree to pool all of the subway operating revenues, on old lines and new, instead of retaining all of the profits from the old lines it operated under Contracts No. 1 and No. 2, as the company had proposed in its December 5 offer. The fare on the expanded system was to be five cents.[15]

On January 19, the Board of Estimate had created a new Transit Committee to replace the one composed of Gaynor, John Purroy Mitchel, and William A. Prendergast. The new Committee was to have the power to confer with the PSC concerning the IRT offer of December 5 or any other plan presented to the Commission.[16] On January 23, Mayor Gaynor appointed McAneny, Bronx Borough President Cyrus L. Miller, and Richmond Borough President George Cromwell to this new committee, with McAneny as chairman.[17] The creation of this new Transit Committee marked a turning point in the history of rapid transit in New York City. President Theodore P. Shonts of the IRT later said that the appointment of this committee "resulted in the practical reopening of the entire question."[18]

By the end of January 1911, an independent Triborough System was no longer being seriously considered as a viable answer to solving New York's subway problem. The consensus on the Board of Estimate was that this would not provide a satisfactory solution. This thinking was reflected in the behavior of the new Transit Committee, which abandoned the plan from the beginning. During the months of subway negotiations that followed, the dominant idea was that the City would participate with either the IRT or the Brooklyn Rapid Transit Company (BRT), or with both companies, to extend New York's transit network. If portions of the proposed Triborough System were put under construction, it would be within the context of expanding the existing system of either or both of these companies.

Moreover, by this time, both the Board of Estimate and the PSC had accepted the political reality that they could not hope to achieve further changes in the constitutional restrictions on the City's borrowing capacity.[19] This reinforced their assessment that private capital would have to be induced to put up a share of the money for new subway construction.[20] Somehow, a compromise would have to be reached between the City's representatives and the PSC, on the one hand, and the companies and their bankers on the other.

The Conferees

The new Transit Committee was dominated from the beginning by Chairman McAneny. In all accounts of the Committee's actions the two other members, Cromwell and Miller, are seldom mentioned and, in fact, had very little impact on the eventual plan that was devised. McAneny, however, devoted most of his time between January and July 1911 to transit planning and to negotiations with the IRT and the BRT, becoming the Board of Estimate's recognized expert on transit matters. Of the Board members, McAneny was most suited to the task of transit planning and negotiating, since he was not only willing to put a great deal of time into studying the problem in detail, but was also attuned to the need for compromise with the private transit companies.[21] On January 19, McAneny stated that New York's needs were so great that it had to be provided with "the largest subway system ever planned" as part of a wider program of controlling city development.[22]

Finding a way to put the largest number of new rapid transit lines under construction was the chief task facing both the PSC and the new Transit Committee. From the beginning, the two bodies worked so closely together that they were soon referred to as one entity, "the conferees." (This term referred only to the public negotiators, not to any of the representatives of the private transit companies or their bankers.) McAneny later said that the new Transit Committee had been created to produce a "working relationship" with the PSC "capable of producing prompt results."[23]

The conferees immediately agreed that all of the meetings between themselves and the IRT or any other company would be held in secret. Chairman Willcox believed that the conferees and company officials would be unable to discuss all aspects of the rapid transit problem in openness and candor if the press were present at the meetings.[24]

Realizing the importance of accurate projections of ridership on proposed subway lines, the conferees authorized studies of future population movement to the outlying boroughs and of projected ridership on each of the proposed new lines. In addition, staff at the City Club were asked to conduct new transportation studies intended for use by the conferees.[25]

While this information about specific routes was being gathered, the conferees held discussions with the IRT to determine whether the company was willing to modify its offer of December 5, 1910, to add a number of routes in Brooklyn and Queens. They also wanted the IRT to agree that some of the profits it was making from existing subways would be used to support deficits expected to arise from the operation of new lines in outlying areas.[26]

The IRT, however, saw little reason to modify its offer. It was public knowledge that expansion of its existing subway network was the only proposal that was seriously being considered by the conferees at the end of January 1911.[27] During 1910, the public negotiators had been able to threaten the IRT with the possibility of an independent, City-built subway system if the company refused to participate in subway expansion. The result had been the IRT offer of December 5, 1910. Now, however, the Triborough System, for all practical purposes, had been abandoned. With this in mind, the IRT was prepared to wait, hoping that the conferees would eventually accept the December 5 offer in substance, rather than making any further concessions to the City. Numerous meetings between the conferees and the IRT took place, but the company refused to budge. One of the main stumbling blocks was the insistence on the part of the conferees that any satisfactory solution to the transit problem had to include new lines going deep into southern Brooklyn.[28]

The BRT Becomes a Player

There was one way of getting new lines in Brooklyn without the participation of the IRT. If the Brooklyn Rapid Transit Company could be induced to participate in new transit development, then perhaps the problem of providing new lines in Brooklyn would be solved. The January 10, 1911, BRT proposal to transform its railroads in southern Brooklyn into rapid transit lines had been laid before the conferees, who had asked the company to amplify it.[29] The BRT had since gone through a reorganization, and its directors had plans for an extensive program of transit expansion. They sought someone to replace President E. W. Winter, who was about to retire, and on February 11, Timothy S. Williams became the new president of the BRT.[30]

Williams decided to enlarge the BRT offer of January 10 to include a main north-south trunk line in Manhattan.[31] His idea was to build a subway under Broadway and other streets from the Battery to 59th Street, which would serve as a distributor for a number of BRT lines entering Manhattan from Brooklyn and Queens. This subway would have the added advantage of being able to pick up profitable short-haul traffic in Manhattan, ensuring the profitability of the feeder lines from the outlying boroughs. The subway in Manhattan would also ensure the long-range profitability of the BRT, which was threatened by extensive additions of the IRT system between Manhattan and Brooklyn.[32] On March 2, Williams submitted to the PSC a detailed offer for transit extensions.[33] (See Map 5.)

Williams prefaced the BRT proposal with a few observations about the subway situation in New York. He noted that there was a very outspoken sentiment for a subway system independent of the IRT, but that there was an equally determined sentiment in favor of reasonable extensions of the existing IRT subway. According to Williams, the people of Brooklyn hoped for more subway extensions to their borough from Manhattan than either municipal or private capital was likely to provide. Both the City and the IRT were reluctant to invest in some of the proposed lines for Brooklyn because of "the almost certain financial loss which would follow such extensions."[34]

Williams argued that public and private capital should be

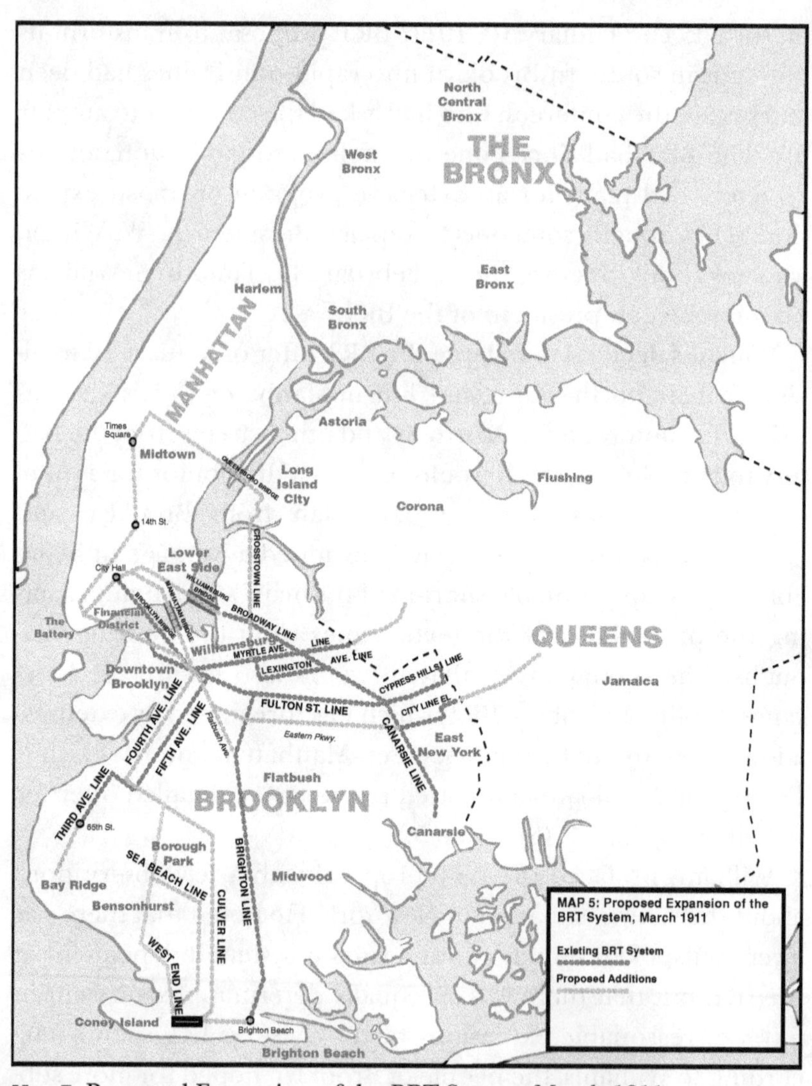

Map 5. Proposed Expansion of the BRT System, March 1911

invested where it would furnish new facilities for the greatest number of people. This could best be achieved by using the existing transit facilities controlled by the IRT and the BRT as a base. In southern Brooklyn, for example, the BRT's existing railroad lines could, at a moderate cost, be converted into feeder lines for the Fourth Avenue subway. Converting the railroads into rapid transit lines would be cheaper than constructing the proposed New Utrecht Avenue branch of the Fourth Avenue subway. This scheme, moreover, would provide service to more people, since several BRT lines were involved.[35]

The BRT plan would provide direct rapid transit service to both the Wall Street area and to the budding business district in Midtown for almost all of southern Brooklyn, accomplishing for these areas what the Jerome, Pelham, and White Plains Road lines of the IRT proposal were to do for the Bronx. The four-track Fourth Avenue subway in Brooklyn would receive trains from four feeder lines in southern Brooklyn and carry them north to Flatbush Avenue. These four lines were the Sea Beach, West End, and Culver lines, as well as the Third Avenue elevated line, which would be extended south into Bay Ridge.[36] At Flatbush Avenue, services from these lines would merge with services from the Brighton line, which would come north from its existing right of way via a new tunnel under Flatbush Avenue.[37] A union station at DeKalb Avenue in Downtown Brooklyn would allow passengers free transfer from the various BRT services from southern Brooklyn to all other services.[38]

Heading for Manhattan, one branch would pass from the DeKalb Avenue station under the East River to the Battery, passing through local streets until it reached Broadway in the vicinity of City Hall. From here, services would proceed north under Broadway. At Canal Street, this line would merge with the other BRT branch from DeKalb Avenue, which would cross the East River via the Manhattan Bridge. North of Canal Street, services would proceed north under Broadway and Seventh Avenue to 57th Street. From 57th Street, a branch would be built extending across 59th Street and across the East River to Long Island City in Queens.

Other services coming across the Manhattan Bridge from DeKalb Avenue would go down the Centre Street loop subway. The BRT plan also called for the extension of this loop subway south through the financial district along Nassau and Broad Streets to a connection with the proposed BRT tunnel passing from Downtown Brooklyn to the Battery. This would allow services on the loop to pass through the heart of the Wall Street area.[39] The BRT also proposed to extend and add third tracks to several of its existing elevated lines in northern Brooklyn, to build a subway on Eastern Parkway, and to construct a new Brooklyn-Queens crosstown elevated line.[40]

In presenting these proposals to the PSC, Williams stated what he believed to be the advantages of his company's new offer. The plan covered every section of Brooklyn and part of Queens. It furnished sixteen separate rapid transit services for travel from Brooklyn and Queens into Manhattan, with through transportation or free transfers via the Broadway subway or the Centre Street loop.[41]

The BRT plan would furnish eighty-two miles of rapid transit routes (old and new) in Brooklyn and Queens, compared to eighteen miles in the IRT's proposal of December 5. It would also offer better facilities for distributing traffic in those parts of Manhattan to which, Williams said, 98 percent of the people living in Brooklyn and Queens wanted to go—namely, the area between the Battery and 59th Street. According to Williams, no other subway or elevated plan for Brooklyn could be constructed within one generation that would serve so large an area or satisfy so many people. The BRT plan, if realized, would greatly benefit more than a million people living in the built-up areas of Brooklyn by providing them with through rapid transit service to Manhattan. It also would stimulate development in southern Brooklyn, of "23,000 acres . . . now substantially unoccupied—an area one and six-tenths as large as the Borough of Manhattan and likely, within ten years after the inauguration of this transportation plan, to house at least a million additional people."[42]

Under the terms of the BRT offer, the City would construct the proposed new subways in Downtown Brooklyn and Manhattan. The BRT would pay for improvements on its elevated lines and for the cost of converting its railroad lines in southern Brooklyn. The BRT would also pay for new equipment on all of the lines. The company proposed to operate all of its existing lines, together with the new lines, as one system with free transfers between old lines. The fare was to be five cents, except for service to Coney Island, which would be ten cents.[43]

In return for its contribution to capital costs, the company proposed that it receive 6 percent per year from operating revenues, representing the profits it was making from the operation of the existing elevated lines, plus interest and sinking funds charges on the money the company would borrow for capital improvements. These deductions from operating revenues would be made before the City received anything from operating revenues to cover the charges on the bonds it would sell to cover its capital costs.[44]

The BRT offer of March 2 was an attempt to ensure the long-term prosperity of the company by obtaining a distribution system in Manhattan for lines from Brooklyn and Queens. So long as Lower Manhattan had remained the core of New York's business district, the BRT had been willing to confine itself to operating lines to this area via the Brooklyn Bridge. By 1911, however, it was obvious that New York's main business center was expanding to include Midtown Manhattan. The BRT would have to extend its system to this new area if it wished to increase its profits.

Moreover, unless the BRT acted quickly, the IRT would be able to capture the cream of the traffic between Brooklyn and Midtown Manhattan by expanding its existing subway network deeper into Brooklyn. Even if the IRT had hesitations about doing so, the PSC and the City were insisting that this be done. In the light of these considerations, the BRT proposal is best seen as what one newspaper termed "an almost Napoleonic stroke" that had the possibility of dramatically altering the course of subway development in New York City.[45]

The day after Williams presented his plan to the PSC, the *Brooklyn Eagle* reported that future meetings of the conferees would be dominated by the effort to coordinate the IRT offer of December 5, 1910, and the new BRT proposal into a new plan for subway expansion.[46] With respect to the City money that would be needed to expand both the IRT and the BRT systems, McAneny said he thought that neither offer would be declined because of the lack of funds. Under both offers, the City and the private companies would put up a portion of the capital necessary to construct and equip the proposed lines, and the City, according to McAneny, had enough to put up its share.[47] A few days later, McAneny revealed that the conferees were trying to prepare a plan involving the total expenditure by the City and the companies of $270 million.[48]

The "Broadway Ultimatum"

Throughout March and April 1911, the conferees negotiated separately with the two transit companies. The aim of the negotiations with the IRT was to see if mutually satisfactory terms could be arranged between the City and the IRT for subway expansion, especially in the light of the BRT offer of March 2. The aim of the negotiations with the BRT was to explore the financial arrangements that might be made between the company and the City to carry out the offer of March 2, as revised by the conferees, and also to ascertain whether the BRT was immediately willing to widen its offer to include other new lines in Manhattan, the Bronx, and Queens if the IRT withdrew from participation in subway expansion.[49] In the negotiations with both the IRT and the BRT, the conferees especially wished to know the companies' positions on new lines to Astoria and Woodside in Queens and on the proposed 14th Street–northern Brooklyn subway.[50]

For most of March, the conferees concentrated their efforts on negotiating with the IRT. They faced a hostile company, which saw its financial arrangement with the Morgan bank, as well as its future profits, threatened by the BRT plan. The IRT was taken aback by the new BRT proposal because of the fact that the Brooklyn company now proposed to invade territory—Manhattan above Canal Street—that the IRT considered its own domain. The IRT feared that a BRT trunk line on Broadway would reduce revenues from the most profitable part of its operations—short-haul traffic in Manhattan. By the middle of March, the IRT was threatening to withdraw from any plan for new subways if the BRT was granted the right to operate a subway under Broadway.[51]

The conferees and the IRT continued to discuss additional routes for the IRT, beyond what the company had included in its December 5 offer. The routes under serious consideration were the Eastern Parkway line, which the conferees now wanted extended out to distant East New York; the lines to Astoria and Woodside in Queens; and the 14th Street–northern Brooklyn subway.[52] The conferees also demanded that the IRT agree to pool the revenues from its existing lines with those from the proposed new lines. They told the IRT that if it agreed to do so, the conferees would be willing to allow the company a guaranteed return on its total investment, to be specified in a new contract. The IRT, however, continued to insist that operating revenues from the existing system be kept separate from revenues from the new lines.[53]

At the end of March, the IRT's board of directors delivered what came to be known as the "Broadway ultimatum": unless the conferees guaranteed that the BRT would not be allowed to operate a subway under Broadway, the IRT would refuse to participate in subway expansion.[54] The conferees now asked the BRT if it would be willing to operate an expanded system that would include all of the lines in its March 2 offer plus the Lexington Avenue line in Manhattan, the Jerome Avenue and Pelham lines in the Bronx, the Woodside and Astoria lines in Queens, and the 14th Street subway.[55]

On April 25, after negotiations with the conferees, Williams made a revised subway offer on behalf of the BRT. He prefaced this offer by saying that the additional lines in the plan had resulted from the opposition of the IRT to a BRT line on Broadway. The April 25 offer included the proposals in the March 2 offer, as well as most of the lines that the conferees had been discussing with the IRT for the Bronx, Queens, and Brooklyn. However, the added lines were to be operated under a separate accounting system, under which the City was to provide all of the capital costs and assume all of the financial risks.[56]

This was unacceptable to the conferees. In meetings between the conferees and the BRT immediately following the new offer, Williams was told that the City intended to begin construction quickly of several lines that the BRT had proposed to be operated under a separate accounting system. He was told that these lines had to be included in the arrangement for the pooling of all receipts on the BRT's expanded network.[57] As a result of these meetings, Williams sent the conferees a letter saying that the BRT was now willing to operate a number of additional lines under the terms it had proposed for the operation of its own expanded network. These lines were the Jerome Avenue line and a portion of the Pelham line (between 138th Street and the Bronx River) in the Bronx; the Astoria and Woodside lines in Queens; and the 14th Street–northern Brooklyn subway and two extensions of the proposed Eastern Parkway subway in Brooklyn.[58]

A Public Plan to Meet Public Needs

After the BRT made its April 25 offer, George McAneny announced that the conferees intended to issue a report containing their own plan for new rapid transit lines. In making this announcement, he said that he himself had "always held that the City should make its own transit plan, placing individual routes where they will do the most good and not necessarily with reference to their earning capacity alone, nor to their relation to enterprise in real estate."[59] Although he did not mention the fact, McAneny himself had assumed the responsibility of drafting this report.[60]

On April 30, the *Standard Union* published an analytical article entitled "The McAneny Subway Plan." Presenting the newspaper's version of the existing subway situation in New York, the article stressed alleged connections between the IRT and real estate interests in Manhattan and the Bronx. The writer contended that, by getting the IRT to agree to expand its system citywide, McAneny and the other conferees believed that they had "broken the power of the real estate cabal which has dictated the policy of the Interborough which has consequently controlled the subway situation in the city for the past ten years." The newspaper alleged that "Interborough directors and lawyers and the politicians who have played into the company's hands are heavily interested in uptown Manhattan real estate and have bought up during the past few years vast tracts of undeveloped Bronx lands." These interests favored "the forced development of the Bronx suburban districts that they control," and were opposed to the opening of large areas of southern Brooklyn and Queens for development since this would reduce the value of their property.[61]

The *Standard Union* praised McAneny for taking the stand that no private sectional influence should predominate. It described his aim as being "to establish a transportation system practically and scientifically adapted" to the city's needs and capable of developing the whole city "symmetrically and fairly." The newspaper admitted that this had not been the work of McAneny alone. He had received the support of a majority of other conferees, some of whom had even greater technical knowledge of the situation than he did. Nonetheless, McAneny deserved the credit for being "their spokesman" and "for leadership in the great subway plan."[62]

McAneny had not yet given up hope that the IRT could be induced to participate in the program of subway expansion. It was evident that the most logical way to expand the city's transit system in northern Manhattan and the Bronx was to complete the Manhattan "H" and to have the IRT operate the Jerome, Pelham, and White Plains Road lines in conjunction with the "H" lines. In addition, without IRT participation a line on Seventh Avenue south of 42nd Street could not be built. This line was to serve the newly opened Pennsylvania Station, which lay between Seventh and Eighth Avenues and 31st to 33rd Streets. As for lines to Queens, the IRT owned the Steinway Tunnel, which connected 42nd Street in Manhattan with Long Island City in Queens, and which could be converted into a subway line at relatively little cost. With these considerations in mind, McAneny conferred on May 4 with Mayor Gaynor, together with President Shonts, August Belmont, and Andrew Freedman of the IRT. The IRT representatives told McAneny that they intended to submit a new subway offer, and he agreed to delay public release of the conferees' report, which he was drafting, until the end of May.[63]

The IRT's new offer, submitted to the conferees on May 9, proposed more new routes and more liberal contract terms than any of its previous offers. The company hoped that in so doing, it could persuade the conferees to confine the BRT to new lines in Brooklyn and in Lower Manhattan below Canal Street. Shonts warned the conferees that if, after extending its lines largely at its own cost, the IRT should be "met immediately with an unnecessary duplication of lines by the city," the result would be the financial ruin of the company.[64]

The new IRT offer included all of the lines in the December 5 offer. In addition, the IRT now proposed to operate two new lines in Queens as part of its expanded subway system. One line would run from Queensboro Plaza north over local streets to Astoria. The other line to Woodside would run from a connection with the Steinway Tunnel line at Jackson Avenue in Long Island City, north over local streets to Queensboro Plaza and a connection with the Astoria line. From the plaza, the line would run over a number of streets eastward to Woodside, a distance of about two miles.[65]

The IRT offer also included a line designed primarily to forestall the possibility of any competitive line on Broadway. This was for a subway that would run from northern Brooklyn across the East River to Broadway and then up Broadway and Seventh Avenue to 59th Street; from here, the line would proceed east over the Queensboro Bridge to a connection with the Astoria and Woodside lines. This route from 14th Street north was identical with the route of the proposed BRT Broadway subway.[66]

The cost of constructing the new lines to be operated by the IRT was to be shared almost equally by the company and the City. The IRT estimated that the total cost for the construction of the lines would be $136 million, of which $68 million would be borne by the company. The IRT would also equip all of the new lines at its own expense, an estimated expenditure of $32 million, bringing the grand total to $168 million. The IRT would operate all of the new lines together with its existing lines as a single system with a five-cent fare.[67]

The Transit Companies Fight It Out in the Press

Following the BRT's March 2 offer, the IRT and the BRT had each waged advertising campaigns in New York's newspapers pointing out the benefits of their respective offers. This war of words intensified with the IRT offer of May 9. The IRT advertisements made the standard argument in favor of expanding the IRT system, that is, that under the IRT proposal there would be a single unified subway system with a uniform five-cent fare. The advertisements also emphasized the substantial amount of money that the company was willing to contribute to the construction and equipment of new lines.[68]

The BRT advertisements were more sophisticated, stressing the social benefits to the city of expanding BRT lines to undeveloped sections of outlying areas. One BRT advertisement in the *New York Times* of May 16, for example, quoted at length an article by Arthur H. Grant, editor of the magazine *American City*. The featured line of the article stated that the BRT proposal would make "all parts of the city available for workers' homes." Grant argued that the most important considerations in subway expansion were the extent of "comparatively unoccupied territory" that would be brought within the area served by rapid transit lines and the comfort, speed of travel, and cost to the passenger. He stressed the point that population should be directed to low-density areas and noted that the IRT proposal of May 9 called for only seven lines into "unoccupied territory," whereas the BRT proposal of April 25 called for eighteen lines. Moreover, the IRT lines proposed for Brooklyn were few and short, with the result that "the worst sort of congestion of population" would be developed along them. The BRT offer, by contrast, would open "a tremendous amount of sparsely settled territory."[69] Another BRT advertisement depicted little men with models of one- and two-family houses in their hands rushing to southern Brooklyn. The caption read: "Tomorrow—the truck farms are gone. In their place are long lines of streets—gently shaded streets—streets lined with neat residences."[70]

Meanwhile, Mayor Gaynor, playing a partisan role on behalf of the IRT, was attempting to get the BRT to drop its plan for a subway under Broadway. He sent Commissioner of Bridges Kingsley Martin to visit Williams to propose a division of subway territory between the IRT and the Brooklyn company.[71] Williams made public his refusal in a letter published in the *New York Times.* He stated that the BRT would not go before the public openly advocating a comprehensive plan of transportation relief while negotiating separately for a "lesser and more selfish plan." Williams accused Gaynor of running a "branch office" of the IRT at City Hall.[72] On June 2, Gaynor replied with a vitriolic attack on the BRT as a "ramshackle road" that was overcapitalized and provided poor service to its customers.[73]

The Report of the Conferees

While the transit companies were attacking each other, George McAneny, with the advice and support of the other conferees, was still at work on a proposal that would allow both companies to participate in subway expansion. He now had a great deal of information not available in January. By mid-May, the staffs of the

PSC and Board of Estimate had gathered specific information on proposed subway lines, including accurate cost estimates, areas to be served, and population projections.[74] In addition, Homer Folks and Henry Wright of the City Club had forwarded information on similar matters to McAneny.[75] Various legal aspects relating to subway expansion had been under intensive study by Commissioner Bassett of the PSC.[76]

The "Report of the Conferees," which was popularly called the McAneny Report, was made public on June 13, 1911.[77] It was signed by all the members of both the Transit Committee of the Board of Estimate and the PSC.[78] The report discussed the course of the negotiations with the IRT and the BRT, as well as some of the issues on which there had been agreement and disagreement. It stressed that the conferees had little disagreement with the BRT regarding the company's offer of April 25, whereas there had been considerable disagreement between the IRT and the conferees regarding the IRT offer of May 9.

The report spelled out the principles governing the deliberations of the conferees. The first of these was: "That future rapid transit lines should follow as closely as possible the development of a logical and well-ordered city plan." The conferees wanted the City to provide, as rapidly as possible, relief of congested areas by opening lines to relatively undeveloped sections of the city.[79] The locations of these lines was to be determined by the City, for its own reasons, and not necessarily to conform to plans proposed by the operating companies. No plan for transit expansion would be adopted that would "prevent the development of the entire city as a social and economic unit or hinder the logical extension of transportation facilities in the future."[80]

The report then listed the new lines to be operated by the BRT and the IRT. The major new route to be operated by the BRT was the Broadway line in Manhattan. In all essentials this route was the same as had been proposed in the BRT offer of March 2. This four-track trunk line would run up Broadway from City Hall to Times Square and then up Seventh Avenue to 57th Street. The Broadway trunk line would serve as the main Manhattan distributor for feeder lines from Brooklyn and Queens. Both express and local services would be operated on this route.[81] (See Maps 6a, 6b, and 6c for the final Dual System plan.)

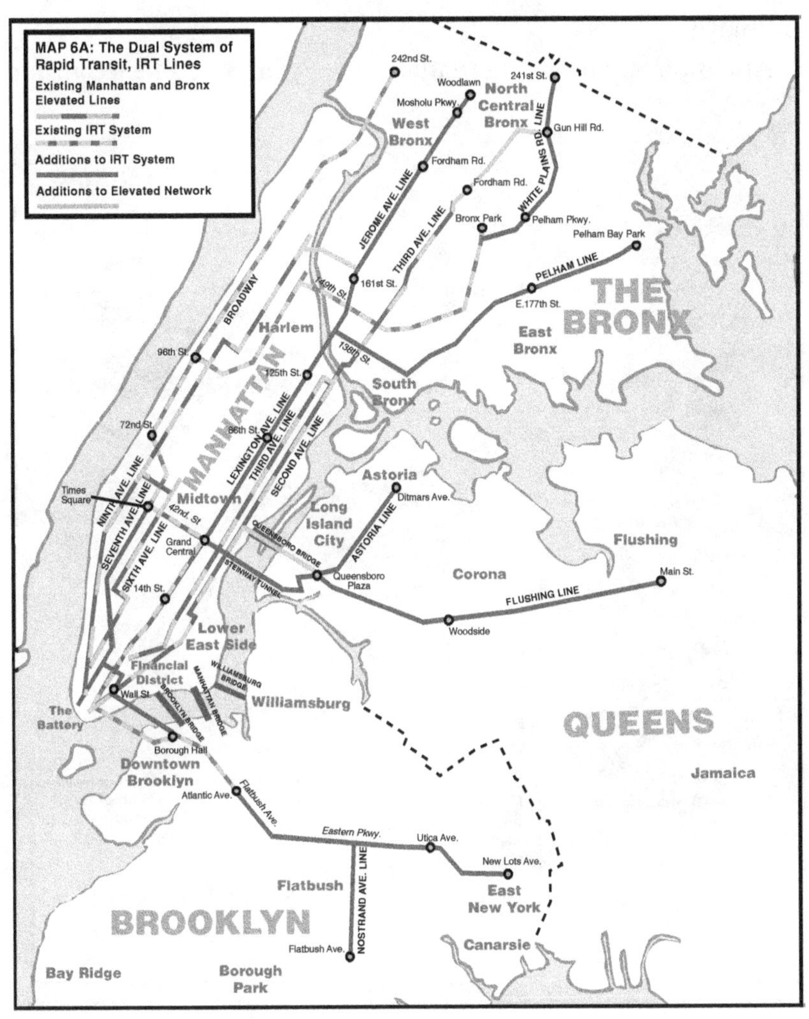

Map 6a. The Dual System of Rapid Transit, IRT Lines

At the Battery, a branch of the Broadway line running south from City Hall would proceed to a new tunnel under the East River and then on to the DeKalb Avenue station in Downtown Brooklyn. The Broadway line would also connect with this station from Canal Street via a branch over the Manhattan Bridge. At the DeKalb Avenue station, the two lines from Lower Manhattan would connect to all of the new BRT services in southern Brooklyn.

At Union Square in Manhattan, there would be a free transfer

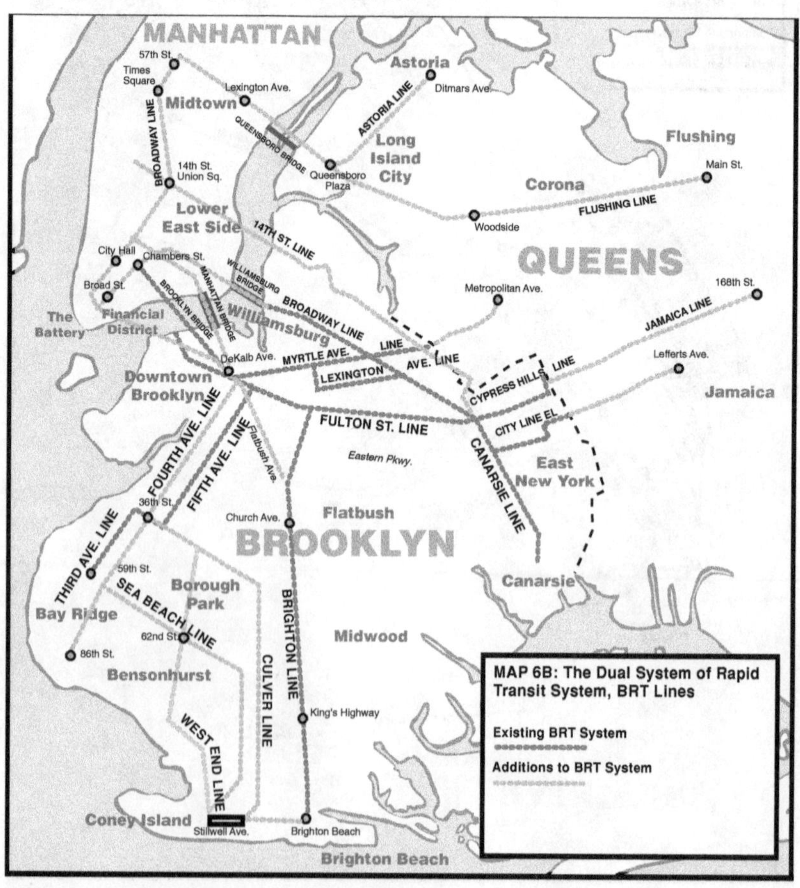

Map 6b. The Dual System of Rapid Transit, BRT Lines

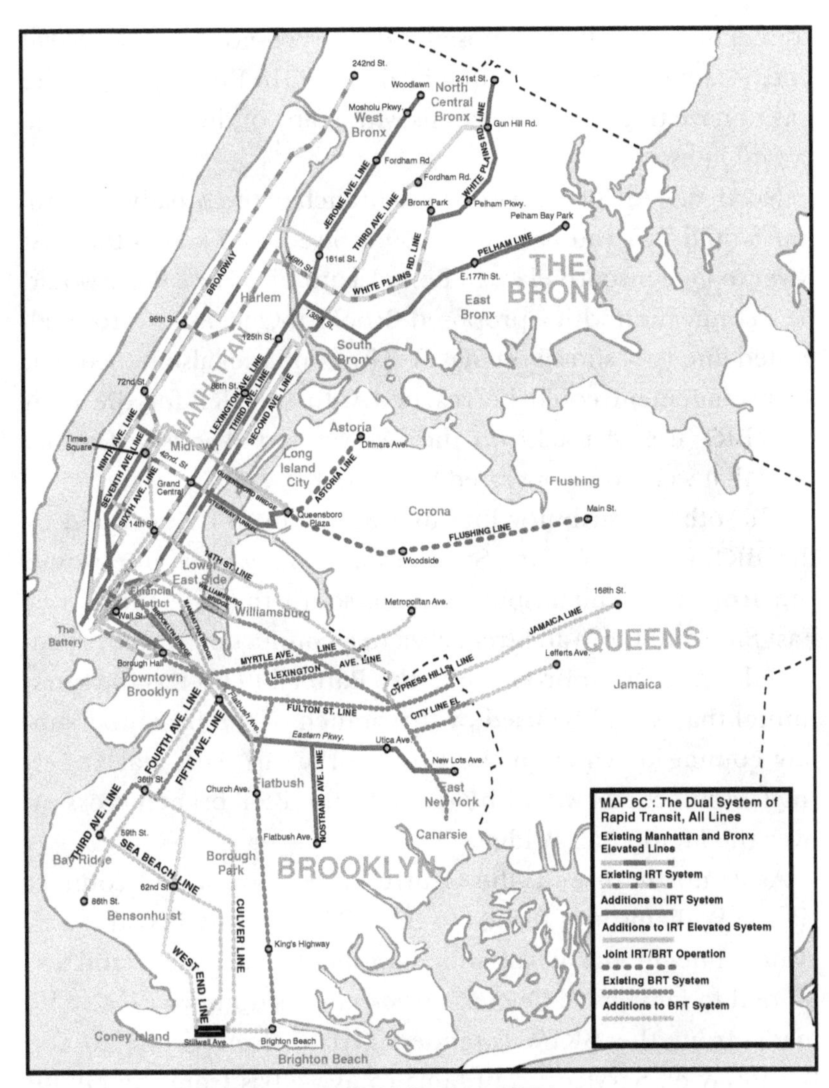

Map 6c. The Dual System of Rapid Transit, All Lines

connection with the proposed 14th Street–northern Brooklyn line, which was to be operated by the BRT. In Brooklyn, this line was to have transfer connections with many of the older BRT elevated lines.

North of 57th Street, a northern branch of the Broadway trunk line would proceed east under 59th Street and across the East River to Queensboro Plaza in Long Island City. Here there would be a connection with a proposed Brooklyn-Queens crosstown elevated line (not shown on maps). The conferees also hoped that an arrangement could be reached with the IRT for the joint IRT/BRT use of tracks on the Astoria and Woodside-Corona lines that were to be operated by the IRT.

The other distributor line in Manhattan to be operated by the BRT was the Centre Street loop subway. This line would run from the Williamsburg Bridge south through the Lower East Side and the Wall Street area to a connection with the proposed tunnel from Brooklyn to the Battery. (This was the same tunnel that would be used by the branch of the Broadway subway coming down from the City Hall area.) At Canal Street, track connections would be made to the BRT branch crossing over the Manhattan Bridge.

At its northern end, the Centre Street loop would connect via the Williamsburg Bridge to the BRT's existing Broadway elevated line in Brooklyn, which would be upgraded and extended to Jamaica in Queens. Track connections would also be made from the BRT's extended Myrtle Avenue line to the Broadway el. Services from Jamaica as well as from the Myrtle Avenue line would come across the Williamsburg Bridge and would then proceed down the loop.

The Centre Street loop also would be used by services from the new lines in southern Brooklyn. These new lines included the Fourth Avenue subway and its branches, the Culver, West End, and Sea Beach lines, as well as the Brighton line. These lines would blanket all of southern Brooklyn with direct rapid transit services to Manhattan. Services on these lines would proceed north to DeKalb Avenue and then on to Manhattan either via the tunnel to the Battery or the Manhattan Bridge. In Manhattan, services from southern Brooklyn would operate either on the Broadway trunk line or on the Centre Street loop.

The City would pay the construction costs of the Broadway subway, the Centre Street loop, the 14th Street–northern Brooklyn line, the branch under the East River to the Battery connecting the DeKalb Avenue station to the Broadway subway and the Centre Street loop, and the Fourth Avenue subway. The BRT would pay the construction costs of the subway to connect the Brighton line to the Fourth Avenue subway. The company also would pay most of the cost of converting its railroad lines in southern Brooklyn into rapid transit lines. In addition, the costs of the extensions and third tracks to existing BRT elevated lines, aimed at increasing their capacity, would be borne by the company, as would the cost of equipment for the expanded BRT system. The fare was to be five cents for a continuous ride anywhere on the expanded BRT system.[82]

The "Report of the Conferees" also listed the new lines to be operated by the IRT in conjunction with its existing subway system. These included the construction of the "H" trunk lines in Manhattan, by building subways on Lexington Avenue north of 42nd Street and Seventh Avenue south of 42nd Street. The Jerome and Pelham lines in the Bronx would be connected to the Lexington Avenue line. In addition, the first subway in the South Bronx would be extended north along White Plains Road. The Seventh Avenue subway would pass through various streets in Lower Manhattan to a new tunnel under the East River and connect with the existing subway in Downtown Brooklyn.

For Queens, a new subway would be built from Times Square east under 41st and 42nd Streets to a connection with the

Steinway Tunnel. In Queens, this line would run to Queensboro Plaza, where it would connect with two new elevated lines, one to Astoria and the other to Woodside and Corona. These lines were to be jointly operated under an arrangement between the IRT and the BRT.

In Brooklyn, a subway was to proceed from the terminus of the existing subway at Atlantic Avenue south under Flatbush Avenue to Eastern Parkway and then along the parkway and other streets to New Lots Avenue in East New York. Another subway was to branch off the Eastern Parkway line and pass south from the parkway under Nostrand Avenue to Flatbush Avenue.[83]

All of the above lines to be granted to the IRT were to be operated in conjunction with the existing IRT subway at a five-cent fare. The construction costs of the new IRT lines would be divided equally between the City and the company. The IRT would pay for the cost of new equipment for the lines.[84]

The conferees estimated the total cost for construction and equipment of all the new BRT and IRT lines in the report at $277 million. Deducting the $27.8 million the City had already committed to the construction of the Centre Street loop subway and the Fourth Avenue subway, the total amount of new money to be invested was $249.2 million. Of this, the municipality would contribute $123 million, the IRT $75.8 million, and the BRT, $50.4 million.[85]

The report also contained a short section on proposed extensions and additions of third tracks for the elevated system operated by the IRT under its lease from the Manhattan Railway Company. Included were recommendations that the Ninth Avenue el be extended across the Harlem River to a connection with the Jerome Avenue line and that the Third Avenue el be extended north to a connection with the White Plains Road line. In addition, several el lines were to have third tracks added to increase capacity and train speeds. Unlike the extensions and third-trackings of the existing BRT elevated lines, however, these elevated lines in Manhattan and the Bronx would continue to operate separately from the IRT subway system. The cost of these improvements was now estimated to be $25 million and would be borne solely by the IRT.[86]

After listing the new subway routes that were to go to each company, the report proceeded to state the general terms that would apply if either or both of the companies were unwilling or unable to come to an agreement with the City. Basically, the conferees recommended that if the IRT was not willing to participate, then many of the lines it would have gotten would be offered to the BRT. If the BRT was not willing to participate, then the IRT would be offered the 14th Street line, but none of the other lines proposed for the BRT. The assumption here was that a deal could be made with the BRT even under a worst-case scenario. If no agreement could be reached with either the IRT or the BRT for the lines assigned to each company in the report, then the City was to proceed at once with the construction of the Triborough System.[87]

The report then went into an extensive discussion of proposed operating terms. Both companies would operate their expanded systems at a five-cent fare for one continuous ride.[88] The City of New York would own all the new subway lines, but would lease them to the private companies for forty-nine years.

After deducting operating expenses, the net revenues derived from operation were to be divided equally between the City and the operator, after provision had been made in a set order for carrying charges on new capital invested. The first carrying charge to be deducted would be for the actual annual carrying charges of the operator for the cost of equipment. The second deduction would be for the actual annual charges of the operator for carrying any portion of the cost of construction not met by City funds. The last deduction was to be for interest payments upon the bonds issued by the City for the costs of construction.[89]

Under this arrangement, the City of New York was to be left holding most of the risk of subway financing. If charges in any one year were insufficient to meet the interest and sinking fund payments upon the City's bonds, however, then the deficit sustained for any such period was to be treated as cumulative and would be a charge in the City's favor against future profits, to be made good before any equal division of profit would proceed between the City and the operator.[90]

No reference was made in the report to one of the major goals of the conferees, namely, the pooling of receipts on the old and new lines of the IRT. Although the report obscured the fact, the conferees had accepted the IRT's demand that the company be allowed to retain its existing profits from the old lines. That is, separate accounts would be kept for operating revenues from the old and new lines. After deducting the proper share of operating expenses on the old lines, to be determined on a cost-per-passenger basis, from the operation of the entire expanded IRT system, the balance of the revenues from the old lines would continue to be distributed as they currently were under Contracts No. 1 and No. 2. The formula with respect to operating terms of the new contracts applied, in the case of the IRT, only to the new lines.[91]

The operating terms applying to the BRT included an annual preferential payment to the company for pooling its receipts. In essence, this was a rental payment allowed to the BRT out of operating revenues from the expanded system in lieu of the profits that the company was making from the operation of its existing, privately owned system. After deducting operating expenses, the contract with the BRT would let the company reserve annually a sum representing the BRT's net profit from operation of the existing lines for the year ending June 30, 1911. This sum was estimated to be about $3.5 million a year. This "preferred" amount, which soon came to be called a "preferential," would be deducted before any payment of interest and sinking fund charges upon the company's investment in new construction and equipment. Last on the list of payments were those upon the City bonds issued for new construction.[92]

The conferees were confident that the estimates of future traffic prepared "from every source" by the statisticians of the PSC justified the vast expenditure necessary to construct and equip the new lines. It was projected that there would be an additional one billion rapid transit fares paid annually by the early 1920s. This would result in an increase of at least $50 million annually in the gross receipts. This meant, according to the calculations, that by the early 1920s the expanded subway system could sustain an investment of $300 million over the investment in existing rapid transit facilities.[93]

If the ridership projections proved to be correct, then within a few years, the revenues derived from the operation of the new lines of the IRT and the expanded BRT system would cover annual operating costs as well as the carrying charges on all the new money invested by the private companies. In addition, by the early 1920s, all of the accruing deficits on the City money invested in new lines would be paid off. From this time on, the Dual System lines would begin to produce an annual profit to be shared between the companies and the City.

Although the report did not mention it, one way the conferees proposed to provide improved transit facilities for areas of low population density was by constructing elevated rather than subway lines.[94] They recognized that elevated lines were eyesores that could blight areas in their immediate vicinity, but such lines had the great advantage of being much less expensive than subways.[95] This was why the conferees had proposed that about half of the Pelham line, most of the Jerome Avenue line, all of the

Woodside-Corona and Astoria lines, and the East New York Avenue extension of the Eastern Parkway line be elevated. On the BRT system, portions of the feeder lines in southern Brooklyn that were to connect to the Fourth Avenue subway would be elevated, as would the extension of the BRT Broadway el to Jamaica.

The conferees' report had little that was new on proposed transit lines or about proposed terms of operation. Its unique feature was that, for the first time, representatives of the public had made concrete proposals for a system of rapid transit to be put under construction simultaneously. By insisting that, as representatives of the public, they had the sole right and responsibility to decide where lines would be built, the conferees had taken from the private transit companies the power to determine which outlying districts of New York would be the next to be developed. The conferees' proposal quickly became known as the Dual System plan, since it embraced the expansion of the two systems operated by the private companies.[96]

Most New York newspapers reacted favorably to the Dual System proposal.[97] The *Post* commented that the McAneny report was "well worth waiting for" and praised the conferees for tackling the problem "absolutely without a suspicion of partisan motive or of any desire whatever except to consult the larger interests of the municipality."[98] The *Times*, crediting McAneny for the report, contended that never had "any city work been more exhaustively discussed" nor "up to this moment has a better plan been produced by anybody. . . . Mr. McAneny has cut a loaf of rather larger dimensions than anybody had anticipated."[99]

The most influential private citizen to support the conferees' report was former mayor Seth Low, who had been a member of the original Rapid Transit Board in the 1890s. Low advocated accepting the Dual System plan, seeing it as representing "a most painstaking desire to secure for the City a comprehensive system of rapid transit, with an eye not only to the present, but also to the future, upon terms which, in the long history of the City, will make its rapid transit system of the maximum value as a distributor of the population."[100]

George McAneny and his allies had produced a subway expansion plan that had the potential to transform New York. Under the plan, most of the less-developed districts of the Bronx and Brooklyn, as well as a sizable portion of Queens, would be provided with direct rapid transit access to an expanded Manhattan Central Business District south of 59th Street. Most of the public officials on the Board of Estimate and the Public Service Commission wanted to implement the plan as soon as possible. The main question was whether agreements could be reached with the IRT and BRT to begin building the Dual System. This question soon hinged on revisions to the financial arrangements to be made with the IRT, which by the end of July 1911 became a matter of sharp controversy.

6. The Battle over Financing the Dual System

The Dual System of Rapid Transit was proposed in June 1911. It did not receive final approval from the Board of Estimate and Public Service Commission (PSC) until March 1913, despite the fact that there was a strong consensus regarding the route structure of the Dual System plan. From June 1911 on, there was almost no debate among public officials over where new subway lines should be located. Instead, the battle was over the financial arrangements to be made with the private transit companies to get the system built. The core of the disagreement, moreover, was over the details of a proposed compromise deal with the Interborough Rapid Transit Company (IRT).

Under the financial arrangements with the IRT that had been proposed in the "Report of the Conferees" outlining the Dual System plan in June 1911, the company was to retain separate accounts for the operation of the existing subway and the new IRT lines.[1] This would theoretically allow the IRT to continue earning substantial profits from its existing subway lines, but there was no guarantee that this would be the case. In addition, the new IRT lines were not expected to produce a profit for several years.

The proposed deal with the Brooklyn Rapid Transit Company (BRT), in contrast, would allow the Brooklyn company a preferred payment annually out of operating revenues. This payment, estimated at $3.5 million, was based on the annual profits the BRT was making from its existing rapid transit system. This "preferential" would be paid ahead of the debt service on the bonds the City of New York would purchase for its share of the cost of the construction of new subways.[2]

The IRT and its banker, J. P. Morgan and Company, soon made it clear that the transit company would not participate in the Dual System plan without receiving a guarantee that it would continue to earn its current profits. This was a most controversial proposal. The proposed preferential for the Brooklyn operator was based in large part on the inclusion of existing company-owned lines, which had been built with private capital, in an expanded BRT system. In contrast, the IRT system had been constructed with public funds and was owned by the City of New York. All the IRT had was a long-term lease from the City for the operation of this system.

Nonetheless, neither the City nor the PSC had the power to compel the IRT to operate additions to the existing subway system. They also could not compel the IRT to provide private capital for the construction of any new subway lines. Without a large amount of private capital, however, not enough new lines could be built at one time.[3] With this in mind, Manhattan Borough President George McAneny and members of the PSC negotiated a tentative deal with the IRT in July 1911 that would allow the IRT a preferential payment for its participation in the Dual System plan.

The proposal to allow the IRT a preferential, however, nearly destroyed the Dual System plan. On several occasions, from the end of July 1911 until early 1913, the Dual System plan was almost defeated at critical points in the decision-making process. Throughout the debates over the preferential payments, however, McAneny, PSC chairman William R. Willcox, and their allies held firm in their argument that the potential financial results of the Dual System plan were secondary to its expected influence on the rational development of the business and residential areas of New York. They reiterated that this development required a massive expansion of the rapid transit system, which was only possible with the participation of private capital, upon terms Wall Street would accept. In the end, their tenacity saved the Dual System.

The IRT Rejects the Dual System

The IRT opposed the Dual System proposal from the start, believing it could block the plan and get a better deal.[4] During June and July 1911, the transit company spent more than $100,000 on a newspaper campaign in which it attacked the authors of the proposal as incompetents. McAneny was personally accused of making an inordinate effort to obtain new lines in Brooklyn and Queens.[5] The IRT argued that the Dual System plan laid out more rapid transit facilities than were necessary from a strictly business point of view, at a financial risk both to the City of New York and the company.[6]

The IRT attacked the preferential payment proposed for the BRT, arguing that it amounted to a guarantee from the City that the BRT would continue to earn its current annual net profits for almost fifty years.[7] The IRT also helped arrange protest meetings along the route of the proposed Lafayette Avenue subway, which had been excluded in the Dual System plan.[8] The IRT continued to insist that it would not participate in any plan for subway expansion if the BRT were allowed a line under Broadway.[9] It believed that such a line, offering quick service throughout the heart of Manhattan, would seriously threaten its profits.[10]

On June, 27, 1911, IRT president Theodore P. Shonts said that if the City wanted the "cooperation of private capital" it would have to propose terms, with respect to old and new investment by the IRT, that would justify embarking on the project. Under the current proposal, however, the risk to the company was too great to warrant cooperation. As a result, Shonts announced that the IRT was withdrawing from its subway offers of December 5, 1910, and May 9, 1911.[11]

In contrast, at the end of June 1911, the BRT agreed to the Dual System plan.[12] The Brooklyn company supported the plan because of the provision that the company would be allowed a preferential payment out of operating revenues and would be compensated, ahead of the City, on the money the company would invest in construction and new equipment. The proposal also allowed the BRT a major trunk line on Broadway, which promised to be lucrative.[13]

Trying to Break the Deadlock

Acceptance by the BRT and rejection by the IRT placed the conferees in a quandary. They could have arranged for routes that were assigned to the IRT in the Dual System plan to be awarded to the BRT. This was the fall-back position that had been suggested in the "Report of the Conferees." The conferees felt, however, that before any final award was made to the BRT, they ought to make one last attempt at compromise with the IRT.[14] In this attempt, former mayor Seth Low was to play a crucial part.

After the IRT's formal rejection, Low worked to resume negotiations between the IRT and the conferees. In this role, he was acting as an independent mediator.[15] Low was aided in his efforts by former comptroller Edward M. Grout, who had been hired by the IRT to discuss the company's position with the conferees and to explore whether or not it was possible to resume negotiations.[16] According to Grout, Shonts at this time "was feeling very much aggrieved" at the terms of the "McAneny Report" and would personally have nothing to do with reopening talks between his company and the conferees.[17]

Low and Grout succeeded in getting Shonts to agree to an appointment with McAneny and Willcox on July 5. As a result of this meeting, Shonts announced that the IRT would participate in the Dual System if the City were willing to grant an annual payment to the company based on its existing profits.[18] After discussions with Low, McAneny and Willcox met with Grout to tell him that they were willing to allow the IRT an annual payment of 8 percent upon the money the company had invested in the existing subway.[19] The IRT made a counterproposal that it receive a guaranteed annual payment of 8 percent not just upon its existing investment, but on its entire investment in old lines and equipment plus its proposed investment in new subways and equipment. McAneny and Willcox were told that the Morgan bank was insisting on such a guarantee.[20]

The IRT's proposed guarantee differed in several ways from what had been offered to the BRT. In the proposed preferential payment to the BRT, the company was to receive a sum from operating revenues based on its existing profits, after which deductions would be made for actual annual carrying charges upon the new capital invested by the BRT in new construction and equipment. The new IRT proposal combined these two items—profit and carrying charges—into one sum. In addition, the IRT proposal was not for a preferential payment that was to come solely out of operating revenues, but for an actual guarantee from the City. That is, if there were not sufficient operating revenues to cover the 8 percent to the IRT, then the City was to make good the difference. The guarantee to the IRT would amount to $10 million a year.[21]

On July 12, the IRT raised its demands even further. Instead of 8 percent, the company now wanted 9 percent, or $11,250,000 annually.[22] The intent was to lock in the minimum amount the IRT board of directors believed the company had to receive annually in order to justify its participation in the Dual System plan.[23]

This 9 percent guarantee was unacceptable to McAneny and other members of the Board of Estimate. Low now attempted to resolve the issue by arguing for compromise. In a memorandum to the Board of Estimate, he stressed his belief that the Dual System plan would provide a needed and equitable distribution of population throughout all the boroughs and pointed out that the cooperation of the IRT was essential to realizing any "ideal system of transit." However, the IRT had more grounds for apprehension about potential profit than the BRT, given that lines to be operated by the BRT were expected to become profitable sooner than those operated by the IRT, that the BRT was to contribute less money toward new construction than the IRT, and that the IRT was uncertain how the BRT line under Broadway would affect its revenues. Since financial uncertainty was the stumbling block to an agreement, he believed that the City "ought to be willing to place its own financial strength in this gap, and offer to supply, year by year, whatever sum may be necessary in the light of the actual experience to make private capital, both old and new . . . safe beyond peradventure."[24]

Numerous conferences and meetings were held to discuss various aspects of the transit problem. By July 18, the question at issue had come down to whether the IRT should be allowed to receive a guarantee from the City of a certain annual return on its investment, or whether it would only be allowed to receive a preferential payment out of operating revenues.[25] On July 19, the IRT accepted the idea of a preferential out of operating revenues.[26] The next day, McAneny and Willcox recommended granting the IRT a preferred payment of 9 percent on the total amount of money it invested in old and new subway lines once the Dual System was complete.[27]

Assuming that the old and new IRT lines by that point would have reached their maximum carrying capacity—estimated at 800 million passengers per year—then, at a five-cent fare, the formula would work as follows:

Gross operating revenue	$40,000,000
Less 45 percent allowance for operating expenses	18,000,000
	22,000,000
Less carrying charges upon the City's bonds for the existing subway	2,700,000
	19,300,000
Less taxes	600,000
	18,700,000
Add non-operating revenue	300,000
Gross income	19,000,000
Preferential allowance to the IRT	11,250,000
	7,750,000
Allowance for new equipment to meet the growth of traffic	1,000,000
	6,750,000
9 percent to the City upon its estimated new investment of $55,000,000	4,950,000
Balance (to be distributed equally between the City and the IRT)	$1,800,000[28]

The conferees made their recommendations in a report to the Board of Estimate that was signed by the entire Transit Committee of the Board of Estimate, that is, Borough Presidents McAneny, Cyrus L. Miller, and George Cromwell and PSC members Willcox, William McCarroll, and John E. Eustis; Commissioner J. Sergeant Cram, who had replaced Edward M. Bassett, refused to sign the report.[29] Commissioner Milo R. Maltbie not only refused to sign it, but issued a statement that contained an extensive critique of aspects of the proposal to allow the IRT a preferential.[30]

On July 19, New York newspapers predicted that the proposal incorporating the preferential for the IRT would be approved by the Board of Estimate the following day, with Comptroller William A. Prendergast, McAneny, and Borough Presidents Miller, Cromwell, and Alfred Steers, holding nine votes, voting in favor. President John Purroy Mitchel, with three votes, was expected to be opposed, and the four votes held by Mayor William J. Gaynor and Borough President Lawrence Gresser were in doubt.[31] As it turned out, the recommendation of the conferees was rejected by a vote of ten to six, with Gaynor, Prendergast, Mitchel, and Gresser voting against it and McAneny, Miller, Cromwell, and Steers voting in favor.[32]

Mayor Gaynor had signaled his opposition to a preferential to either the IRT or the BRT in a press release issued prior to the vote. His position at this time was that no company should be allowed to make a profit from subway operation before interest and sinking fund payments were made on City bonds issued for subway construction.[33] Gaynor said he still believed that the best plan for new subways was the IRT offer of December 5, 1910, as modified by its offer of May 9, 1911.[34]

The Mayor aimed to delay subway expansion in hopes that he would soon have the sole power to determine who would operate new subway lines. This power was currently held by the Board of Estimate, but a new City Charter proposed by Democratic governor John A. Dix would place this power in the mayor's hands.[35] Once Gaynor had this power, he thought he could force new negotiations with the IRT and BRT and come to agreements with these companies that would be without preferentials or guarantees. He wanted a decision on new subways postponed until the State Legislature considered the proposed charter.[36]

President Mitchel's vote was based in part on his political aspirations. Mitchel was an ambitious young man who wanted to be mayor. To accomplish this goal, he needed the support of William Randolph Hearst. The publisher strongly opposed the proposed deal with the IRT. Not surprisingly, therefore, Mitchel was also strongly against granting the IRT a preferential.[37] The latest proposal of the IRT, he said, was a barefaced attempt to involve the City of New York in a contract that would assure the company all of the profits and would leave to the municipality all of the risks. It was, to his mind, "the most outrageously unjust proposition to the City which has ever been put forward in the whole course of the rapid transit history of the city."[38]

Comptroller Prendergast's opposition had been pressured by Bradford Merrill of Hearst's *New York American.* At a meeting on the evening of July 19, Merrill demanded that Prendergast tell him whether he was going to vote according to the pledge he had made in the 1909 election campaign and the private assurances he had made to Hearst that he would support City ownership and control of new subways. He reminded Prendergast of his opposition to the IRT offer of December 5, 1910, and presumably insinuated that Hearst would oppose him politically if he voted for the compromise. Thereupon Prendergast wrote a letter in which he said that although he would have liked to see both the IRT and the BRT participate in subway expansion, his perusal of the present IRT proposal convinced him that the City should award an operating contract only to the BRT.[39]

Gaynor Tries to Get Control over New Subways

After the defeat of the conferees' recommendation, McAneny introduced a resolution granting new subways to the BRT under the provisions outlined in the conferees' report. This resolution was carried on the Board of Estimate by a vote of eleven to five, with Gaynor, Gresser, and Miller in opposition.[40]

The IRT position at this time was to wait to see what transpired in the fall.[41] IRT director Andrew Freedman informed A. J. County, an assistant to the president of the Pennsylvania Railroad, that in the fall the IRT would help start a "concentrated movement of property owners and taxpayers" that would generate public support for expansion of the IRT system. The Dual System plan would be defeated in the end and the City would be saved "from the monumental act of insanity" that the plan entailed.[42]

While the IRT was biding its time and Gaynor was anticipating passage of a new City Charter, the PSC was taking action to see that subway construction actually began. On July 26, 1911, the PSC awarded additional contracts, for subway construction alone, on sections of the Lexington Avenue line. These were portions of the old Triborough System that would now presumably be operated by the BRT. On July 31, construction work began.[43]

What happened next depended on what action the State Legislature took on the proposed City Charter.[44] In his efforts to increase his control over subway development, Gaynor had the support of the Democratic Tammany Hall machine, which had traditionally favored expansion of the IRT system.[45] In September, however, the Brooklyn Democratic organization, which had originally supported the transit provisions of the revised charter, split with the Manhattan-based Tammany machine over the issue.

Numerous state legislators from Brooklyn now publicly opposed the scheme to grant the mayor more power over new subways. They believed that the plan for extensions of BRT lines in Brooklyn would benefit their constituents more than expansion of the IRT system.[46] Facing this strong opposition, Governor Dix announced on September 20 that he would veto any charter passed by the Legislature if it gave the mayor the power to veto subway expansion plans.[47] On September 30, the Democratic majority leadership of the Legislature, deciding that they could not control their own ranks on this matter, abandoned the attempt to revise the City Charter.[48]

Making a Deal with the IRT

After the defeat of the proposed charter, Gaynor continued to appeal for what he called "subway sanity," citing the need for a subway line on Seventh Avenue south of 42nd Street to serve Pennsylvania Station and arguing that the City did not have the borrowing capacity to build a complete subway system with its own funds.[49] It was clear, however, that the most the mayor could now do was force another stalemate by refusing to consent to the use of City streets for whatever new lines were approved by the Board of Estimate and the PSC.[50]

At this juncture, representatives of the Pennsylvania Railroad entered the picture as mediators, hoping to bring about a renewal of negotiations between the mayor, the Board of Estimate, the PSC, and the IRT. The goal was to reach a compromise acceptable to all sides that would allow the IRT to participate in the Dual System plan. The Pennsylvania Railroad had invested $116 million of its own funds in new facilities in New York in recent years, including the construction of Pennsylvania Station.[51] Without a subway line on Seventh Avenue, this station was without direct subway connections to the Wall Street business district and to sections of Midtown Manhattan that were beyond walking distance from the station.[52]

Pennsylvania Railroad representatives urged Mayor Gaynor to try to restart negotiations with the IRT, after which he asked Prendergast to meet with him. Gaynor asked the comptroller if he did not think that the whole transit situation "had been left in an unsatisfactory state" in July. Prendergast answered that the situation was unsatisfactory, and that he believed it would be best if the IRT participated in the Dual System plan along with the BRT. Gaynor then asked Prendergast if he would be willing to reopen negotiations with the IRT, to which the comptroller answered that this would be desirable.[53]

Gaynor and Prendergast had been at odds over transit expansion since the beginning of 1910.[54] Now, however, Gaynor proposed that he and Prendergast set aside their differences and "work together upon this question and work harmoniously."[55] From this time on, Gaynor accepted the concept of allowing a preferential payment to both the IRT and BRT in the final Dual System contracts, and Prendergast was willing to negotiate with the IRT on the exact details of this allowance. Gaynor also asked Prendergast to serve as his representative in the final negotiations with the IRT and BRT.[56]

Comptroller Prendergast later explained that he had changed his mind about the deal with the IRT because he had become convinced that the participation of both the IRT and the BRT in the Dual System plan "would be more satisfactory to the people of the city as a whole" than if just one of the companies was involved.[57] He also said that in the negotiations over the details of the proposed contract that followed his meeting with Gaynor, the IRT had made several concessions to the public negotiators, such as joint operation of new lines with the BRT in Queens. These concessions made the final arrangements a better deal than the one that had been under consideration in July 1911.[58]

The reconciliation between Gaynor and Prendergast opened the possibility that a successful compromise could now be negotiated with the IRT for participation in the Dual System plan. A majority of the Board of Estimate was now disposed to accept an arrangement with the IRT that would include a preferential payment to the company out of subway operating revenues.[59] On the

PSC, a majority of the members were also in favor of working out a final deal with the IRT.[60]

After receiving notice from public officials that they were willing to resume negotiations with the IRT, Vice President Samuel Rea of the Pennsylvania Railroad, acting as an impartial mediator, set up a meeting of interested parties at the Century Club on November 9. This meeting included representatives of the Morgan bank, but not the IRT.[61] The only major issue to be resolved was the amount of the preferential payment the company was to be allowed to retain annually out of subway revenues.[62] After much discussion, the conferees agreed to allow the IRT a preferential amounting to 8.5 percent on its investment in old and new subway lines. The representatives of the Morgan bank and the Pennsylvania Railroad said that this would not be acceptable to the IRT and the conference adjourned.[63]

Prendergast now asked Duncan MacInness, the chief accountant of the City's Finance Department, to examine the figures on the construction costs and estimated future traffic of the expanded IRT system to determine what the results of operation would be if the IRT were allowed a preferential payment of 8.76 percent on its total investment in old and new subway lines. This percentage was arrived at by assuming the IRT would receive as a preferential an amount equivalent to its average profits for the two fiscal years ending June 30, 1911, plus 6 percent on the money the company would invest in new lines and equipment.[64]

Using IRT estimates of future traffic, MacInness concluded that if operation of the new lines began on January 1, 1917, it would take until 1933 for the City to be compensated for interest and sinking fund charges on the money it invested in new construction. That is, not until 1933 would subway revenues be sufficient to have completely provided for the cumulative finance charges on the money the City was to invest in new IRT subway lines.[65]

The main point of MacInness's report was that the City would probably be paying at least a portion of the interest and sinking fund charges on its investment in new IRT lines out of tax revenues until 1933, during years in which the IRT would be receiving its preferential payment. McAneny, Willcox, and Prendergast were willing to accept this possibility, especially since their estimates of future travel on the expanded IRT system were more optimistic those of the IRT.[66] When MacInness was later asked why the public officials were willing to accept a financial arrangement as potentially unfavorable as he had outlined, he replied that this was necessary if one believed that the Dual System were the only plan "by which the city's congestion could be relieved" and New York "be made one great city in fact, by a system of transportation."[67]

MacInness was also asked to determine the probable results of the proposed financial arrangements with the BRT. Expanding the BRT system was more cost effective than expanding the IRT system, in part because the per mile cost of transforming existing railroad lines into rapid transit lines was cheaper than that of building completely new lines. The portion of the BRT's preferential based on its existing profits, $3.5 million, was also to be considerably less than that of the IRT's. According to MacInness, the proposed BRT contract promised "splendid returns . . . after the first few years of operation for the city."[68]

Negotiations on the details of the proposed financial deal with the IRT went on for another two months before all the issues were straightened out. After this, the City negotiators drew up a memorandum saying that they were willing to allow the IRT a preferential consisting of $6,335,000 a year plus 6 percent on the money to be invested by the company in new construction and equipment. This represented 8.76 percent on the total amount the IRT invested in old and new subway lines and equipment. The IRT quickly indicated that it would accept these terms and would incorporate them into a new offer from the company to the City.[69] On January 24, 1912, the IRT sent a draft of a new subway offer to Mayor Gaynor.[70]

The agreement on the financial terms of the IRT's participation in the Dual System settled all major issues between public officials and the transit company. Since the BRT was already on board, what was left was to work out the details of the financial arrangements and to obtain formal approval of the entire plan from the Board of Estimate and the PSC. In addition, changes in New York State law were required for the specifics of the Dual System's financial arrangements to be implemented. Meanwhile, however, the proposed subway deal once again became a subject of public controversy.

Another Round of Rhetoric

While IRT participation in the Dual System plan was being negotiated, the city's newspapers had occasionally reported that a deal might be imminent.[71] Since the actual details of the negotiations were kept secret, however, there was little public debate on the issue. Once the draft offer presented by the IRT to Gaynor was made public, the situation changed dramatically and new subways again became front-page news. Opponents of the IRT offer derided the plan to allow the IRT a preferential based largely on its existing profits, while proponents of the Dual System plan went on the stump, giving speeches extolling the merits of the plan.

The most influential opponent of the proposed agreement was Hearst, who used his newspapers to mount a vicious attack on the public negotiators.[72] Hearst was trying to stop the Dual System. He also was setting the stage for the next mayoral election in September 1913.[73]

Cartoon 1. The three monkeys who see no evil, hear no evil, and speak no evil—Manhattan Borough President George McAneny, Mayor William J. Gaynor, and Comptroller William A. Prendergast. *New York American*, January 27, 1912. (Courtesy of the New York Public Library)

A headline in Hearst's *New York American* on January 24, 1912, asserted the "Triumph of Private Interests over Public Interests in New Subway Deal." An accompanying cartoon pictured Morgan bankers dominating McAneny and Prendergast.[74] On January 27, a cartoon on the front page of the *American* portrayed McAneny, Prendergast, and Gaynor as the three monkeys who see no evil, hear no evil, and speak no evil, and who were thus "deaf, dumb and blind to all Evil" in the form of the Morgan bank.[75] (See Cartoon 1.) Yet another cartoon in the *New York Evening*

Journal on January 30 showed a tiny figure of Mayor Gaynor on a small pedestal next to a huge J. P. Morgan, Senior. Gaynor was holding a sign saying "New York Is Too Poor to Build Subways. Let Mr. Morgan Build Them." A caption on the bottom of the cartoon said: "J. Pierpont Morgan is a great collector. But he never collected anything as precious or valuable to him as that little, obedient Mayor Gaynor, faithful to the Street Car Trust and obedient to his master, J.P.M."[76]

While the Hearst newspapers attacked the proposed arrangement with the IRT, proponents of the Dual System argued the merits of the plan.[77] One speech by McAneny, "The Responsibility of the City Administration in Regard to Subway Construction," contained all of the arguments he and his allies used to justify the proposed Dual System contracts from this time until the contracts were signed. In this speech, McAneny called current attacks on the IRT unfair. When the first subway was built, August Belmont and the other financiers involved were taking a major risk. The IRT subway, however, had proved to be a great success. On its investment of about $48 million, the IRT had earned unusual profits—16 percent in 1909 and 13.5 percent in 1910. Even before the first subway was opened, plans had been made for additional lines, but little had been accomplished because of political difficulties. Now, however, there was hope that New York would be able to get a transit system adequate to its present and future needs.[78]

In order "to keep up with the extraordinary growth of New York," McAneny said that the City now had planned "a new and broad system of transit—a system that will go forward, that will not only keep up the lines into districts at present congested, and run these lines into districts that are not congested, but which offered opportunity for the building of small homes." This system could not be built piecemeal, if the desired results were to be achieved. If only one or two new lines were constructed at one time, congestion of population would repeat itself in newly developed areas, as had happened in the South Bronx between 1900 and 1910 along the route of the first subway. The proposed "Dual Subway System" could not "relieve the crowded districts" unless the City was willing to build many new lines at the same time, taking "the risk of going into districts that do not seem at present to offer anything at all in the way of traffic." Under the Dual System plan, the City was "going to get the people out of the crowded places, distributing them evenly, and equalizing the whole thing, all in time."[79]

To do such a thing, McAneny said, was "not mere railroading," that is, it was not something in which the City of New York necessarily sought a profit. Rather, the conferees saw transit expansion as an essential element of city planning, providing "a means of relief for the people, a means of daily comfort in their travel and in their living conditions." To achieve these ends, the City was warranted in spending up to the limit of its means. But, McAneny asserted, since municipal funds were limited and since the logical way to expand the transit network was to add new lines to the systems controlled by the IRT and the BRT, the best plan was one whereby the private companies would contribute part of the money necessary to cover the costs of transit expansion.[80]

According to McAneny, "better transit" always meant a "better city," and transit expenses were just as proper an item as any other in the municipal budget. McAneny noted that New York had spent more than $90 million on the East River bridges and was running a deficit of $700,000 a year on the Staten Island ferry, but "when we come to these greatest of all highways . . . there are some people who stop to cavil about a little margin of City expense because there happens to be a private operator whose property is involved and who asks a fair return upon that property." Such arguments were false, McAneny said, because "if cities stop to measure the time when they will 'make money' out of their railways, without regard to anything else, they will never make progress as cities." In expanding the existing IRT system, New York City had to be willing to take the major risk since the company naturally wanted its "full money's worth . . . now." The municipality was justified in doing so, however, because even "if the risk does run against it for some years to come . . . every penny expended would be expended upon right principles in city-building."[81]

McAneny predicted that the proposed contracts with the IRT and the BRT would be favorable financially to the City in the long run. He estimated that there would be one billion additional rapid transit passengers within ten years from the opening of the new lines.[82] Even if this figure were reduced to reflect a more conservative estimate, there would still be enough revenue from future traffic over the forty-nine years of the proposed leases to cover all the new money invested by the companies as well as "every dollar which the City spends," and still leave the City with "a handsome profit." This could not be accomplished "in one year, or five years, or ten years. It means for a time the City must carry its share of the burden." As a long-range proposition, however, McAneny and the other public negotiators had "no doubt whatsoever about the safety of the future."[83]

Taking Care of Details

On February 27, 1912, the IRT formally sent the PSC a new offer covering both expansion of the IRT subway and the Manhattan Railway elevated lines controlled by the IRT. The proposed subway routes listed in this offer were the same as those in the conferees' report of June 5, 1911. The only major change had to do with trackage rights, with the IRT now offering to allow the BRT trackage rights on the proposed new lines to Astoria and Corona in Queens.[84] The IRT was to furnish $56 million for new construction and $21 million for equipment, while the City was to provide $56 million for new construction. The lease for the new lines was to run for forty-nine years and the IRT leases for the existing subway were to be leveled so that the old and new leases would expire at the same time. The fare would be five cents.[85]

The gross receipts from the operation of the old and new IRT lines would be pooled. From these receipts, deductions would be made annually in the following order:

1. Operating expenses and rentals under the existing contracts.
2. A total of $6,335,000 to the IRT.
3. A sum equal to 6 percent on the IRT's investment in new subway construction and equipment.
4. Payment to the City of New York of its preferential, consisting of interest and sinking fund charges upon the capital provided by the City for new construction and such a further sum as would bring the payments made to the City during the entire course of the lease up to an amount equal to 8.76 percent of new capital.
5. Division of the remainder of the revenue equally between the City and the IRT.[86]

The IRT offer also contained proposals for the third-tracking and extension of certain Manhattan Railway elevated lines that would continue to operate under a separate fare.[87]

President Shonts also advised Willcox that he had informed the IRT's bankers that the company had reserved the right to submit to the proper court the determination of any and all questions regarding the legal validity of the proposed contract for new subways.[88] This was a point insisted upon by the Morgan bank in January.[89] The question at issue was whether the proposed preferential to be allowed to the IRT violated the New York

State Constitution, which forbade lending the credit of the City of New York to a private corporation. The public negotiators had agreed to this point in private in January. They had also agreed that the Rapid Transit Act needed to be amended by the New York State Legislature before any contract could be signed between the company and the City.[90]

On March 13, 1912, the PSC gave preliminary approval to the new IRT offer by a vote of three to two, with Commissioners Willcox, Eustis, and McCarroll voting in favor and Commissioners Cram and Maltbie against. The PSC forwarded the offer to the Board of Estimate for its consideration.[91]

In late January 1912, once a tentative agreement had been reached with the IRT, intensive negotiations had been resumed with the BRT. This company was willing to accept the original routes assigned to it in the conferees' report, since it had never been particularly interested in operating lines in northern Manhattan and the Bronx.[92] Certain details regarding BRT participation in the Dual System plan, however, remained unresolved. Chief among these was the precise location of new rapid transit routes in southern Brooklyn, which previously had been discussed only generally pending further analysis.

The State Legislature Allows the Dual System

While negotiations continued with the BRT, the public negotiators moved to have the Rapid Transit Act amended by the State Legislature. The purpose of the changes they proposed was to widen the powers of the PSC to enable it to enter into contracts with the IRT and the BRT to carry out the Dual System plan.[93] The PSC also wanted the law amended to allow a private company to contribute part of the construction costs for new subway lines.[94]

A bill containing these amendments was drafted by the PSC and submitted to the Legislature. On March 18, this bill was introduced in the New York State Senate by Democratic Majority Leader Robert F. Wagner.[95] The choice of Wagner meant that the bill had the support of the Tammany Democratic organization, since Wagner, at this point, made no major move without consulting Tammany boss Charles F. Murphy.[96] That the Wagner bill had the full support of Tammany was of fundamental importance, because it signified that the most powerful Democratic organization in New York City now favored the Dual System plan. The Wagner bill also was supported by most civic organizations, including the Citizens Union and the Merchants Association.[97]

McAneny and Willcox were the major defenders of the bill in Albany, once again citing the primary purpose of the Dual System plan as the relief of congestion of population.[98] Opposition to the bill was led by Hearst's counsel, Clarence J. Shearn, and by other Hearst supporters.[99] The most significant opposition came from Commissioner Maltbie, who objected to certain provisions of the bill, and from Commissioner Cram, who believed that the entire Dual System plan was unconstitutional.[100]

The vote on the Wagner bill indicated that both the Republican Party and the machine Democrats were solidly behind the Dual System plan. The bill passed the Senate by a vote of 38 to 3 and the Assembly by a vote of 120 to 6, the only opposition coming from legislators who were allied with Hearst.[101]

As a bill affecting only New York City, the Wagner Act needed the consent of the mayor. On April 8, 1912, Mayor Gaynor approved the Wagner bill and Governor Dix signed it into law the following day.[102] Dix had previously indicated his support of the Dual System plan by his appointment of a new Public Service Commissioner, George V. S. Williams, at the beginning of April, to replace outgoing Commissioner McCarroll. The appointment of Williams, who was known to favor the plan, was critical since two of the present commissioners were opposed to the proposed contract with the IRT.[103]

On April 9, Shonts informed J. P. Morgan and Company that the IRT and the City had agreed upon a contract for the construction and operation of new subway and elevated lines. The bank immediately replied, outlining the terms of the proposed financial arrangements with the IRT.[104] On April 12 Shonts notified the Morgan bank that the IRT's board of directors had confirmed the agreement.[105]

The Courts Allow the Dual System

On April 12, Justice Abel E. Blackmar of the State Supreme Court in Brooklyn issued a ruling on the constitutionality of the proposed Dual System contracts. The case involved three suits, one instigated by the IRT, one by the BRT, and one by Hearst, begun earlier in 1912. Blackmar had joined the three together into one suit referred to as *Admiral Realty Co. v. City of New York*. All of these suits alleged that the PSC did not have the power to enter into the proposed contracts because the preferential payments that were to be allowed in the contracts violated the New York State Constitution, which said that no city was to give any money or property or loan its money or credit to or in aid of any corporation. Blackmar had deferred his decision purposely until the Wagner Act received final approval so that the issue of whether the Rapid Transit Act allowed such contracts did not have to be discussed.[106]

Blackmar ruled that the proposed Dual System contracts were constitutional. Under the contracts, the City of New York would not give its property, but would lease it. Nor did the City guarantee the annual preferential payment to either company, since these were to come solely out of operating revenues. The City was therefore not lending its credit to a private corporation. Previous cases had established that a rapid transit line served a City purpose as much as streets, bridges, ferries, and the like. Profit could arise incidentally, but the City purpose in extending its rapid transit system was to promote the welfare and convenience of its citizens. In pursuit of a City purpose, the City was justified in extending its rapid transit system, even though "such extensions must necessarily be operated at a loss."[107]

Blackmar's decision, and the decisions of the Appellate Division of the Supreme Court and the Court of Appeals (the state's highest court) that followed, were absolutely critical to the success of the Dual System plan. Had the courts decided that the proposed contracts were illegal, then there was no way in which the plan could have been carried out.[108]

The Board of Estimate Allows the Dual System to Proceed

Once the State Legislature and the courts allowed the Dual System plan to proceed, McAneny was given the task of writing another report for the Board of Estimate outlining the terms of the proposed contracts with the private companies. After the Board approved the recommendations in this report, thereby indicating its willingness to agree to final contracts incorporating these terms and provisions, then the lawyers and engineers of the PSC were to draft the final contracts and prepare the final engineering plans for the approval of the PSC and the Board of Estimate.[109]

McAneny presented his "Supplementary Report" to the Board of Estimate on May 22, 1912. He first presented the history of the transit negotiations with the IRT and the BRT and then argued at length that the Dual System was necessary to spread out the population. He noted that the new routes to be operated by the IRT and BRT were the same as those recommended in the "Report of the Conferees," except that the route structure for southern Brooklyn had now been finalized and the Brooklyn-Queens crosstown line had been eliminated. The operating and financing terms of the proposed Dual System contracts summarized in the "Supplementary Report" were, in all essential matters, the same as those in the actual contracts.[110] (These contracts are summarized in Appendix 1.)

McAneny's report contained charts and tables, prepared by the New York City Department of Finance, showing the anticipated financial results of the operation of the Dual System lines. These studies were more optimistic than the one MacInness had prepared in December 1911. They indicated that under the proposed contract with the IRT, after just six years of operation, starting in 1917, there would be no deficiencies in the City's annual account covering its interest and sinking fund payments, and that the City's cumulative deficit account would probably be wiped out in the year 1928, not 1933. Under the proposed contract with the BRT, the cumulative amount of the City's deficiencies would disappear eight years after the beginning of operation, or in 1925.[111]

At a meeting on May 24, 1912, McAneny moved that the Board of Estimate adopt the "Supplementary Report."[112] Seth Low spoke before the Board, predicting that in the future the public negotiators who had formulated the Dual System plan would be held up as "the real designers of Greater New York."[113] When the vote was taken, the Board approved the report thirteen votes to three. The only person in opposition was John Purroy Mitchel.[114]

Problems with the BRT

After this decision by the Board of Estimate, the PSC's lawyers and engineers continued to work on the details of the final drafts of the contracts and on the engineering plans. In addition, the Commission strove to legalize Dual System routes that had not yet received the necessary consent of affected property owners. This work was time consuming, and it was not expected that the contracts would be ready for final approval until late fall.[115]

No problems arose with the IRT at this time, but in October it became apparent that there were sharp disagreements between the BRT and the conferees over aspects of the financial plan the company had made with its bankers in order to cover its share of the cost of new construction and equipment. On June 10, 1912, the BRT had entered into an agreement with its bankers, Kuhn, Loeb, and Company, Kidder, Peabody, and Company, and the Central Trust Company, to sell $60 million of its six-year notes on a 6 percent basis. The BRT would use the proceeds of this sale to buy the bonds of a new railroad company, to be created by the BRT.[116]

The BRT had to resort to such an arrangement because it was a holding company, not a railroad company, and could not legally enter directly into an operating contract.[117] The plan was thus for the new company, which came into existence on September 27, 1912, as the New York Municipal Railway Corporation, to take the actual contract. The BRT would purchase the bonds of the New York Municipal Railway with the proceeds of its sale of notes once the proposed contract was signed with the City.[118]

On October 1, 1912, the BRT sold $40 million of its notes to its bankers.[119] Soon after, the PSC informed the BRT that it objected to so much money being borrowed at one time, even before the actual operating contract was signed. The Commission knew that some of this $40 million could not possibly be used for one or two years and saw no reason why interest on this money should be allowed toward the cost of construction for such a long period before it was used.[120]

The BRT responded to the Commission's criticism by saying that it felt it was imperative to have the money on hand before the contract was made and that its bankers had insisted that the $40 million be taken on October 1, 1912.[121] The PSC, however, argued that the proper course would have been for the BRT to borrow the money quarterly or at least on an annual basis and that the BRT alone was responsible for absorbing the additional interest that would have to be paid because the money had been borrowed so far in advance. Chairman Willcox felt so strongly about this that he was willing to break off negotiations with the BRT over it if the company did not accept the Commission's interpretations.[122] McAneny and Prendergast, however, insisted that a compromise be worked out. After two months of stalemate, an agreement was finally reached between the BRT and the conferees at a meeting at McAneny's home on December 23.[123]

This agreement cleared up the last area of contention with the two operating companies. The conferees now expected that the final form of the proposed operating contracts would be quickly approved by the PSC and the Board of Estimate and would be formally signed by the end of January 1913.[124] On December 31, the PSC released the drafts of what were intended to be the final contracts to the public in preparation for a series of public hearings in mid-January. Willcox believed that the hearings on the contracts and the related certificates would be a "mere formality," and many New Yorkers seemed to agree. A group of supporters of the Dual System plan, for example, made arrangements for a "Subway Signing Banquet" for late January.[125]

The Last Battle

Quick approval, however, did not come, and by the end of January 1913 there was even doubt as to whether the Dual System contracts would ever be signed. Proponents of the Dual System plan failed to take sufficient account of the force of the opposition to the contracts. This opposition, once again, consisted of a number of elements, including President Mitchel on the Board of Estimate, Commissioners Maltbie and Cram of the PSC, and Joseph Pulitzer's *New York World*.[126] The "head and the front, the soul and the body" of the opposition, however, came from Hearst, who used every means possible to delay the approval and execution of the contracts.[127]

Almost all of the criticism leveled at the Dual System plan in 1912 and 1913 had to do with the financial terms of the proposed contracts and the arrangements that the companies had made with their bankers; the route system of the plan, on the other hand, was generally regarded as excellent. The one major exception on this score was criticism from residents of the Williamsburg and Bushwick sections of Brooklyn, which were densely populated areas that lay along the existing BRT elevated lines, across the East River from the Lower East Side of Manhattan.[128]

Local residents alleged that they had been shortchanged by the Dual System, the final version of which had eliminated the proposed Lafayette Avenue Subway line (part of the old Triborough System plan) through these communities. McAneny and Willcox had justified the elimination of the proposed subway on Lafayette Avenue on the grounds that it was more important to build new transit lines to areas that had not yet been developed than to build them in congested areas that were already served by elevated lines.[129] They also noted that under the Dual System plan, the BRT elevated lines in these areas were to be upgraded.[130]

Many of the more than 600,000 people living in these areas, however, disagreed with these arguments.[131] They found a vocal spokesman in local Democratic politician John F. Hylan, who was president of the Allied Board of Trade of the Eastern District. Hylan contended that if the PSC were really doing its duty, "it would lay out lines in the thickly populated sections where they would be self supporting, instead of developing farm lands."[132]

The opponents of the Dual System hoped that PSC approval of the contracts could be delayed until Willcox's term expired at the end of January 1913. Two of the five members of the Commission, Maltbie and Cram, were on record as opposing the contracts, so all that was necessary to defeat them once and for all would be to delay approval until the newly elected Democratic governor, William G. Sulzer, could appoint a new PSC chairman. If Sulzer appointed an opponent of the plan, the Dual System was dead.

Part of this tactic was to discredit Willcox so that Sulzer would not reappoint him. One of Hearst's newspapers, the *Journal*, contended that Willcox was largely responsible for the negotiations with the private companies that, it said, had been "held in the exclusive clubs of the rich, to which no ordinary individual might hope to gain access." Part of this populist rhetoric was the charge that in these clubs, "the deals which led to the transportation enslavement of the community were arranged."[133]

The opposition also tried to sway the public against the contracts at the public hearings held by the PSC. To judge from the newspaper accounts, sentiment at the hearings was heavily in favor of the proposed contracts.[134] However, opponents such as Hylan led large groups of people to the hearings, at one point creating a situation that was "strikingly similar to a riot," when 1,200 people, both for and against the contracts, surged into the hearing room and exchanged charges of corruption.[135]

At the final public hearing, President Mitchel delivered what the *New York Times* called a "blow" to the contracts, so timed that the contracts might have to "hang fire" until Willcox was replaced.[136] Mitchel accomplished this by attacking details of the proposed contracts item by item with such effect that even the public negotiators were forced to admit that they had erred and that the final contracts would have to be amended.[137] On January 23, Willcox announced that these revisions would require time and that, as a result, the proposed contracts could not be printed and approved before his term expired.[138] Since Governor Sulzer had recently announced that he would not reappoint Willcox, this meant that whoever became the new PSC chairman would hold the deciding vote on the contracts.[139]

Governor Sulzer was now in a dilemma. He had hoped that the contracts would be approved before Willcox's term expired because he feared the political risks of any involvement with the Dual System plan. Sulzer had been elected in 1912 with the support of the Tammany organization, and Tammany boss Murphy was now strongly in favor of the contracts. Sulzer desired, however, to become more independent of Murphy, and to do this he needed Hearst's support.[140]

Hearst wanted his friend and counsel, Clarence J. Shearn, to be appointed to the PSC, but State Senate majority leader Robert F. Wagner let it be known that Shearn was unacceptable.[141] Hearst then openly challenged Murphy and the Tammany Democratic machine by demanding that he himself be appointed chairman of the PSC. This made it obvious that Hearst intended to use the subway issue as a "pretext for hullabaloo" to put himself in a position in which he could either hitch Tammany to his own political ambitions or, if Tammany refused to go along, defeat the regular Democratic organization in the 1913 municipal election.[142]

While Sulzer was considering whom to appoint, Hearst continued his attacks on the public negotiators of the Dual System contracts. His newspapers ran a number of front-page cartoons, the first of which showed Willcox carrying the City treasury into the IRT subway.[143] This was followed by a cartoon showing McAneny, Prendergast, and Gaynor sharing a pedestal with former Tammany boss William Marcy Tweed, who had been convicted of felonies for swindling public funds.[144] Another cartoon portrayed a scene in which Willcox, McAneny, Prendergast, and Gaynor were manipulated as puppets on strings controlled by J. P. Morgan (see Cartoon 2).[145] Hearst also helped organize a mass meeting at Cooper Union to oppose the contracts. At this meeting, Mitchel charged that "the same old bunch was getting away with the swag." Other speakers attacked Willcox, McAneny, and Prendergast as crooks, and one speaker singled out McAneny as a "conscious tool of the looters."[146]

Commissioner Maltbie, who had consistently opposed the proposed contracts, now felt obligated to defend Willcox, saying that Willcox believed "in these contracts just as honestly and sincerely as I disagree with him." Maltbie contended that there was no issue of right or wrong involved, because rational arguments could be made both for and against the contracts. In his opinion, it was the responsibility of the public officials to decide which argument held the balance of advantage for the City.[147]

The public officials supporting the Dual System plan, including McAneny, Willcox, and Prendergast, defended the proposed contracts in a series of speeches and public statements. Once again they argued that many new subway lines had to be built at the same time in order to break up congestion of population and promote rational city development.[148]

The most important of these public arguments, because it swayed Governor Sulzer to support the Dual System plan, was presented by Seth Low.[149] Low wrote a letter to Sulzer on January

Cartoon 2. J. P. Morgan holding PSC Chairman William R. Willcox, Manhattan Borough President George McAneny, Comptroller William A. Prendergast, and Mayor William J. Gaynor on puppet strings. *New York Evening Journal*, January 28, 1913. (Courtesy of the New York Public Library)

22, which was printed in its entirety in the *New York Times* the following day. The letter said: "You, Sir, have lived upon the East Side of Manhattan Island, and you know by experience what the congestion of population means. I am greatly mistaken in my estimate of your human sympathy if a plan does not appeal to you which promises to make any such congestion impossible again in any part of the City of New York." Low went on to say that, so long as only trunk lines of rapid transit existed in the older areas of the city, the growth of population would be largely centered along these lines. The Dual System plan, however, would add to the trunk lines the essential branches that were necessary to allow the population to spread to the outskirts. The plan would "have a maximum effect in distributing population because it avails of every rapid transit line that now exists, and, instead of offering competition in the same territory with existing lines, completes these lines, and brings into vital touch with the throbbing heart of the City of New York, on Manhattan Island, the remotest sections of its territory."[150]

Even the House of Morgan got into the public debate. The bank sent PSC Chairman Willcox a letter on January 27, which was reproduced in its entirety starting on the front page of the *New York Times* on January 28.[151] The Morgan letter explained publicly the arrangements the bank had made with the IRT the previous spring. The letter said that the investment bank had been asked to provide about $160 million to the IRT. This meant that approximately $170 million in new bonds would have to be issued (since they would be sold at a discount). In addition, a sinking fund was needed to retire the bonds before the expiration of the operating lease. To provide for bond interest and the sinking fund, the IRT was relying upon a preferential claim to earnings from the operation of its expanded subway network.

To determine the price to be paid to the IRT for its bonds, the Morgan bank said that "it was obviously necessary to have regard to the ruling prices of other bonds of like grade, and to the fact that the money for this issue of $170,000,000 (the largest single corporate transaction that we can recall) must be furnished from year to year in amounts specified."[152] The Morgan bank said that it had formed a syndicate, with about 280 participants, which was to profit to the extent that the price at which the bonds were sold exceeded the syndicate's cost.[153] At the end of the letter, the bank said that there could be no question that the entire financing was for the account of the IRT "and comes out of its fixed five cent fare."[154] This statement was aimed at the Hearst press and other newspapers that were alleging that the City was guaranteeing the IRT a profit from the public treasury.

The House of Morgan's public explanation was intended to show that the deal was a straightforward financial arrangement, with nothing underhanded about it.[155] As Mayor Gaynor told a group of businessmen the day the letter was released, the arrangement that the IRT had made with the Morgan bank, as well as the arrangement the BRT had made with "Schiff and Co." (that is, with Jacob H. Schiff's banking house, Kuhn, Loeb, and Company), simply reflected what the companies had to do in a competitive market to raise money for their businesses.[156]

On February 3, the Dual System plan was saved when Governor Sulzer appointed Edward E. McCall as the new chairman of the PSC. McCall, a Tammany man and a justice of the State Supreme Court, was known to favor the plan. He was the brother of John A. McCall, the president of New York Life Insurance Company, who was a close friend of Tammany boss Murphy. The State Senate confirmed McCall the same day he was nominated.[157]

Before his defeat in Albany, Hearst had obtained an injunction halting the PSC from approving the Dual System contracts, the final copies of which were being printed at the end of January. Some of Mitchel's criticisms regarding financial terms had been resolved in these revised contracts, but essentially the contracts were the same as those discussed at the public hearings in January. Because of this injunction, and because McCall announced that he would need time to consider the contracts, it was predicted that the contracts would not be signed for at least a month.[158]

After the injunction was vacated on February 11, McCall held another set of hearings on the contracts in mid-February, although these hearings were not legally required. At these hearings, the proposed contracts were opposed by Mitchel and Hylan and defended by McAneny and Prendergast.[159] Mitchel offered an alternative plan, which he had devised with Maltbie, for a municipally built, owned, and controlled rapid transit system that would cost $207 million. The virtue of this plan, said Mitchel, was that it would be independent of J. P. Morgan and Company and the IRT. The lines could be operated by William G. McAdoo (who operated the Hudson tubes), the BRT, another private operator, or the City itself.[160] McAneny responded that this plan was insufficient to meet the transportation needs of New York.[161]

The Dual System Is Approved

The PSC gave its final approval to the Dual System contracts on March 4, 1913, by a vote of three to two, with Commissioners McCall, Williams, and Eustis in favor and Maltbie and Cram opposed.[162] The Commission then referred the contracts to the Board of Estimate for its final approval. That same day, Commissioner Maltbie submitted a memorandum to the Commission explaining in detail why he opposed the contracts. A similar memorandum by Mitchel was presented to the Board of Estimate on March 11.[163] Maltbie and Mitchel's final arguments against the Dual System contracts had no effect on the Board of Estimate, which approved the contract by a vote of thirteen to three on March 18, with Mitchel casting the only negative vote.[164]

All that remained was the formal execution of the documents, which took place at a ceremony at the offices of the PSC on March 19, 1913.[165] On this date, Contract No. 3 was signed between the PSC and the IRT, and Contract No. 4 was signed between the PSC and the New York Municipal Railway Corporation, for the BRT. The PSC also issued the necessary certificates for the addition of third tracks and extensions of various elevated lines of the Manhattan Railway Company and the BRT, through its subsidiary, and agreements were made for joint trackage rights on a number of new lines.[166] (See Appendix 1 for a detailed summary of each contract.)

Both contracts specified that the fare on each of the expanded systems would be five cents for the life of the contracts.[167] There would continue to be a separate five-cent fare for services on the lines of the Manhattan Railway Company, controlled by the IRT.[168]

The new rapid transit lines of the Dual System represent the largest single expansion of New York's subway system.[169] All of the lines included in the plan were constructed and placed in operation. The new lines would more than double the total track mileage of the rapid transit system in New York City from 296 to 621 miles.[170] Route mileage would increase from 119 to 233.[171]

The track mileage to be added by the Dual System exceeded the existing rapid transit mileage of any city in the world. Moreover, the total track mileage of the entire Dual System, including old and new lines, exceeded the combined mileage of all other cities in the world with rapid transit systems, which at that time included Chicago, Philadelphia, Boston, London, Liverpool, Paris, Berlin, Hamburg, and Budapest.[172] In the late twentieth century, the remaining Dual System lines constituted most of the subway route mileage operated by MTA New York City Transit.[173]

Track mileage alone, however, is not a complete measure of capacity. According to PSC Deputy Engineer Daniel L. Turner, although the Dual System would double the track mileage of New York's rapid transit network, it would triple the number of passengers that could be served during peak periods.[174] The existing subway and elevated lines could carry a total of 352 trains, with 126,300 seats, per hour in one direction. The new facilities would add 499 trains, with 248,000 seats, per hour, providing a grand total of 851 trains, with 374,000 seats, on all of New York's rapid transit lines during the peak hour of service.[175]

For McAneny and his allies, the extent and carrying capacity of the Dual System lines were important largely because they would allow huge amounts of land to be opened for development at one time. Under the plan, most neighborhoods in the Bronx would have direct access to rapid transit service.[176] In addition, many of the outlying sections of Brooklyn and Queens would now have direct access by subway to all of Manhattan below 59th Street.[177]

On both the IRT and BRT networks, one of the main operating features would be the two types of services provided—express and local.[178] Making fewer stops, express services were aimed at reducing travel times for passengers. The express services on the Dual System lines would allow quick access (within fifty minutes) to Midtown and Lower Manhattan for almost all commuters in the new "subway suburbs," extending out up to fifteen miles from City Hall.[179]

Turner concluded that when the Dual System was completely in operation, instead of being a collection of separate borough communities, New York would be a unified city in fact as well as in name. The city's future growth, he predicted, would take place along the transportation skeleton provided by the Dual System. As a result, the Dual System would be "the real foundation for the city plan of the future."[180]

Lines of the Dual System

A detailed summary of the provisions of Contracts No. 3 and No. 4 and the related certificates is contained in Appendix 1. What follows is an explanation of the route structure of the Dual System as outlined in the contracts. For all intents and purposes, the routes of the Dual System were the same as those outlined in the original Dual System plan of June 1911.[181] (See Maps 6A, 6B, and 6C for the final Dual System plan.)

Under the provisions of Contract No. 3 and its related certificates, new IRT lines were to be constructed in Manhattan, the Bronx, Brooklyn, and Queens. In Manhattan, the "H" lines, the two north-south trunk routes, would finally be built. On the West Side, a new subway would be constructed under Seventh Avenue south of 42nd Street, extending through Lower Manhattan and then across the East River into Downtown Brooklyn. Joined to the existing subway on Broadway north of 42nd Street, this line would form one leg of the "H." On the East Side, a subway would be constructed north of 42nd Street under Lexington Avenue. Connected to the existing subway coming up to the Grand Central area, the "Lexington Avenue subway" (the common name for the entire line) would form the other leg of the "H." A portion of the first subway between the Grand Central and Times Square stations would become the 42nd Street Shuttle. All of the IRT services from the Bronx and Brooklyn would feed into the "H" trunk lines. In addition, the IRT's line to 42nd Street from Corona and Flushing, Queens, would have easy transfers to the "H" lines at the Grand Central and Times Square stations.

Except in the densely developed southern portion of the borough, the new IRT "subways" in the Bronx would actually be on elevated structures. (They are commonly referred to as "the subway," despite this fact.) In the West Bronx, the Jerome Avenue line would proceed to a terminal near the northern border of the city. In the East Bronx, the Pelham line would go up to the far northeastern corner of the borough. Services on both the Jerome Avenue and Pelham lines would feed into the Lexington Avenue trunk line. In the North Central Bronx, the existing IRT elevated line was to be extended up White Plains Road, almost to the Westchester County line. Service on this line would feed into either the existing Lenox Avenue subway or, via a connection to be made at 149th Street, into the Lexington Avenue line.

Under the certificates for improvements to the Manhattan Railway elevated lines, a connection was to be made between the Jerome Avenue line and the Ninth Avenue el, via a tunnel under the Highbridge neighborhood and a bridge across the Harlem River. This would provide West Bronx residents with direct rapid transit access to the West Side of Manhattan. In addition, the Third Avenue el was to be extended from Fordham Road up Webster Avenue to a connection with the White Plains Road line at Gun Hill Road and a connection was to be made between the existing IRT subway and the Third Avenue el at 149th Street and Third Avenue. A third track would be added to the Second, Third, and Ninth Avenue els to increase capacity and allow for express service.

In Brooklyn, the expanded IRT network was less extensive than in the Bronx, since most new services in the borough would be operated by the BRT through its subsidiary. The existing IRT subway was to be extended down Flatbush Avenue and then out Eastern Parkway. From Nostrand Avenue there would be two branches, one continuing out Eastern Parkway and other streets to New Lots Avenue in East New York, the other passing south under Nostrand Avenue to Flatbush Avenue. Except for the outer portion of the line to New Lots, these lines would be underground. Services on the expanded IRT network would connect to both of the Manhattan "H" trunk lines.

For Queens, the Dual System plan provided the first direct rapid transit services to Manhattan. The Steinway Tunnel from 42nd Street in Manhattan to Queens, controlled by the IRT, would be converted into a rapid transit line and extended north to Queensboro Plaza, where a large transfer station would be built. This station would also be used by Second Avenue el trains coming across an extension of the line over the Queensboro Bridge. In addition, Contract No. 4 provided that BRT services passing across 59th and 60th Streets would cross the East River to the station at Queensboro Plaza.[182]

From the Queensboro Plaza station, two lines would extend into the borough. The Astoria line would go to the northwestern corner of Queens; the other line would travel northeast to Corona and Flushing. (At the time Contract No. 3 was signed, plans were being made to extend this line to Main Street, Flushing. This extension received final approval in December 1913, and is best regarded as an integral part of the Dual System.)[183] Both of these lines would be largely on elevated structures. The Astoria and Flushing lines would be leased to the IRT, but the BRT, through the New York Municipal Railway, would have trackage rights on both lines.[184] Both lines would have three distinct services to Manhattan—on the IRT via the Steinway Tunnel, on the Second Avenue el via the Queensboro Bridge, and on BRT trains connecting to the Broadway trunk line via 60th Street.

Under Contract No. 4 and its related certificates, the BRT, through the New York Municipal Railway Corporation, would operate a vast, unified network of rapid transit lines in Brooklyn and Queens, together with new subways that would distribute services on these lines throughout the Manhattan Central Business District south of 59th Street. The most important BRT line was the Broadway trunk subway in Manhattan, which would extend from the City Hall area up Broadway to Times Square and then up Seventh Avenue to 57th Street. At its southern end, this line would connect to a branch extending from DeKalb Avenue station in Downtown Brooklyn, under the East River to the Battery and then up local streets to Broadway. Another branch would pass across the Manhattan Bridge from DeKalb Avenue station, joining the Broadway line at Canal Street. A station at Union Square would allow passengers to transfer to the new BRT line that was to cross 14th Street and go under the East River to northern Brooklyn. At its northern end, a branch of the Broadway line would proceed across 59th and 60th Streets and then across the East River to the union station at Queensboro Plaza.

The Centre Street loop subway would also be a distributor for BRT services. This line had already been constructed by the PSC from the Williamsburg Bridge to Chambers Street. It would now be extended south through the Wall Street area to connect to the new BRT tunnel from Downtown Brooklyn to the Battery. (This was the same tunnel used by the southern branch of the Broadway line.) In addition, track connections would be made between the loop and the BRT branch coming across the Manhattan Bridge.

Most BRT services from Brooklyn and Queens would use the Broadway trunk line or the Centre Street loop to distribute passengers in Manhattan. This included all of the services on the new BRT rapid transit lines in southern Brooklyn—the Fourth Avenue, Culver, West End, and Sea Beach lines—plus the Brighton line. Services on these lines would feed into DeKalb Avenue station in Downtown Brooklyn, where passengers could transfer from one line to another, depending on their final destination in Manhattan. All of the services from southern Brooklyn would travel into Manhattan either via the tunnel to the Battery or the Manhattan Bridge, passing into either the Broadway trunk line or the Centre Street loop. The Fourth Avenue line would be underground; most of the other BRT lines in southern Brooklyn would be on elevated structures, on grade-separated embankments in open cuts.

Services to northern Brooklyn and southern Queens would also be substantially improved. A new subway line would pass from 14th Street under the East River to northern Brooklyn and through a number of local streets to a connection with existing BRT el lines in East New York.[185] The Broadway (Brooklyn) elevated line would receive a third track and be extended to Jamaica, Queens. The Myrtle Avenue el would also receive a third track and be extended into Queens. Services on both the Broadway-Jamaica line and the Myrtle Avenue line would cross over the Williamsburg Bridge and into the Centre Street loop. South of these lines, the Fulton Street el would receive a third track and be extended into Queens.

In northwestern Queens, the BRT would operate services on the Astoria and Corona-Flushing lines under a trackage agreement with the IRT. These services would meet at the Queensboro Plaza station and then cross the East River, passing through 60th and 59th Streets and then into the Broadway trunk line.

Cost of the Dual System

The cost estimates for the construction and equipment of the Dual System were still being refined when the contracts were signed on March 19, 1913. On this date, the estimated cost for the work to be done under Contracts No. 3 and No. 4 was $301,792,628.[186] In addition, the cost of the extensions and third trackings of the Manhattan Railway lines by the IRT was estimated at $25 million.[187] According to Comptroller Prendergast, this proposed expenditure was “the largest in financial volume” in the history of New York City for any municipal project.[188]

The cost estimates for the Dual System were expected to be revised as more detailed engineering work was carried out.[189] With respect to the final share of costs for various types of work, the Dual System contracts and the related certificates were specific about the financial responsibilities of the City of New York and the two companies. Contract No. 3 specified that the IRT would contribute at least $58 million toward construction of the new IRT lines, all of which would be owned by the City. The City would provide at least an equal amount. Any costs beyond $116 million would be the responsibility of the City. The IRT would purchase new subway cars, at a cost of at least $22 million. Any additional costs for equipment would be borne by the company. Under the related certificates, the IRT was also responsible for the improvements to the Manhattan Railway Company els, estimated at $25 million in March 1913.[190]

Contract No. 4 specified that the New York Municipal Railway Corporation would provide at least $13.5 million toward the construction of the new subway lines, which would be owned by the City of New York. (These included all of the major new construction, including the Broadway subway and the Fourth Avenue subway. See Appendix 1 for a summary.) The City would pay the balance of the costs for these lines. The BRT subsidiary would also be responsible for transforming the Sea Beach and Brighton lines into rapid transit facilities and for the improvements to the BRT elevated lines, at an estimated cost of $21 million. It would also pay the entire cost of equipping all of the new services, estimated at $26 million.[191]

By June 1913, the official PSC figure for the cost of the Dual System and related improvements to the Manhattan Railway lines was $337 million.[192] By the end of 1913, the official figure published by the PSC was $366 million, of which $200 million was to be provided by the City of New York, $105 million by the IRT, and $61 million by the BRT.[193] This is the best base cost estimate for the package.[194] In 1999 dollars, the $366 million figure, when inflated using a construction cost index, would total about $22 billion.[195] The Dual System was the most expensive public works project ever implemented in the United States up to that time.[196]

Distribution of Revenues

Both Dual System contracts provided that the annual operating revenues from the expanded IRT and BRT networks would be distributed in a precise order. Under Contract No. 3, all of the operating revenues of the old and new IRT lines would be pooled. The first charge against these revenues would be rental payments to the City of New York under Contracts No. 1 and No. 2. The next charges were for operating expenses, maintenance, and depreciation. Following this, the IRT would receive its preferential payment, consisting of $6,335,000 plus 6 percent of the IRT's contribution to the cost of new lines and equipment.[197] Next, the City of New York would receive an amount equal to 8.76 percent of its share of the cost of construction of new IRT lines.[198] Deficits in these payments in any given year would be cumulative and would be paid from operating revenues in future years.[199] Any amounts remaining after the distribution of specified payments would be divided equally between the IRT and the City.

Under Contract No. 4, the first charge against annual operating revenues would be for rentals payable to the City. Then came deductions for operating expenses, maintenance, and depreciation. Following this, the BRT subsidiary would receive a preferential payment of $3.5 million plus 6 percent of the New York Municipal Railway's contribution to the cost of new lines and equipment.[200] Next, the City of New York would receive an amount equal to the annual interest payable by the City for its share of cost of construction of new lines.[201] Any amounts remaining after the distribution of specified payments would be divided equally between the company and the City. (For a detailed summary of the division of revenues for both contracts, see Appendix 1.)

The public officials responsible for the Dual System contracts were proud of what they had accomplished.[202] Most outspoken at the time the contracts were signed was Mayor Gaynor, who would die unexpectedly just a few months later:[203]

> The great matter has now been brought to a conclusion. It is the greatest accomplishment of our day. The effect it is to have on the City of New York is something larger than any mind can realize. I suppose all intelligent people realize . . . the immense amount of work we have done, and the wear and anxiety we have suffered over it for three years. Never were greater difficulties, legal, engineering and financial, developed and solved. And think of the abuse and charges of dishonesty and theft we have endured on account of it from certain newspaper proprietors and others. [The treatment of the public negotiators] by two sets of newspapers here has been false, cruel and unjust to the last degree of vice and infamy. . . . But it was always so, and always will be, that those who do right, and lead in large matters, must endure much, and even wear out their reputations, if not their lives.[204]

7. Impact of the Dual System

The new subway lines of the Dual System achieved their main purpose. They helped save New York from the problems caused by rapid population growth by making it possible for hundreds of thousands of middle- and working-class families to move out of the overcrowded tenement districts. Most of the Dual System lines were in operation by 1920.[1] (See Appendix 2 for the opening dates of the individual Dual System lines.) Almost all of the net population growth in New York City from 1910 to 1940 was in the "subway suburbs" that sprung up along the new lines, while population declined in the older congested districts.[2]

For the great majority of families who moved to the new subway suburbs, daily life was far superior to that in the overcrowded tenements they left behind. The new "subway suburbs" covered twice the land of the city's existing built-up districts.[3] Largely because so much land was opened for new residential development by the Dual System lines, most of the neighborhoods by the 1940s had a mix of apartment houses and single- and two-family homes.[4] For the average working family, the new homes were almost all of better quality than those in the old neighborhoods. Private homes and apartments were all equipped with the simple amenities of everyday life, including a separate bathroom, with a toilet, sink, and bathtub, and a separate kitchen. Most were well lighted and ventilated.[5]

By helping to assure decent places to live for millions of middle- and working-class people, the Dual System lines also sustained the long-term vitality of New York as the nation's premier business center. The new neighborhoods were within easy commuting distance of the Manhattan Central Business District. Without the subways, hundreds of thousands of Manhattan employees would have had no convenient way of getting to and from work each business day. More than any other single factor, the Dual System lines shaped the current geography of New York City.[6]

Manhattan Borough President George McAneny and his allies viewed the Dual System as part of a larger effort to plan the growth of New York in the interest of its citizens. Other aspects of this effort included zoning laws, building height and volume restrictions, and creation of a city planning commission.[7] After 1913, the attempts to implement other planning measures were only partially successful.[8]

The financial arrangements of the Dual System contracts proved the most problematic. Over the life of the contracts, the five-cent fare on each of the expanded networks of the Interborough Rapid Transit Company (IRT) and Brooklyn Rapid Transit Company (BRT) was supposed to pay for all operating expenses as well as all of the capital costs of building and equipping the system. However, inflation sparked by World War I, which started in Europe in 1914, caused substantial increases in both operating and capital costs. Operating revenues were not sufficient to cover the payments on the bonds the City of New York sold to pay for its contribution to the construction costs. This meant that the payments had to be made annually out of tax revenues from 1920 on.[9]

Construction and Operation of the Dual System

The Dual System lines were designed by engineers of the Public Service Commission (PSC) and were constructed by private companies under contracts prepared, bid, awarded, and supervised by Commission staff.[10] Almost all of the lines were placed in operation between 1915 and 1920.[11] Portions of a few of the BRT lines did not open until much later, however, because of the refusal of Mayor John F. Hylan (1918–1925) to approve contracts for construction.[12] The last section of the Dual System opened in 1931.[13] All the routes that had been agreed to in 1913 were eventually built.[14] (See Appendix 2 for the opening dates of individual lines.)

The number of trips made on the expanded IRT and BRT networks was close to what the planners of the Dual System had forecast in 1912. The IRT system carried almost 303 million passengers in 1912; by 1926, the expanded system carried about 785 million people. In 1930, the IRT carried an all-time high of more than 986 million passengers. The BRT system carried 172 million passengers in 1912; by 1926, the expanded system, now run by the Brooklyn Manhattan Transit Corporation (BMT), was carrying 621 million riders. In 1930, 714 million trips were made on the BMT lines, a figure that was never again equaled.[15] In 1930, the total number of trips on all of New York's rapid transit lines—that is, the IRT network, the BRT network, and the elevated lines of the Manhattan Railway Company—was just over two billion.[16] (See Table 2 for annual rapid transit ridership from 1901 to 1998.)

Financial Results

Under the calculations of projected subway ridership and revenues made by the PSC and Board of Estimate in 1912, the City would accrue deficits on its payments during the early years of operation for the bonds it had sold for construction of the Dual System lines. It had been projected, however, that by the early 1920s subway operating revenues would be sufficient to pay off all accumulated deficits accruing to the City's account. The expanded networks would then begin to produce a profit, to be divided between the City and each of the transit operators.[17]

In 1922 and 1923, engineers and accountants from the New York State Transit Commission analyzed the original ridership projections on which the revenue estimates had been made and determined that the estimates of the number of passengers had been "accurate within a small fraction of 1%." This meant that the revenue estimates that had been projected from transit operations were also correct. The study concluded "that if costs obtaining in 1913 had held true and not been affected by the war, by 1921 all deficits—Company and City alike—would have been absorbed and there would have been a substantial division of profits."[18]

This, however, is not what happened. Between 1913 and 1920, construction and operating costs increased substantially, wrecking the financial structure on which the Dual System was based.[19] New subways cost more to build than had been expected, and operating revenues did not cover payments on the debt the municipality had incurred for subway construction.[20] By 1936, the City's contribution for construction of the new subways built under Contract No. 3 with the IRT totaled $120,527,000.[21] The revenues from the expanded IRT system, however, covered only a small portion of the interest and sinking fund charges on the City's investment. The difference between the debt service cost and the amount received from the IRT had been made up in the City's budgets from tax revenues.[22]

By 1936, the City's investment in construction of new BRT lines under Contract No. 4 totaled $189,814,000.[23] The City never received anything from the BRT or its successor, the BMT, on this investment. All of the City's debt service was paid out of tax revenues.[24]

Other commentators have similarly blamed these unfavorable financial results on the rise in the cost of labor and materials that resulted from World War I.[25] According to Joseph L. Weiner, by the time the construction plans for the Dual System lines were ready, "the World War had commenced and the cost of construction and equipment mounted enormously. The ultimate cost was almost twice that originally estimated."[26] Cynthia Morse Latta, who conducted an extensive investigation of the IRT's finances, concluded that the expectations underlying Contract No. 3 with the IRT were shattered by inflation. Latta notes that had there been no inflation, then Contract No. 3 would have produced favorable results both for the IRT and the City.[27]

Furthermore, the Dual System contracts had fixed the fare at five cents for the forty-nine-year term of the leases with the private companies. Both the companies and the City agreed to this because for decades up to 1913 there had been little experience with high inflation rates.[28] Under the contracts, the fare could only be changed by mutual agreement between each company and the City of New York. If the IRT and BRT had been able to increase the transit fare after World War I, as was done in most other major American cities, then the City might have been able to receive revenues from subway operations to cover its debt service costs, not to speak of making a profit.[29]

In New York, however, during the administration of Mayor Hylan the five-cent fare became a political shibboleth. Hylan had come into political prominence as a fierce opponent of the Dual System plan. His election in 1917 was the result of strong support from William Randolph Hearst. Hylan refused to allow the IRT or the BRT a fare increase, blaming the companies for all problems relating to transit construction and operation. This was extremely effective politically, helping to ensure his reelection in 1921.[30] From this time on, the five-cent fare was a major issue in municipal politics.[31] The fare remained at five cents until 1948, when it was raised to ten cents.[32]

If the City did not benefit financially from the Dual System contracts, neither did the private companies do very well.[33] The BRT was forced into receivership on December 31, 1918, and remained in this state until June 15, 1923, when it was successfully reorganized as the BMT.[34] Revenues from the operation of the BRT/BMT lines were never sufficient to cover the total amount of the company's preferential payment, including debt service.[35]

In the case of the IRT, Latta's study reveals that the average IRT stockholder did not fare well from Contract No. 3.[36] By 1936, the IRT had received most of the preferential payments provided for in Contract No. 3. It had, however, lost money on the improvements to the Manhattan elevated lines.[37] In 1932, the IRT went into receivership, where it remained until 1940. Reacting against allegations made "throughout the Interborough Company's corporate life" that the IRT was exploiting the City, Latta claims that "overall, it was clearly the City that exploited the Interborough Company." By refusing to allow a fare increase at a time of rapid inflation, City politicians ensured the company's demise.[38]

Mayor Hylan and other politicians were also responsible for the fact that the last major addition to New York's subway network, the Independent System (IND), was designed to compete with, rather than complement, the Dual System lines. The decision to build the IND was made in 1924, after yet another intense political battle over how to expand the rapid transit network.[39] Operated by the Board of Transportation of the City of New York, the IND lines opened between 1932 and 1940.[40] Except for the area along Queens Boulevard, in the central part of the borough, and a portion of northern Manhattan, the IND lines did not open any new areas for residential development. Instead, they were intended to replace older elevated lines of the IRT and BMT, or to compete with the new Dual System lines.[41]

Unification and Public Operation

From 1932 on, as the new IND lines began to syphon off riders from the IRT and BMT systems, the financial condition of the private companies worsened. Negotiations went on throughout the 1930s to unify the rapid transit network.[42] Finally, on June 12, 1940, the system was unified.[43] The City of New York purchased all of the rights of the private rapid transit operators, paying $175 million for the rights of the BMT and $161.5 million for those of the IRT and the Manhattan Railway Company.[44] After 1940, the IRT and BMT lines were operated, together with the IND lines. In 1953, operation was transferred to another agency created by the State of New York, the New York City Transit Authority. In 1968, this agency became part of a larger regional organization, the Metropolitan Transportation Authority (MTA).[45]

In 1947, New York's subway system, including the new IND lines, carried just about the same number of passengers—two billion a year—as the Dual System lines had in 1930. From this time on, however, ridership began to decline. By 1977, the subway system was serving less than a billion riders annually. The reasons for this decline are complex. Internal factors such as disinvestment in the physical infrastructure made subway service less attractive.[46] External factors encouraged other means of transportation. Massive amounts of government funds were spent by Robert Moses and others on the construction of an extensive network of limited access highways and related bridges and tunnels.[47] Many of these highways were paid for largely by the federal government. Meanwhile, federal mortgage policy encouraged the construction of new housing on open land in the region, most of it in suburban counties outside New York City. At the same time, federal policy made it more difficult to obtain mortgages in the neighborhoods that had been built up along the elevated and subway lines.[48] These policies encouraged a rapid increase in automobile ownership and use, as well as the relocation of many businesses, particularly manufacturing, outside New York City.[49] New York's subway was still essential for hundreds of thousands of workers traveling to and from Manhattan, but for many other types of trips (such as shopping or medical visits), many people now chose to use private vehicles.

Another factor that contributed to the decline in subway ridership in New York is that the system has been largely frozen in time since the 1950s. Since the completion of the IND in 1940, the only completely new routes added to New York's rapid transit network have been the incorporation of portions of two railroad lines into the system, the Dyre Avenue line in the Bronx (1941) and the Rockaway line in Queens (1956).[50] With few new lines being added, the subway system has not been able to adapt adequately to changing demographic and employment patterns. Moreover, in some districts, such as the East Side of Manhattan, the amount of rapid transit service available has actually declined. Under the 1929 second-stage plan for the IND, a subway was to be constructed under Second Avenue to replace the Second and Third Avenue els. In the end, these old elevated lines were torn down, cutting the amount of service on the East Side by half, but the Second Avenue subway was not built.[51]

The lack of progress on the construction of new subway lines from the late 1940s on was mainly due to inadequate financing. From the 1950s on, almost all capital funds came from the various levels of government. The money that was provided from 1950 to 1980, however, was insufficient even to meet the capital renewal needs of the existing physical plant and to replace old subway cars. There was never enough money to complete plans for expansion. As part of a grandiose MTA capital plan approved in 1968, construction was started on portions of the Second Avenue subway. Work also began on new lines for Queens. The Second Avenue construction was halted in the mid-1970s, however, when it became clear that large portions of the physical plant of the existing subway system were falling apart.[52]

In 1981, the New York State Legislature approved a five-year capital renewal plan for 1982–1986, aimed at restoring the region's subway, bus, and commuter rail network to a state of good repair.[53] This plan more than tripled the amount of annual funding for capital rehabilitation. Under the first MTA five-year capital plan for 1982–1986, and two subsequent plans ending in 1996, more than $25 billion was spent on capital improvements to the existing MTA transit systems, about $16 billion of which was for the subway system. The result was substantial improvements in service quality and reliability.[54] New York City's economy also has remained strong, with overall employment levels holding steady, and increasing in some areas.[55] The improvements in subway service and the buoyant economy led to ridership increases. About 1.2 billion passengers used the system in 1998, or about 3,975,000 riders on an average business day.[56]

In the late 1990s, after much of the subway system had been returned to a state of good repair, plans were once more being made to construct a subway under Second Avenue. Meanwhile, portions of a new line to Queens were opened in 1989 and additional sections of this line were under construction in the late 1990s.[57] Building the Second Avenue subway, as well as other proposed new lines, will cost billions of dollars.[58] The debate now centers around how to finance expansion of the region's rail network, while at the same time finding the capital funds to keep existing services running properly. Devising a financing plan to achieve both goals is the major challenge facing the rail system and its managers at the start of the twenty-first century.

The Dual System and City Planning

From the point of view of producing favorable financial returns, the Dual System plan was a failure, although it can be argued that this was largely because City politicians acted irresponsibly from 1918 on in refusing to allow a fare increase. The major justification used by George McAneny, William R. Willcox, Seth Low, and others in favor of the Dual System contracts, however, had not been that the new subways would produce a monetary profit for the City. Rather, it was that the Dual System lines would foster the movement of population to the outlying boroughs, thereby reducing congestion of population and the social problems that reformers alleged were the natural result of congestion. The most important question in evaluating the success of the Dual System plan, therefore, is what effect the new lines had on the movement of population. In addition, the progressive reformers who devised the plan had regarded it as only part of a larger program of city planning. So the success of other actions taken to control growth and development in New York are also integral to the final evaluation.

McAneny regarded new rapid transit lines as the "basis for city building" but did not believe that new transit lines alone would ensure rational city growth.[59] In order to be most effective, the new subways had to be accompanied by other measures such as the creation of a city planning commission and the passage of zoning laws and building height restrictions.[60] One responsibility of a city planning commission would be to devise a logical plan for public improvements in the outlying boroughs coordinated with the new Dual System lines. The commission would also regulate private development through a zoning code.[61] In the years after the Dual System contracts were approved, McAneny, together with other reformers, tried to translate these ideas into action.

Throughout 1912 and 1913, McAneny strove to have a planning committee created within the Board of Estimate.[62] In the 1913 municipal elections, reformers carried all the positions on the Board of Estimate, with McAneny being elected president of the Board of Aldermen. The new Board took office on January 1, 1914, and one of its first official acts was the creation of the Standing Committee on the City Plan, chaired by McAneny.[63] This committee delivered a report to the Board of Estimate on December 31, 1914, which asserted that the Dual System was a "distinct achievement in city planning," fixing lines of development for at least twenty-five years.[64] Now that it was known where new rapid transit lines would go, comprehensive plans had to be made for new public facilities, such as schools and parks. These plans would be made by a permanent city planning commission, staffed by experts, who would serve for a fixed number of years and would not be subject to political removal.[65] Late in 1916, McAneny called for the creation of such a permanent commission.[66]

McAneny's high hopes were dashed by the election of Mayor Hylan, who opposed the creation of a planning commission.[67] During Hylan's two administrations, from 1918 to 1925, and for much of the time that his successor, James J. Walker, was mayor, planning for parks, schools, and other public facilities went on in the same haphazard way as in the past. No public agency had responsibility for comprehensive planning of public works in the areas opened for development by the Dual System lines.[68]

McAneny and his allies were more successful in setting controls for private development through building regulations and zoning.[69] Regulating building heights and volumes was a negative form of planning, aimed at preventing the construction of more tall, bulky skyscrapers taking up the entire lot areas. Zoning had more creative possibilities. The City would district all five boroughs into "use areas." In some areas, only residential buildings would be allowed; in some, only commercial buildings; in others, only factories.

Under a strong zoning law, the City could also determine the density of residential development. Certain areas could be zoned only for single- and/or two-family houses, whereas others would allow a mixture of small homes and apartment buildings. Zoning could thus ensure that in the future no area would be built up exclusively with tenement houses.[70] In addition, in the older tenement areas, stores, bars, and restaurants had been allowed on the lower floors of each building. In the new neighborhoods to be built up along the Dual System lines, the hope was that zoning would restrict such activities to designated commercial strips.[71]

On February 27, 1913, the Board of Estimate passed a resolution establishing a temporary Commission on Building Heights. Support for the proposal had come from reports issued by the Fifth Avenue Association and the City Commission on Congestion of Population, which had recommended limitations on building heights and comprehensive zoning throughout the five boroughs. The Fifth Avenue Association wanted such regulations to halt the spread of the garment district into the Fifth Avenue retail district. The Congestion Commission wanted to use zoning to ensure that congestion of population would not spread to outlying areas.[72]

The Commission on Building Heights was chaired by McAneny's old ally, former PSC commissioner Edward M. Bassett. On December 5, 1913, the Commission submitted a report to the Board of Estimate recommending an amendment to the City Charter to allow the municipal government to divide New York into zones and to regulate the heights of buildings and the location of trades and industry within each zone. The Commission made it clear that it was concerned not just with the development of business areas in Manhattan, but also with preventing the repetition of the overcrowded conditions in the tenement districts.[73] In April 1914, the New York State Legislature revised the Charter to allow for zoning, but provided that, before the City established zones, the Board of Estimate should appoint another commission to recommend the boundaries of the zones. On May 22, 1914, the Board of Estimate created the Commission on Building Districts and Restrictions. Bassett was once again chosen to serve as chairman.[74]

Between 1914 and 1916, the Commission on Building Districts and Restrictions worked out the details of a plan for comprehensive zoning. McAneny strongly supported the zoning proposal.[75] On July 25, 1916, the Board of Estimate approved a zoning resolution based on the recommendations of the Commission. New York was divided into three types of zones: residential, business, and unrestricted. It was assumed that the unrestricted districts would become industrial areas. The resolution also contained restrictions limiting the heights and volumes of buildings within each zone.[76]

Unfortunately, the final zoning ordinance achieved less than the planning reformers had hoped with respect to residential development, since it was the result of a negotiated process with input from private developers.[77] The reformers' ideal had been to have many areas zoned exclusively for single- and two-family homes. In the end, however, most of the communities along the new subway lines were zoned to allow most streets to be lined with five- and six-story apartment houses. In a small number of areas close to the subway lines, the zoning regulations aimed at promoting single- and two-family homes, but even in these areas apartment houses were allowed. The only districts zoned for single-family homes were far from the subway lines.[78] Kenneth T. Jackson has observed that the 1916 zoning law by itself had little impact on congestion because much more land was zoned for high-density residential buildings than could ever have been developed for such purposes.[79]

The 1916 zoning regulations accomplished two of the reformers other goals, however. In areas such as the Lower East Side, factories and tenement houses had existed on the same block. In addition, retail stores, bars, and restaurants had been allowed in all the buildings. Tenement dwellers had been forced to live with the noise, smell, and smoke of the factories, stores, and restaurants. The 1916 zoning law forbade factories, warehouses, slaughterhouses, bottling plants, and the like in residential areas. Secondly, it restricted retail and other commercial activities to designated streets, usually those served by subway stops.[80]

Richard Plunz, author of a major history of housing in New York, has commented that the impact of the 1916 zoning resolution on the outer boroughs is more difficult to trace than its impact on high-rise buildings in Manhattan's Central Business District. He concluded that in the outer boroughs the zoning code "worked in league with other forces, including the building code, the extension of mass transit routes, and the city's political economy, to produce the new development and the new forms of urbanism that emerged throughout much of the boroughs during the boom decade of the 1920s. What the resolution produced could be called a new horizontal city, a city characterized by neither the towers nor the tenements of Manhattan."[81] According to Plunz, of the three factors subject to public decision making—the zoning resolution, the building code, and mass transit—the new subways were the most important.[82] The new residential districts in the outer boroughs, which Plunz calls "a new horizontal city," can also be viewed as "subway suburbs."[83]

The Subway Suburbs

The Dual System lines served as a catalyst for the development of new residential areas in the Bronx, Brooklyn, and Queens. These areas, built up after World War I, are the "subway suburbs" of the interwar years. At the peak of their development around 1940, these neighborhoods had relatively low population densities and a mix of housing that allowed much more open space, grass, and trees. They were inhabited mainly by middle- and working-class people who largely commuted to work in other parts of the city. Most importantly, many of the residents themselves believed they were living in a suburban area and had greatly improved their quality of life by moving there.[84]

If the subway suburbs might not seem "suburban" to many Americans at the turn of the twenty-first century, this is perhaps because the term is now popularly regarded as applying solely to communities that are totally dependent on cars and dominated almost exclusively by single-family homes. The 1929 Regional Survey of New York, however, noted: "the word 'suburb' must not be interpreted too narrowly. The contrast is between neighborhoods in which the land is heavily covered with buildings and others where a good deal of it is open in the form of parks, gardens or ground surrounding detached homes. . . . Compared to Manhattan and the old wards of Brooklyn, large portions of the outer boroughs are definitely suburban in character."[85]

Ninety percent of the net population increase in New York City between 1910 and 1940 occurred in the subway suburbs. During this time, the city's population grew from 4,767,883 to 7,454,995, a rise of 2,688,112, or 56 percent. Over the same period, the population of the subway suburbs increased from 788,202 to 3,206,092, a rise of 2,418,090, or 307 percent.[86] The subway suburbs covered more than twice the area of the older developed districts. For the first time, enough land was opened for new housing so that population densities in New York, which had risen steadily since the 1840s, began to decline.

The population of the older developed areas, including all of Manhattan, the South Bronx, and the older areas of northern Brooklyn, actually decreased during this period, from 3,773,718 to 3,545,700.[87] The most dramatic changes were in the four oldest and most crowded tenement districts, which together lost 45 percent of their residents between 1910 and 1940, dropping from 1,313,383 to 727,160. The largest population decline was in the Lower East Side south of Houston Street, which fell from 397,842 in 1910 to 181,715 in 1930 and 147,118 in 1940, a total decrease of 63 percent.[88] (See Table 3 for population changes by district, 1910–1940.)

In his massive *Population of the City of New York, 1890–1930* Walter Laidlaw noted that the most extreme congestion in New York was concomitant with the "huge Southeastern European immigration" during the first decade of the century and reached a peak in 1910.[89] In 1910, there were sixty-seven census tracts in the city with more than three hundred people per acre, with a total population of 1,313,969. By 1930, all but one of these tracts had decreased in population, many of them substantially, and their total population was 779,358.[90] Laidlaw attributed the breakup of congestion to the construction of the new subway lines.[91]

Most of the subway suburbs grew spectacularly between 1910 and 1940.[92] For example, the district along the Jerome Avenue line in the West Bronx had 96,781 residents in 1910. By 1920, the figure had climbed to 215,021; by 1930, it was 460,527; and by 1940, it had reached 514,782. The East Bronx, served by the Pelham line, had 50,267 people in 1910 and 334,555 in 1940.[93] Similar growth took place along the Dual System lines in several districts in southern Brooklyn and in Queens.[94]

Table 3

Population Change in New York City by Districts, 1910 and 1940

	1910	*1940*	*% Change 1910–1940*
1. Lower East Side[a]	397,842	147,118	–63.0
2. Stuyvesant	355,564	212,890	–40.1
3. East Side	271,653	211,391	–22.2
4. East Harlem	335,266	235,813	–29.7
5. Lower West Side	246,469	131,786	–46.5
6. West Side	239,451	200,463	–16.3
7. Upper West Side	178,066	262,691	47.5
8. Harlem	191,454	231,283	20.8
9. Washington Heights	54,331	236,414	335.1
MANHATTAN TOTAL	2,331,542	1,889,924	–18.9
10. South Bronx	283,932	545,374	92.1
11. West Bronx	96,781	514,782	431.9
12. East Bronx	50,267	334,555	565.6
BRONX TOTAL	430,980	1,394,711	223.6
13. Long Island City	62,763	233,587	272.2
14. Jackson Heights	32,932	199,987	507.3
15. Flushing/Bayside	37,165	154,327	315.3
16. South Queens	138,705	670,938	383.7
17. Rockaway	12,476	38,795	211.0
QUEENS TOTAL	284,041	1,297,634	356.9
18. Williamsburg	313,508	235,366	–24.9
19. Old Brooklyn	370,014	318,894	–13.8
20. Bedford	204,204	283,475	38.8
21. Bushwick	270,518	272,667	0.8
22. Bay Ridge	166,261	489,116	194.2
23. Flatbush	79,846	394,215	393.7
24. Brownsville	196,439	361,927	84.3
25. Coney Island	33,561	342,625	921.0
BROOKLYN TOTAL	1,694,351	2,698,215	65.1
26. Staten Island	85,969	174,441	102.9
NEW YORK CITY TOTAL	4,766,883	7,454,995	56.4

[a] Districts devised by Consolidated Edison Company.
SOURCE: Irving M. Plant, *Population Growth of New York City by Districts, 1910–1948* (Report prepared for Consolidated Edison Company of New York, December 1948).

As New York's population continued to grow from 1910 on, its residential areas were extended farther and farther from the core. In 1910, 54 percent of the city's population lived within four miles of City Hall; by 1930, the figure had fallen to 22 percent, and 72 percent of the population lived between four and twelve miles from City Hall.[95]

By 1940, when the areas opened by the Dual System lines had neared the peak of their development, they all had significantly lower population densities than older sections of the city. Population per acre in the newly developed areas ranged from 28 in the East Bronx to 105 in the West Bronx (the latter attributable in part to the opening of the Grand Concourse subway line of the IND in 1932). The figure for Long Island City was 53; for Jackson Heights, 40; for South Queens, 38. In Brooklyn, Bay Ridge had 91 people per acre; Flatbush had 59; and Coney Island had 54.[96]

The above statistics are from a study of the movement of population within New York City conducted by the Consolidated Edison Company in 1948 in order to plan for future utility needs. The general conclusion of the study was that "the direction and growth of the city has been dominated by the direction and growth of the city's transit facilities."[97] Similarly, in 1926 a Queens Chamber of Commerce brochure said, with respect to the Dual System lines to that borough, "It is almost impossible to exaggerate the effect of this improvement on the development of Queens borough."[98]

Almost all of these new subway suburbs were within fifty minutes commuting time from the Manhattan Central Business District.[99] Because of the new accessibility of these districts to job sites, mainly in Manhattan, the value of land increased substantially.[100] In many of the older residential districts, however, values dropped, as the population moved out and demand decreased.[101]

Impact on the Manhattan Central Business District

The Dual System lines also helped spur the rapid growth of Midtown Manhattan as a business district. Until the 1890s, much of central Midtown had been an upscale residential area.[102] From this time on, however, it was transformed into a commercial district. New transportation lines were the catalyst for this transformation. The Dual System lines provided excellent service to Midtown from the outer boroughs via the IRT's "H" trunk lines, the BRT's Broadway trunk line, and the crosstown lines under 42nd Street and 59th/60th Streets.[103]

The growth of Midtown was also encouraged by the opening of Pennsylvania Station in 1910, which gave commuters from New Jersey and Long Island direct service to Manhattan for the first time. Grand Central Terminal, which opened in 1913 on the site of an older railroad building, also provided expanded service.[104] The trains coming into the commuter stations were powered by electricity, which made underground operations possible.[105]

With these improvements in subway and railroad infrastructure, Midtown grew rapidly as an office and retail district.[106] In addition, the garment center moved to lofts on the streets along Seventh Avenue north of 34th Street.[107] In 1920, there was about 40 million square feet of office space in Lower Manhattan, and a little over 20 million in Midtown. By 1935, Midtown had 60 million square feet, and the Wall Street area 55 million; in 1963, the numbers were 160 million and about 98 million, respectively.[108]

From World War I on, the number of office jobs in Manhattan rose dramatically. By 1947, Manhattan had about 725,000 office jobs and 875,000 production jobs; another 800,000 people worked in other sectors, including wholesale, retail, transportation, and construction.[109] Employment in the nine square miles of the Manhattan Central Business District south of 59th Street was heavily dependent upon the subway system to get people to and from work. On an average business day in 1948, more than a million workers traveled to jobs in the district from homes in the Bronx, Queens, and Brooklyn, 83 percent of them using the rapid transit system. For all purposes—work, shopping, leisure, and so on—about 3.7 million people a day entered the district on an average business day in 1948, 2.4 million of them coming by subway.[110] In 1950, more than two-thirds of all subway passengers boarded on stations of the Dual System lines.[111]

Better Housing

Plunz attributes the "mass improvement of working-class housing" after World War I largely to the development of transportation infrastructure, particularly the subways, which made accessible the relatively inexpensive open land of the outer boroughs.[112] In addition, in 1920 the State Legislature passed a law permitting real estate tax exemptions for construction of new residential buildings.[113]

The combination of cheaper land and tax exemptions sparked small-scale developers to invest in apartment houses and private residences. Between 1921 and 1929, 420,734 new apartments, 106,384 single-family houses, and 111,662 two-family houses were built in New York City. This volume of new housing "has never again been equaled, quantitatively or qualitatively."[114] Because of the 1901 Tenement House Act and the 1916 zoning resolution, all new apartments had to meet much higher standards for sunlight, ventilation, and sanitary facilities than for tenements built before 1901.

The new subway lines of the Dual System did not alone cause this construction boom, but they had to be in place for it to happen.[115] Other factors included increasing economic prosperity and the entrepreneurship of New York's real estate developers. After World War I, wages rose and the number of hours worked fell. This economic prosperity helped promote the exodus to the new residential communities along the Dual System lines. It also enabled working families to demand better-quality housing in these new neighborhoods.[116] Private developers responded, and strove to build good-quality housing as fast as possible.[117] With so much land for residential use now available at reasonable prices in the subway suburbs, this was the place to do it.

Although many families were better off financially, one of the most striking aspects of the migration from the older tenement districts is that it did not require improvement in a family's economic circumstances. Historian Marion Casey has noted that much of the residential mobility in New York from the 1920s to the 1950s had "little relation to vertical mobility in either occupation or class."[118] According to Casey, "Dissatisfaction with . . . outmoded accommodations in older sections of Manhattan created an incentive for mobility, encouraging families with children to explore the greater 'spatial amenities' of the outer boroughs."[119] The move to the subway suburbs reflected a "search for a better quality of life" than was possible in the older neighborhoods. For the first time, physical conditions in New York "offered a unique opportunity to obtain a standard of living that was both comfortable and respectable, yet not dependent upon occupational advancement or even better wages." For the same monthly rent, a family living in a cramped tenement apartment in Manhattan could move to a much larger modern apartment in Fordham in the Bronx, Woodside in Queens, or Bay Ridge in Brooklyn.[120] This geographic mobility "enabled blue-collar workers to enjoy middle-class amenities in their housing and neighborhoods—a style of living that in the more traditional definition of mobility should have taken a generation or two longer." Casey argues that the subways were "the real key" to this large scale working-class mobility.[121]

The quality of much of the housing in the subway suburbs exceeded the new regulations. Many apartment buildings had self-service elevators, modern bathrooms, and kitchens. Many were garden apartments, with large interior courtyards.[122] The new apartment buildings, which were technically "tenements" under the law, were no longer called by that name. Instead, residents called them "apartment houses." In the 1920s, all of the new housing was constructed by the private sector.[123]

The housing in place in the subway suburbs by the early 1940s was a mix of apartment houses and single- and two-family homes. In all but one of the areas that grew up along the Dual System lines, more than half of the total number of buildings in place by the early 1940s were single- and two-family houses. In most districts, such dwellings accounted for 65 to 75 percent of all buildings.[124] Moreover, many of the private houses were detached or semi-detached and surrounded by yards.

This mix of housing types gave the subway suburbs, as a whole, a very different look from the older areas of the city, including those built up along the elevated lines and the first subway. In Manhattan, only 2 percent of the residential buildings in the early 1940s were single- and two-family homes. In most of the areas along the elevated lines in Brooklyn, single- and two-family homes accounted for less than 40 percent of all buildings in the early 1940s; this was also the case in the South Bronx. Moreover, in these older areas there were few detached houses; the single- and two-family homes were row houses. The look of almost all residential areas in Manhattan was of wall-to-wall brick buildings, attached to one another, with no space between the structures. The streetscape of the older areas of Brooklyn and the South Bronx was also dominated by block after block of attached masonry structures.[125]

In the subway suburbs, the typical streetscape contains a combination of apartment buildings and detached homes. The apartment buildings are usually on the corners, the single- or two-family homes in the middle of the blocks. As compared to much of Manhattan, all retail activity is on designated streets, usually the major thoroughfares served by subway stops.[126] This streetscape resulted in part from the 1916 zoning law, but the main influence was the large amount of relatively vacant land that was opened for development by the new subway lines.

According to Plunz, the 1920s housing boom in the outer boroughs rendered the New Law tenement obsolete.[127] The economic formulas that had resulted in the construction of block after block of this type of building along the route of the first subway in the South Bronx, for example, were no longer operative because the price of land opened for development by the Dual System lines "meant that maximizing density was no longer the primary factor that determined the profit that could be made by building affordable housing."[128] So much land was made available for residential use that the cost per lot was low enough to construct many new single- and two-family homes in communities such as Borough Park and Bensonhurst in southern Brooklyn and Corona in Queens.[129]

In the Bronx, only 19 percent of the new housing constructed in the 1920s was of this type.[130] However, a substantial number of single- and two-family homes were already in place by 1920. Much of this housing had been constructed to serve residents working in local industries, although some Bronx communities, such as Bedford Park, had been built up as commuter railroad suburbs in the late nineteenth century. In the 1920s, there was so much vacant land available near these detached single- and two-family homes that it did not make economic sense to buy up the buildings and tear them down, as had been done in Manhattan and the South Bronx. Instead, vacant lots were filled in with new apartment houses and the older buildings remained, resulting in a mix of housing.[131]

A 1942 market analysis provides descriptions of neighborhoods in the subway suburbs, along with pages of photographs. In the Bronx, for example, University Heights was said to have many private homes, as well as several streets lined with apartment houses. The Pelham Bay Park neighborhood was filled with "attractive two-story homes . . . and a sprinkling of apartment houses." The district in the North Central Bronx along White Plains Road was "suburban in character with attractive one and two-family dwellings . . . and a number of modern apartment houses."[132] In Brooklyn, Borough Park had "plenty of one and two-family homes," interspersed with elevator apartment houses, and Bensonhurst had "a large number of one and two-family homes," with apartment houses on the main streets. In Queens, Jackson Heights counted "many one and two-family homes," although most of the residents lived in apartment houses.[133]

The subway suburbs ended up being denser than the planners of the Dual System had wanted, but much less crowded than the older tenement districts. Most of the dwelling units were in apartment buildings, and most families rented rather then owned.[134] Even so, the apartments were of good quality, and the mix of single- and two-family homes with apartment houses gave most neighborhoods a look quite different from the dense urban neighborhoods of Manhattan. Most importantly, the new residents of the subway suburbs thought they had taken a major step upwards.

The People Who Moved to the Subway Suburbs

The vast majority of those moving to the subway suburbs up to 1940 were of European descent.[135] They included Jews and Italians of the "new immigration," as well as Irish and Germans and a host of other nationalities. Most were second- or third-generation Americans. In their new homes they created new "hyphenated" American cultures—Jewish-American, Irish-American, Italian-American, and so on—that were different from those of their first-generation parents. Most of the new communities had a mix of people from different ethnic backgrounds, although in many neighborhoods one group predominated.[136]

For second-generation American Jews, the improvements in living conditions were perhaps the most striking, since their economic mobility was greater than that of most other groups.[137] Many Jews had achieved middle-class status by the 1920s and were looking for better places to live. During the decade, a mass migration took place from the Lower East Side, East Harlem, Williamsburg, and Brownsville to new neighborhoods in the Bronx and Brooklyn. Neighborhoods along the Grand Concourse and Pelham Parkway in the Bronx and Eastern Parkway, Flatbush, Borough Park, Brighton Beach, and other areas in Brooklyn now became major centers of Jewish-American life.[138]

Most of the buildings in these communities were constructed by small developers who were themselves Jewish. They produced a quality product that catered to a market that had many choices.[139] In their new dwellings, second-generation New York Jews felt "at home in America," no longer being regarded, or regarding themselves, as foreigners. Here they "devised the grammar of American Jewish life," as they created communities of their own.[140] As author Ruth Gay describes it, once past the first shock of entry in places such as the Lower East Side, Jews "moved to their dream neighborhoods . . . where they invented their own version of America. Reveling in the luxuries of steam heat and indoor plumbing, they built a familiar world of synagogues, schools and stores."[141]

Many Irish-Americans moved out of the older tenement districts to new homes in the subway suburbs. By 1940, the Irish were heavily concentrated in Fordham, University Heights, and Highbridge in the Bronx, Woodside and Sunnyside in Queens, and Bay Ridge and Flatbush in Brooklyn, although they could be found in almost all of the new neighborhoods.[142] Second-generation Italian-Americans moved from the Lower East Side and East Harlem to new neighborhoods, particularly the northern Bronx and southern Brooklyn.[143] Along with the Jews, Irish, and Italians came immigrants and the descendants of immigrants from many other lands.[144] The anecdotal accounts of the lives these migrants found in the new neighborhoods of the Bronx, Brooklyn, and Queens are very positive. Living in places such as "The Beautiful Bronx" from 1920 to 1950 was an experience many residents remembered fondly.[145]

In terms of income, in the early 1940s, the subway suburbs were solidly middle class.[146] Despite this, residents were not dependent upon the private automobile for mobility. As late as the 1940s, most households did not own cars and used public transit to traverse the city.[147] Local trips could easily be made by streetcar (later by bus), and the subway was always available, twenty-four hours a day, seven days a week, for local travel as well as for journeys to Manhattan and the other boroughs. The great majority of people living in the Dual System suburbs who were employed in Manhattan used the subway to travel to and from work.[148]

The People Left Behind

The Dual System subways relieved many of the worst problems caused by overcrowding. Through the early 1940s, however, there still were hundreds of thousands of people, mostly the poorest New Yorkers, living in the older tenement districts with the cheapest housing.[149] In addition, population densities were increasing in several older areas of the city, including Harlem and Bedford-Stuyvesant, as African-Americans, and later migrants from Puerto Rico, were restricted by segregation to living in specified neighborhoods.[150]

Conditions in these areas were discussed in a confidential report to the savings banks of New York State in 1942. The report noted that during the nineteenth century, high real estate values for residential use in Manhattan had "developed primarily because of a large population confined in a small area of land too great to be crossed daily in going to and from work." Now, in the oldest tenement districts, these high values had been "dissipated by rapid transit, bridges and tunnels, which removed these barriers, making a vast area available for residential use." As a result: "All barriers have been leveled and the process of decentralization is well advanced."[151]

This was true largely for people of European descent, who had quickly filled up most of the subway suburbs. For African-Americans, the report went on, it was another matter. They continued to live in overcrowded housing. The barriers that confined them to certain areas of the city, however, were not physical ones. They were in part due to economic status, but were mainly the result of the reluctance of whites to rent to blacks.[152] In other older residential neighborhoods, where abandonment of the oldest tenement buildings had begun as early as the 1930s, the poorest families also were having trouble finding decent housing. These areas included the older tenement districts of Manhattan, the South Bronx, and northern Brooklyn.[153]

The poor condition of much of the housing in the older areas led to efforts to tear down the worst tenements and replace them with public housing, funded in part by the federal government. The first public housing opened in 1935, a rehabilitation of a set of pre–Old Law tenements on the Lower East Side.[154] This proved very expensive, so almost all public housing from then on was new construction in which older buildings were demolished and replaced by high-rise buildings surrounded by grass and trees.[155] Thousands of old buildings were torn down in the tenement districts of Manhattan, the South Bronx, and the older areas of Brooklyn. On these sites, as well as on vacant land in portions of the subway suburbs, hundreds of high-rise, "tower in the garden," public apartment buildings were constructed.[156]

The Subway Suburbs Hold Their Own in a Changing City

Since the early 1950s, New York City has undergone a series of major transformations. Its major job base in Manhattan has shifted from a balance of factory and service jobs to one based largely on service industries.[157] The amount of office space in Manhattan has continued to increase while the total number of jobs in the borough has remained relatively stable.[158]

In the 1990s, the Manhattan Central Business District led all world cities in the amount of office space, with over 360 million square feet. It was the premier center in the global economy, serving as a command post for multinational businesses, world financial markets, and world government (the United Nations and a host of related non-governmental organizations), as well as a global center of culture (arts, fashion, media, and publishing) and a major tourist destination. Manhattan was the headquarters of the three major broadcast television networks and several major entertainment conglomerates, home of six of the ten largest book publishers, the leading center of magazine and newspaper publishing, and a growing center for on-line information providers. Manhattan also continued to outpace all other locations as a center of banking and was still the headquarters to about fifty Fortune 500 companies. The business district south of 59th Street was the economic engine of an metropolitan region extending out in a radius more than sixty miles from Manhattan.[159]

In large part powered by the strength of the New York economy, the subway suburbs continued to hold their own during the second half of the twentieth century, while undergoing major demographic changes.[160] In several of these communities, the population continued to be largely of European descent.[161] In many of the communities built up along the Dual System lines, however, the population of European descent began to move out during the 1950s. This included many of the children of the original migrants, who moved to outlying parts of the city, such as eastern Queens or Staten Island, and to more distant suburbs north of the city, on Long Island, or in New Jersey.[162]

This outward movement to areas of lower population density was fostered by the transportation and housing policies of the federal government, as discussed earlier.[163] New highways and the availability of cheap mortgages, however, were only the means to an end. For most families, the major motivation for moving out of the subway suburbs was the pull of even better housing. Instead of renting an apartment, they could now own a single-family home.[164] For these people, the neighborhoods that had grown up along the Dual System lines were only a one-generation stop on the journey "from tenement to split level."[165]

As the older population moved out from many of the subway suburbs from the 1950s on, new groups saw an opportunity to improve their living conditions. The residents who initially replaced the older population were mainly African-American and Latino.[166] In addition to the "pull" of better housing and more attractive surroundings in the subway suburbs, they were also being "pushed" out of the older tenement neighborhoods by deteriorating housing, fires, crime, drugs, and a host of other factors.[167]

During ensuing decades, many of the subway suburbs became the new neighborhoods of African-Americans and Latinos. They were joined by of tens of thousands of new immigrants from many nations of the Caribbean, Latin America, Africa, and Asia. This was the result of new federal immigration laws, which sparked a new wave of foreign immigration to New York, equal to that of the early years of the twentieth century.[168]

The continued supply of good housing at prices working families could afford was the main reason for this new migration to the subway suburbs.[169] While many older neighborhoods were experiencing severe problems from the 1950s on, the housing stock in the subway suburbs had remained largely in place. With one exception, the areas built up along the Dual System lines did not experience the same cycle of decline and rehabilitation as the older tenement districts.[170]

A good example of a subway suburb that has held its own is Norwood in the North Central Bronx. Since 1918, this area has been served by the Jerome Avenue line. Fashion designer Ralph Lifshitz—who changed his name to Ralph Lauren—grew up here during the 1940s, as did Calvin Klein.[171] An article in the *New York Times* on September 5, 1999, headlined this community as "A Miniature U.N. Bordered by Parkland," with the subheading "Diverse Bronx area has accommodated waves of immigrants." The article quoted Dart Westphal, president of the Mosholu Preservation Corporation, who noted, "Norwood never fell apart. It never experienced the kind of abandonment that happened in other parts of the Bronx."[172]

The newest arrivals to the subway suburbs still found an excellent supply of good housing in apartment houses and one- and two-family homes. All of the physical infrastructure on which public health and safety depend, including water supply, sewerage, and sanitation, was in place. An excellent network of public transit enabled people to get to and from jobs, as well as other activities, without having to depend on automobiles.[173]

A February 1998 study profiled the fifty-one City Council districts in New York. One of the purposes of the study was to show that New York City is not, as is often argued, two cities, one rich and one poor.[174] Instead, the study said that there are three New Yorks—one that is poor and largely minority (twelve Council districts), a relatively small one (six districts) that is wealthy, and another New York with a large number of low- to middle-income people of all races and ethnic groups (thirty-three districts).[175]

With the exception of the West Bronx and the Lower East Side, all of the poor districts (with average household incomes under $22,000 per year) were in areas that developed along the elevated lines and the first subway. Three of the wealthy districts (household incomes over $40,000) were in Manhattan, two in the outer parts of Queens, and one on Staten Island. Not surprisingly, all of the subway suburbs except the West Bronx were in the low- to middle-income grouping (household incomes of $22,000 to $40,000).[176] The population of all the Council districts in the subway suburbs, with the one exception, also had higher levels of education, lower levels of public assistance, and better health (measured by rates of asthma, tuberculosis, and AIDS) than any of the poor districts. Many of the districts in the subway suburbs had large numbers of African-Americans and/or Latinos; in Queens, a number of them had many people of Asian descent.[177]

Creating and maintaining a decent living environment for generations of middle- and working-class residents in New York City was a major accomplishment. A public television show, "Journey to Planet Earth," aired on April 18, 1999, cited New York as "a mega-city that works." This was attributed in part to the fact that the city had built its basic physical infrastructure to serve all the people—and had built it decades ago, in advance of development.[178]

At a public health conference in 1999, Ximena de la Barra, a senior urban advisor at UNICEF, noted that more than three billion people in urban areas worldwide lack proper sanitation, leading to epidemics of cholera and other diseases. These areas also have severe problems with housing and transportation. De la Barra noted that housing overcrowding and concern about disease had been a major issue in New York in the early 1900s. She cited the Dual System as a successful effort to alleviate these problems, using it as an example of the type of planning that needs to be done to address current public health issues.[179]

Planner Peter Hall, discussing what he calls "the mass transit suburb" as it developed in London, Paris, Berlin, and New York between 1900 and 1940 notes that in London, as in New York, lower-middle- and working-class families had moved to their new neighborhoods from inferior housing, without bathrooms or indoor toilets, in the older congested districts of London. The people who moved to the new neighborhoods "were enjoying a quantum leap in their quality of life," and were very positive about their move.[180] Hall points out that "whether by the crudest of speculative mechanisms or the guiding hand of social purpose, transport did prove to be the maker of cities—and also, if it failed, its breaker." He cites the Dual System as a public plan that had a major impact on the development of New York in the twentieth century.[181]

As was intended by the reformers who planned them, the new subways of the Dual System helped New York to meet the challenges of rapid urban growth. They saved New York from the many problems resulting from poor living conditions in the tenement districts. For decades, the subway suburbs built up along the Dual System lines have been the neighborhoods where millions of New Yorkers have found a better life.

Conclusion

The Dual System of Rapid Transit was of unrivaled significance for the development of New York City in the twentieth century. More than any other public work, it set the pattern of growth for residential areas in much of the city for three decades. It was also the largest and most expensive single municipal project ever built. The new subways saved New York from the problems resulting from rapid population growth and made it possible for millions of average New Yorkers to move to good housing in a decent environment. The Dual System subways also helped lay the basis for the development of Midtown Manhattan as one of the world's largest employment centers.

Three specific conclusions can be made about the decision by public officials to build the largest single addition to New York City's subway system. The first is simply that the process required to reach the decision was extraordinarily complex. In fact, given the number of people and groups involved, it is surprising that any decision at all was reached to provide New York with a rapid transit system adequate to its needs.[1] Struggles among these individuals and groups hindered subway development, since the structure of law and government required that a strong consensus exist as to the method of obtaining new rapid transit lines before major additions could be built. This problem was most evident from 1902 to 1909, when almost no major decision was made to expand the city's rapid transit network, despite an obvious need for such expansion. The principals involved, including the representatives of the private transit companies, could not reach agreement about how transit expansion was to be accomplished.

After a new Board of Estimate came into office in New York City in 1910, the situation changed. The new Board was willing to cooperate with the New York State Public Service Commission, which had been at odds with the former Board. More importantly, some of the members of the new Board shared a set of ideas similar to those of the Public Service Commission regarding the necessary expansion of the subway network and the reason why such expansion was crucial to New York's long-term well being. This brings us to our second conclusion, namely, that this common set of ideas was largely responsible for the fact that the deadlock over subway expansion was finally overcome.

By 1910, Manhattan Borough President George McAneny on the Board of Estimate and William A. Willcox, Edward M. Bassett, and others on the Public Service Commission had concluded that a vast expansion of New York's rapid transit network was necessary to reduce congestion of population in the older residential districts. Transportation lines would be extended into undeveloped areas in outlying boroughs in which new homes could be built. These men saw the construction of new transit lines as intrinsic to the development of a rational plan for city growth under which past mistakes could be avoided and the city would expand more harmoniously.

The principles on which the Board of Estimate and the Public Service Commission acted were not conceived by these officials, but were part of a new paradigm of urban development and the role of government in the provision of new transportation lines, which had been under discussion since the 1890s. What McAneny, Willcox, Bassett, and others did, from January 1911 on, was to take the new paradigm and apply it pragmatically to the situation in New York City. The result was the Dual System of Rapid Transit.

The need to promote the rational growth of New York for all its citizens was the justification used by the public officials for the compromises made with the operators of the existing rapid transit systems, the Interborough Rapid Transit Company and the Brooklyn Rapid Transit Company. They countered every attack on the proposed Dual System contracts, including the financial arrangements that were made with the transit companies, by arguing that compromise was in New York's best interest. According to these progressive reformers, new subway lines were the only way to relieve housing congestion. They would enable middle- and working-class families to move to better homes in less crowded neighborhoods. This expected result was worth the financial risks assumed by the City of New York under the Dual System contracts.

In the end, these arguments won out. At critical moments, when it seemed as if the Dual System plan might fall through, such as when Governor William G. Sulzer had to appoint a new Chairman of the Public Service Commission, the emphasis on the relief of population congestion saved the day. This new paradigm of urban development thus served as a powerful tool to bring about the consensus necessary for the subway expansion plan to be adopted, ensuring that New York City would finally receive a rapid transit network adequate to its needs and its future.

Critics of the Dual System plan contended that McAneny, Willcox, and other public officials were tools of financial interests that wanted to use transit expansion for their own gain. They argued that the public officials' justification for the financial arrangements in the contracts was really just a rationalization for corporate greed.[2] This accusation can never be completely disproved, although the speeches, letters, and public statements of men such as Comptroller William Prendergast, Mayor William J. Gaynor, Mayor Seth Low, George McAneny, William R. Willcox, and other supporters of the Dual System plan attest to the sincerity of their belief that it would greatly benefit the city.[3]

The public servants who implemented the Dual System plan certainly thought that they had done the right thing, and that a careful analysis of the evidence would bear them out. McAneny, Prendergast, and Gaynor all took part in the opening ceremonies of the Municipal Reference Library on March 31, 1913. Mayor Gaynor gave a speech at this event in which he referred to the Dual System contracts:

> Here all the facts with regard to municipal government can be found—the good and the bad. I suppose we are to exclude nothing, are we? (laughter). They will read them here in the future from certain corrupt newspapers how we three people (turning to the Comptroller and Borough President McAneny) sold out the city's subways, and how corrupt we were, and those to whom we sold them. I believe everything will be told except the price (laughter). I never saw the price mentioned, but presumably it was considerable (laughter). The cartoons in which two out of the three—I will not say which two they were—were painted with striped clothes, and in one case with a ball and chain, will be here in connection with the history of the subways. . . . But it is done now and it is too late to retract. But I think that we all are perfectly willing to have it done, and we have no fear for the future. The truth seeps out, and leaks out, one way and another. The only trouble is that sometimes it takes too long, but it gets out after a fashion. . . .
>
> But all will be collected, good and bad, the writings of the good man and the writings of the evil man—the writings of the competent man, and to some extent, I suppose, the writings of

> the dunce who does not know what he is talking about (laughter). It will all be here. And through all that all the intelligent writers and historians who come here will get at the truth one way and another.[4]

This book is based largely on records at the Municipal Reference Library and other collections of primary sources. After going through the evidence, it seems obvious that the worst thing that can be said about the Dual System contracts is that they were an honest, if somewhat complicated and controversial, attempt to come to terms with some of New York's most pressing social issues. As another historian of the New York subway, Brian J. Cudahy, has noted: "Hindsight wisdom may be critical of the Dual Contracts. . . . But the fact is that the city was totally unable to undertake such a massive transit project on its own; it had to have the cooperation of private enterprise and private investment. Private firms, on the other hand, could not go into the 1913 money market for financing without the guarantees provided by the Dual Contracts profit provisions." Cudahy sees the Dual System subways as "a solution . . . that was total in scope" and notes that few other municipal undertakings can be so characterized.[5]

The third conclusion is that the Dual System had almost precisely the impact on the development of New York City that was expected. Residential growth from 1910 to 1940 occurred largely in corridors along the new subway lines, and ridership was almost exactly what had been projected. The spectacular growth of Midtown Manhattan as a business center also required the new subway lines to carry hundreds of thousands of workers to and from their homes each day. If the financial results of the Dual System were problematic, this was due in large part to the fact that local politicians made a political issue out of the five-cent fare and refused to allow it to increase, even at the rate of inflation.

The Dual System lines strengthened New York's economy and

provided the necessary means whereby millions of families have been able to find a better life in the subway suburbs of the Bronx, Brooklyn, and Queens. This includes not just the first generation of people of European descent who moved out from slums such as the Lower East Side, but succeeding generations of migrants, first African-Americans and Puerto Ricans, and then people from "all the nations under Heaven."[6] In 1928, after hundreds of thousands of new apartments and homes had been constructed in the outer boroughs, McAneny commented that the Dual System subways had "proved the city's physical salvation."[7] Given the impact of the Dual System, it was the most important decision made by New York's government in the twentieth century.

Appendix 1

Summary of the Dual System Contracts and Related Certificates

The complete text of the Dual System Contracts and related certificates for elevated extensions and additions of third tracks is contained in the fourth volume of the Public Service Commission's Annual Report for 1913.[1] What follows is a detailed summary of the provisions of these agreements.

Contract No. 3 and Related Certificates

Under the terms of Contract No. 3, between the City of New York by the Public Service Commission (PSC) for the First District and the Interborough Rapid Transit Company (IRT), the IRT agreed to contribute at least $58 million toward the cost of construction of new rapid transit lines. The IRT would also pay for the new subway cars for these lines, at a cost of at least $22 million. The IRT would maintain and operate the new lines in conjunction with the existing IRT subway for a single five-cent fare. The City agreed that if the IRT contributed toward the cost of construction, the City would construct the new lines and lease them to the IRT for a term of forty-nine years from the beginning of operation.

As a result of Contract No. 3, the IRT's "H" lines in Manhattan were finally to be built. On the West Side south of 42nd Street, a new line would be built down Seventh Avenue, Seventh Avenue South (a new street connecting Seventh Avenue to Varick Street in Greenwich Village, carved out from the local grid of streets to allow the building of the subway), Varick Street, and a number of local streets. This line would end at South Ferry, at the southern tip of the island. From Chambers Street south, a branch of this line would pass through the Wall Street area and through a new tunnel under the East River to Downtown Brooklyn, where it would merge with the existing IRT subway to Brooklyn. The new Seventh Avenue subway would have four tracks from Chambers Street to 42nd Street, where it would join with the existing four-track subway running up Broadway. This would allow express and local services on the West Side between Chambers Street and 96th Street. (See Maps 6a and 6c in Chapter 5.)

On the East Side, a similar realignment would take place. The existing subway between Lower Manhattan and 42nd Street would be joined to a new subway going north under Lexington Avenue. The new subway would have four tracks between 42nd Street and 125th Street. Together with the four tracks of the existing subway, this would allow for both express and local service on the East Side between the Brooklyn Bridge Station and northern Manhattan. The new north-south trunk lines on the East and West Sides would be connected at 42nd Street by a shuttle service along the route of the first subway from Grand Central to Times Square.

All of the IRT services in the Bronx and Brooklyn would feed directly into the "H" trunk lines. In addition, IRT services coming into Manhattan from Queens via a new line to Times Square would have easy transfer connections to both the Lexington Avenue and Seventh Avenue lines.

In the Bronx, the Jerome Avenue, Pelham, and White Plains

Road lines would all be built. Except for those portions of the first two lines that passed through neighborhoods already developed in the South Bronx, these lines were to be on elevated structures in order to reduce construction costs. All of the new lines were to have at least three tracks, allowing for peak-period express service in one direction.

Jerome Avenue line services in the West Bronx would feed into the Lexington Avenue subway, providing direct access to the entire East Side of Manhattan. In addition, as provided in the related certificate for the Manhattan Railway Company's elevated lines, a connection would be built from the northern terminus of the Ninth Avenue elevated, at 155th Street, across the Harlem River to connect to the Jerome Avenue line. This would provide West Bronx passengers with direct access to the entire West Side of Manhattan.

In the East Bronx, Pelham line services would feed into the Lexington Avenue trunk line, providing access to Midtown and Downtown. For the North Central Bronx, the White Plains Road extension of the first subway would have services feeding into the West Side via the existing Lenox Avenue subway, as well as to the Lexington Avenue line. In addition, under the terms of a related certificate, the Third Avenue elevated was to be extended north from Fordham Road to a connection with the White Plains Road line at Gun Hill Road, providing riders with more options for travel to the East Side. Also, a connection was to be made between the Third Avenue el and the existing IRT subway at 149th Street and Third Avenue, allowing further travel options.

In Downtown Brooklyn, IRT services from both the East Side and West Side would merge into an expanded four-track trunk line running south to the existing terminal at Atlantic Avenue (where transfers could be made to Long Island Rail Road trains). From here, a new four-track line would go south under Flatbush

Avenue and then east along Eastern Parkway. From Nostrand Avenue there would be two branches, one continuing out the Parkway and other streets to New Lots Avenue in East New York, the other passing south under Nostrand Avenue. Except for the eastern portion of the New Lots line, which was elevated, these lines were to be underground. Passengers on IRT services from Brooklyn would have the choice of service to either the Lexington Avenue line or the Seventh Avenue line, to the Wall Street district or Midtown, using express or local services.

Contract No. 3 also provided for direct rapid transit from Queens to Manhattan for the first time. A new subway would run east from Times Square to Grand Central and then via the Steinway Tunnel to Long Island City. From the Queensboro Plaza station there would be two branches, one to Astoria in northwestern Queens, the other to Woodside and Corona (soon to be extended to Flushing) in northern Queens.[2] Both of these branches would be three-track elevated lines. They were to be operated jointly by the IRT and the BRT under an operating arrangement between the two companies covered under a supplemental agreement.[3] BRT trains would reach the Queensboro Plaza station via a new tunnel under the East River from 60th Street in Manhattan. In addition, as provided by a related certificate, a branch of the Second Avenue elevated of the Manhattan Railway Company would be built across the Queensboro Bridge to this same station. This would give passengers still more options for trips to the East Side.

On March 19, 1913, in addition to signing Contract No. 3, the PSC approved certificates for the extension and third-tracking of the elevated railroad lines controlled by the IRT. One of these certificates was issued to the IRT for the extension of the elevated lines of the Manhattan Railway Company, as discussed above. The other was issued to the Manhattan Railway Company directly for the addition of a third track on its

Second, Third, and Ninth Avenue lines.[4] The additional third track was to allow these lines to carry more trains and to increase train speeds. This was needed in part to serve the new extensions in the Bronx and Queens.

Under Contract No. 3, the IRT agreed to contribute up to $58 million toward the cost of constructing the new IRT lines (exclusive of the improvements and extensions to the elevated lines). The City would provide the funds for the additional construction costs, which would be at least as much as the IRT's contribution. This meant that the City would be responsible for covering any of the construction costs of the new lines to be operated by the IRT above $116 million. The IRT also agreed that it would be responsible for equipping the new lines, for which the company would contribute a minimum of $22 million.[5] If the eventual cost of rolling stock was higher, the IRT would cover the increase. Under the terms of the related certificates, an estimated $25 million would be provided for the improvements to Manhattan Railway Company's elevated lines.

The construction contracts for the new IRT subways, together with the contract drawings for them, would be prepared by the PSC. The new lines would be built under separate construction contracts that would be awarded by the PSC after publicly advertised bids were received. The PSC also would undertake the sole supervision and direction of work on the construction contracts. Title to all of the new IRT subway lines and equipment would be vested in the City.

By signing Contract No. 3, the City of New York leased to the IRT the operation of the new lines and the new equipment, for operation in conjunction with the existing subway and the existing equipment. The lease was to run from January 1, 1917, to December 31, 1965, or a period of forty-nine years. Provisions were made in the contract to cover the eventuality that the new lines might not be ready for operation on January 1, 1917. The existing leases held by the IRT under Contracts No. 1 and No. 2 were modified in Contract No. 3 so that they would also expire on December 31, 1965.

The fare on the expanded IRT network was to be five cents for the life of the contract, unless both parties agreed to change it. This was a flat fare, not distance-based, with free transfers among lines for one continuous trip. A separate five-cent fare would continue to be charged on the Manhattan Railway elevated lines.

Contract No. 3 specified that the gross receipts from the operation of the new IRT lines and the existing IRT lines were to be combined during the term of the lease. From this income, derived from operating revenues, deductions were to be made annually in the following order:

1. The rentals required to be paid to the City under Contracts No. 1 and No. 2 for the existing subway.
2. Taxes, if any.
3. All expenses, exclusive of maintenance, actually and necessarily incurred by the IRT in the operation of the expanded system.
4. An amount equal to 12 percent of the revenue for maintenance.
5. Depreciation (calculated under a complex formula).
6. $6,335,000 to be retained by the IRT, representing the average annual income from the operation of the existing subway.
7. Six percent of the IRT's contribution toward the cost of construction of the new lines and the cost of equipment, out of which the IRT was to set aside amounts sufficient, with interest and accretion therein, to amortize within the term of the lease such contributions and such cost. (Items 6 and 7 constituted the IRT's preferential payment.)

8. If additional equipment were provided by the IRT, then the company was to receive payment covering its actual interest on the money borrowed to pay for this, plus 1 percent for amortization.
9. If the IRT shared in the cost of construction of additions to its system not specified in the contract, then the company was to receive payment covering its actual interest on the money provided, plus 1 percent for a sinking fund.
10. An amount to be paid to the City equal to 8.76 percent of the portion of the cost of construction of new lines paid for by the City. (This was the City's preferential payment.)
11. An amount to be retained by the City equal to interest charges, plus a 1 percent sinking fund, on any money provided in the future for additions to the IRT system not provided in the contract.
12. One percent of the revenue to be paid into a separate fund to be controlled by a Depreciation Fund Board. This fund was to be used to meet any deficits in operation of future additions to the IRT system.

The amount remaining after taking all of the above deductions was to be deemed the income, earnings, and profits of the expanded IRT system and was to be divided equally between the IRT and the City.

If the revenues from the operation of the expanded IRT system in any one year were insufficient to cover the obligations and deductions listed above, then the deficits for the items not covered were to be cumulative. Payments of such deficits were to be made in full before deducting any amounts for any item in the succeeding revenue periods. Interest on such deficits was to be payable at the actual rate payable by the IRT or the City and such interest would form a part of the cumulative deficits.[6]

Contract No. 4 and Related Certificates

Contract No. 4 was between the City of New York by the Public Service Commission for the First District and the New York Municipal Railway Corporation, a subsidiary of the Brooklyn Rapid Transit Company (BRT). Under the terms of the contract, this corporation agreed to contribute toward the cost of construction of new rapid transit lines and to equip and operate these new lines in conjunction with its existing lines for a single five-cent fare. The City agreed that if the New York Municipal Railway Corporation contributed toward the cost of construction, the City would construct the new municipal lines and lease them to the company for forty-nine years from the beginning of operation.

Although the City of New York was to own all the new IRT lines, this was not the case with the expanded BRT system. In Contract No. 4, the new rapid transit lines to be owned by the City were termed the "Railroad." The "Railroad" to be constructed for initial operation and to be equipped, maintained, and operated under Contract No. 4 included the Broadway trunk line and Centre Street loop in Manhattan and the Fourth Avenue, West End, Culver, and Fourteenth Street–Eastern District lines in Brooklyn. The "Existing Railroad," to be operated as one system with the "Railroad" lines, was defined as the rapid transit lines and equipment belonging to the BRT through various subsidiaries. The lines of the "Existing Railroad" were listed as the Broadway (Brooklyn), Fulton Street, Myrtle Avenue, Lexington Avenue (Brooklyn), Fifth Avenue (Brooklyn), Brighton, Canarsie, and Sea Beach lines. These lines would all continue to be owned by the BRT through its subsidiaries.

The expanded BRT system's network was more complicated than that of the IRT. The enlarged IRT system used the original subway network as a base, and all new services connected with the Manhattan "H," either directly or via a simple transfer. The enlarged BRT system would consist of brand-new subways in Manhattan and Brooklyn, as well as existing railroads in southern Brooklyn that were to be transformed into rapid transit lines and connected to the new subways. In addition, the enlarged system included all the lines of the older BRT elevated network, which would be expanded and improved and whose services were to be integrated with those of the new subways as much as possible. Lastly, it would include new BRT services in Queens, to be operated over the new IRT lines. The expanded BRT system would include almost all of the lines in the original Dual System plan of June 1911, as refined in subsequent discussions between the company and PSC engineers. (See Maps 6b and 6c in Chapter 5.)

In Manhattan, the work horse of the expanded BRT system was to be a four-track trunk line extending up Broadway from a station near City Hall to 42nd Street and then up Seventh Avenue to 57th Street. Both express and local services would operate over the Broadway trunk line. Together with the express tracks on the lines in southern Brooklyn and Queens, this would allow fast service to Midtown and the Wall Street area from these residential areas.

The Broadway trunk line would have several connections to the feeder lines from Brooklyn and Queens. From City Hall station south, a two-track line would proceed through Lower Manhattan to a new tunnel to Brooklyn at the Battery. At Canal Street, just a few blocks north of City Hall, the Broadway trunk subway would be joined by a branch from Downtown Brooklyn crossing over the East River via the Manhattan Bridge. At Union Square, there would be transfer connections between Broadway line services and services on the new 14th Street crosstown subway to northern Brooklyn.

From 57th Street and Seventh Avenue, a two-track line would go east, proceeding under 59th and 60th Streets and then crossing over the East River via the Queensboro Bridge to the

Queensboro Plaza station. (After Contract No. 4 was signed, this route was modified so that instead of passing over the Queensboro Bridge, a tunnel would be built from 60th Street to Queens for BRT services.)[7] At the Queensboro Plaza station, BRT services from Manhattan would connect to the Astoria and Corona (later Flushing) lines to be jointly operated with the IRT.

The other BRT line in Manhattan was to be a four-track loop subway extending from the Williamsburg Bridge through local streets in the Lower East Side to Centre Street and then south to a station at Chambers Street–Brooklyn Bridge. From this point, two tracks would continue further south through the Wall Street area under Nassau and Broad Streets to a connection with the new tunnel from the Battery to Brooklyn (this tunnel was the same as that to be used by Broadway subway services on the line coming down from City Hall). North of Chambers Street, two of the four tracks coming across the Manhattan Bridge would also pass into the loop, allowing services from southern Brooklyn coming across the bridge to pass through the heart of the financial district.

All of the new BRT services from Brooklyn and Queens to Manhattan, except the 14th Street line, would feed into either the Lower Manhattan loop subway or the Broadway trunk line. This would mean that passengers would have easy access to the Wall Street area and Midtown, as well as to the commercial districts between the two office hubs. In addition, trains from the old BRT elevated lines would continue to operate over the Brooklyn Bridge to the existing terminal opposite City Hall.

In Downtown Brooklyn, the two lines from Lower Manhattan—the one passing from the Battery to Brooklyn via tunnel and the one crossing the Manhattan Bridge—would merge at a union station at DeKalb and Flatbush Avenues. This huge six-track station would receive trains from all of the new BRT rapid transit lines in southern Brooklyn. Passengers could transfer easily between services at this station. At the other end of Brooklyn, all of the southern Brooklyn lines, except the Fourth Avenue spur to the southwestern corner of the borough, would unite again at a vast terminal station at Coney Island, where transfers could be made between lines.

From DeKalb Avenue station south, the six-track BRT trunk line would pass south under Flatbush Avenue Extension to the vicinity of Fourth Avenue, where it would split into two branches. The Brighton line would continue south with two tracks under Flatbush Avenue to a connection with the old Brighton railroad. This railroad would now operate as a rapid transit line with direct service to both Midtown and Lower Manhattan. Four tracks to Coney Island would allow express and local services.

From the split with the Brighton line, the Fourth Avenue subway was to proceed south to 59th Street, at which point it would become a two-track line to 86th Street in Bay Ridge.[8] The Fourth Avenue subway had been the main line of the proposed Triborough System in Brooklyn and was already well under construction with City funds. This trunk line would now be joined by three feeder lines. South of the 36th Street station, the Culver and West End lines would split off to the east. Both would be rebuilt as three-track elevated lines, allowing for express and local services. South of 59th Street, the reconstructed Sea Beach line would split off the Fourth Avenue trunk, passing to the east, mostly on a four-track open cut, with express and local services. The Culver, West End, and Sea Beach lines would meander through many of the neighborhoods of southern Brooklyn, ending at the terminal station at Coney Island. The new BRT services in southern Brooklyn would bring almost all of the area within one-half mile of direct rapid transit connections to where most of New York's jobs were located—Manhattan south of 59th Street.

Service to the northern tier of Brooklyn would also be improved substantially. Most of the neighborhoods in this area had been built up along the BRT elevated lines constructed in the late nineteenth century; they contained the bulk of Brooklyn's population and most of its tenements.[9] Northern Brooklyn was then served by five elevated lines. From north to south these were the Broadway, Myrtle Avenue, Lexington Avenue, Fulton Street, and Canarsie lines. Contract No. 4 called for a new line to be constructed north of these existing lines from 14th Street in Manhattan. This 14th Street–Eastern District line, as it was then called, would end at Broadway Junction in East New York (a junction of the BRT elevated lines) where connections could be made to the Canarsie line and the Broadway line to Jamaica. It was to have two tracks and would be partly subway and partly elevated.[10]

Several of the existing elevated lines in northern Brooklyn were to be extended and have third tracks added to them, to increase capacity and reduce passenger travel times. The existing Broadway (Brooklyn) elevated would be extended to Jamaica, Queens, and the Myrtle Avenue elevated would be extended into Queens. Both lines would have third tracks added. Track connections would be made between the Broadway/Jamaica line and the Myrtle Avenue line. Both Jamaica and Myrtle Avenue line services would travel over the Broadway elevated line and feed into the Centre Street loop subway via the Williamsburg Bridge. Further south, the Fulton Street elevated would also be extended into southern Queens, along Liberty Avenue, and receive a third track. Except for the Myrtle Avenue line extension, these improvements were not covered directly by Contract No. 4 but were provided for in certificates issued to the New York Municipal Railway Corporation by the PSC on March 19, 1913, for the extension and third-tracking of these elevated railroads.[11]

Under Contract No. 4, the BRT, through its subsidiary, would contribute at least $13.5 million toward the construction costs of the new subway lines, called the "Railroad," which would be owned by the City of New York. The City would pay for the balance of the construction costs of these lines.[12] As with the IRT contract, this meant that the City would be responsible for any increases in the estimate cost of construction of these lines. The New York Municipal Railway Corporation would pay for the entire cost of reconstructing the existing BRT elevated and railroad lines, the "Existing Railroad," which would be operated as part of the expanded system. These existing lines would continue to be owned by the private company.[13] The private company would also pay for the entire cost of equipping the new lines with rolling stock.[14] Any cost increases for the reconstruction of existing lines or for equipment would be borne by the company.

Under Contract No. 4, the construction contracts for the new City-owned lines, together with the contract drawings thereof, would be prepared by the PSC. Proposals for construction contracts would be the subject of public bidding. The PSC would undertake the sole supervision and direction of work on any construction contract.

By signing the contract, the City leased the "Railroad" and the equipment of the Railroad to the New York Municipal Railway Corporation for operation in conjunction with the "Existing Railroad." The lease was to begin on January 1, 1917, and would expire on December 31, 1965. Provisions were made, however, in case portions of the new lines were not ready for operation on January 1, 1917.

The fare on the expanded BRT network was to be five cents for the life of the contract, unless both parties agreed to change it. This was a flat fare, not distance-based, with free transfers among lines for one continuous trip.

The gross receipts from the operation of the entire expanded

BRT system were to be combined during the term of the lease and deductions from these receipts were to be made in the following order:

1. Rentals payable by the New York Municipal Railway to the City. (Such rentals were payable for certain improvements to be made on the existing BRT elevated lines.)
2. Taxes, if any.
3. All expenses, exclusive of maintenance, actually and necessarily incurred by the New York Municipal Railway in the operation of the expanded BRT system.
4. An amount equal to 12 percent of the revenue for maintenance, exclusive of depreciation.
5. Depreciation (calculated under a complex formula).
6. $3.5 million, to be retained by the New York Municipal Railway, representing the average annual income from the operation of its existing services during the prior two years.
7. An amount, to be retained by the New York Municipal Railway, equal to 6 percent of the company's contribution toward the cost of construction of the railroad and for equipment.[15] (Items 6 and 7 represented the New York Municipal Railway's preferential payment.)
8. If additional equipment was provided by the New York Municipal Railway, the company was to receive payment covering its actual interest on the money borrowed to pay for this.
9. If the New York Municipal Railway shared in the cost of construction of additions to its system not specified in the contract, then the company was to receive payment covering its actual interest on the money provided, plus 1 percent for a sinking fund.
10. An amount to be paid to the City equal to the annual interest payable by the City upon its share of the cost of con-

struction provided for in the contract, plus 1 percent for amortization.

11. An amount to be paid to the City equal to the annual interest payable by the City upon its share of the cost of any additional construction, plus 1 percent for amortization.
12. One percent to a contingent reserve fund.

The amount remaining after the above deductions was to be considered the income, earnings, and profits of the expanded system and was to be divided equally between the company and the City.

If the revenues from operation were insufficient to meet the obligations and deductions listed above, the resulting deficits were to be cumulative and payments of such deficits were to be made in full before deducting any amounts during succeeding revenue periods.[16]

Appendix 2

Opening Dates of the Dual System Lines

Contract No. 3 (IRT Lines)

1. Seventh Avenue Line	July 1, 1918
2. Lexington Avenue Line	July 17, 1918
"H" System	August 1, 1918
3. Jerome Avenue Line	July 17, 1918
4. Pelham Line	December 20, 1920
5. White Plains Road Line	December 13, 1920
6. Seventh Avenue Line Connection	
To Brooklyn	April 15, 1919
7. Flushing Line	
GCT to Queensboro Plaza	June 22, 1915
Queensboro Plaza to 103rd St.	April 21, 1917
To Times Square	March 14, 1927
To Main St.	January 21, 1928
8. Astoria Line	February 1, 1917
9. Eastern Parkway Line	
To Utica Ave.	August 23, 1920
To New Lots Ave.	October 16, 1922
10. Nostrand Avenue Line	August 23, 1920

Contract No. 4 (BRT Lines)

1. Broadway Line	
Whitehall St. to Times Square	January 5, 1918
To Queensboro Plaza	August 1, 1920
Connection to DeKalb Ave. Station via Manhattan Bridge	September 4, 1917
Connection to DeKalb Ave. Station via Tunnel	August 1, 1920
2. Centre Street Loop	
Williamsburg Bridge to Chambers St.	August 4, 1913
Chambers St. to Battery	May 30, 1931
3. Astoria Line	February 1, 1917
4. 14th St.–Eastern District Line	
Sixth Ave. to Montrose Ave.	June 30, 1924
To Broadway Junction, Brooklyn	July 14, 1928
To Eighth Ave.	May 30, 1931
5. Jamaica Line	July 3, 1918
6. Brighton Line	August 1, 1920
7. Fourth Ave. Line	
To 86th St.	January 15, 1916
To 95th St.	October 31, 1925
8. West End Line	July 21, 1917
9. Culver Line	March 16, 1919
10. Sea Beach Line	June 22, 1915
11. Myrtle Ave. Extension	February 22, 1915
12. Fulton St. (Liberty Ave.) Extension	September 25, 1915

SOURCES: Robert A. Hall, Jr., *New York City Rapid Transit Chronology* (Ann Arbor, Mich.: privately printed, 1945), 6–8. Stan Fischler, *Uptown, Downtown: A Trip through Time on New York's Subways* (New York: Hawthorn Books, 1976), 236–237, 240–241. *New York Times*, September 9, 1932.

Notes

NOTES TO THE INTRODUCTION

1. The cost estimate was about $327 million as of March 19, 1913. *New York Times*, March 19, 1913. By the end of 1913, as more detailed engineering work was done, the Public Service Commission's cost estimate was $366 million. New York State, Public Service Commission for the First District, *New Subways for New York: The Dual System of Rapid Transit* (New York: PSC, December 1913), 3. This is the best base cost estimate. When inflated using the "Construction Cost Index History (1910–1999)" from *Engineering News Record*, March 22–29, 1999, 100, $1 in 1913 was worth $60 in 1999. This means that $366 million in 1913 was equivalent to $21.96 billion in 1999.

2. All of the new subway lines were owned by the City of New York. Some of the older rail facilities that were improved and incorporated into the Dual System were owned by private companies. The dates for the openings of the lines are in Robert A. Hall, *New York City Rapid Transit Chronology* (Ann Arbor, Mich.: privately printed, 1945), 6–8.

3. In 1994, Manhattan's Central Business District (CBD) south of 60th Street had 360 million square feet of nonresidential floor space; the next largest CBD in the United States was Chicago, with 115 million square feet. London had 284 million square feet; all of Greater Paris had 316 million. Urbanomics, *The Future of the Extended Core in the Global Economy* (New York: Report to the Access to the Region's Core Study, June 16, 1995), 5.

4. New York City, Commission on Congestion of Population, *Report of the New York City Commission on Congestion of Population* (New York, February 28, 1911), 85. Hereafter cited as *Congestion Commission Report.*

5. George McAneny, "From Cow Path to Subway: How New York Has Solved Many Problems of Rapid Growth," *Current Affairs in New England* 15 (November 24, 1924): 13, 32.

6. Edward Ewing Pratt, *Industrial Causes of Congestion of Population in New York City*, Columbia University Studies in History, Economics and Public Law no. 109 (New York: Columbia University Press, 1911), 31–32. For maps of the poor areas of New York and of the tenement districts at the turn of the century, see Clara Cardia, *Ils ont construit New York: Histoire de la métropole au XIXe siècle* (Geneva: Georg Editeur, 1987), chap. 5.

7. *Congestion Commission Report*, 80.

8. Pratt, *Causes of Congestion*, 14. By 1910, reformers feared that unless immediate action was taken, many areas in the outlying boroughs would become instant slums. See George McAneny, "Bulletin for Press Release

on Congestion," February 26, 1910, George McAneny Papers, Princeton University.

9. Pratt, *Causes of Congestion*, 32.

10. Lawrence Veiller, "Reminiscences," Lawrence Veiller Oral History Project, Oral History Collection, Columbia University, 1950, 42. Real estate maps of Manhattan circa 1910 show block after solid block of mostly five- and six-story tenements on the entire East Side, east of the Bowery and Third Avenue up to East Harlem, and along much of the West Side west of Eighth Avenue up to around 60th Street (including the area later made famous by *West Side Story*). George W. Bromley and Walter S. Bromley, *Atlas of the City of New York, Borough of Manhattan* (Philadelphia: G. W. Bromley and Co., 1911).

11. Thomas Adams, "The Peculiar Social and Economic Conditions of New York and the Need for a City Plan," *Town Planning Review* 2, no. 3 (October 1911): 190.

12. *Congestion Commission Report*, 85; Pratt, *Causes of Congestion*, 30. Pratt's figure is for 1905. His definition of the Lower East Side includes the area on the East Side up to 14th Street. On the Lower East Side, there were 122 blocks that contained more than 750 persons per acre and 30 blocks containing more than 1,000 per acre. *Congestion Commission Report*, 86.

13. The conditions in New York's tenement areas at the turn of the century are described in Irving Howe, *World of Our Fathers* (New York: Harcourt Brace Jovanovich, 1976), chaps. 6 and 8. See also Moses Rischin, *The Promised City: New York's Jews, 1870–1914* (New York: Harper and Row, 1970), chap. 5.

14. These problems were the subject of the Exhibit on Congestion of Population in New York held at the American Museum of Natural History and at the Brooklyn Institute in spring 1908. Committee on Congestion of Population in New York, *Program of the Conference Held at the Exhibit of Congestion of Population in New York* (New York, 1908). The exhibit was widely reported in the press.

15. Benjamin C. Marsh, "The Public Health as Affected by Congestion of Population," in *Proceedings of the Tenth New York State Conference of Charities and Corrections* (1909), 250. Alan M. Kraut, *Silent Travelers: Germs, Genes, and the "Immigrant Menace"* (Baltimore: Johns Hopkins University Press, 1994), 158–159. René Dubos and Jean Dubos, *The White Plague: Tuberculosis, Man and Society*, rev. ed. (New Brunswick, N.J.: Rutgers University Press, 1996). Katherine Ott, *Fevered Lives: Tuberculosis in American Culture since 1870* (Cambridge: Harvard University Press, 1996). Thomas M. Daniel, *Captain of Death: The Story of Tuberculosis* (Rochester, N.Y.: University of Rochester

Press, 1997). Claude H. Miller, "The Menace of Crowded Cities," *World's Work* 16 (May 1908), 10269. Hermann M. Biggs, "Tuberculosis and the Tenement House Problem," in Robert W. DeForest and Lawrence Veiller, eds., *The Tenement House Problem* (New York: Macmillan, 1903), 1:447.

16. Lawrence Veiller, "Tenement House Reform," in Robert W. DeForest and Lawrence Veiller, eds., *The Tenement House Problem* (New York: Macmillan, 1903), 1:115.

17. N. O. Nelson, "The Remedy for City Congestion," *Independent* 65 (September 24, 1908): 703. In 1908, Mary Simkhovitch, the head of Greenwich House, noted that settlement house workers and reformers were convinced that "back of all the evils of city life lay the dominant evil of congestion of population." Quoted in Richard E. Foglesong, *Planning the Capitalist City: The Colonial Era to the 1920s* (Princeton: Princeton University Press, 1986), 168.

18. New York City, Board of Estimate and Apportionment, Committee on the City Plan, *Development and Present Status of City Planning in New York City* (New York, December 1914). George McAneny, "Program for Comprehensive City Planning in New York City for 1917," typescript, December 21, 1916, George McAneny Papers, Princeton University.

19. The debt limit was set by the New York State Constitution to 10 percent of the assessed value of New York's taxable real estate.

20. Louis Roth, "History of Rapid Transit Development in the City of New York" (Memorandum for Public Service Commissioner Travis H. Whitney, April 3, 1917), 10.

21. Studies conducted by the Public Service Commission had shown that new transit lines to the far reaches of the city would not reap a profit for more than a decade, and that some might never be profitable. The findings of the Public Service Commission are summarized in its *Annual Report, 1908*, 1:28. Bion J. Arnold, *The Traffic of the Subway of the Interborough Rapid Transit Company* (New York, December 31, 1908).

22. William R. Willcox, "The Transportation Problem in New York City," *Harper's Weekly* 54, no. 13 (March 5, 1910): 13.

23. The Brooklyn Rapid Transit Company went into bankruptcy in 1918 and was reorganized as the Brooklyn Manhattan Transit Corporation (BMT) in 1923.

24. For nearly two years, Hearst's *New York American* and *New York Evening Journal*, as well as Pulitzer's *New York World*, attacked in the severest terms the public officials who were negotiating the Dual System contracts. A cartoon in the *Evening Journal* on January 28, 1913, for example, showed a picture of banker J. P. Morgan pulling puppet strings at the end of which

dangled George McAneny, together with Mayor William J. Gaynor, Comptroller William Prendergast, and the Public Service Commission Chairman William R. Willcox. The *American* for the same day had a headline that read: "Twin Forces of Syndicate—Avarice and Monopoly Dictate Subway Deal."

25. George McAneny, "The Responsibility of the City Administration in Regard to Subway Construction," address given at the City Club of Philadelphia, January 27, 1912, George McAneny Papers, Columbia University.

26. *New York Times,* March 19 and 20, 1913.

27. D. L. Turner, "The New Municipal Transportation System for New York City, and Its Relation to the City Plan," *Landscape Architecture* 3, no. 4 (July 1913): 193–194.

28. See Appendix 2. The dates for the openings of the lines are in Hall, *New York City Rapid Transit Chronology,* 6–8.

29. See Table 2 in Chapter 1 for rapid transit ridership from 1901 to 1998.

30. From 1921 to 1929, 420,734 new apartments were constructed in New York City, together with 106,384 single-family and 111,662 two-family homes, a rate never equaled in New York. Richard Plunz, *A History of Housing in New York City: Dwelling Type and Social Change in the American Metropolis* (New York: Columbia University Press, 1990), 123.

31. Marion R. Casey, "'From the East Side to the Seaside': Irish Americans on the Move in New York City," in Ronald H. Bayor and Timothy J. Meagher, eds., *The New York Irish* (Baltimore: Johns Hopkins University Press, 1996): 398–399.

32. Almost all of New York's net population growth between 1910 and 1940 occurred in the districts opened for development by the new Dual System lines. The city's population changes are summarized in Irving M. Plant, *Population Growth of New York City by Districts, 1910–1948* (Report for Consolidated Edison Company, 1948), 4, 17.

33. By 1948, most of the Dual System's subway suburbs had been built up. For this year, one study has estimated that 1,930,000 people traveled to jobs in the Manhattan Central Business District south of 59th Street from all places during 6 to 10 A.M. on an average business day. Of these, 1,025,000 traveled from homes in the Bronx, Brooklyn, and Queens. Of these, 854,000, or 83 percent, took the subway to work, most of them on the lines of the Dual System. Another 575,000 people lived in Manhattan and worked in the Manhattan CBD, 418,000 of them using the subway. Joseph M. Leiper, "Analyze Transit Travel Trends," *Interim Technical Report, Preliminary Summary Tables* (New York: Report to the Transit Service Demand and Supply Evaluation Study, May 1, 1984).

NOTES TO CHAPTER 1

1. The term is from Edward K. Spann, *The New Metropolis: New York City, 1840–1857* (New York: Columbia University Press, 1981).

2. In 1874, the western portion of what is now the Bronx was annexed; in 1895, the district east of the Bronx River became part of New York. In 1898, Greater New York took on its current boundaries, with Brooklyn, Queens, and Staten Island being consolidated with Manhattan and the Bronx. Table 1 shows the population of what is now New York City by borough from 1790 to 1997.

3. Eugene P. Moehring, "Space, Economic Growth, and the Public Works Revolution in New York," in Public Works Historical Society, *Infrastructure and Urban Growth in the Nineteenth Century,* Essays in Public Works History no. 14 (Chicago: Public Works Historical Society, 1985), 45. Spann, *The New Metropolis,* 174–175. George Rogers Taylor, "Building an Intra-Urban Transportation System," in Allan M. Wakstein, ed., *The Urbanization of America: An Historical Anthology* (Boston: Houghton Mifflin, 1970), 144–145.

4. *Sanitary Condition of the City, Report of the Council of Hygiene and Public Health of the Citizens' Association of New York* (New York, 1865), cxxv.

5. Rapid transit is defined as rail lines having their own rights of way, apart from the streets. Trains can operate on elevated structures above the streets, underground in subways, or on grade-separated open-cuts, viaducts, or embankments. In New York, rapid transit service has usually had trains running on frequent headways. All of the rapid transit lines built in the twentieth century in New York are commonly referred to as "subways." These lines are underground in Manhattan, but some are on elevated structures in the outer parts of the city.

6. LeRoy T. Harkness, "The Dual System Contracts in Their Relation to the Rapid Transit History of New York City," in Municipal Engineers of the City of New York, *Proceedings for 1913* (1914), 226.

7. Ibid. Jacob A. Riis, *How the Other Half Lives: Studies among the Tenements of New York* (1890; reprint, New York: Penguin Books, 1997). Housing overcrowding continued to worsen until 1910. Edward Ewing Pratt, *Industrial Causes of Congestion of Population in New York City,* Columbia University Studies in History, Economics and Public Law no. 109 (New York: Columbia University Press, 1911), 26–37.

8. Eric Homberger, *The Historical Atlas of New York City: A Visual Celebration of Nearly 400 Years of New York City's History* (New York: Henry Holt, 1994), 110. Pratt, *Causes of Congestion,* 35.

9. Louis Roth noted that "the recipients of rapid transit franchises were willing to construct only such routes as would yield an immediate return on their investment." Louis Roth, "History of Rapid Transit Development in the City of New York" (Memorandum for Commissioner Whitney, April 3, 1917), 7.

10. In 1907, the New York State Public Service Commission determined that subway lines to outlying areas of the city would be generally unprofitable for the first decade or more after operation began, and that some of them would never cover all of their capital and operating costs. The only subway lines that could make a quick profit were those that traversed heavily developed areas. *New York Times*, September 6, 1907. This finding was reinforced by subsequent studies, including Bion J. Arnold, *The Traffic of The Subway of The Interborough Rapid Transit Company* (New York, December 31, 1908). One of the most significant limitations on potential profits was the fare. From the 1880s on, it became public policy to keep transit fares low, with a five-cent fare becoming the norm. Private companies soon realized that, due to the high costs of subway construction, they could only make substantial profits if trains were very crowded.

11. See Chapter 3 for a discussion of how new rapid transit lines came to be seen primarily as a public responsibility by 1910.

12. Real Estate Analysts, Inc., *Real Estate Trends in New York City with Special Emphasis on the Island of Manhattan* (report prepared for the Committee on Real Estate Trends of the Joint Committee of the Savings Banks Association of the State of New York, Saint Louis, 1942), 1–2.

13. George J. Lankevich, *American Metropolis: A History of New York City* (New York: New York University Press, 1998), 4. Edwin G. Burrows and Mike Wallace, *Gotham: A History of New York City to 1898* (New York: Oxford University Press, 1999), 23–26.

14. Burrows and Wallace, *Gotham*, 62.

15. See Table 1. The area of what is now New York City had 49,000 inhabitants.

16. Paul E. Cohen and Robert T. Augustyn, *Manhattan in Maps, 1527–1995* (New York: Rizzoli, 1997), 96–97.

17. Irving Howe, *World of Our Fathers* (New York: Harcourt Brace Jovanovich, 1976), 151. Robert I. Goler, "George Washington," in Kenneth T. Jackson, ed., *The Encyclopedia of New York City* (New Haven: Yale University Press, 1995), 1242.

18. The plan was devised by surveyor John Randel and approved by a commission established by the New York State Legislature. Edward K. Spann, "The Greatest Grid: The New York Plan of 1811," in David Schaffer, ed., *Two Centuries of American Planning* (Baltimore: Johns Hopkins Univer-

sity Press, 1988), 11–39. Since Manhattan Island does not run directly north to south, the directions are only approximate.

19. The 1811 plan only extended up the island to 155th Street because it was believed that "it is improbable that (for centuries to come) the grounds north of Harlem Flat will be covered with homes." Although this proved incorrect, the 1811 plan largely set the street system of Manhattan south of 155th Street. Quoted in Burrows and Wallace, *Gotham,* 422.

20. In the 1830s, two additional avenues, Madison and Lexington, were inserted. Madison Avenue was placed between Fourth (now Park Avenue north of 32nd Street) and Fifth Avenues; Lexington Avenue was placed between Third and Fourth Avenues. The biggest change to the grid's rigid dominance of the Manhattan landscape was the establishment of Central Park, from 59th to 110th streets, Fifth to Eighth Avenues, from the late 1840s on. Spann, "Greatest Grid," 29, 34.

21. The resulting intersections later became the city's major centers of activity: Union Square (intersection of Broadway and Fourth Avenue at 14th Street), Madison Square (at Fifth Avenue and 23rd Street), Herald Square (Sixth Avenue and 34th Street), Longacre (now Times) Square (Seventh Avenue, north of 42nd Street), and Columbus Circle (at Eighth Avenue and 59th Street).

22. Spann, "Greatest Grid," 19. Burrows and Wallace, *Gotham,* 420–422.

23. Frederick Law Olmsted, one of the designers of Central Park, blamed the grid plan's narrow lots for "the cramped housing which had become a major social and physical curse for New York." Spann, "Greatest Grid," 33.

24. Robert Greenhalgh Albion, *The Rise of New York Port (1815–1860)* (New York: Charles Scribner's Sons, 1939). Lankevich, *American Metropolis,* 112–113. Spann, *The New Metropolis,* chap. 5. Burrows and Wallace, *Gotham,* chap. 38. Moehring, "Public Works Revolution," 33–36.

25. Moehring, "Public Works Revolution," 32, 36–37.

26. Kenneth T. Jackson, *Crabgrass Frontier: The Suburbanization of the United States* (New York: Oxford University Press, 1985), 27–28.

27. Charles Lockwood, *Manhattan Moves Uptown: An Illustrated History* (New York: Barnes and Noble Books, 1995), 42–71, and *Bricks and Brownstone: The New York Row House, 1783–1929: An Architectural and Social History* (New York: McGraw-Hill, 1972), 75–86.

28. John Anderson Miller, *Fares, Please! A Popular History of Trolleys, Horsecars, Streetcars, Buses, Elevateds, and Subways* (New York: Dover Publications, 1960), 1–2.

29. Taylor, "Transportation System," 135–138, 145.

30. Lockwood, *Manhattan Moves Uptown,* chaps. 3–7.

31. By this time, most residential neighborhoods in Manhattan were becoming sharply segregated by class and income level. This was a trend that continued throughout the remainder of the century. Elizabeth Blackmar, "Accountability for Public Health: Regulating the Housing Market in Nineteenth-Century New York City," in David Rosner, ed., *Hives of Sickness: Public Health and Epidemics in New York City* (New Brunswick, N.J.: Rutgers University Press, 1995), 48–61; and Elizabeth Blackmar, *Manhattan for Rent, 1785–1850* (Ithaca, N.Y.: Cornell University Press, 1989), 250–267. See also Anthony Gronowicz, *Race and Class Politics in New York City Before the Civil War* (Boston: Northeastern University Press, 1998), 152–171. Christine Stansell, *City of Women: Sex and Class in New York, 1789–1860* (New York: Alfred A. Knopf, 1986), 217–220.

32. Jackson, *Crabgrass Frontier*, 28.

33. Taylor, "Transportation System," 142–143. Brian J. Cudahy, *Over and Back: The History of Ferryboats in New York Harbor* (New York: Fordham University Press, 1990).

34. Robert C. Brooks, "History of the Street and Rapid Transit Railways of New York City" (Ph.D. diss., Cornell University, 1903), 18.

35. Ibid., 20. Jackson, *Crabgrass Frontier*, 39.

36. Moehring, "Public Works Revolution," 37. Spann, *The New Metropolis*, 107–115, 143–149. John A. Kouwenhoven, *The Columbia Historical Portrait of New York: An Essay in Graphic History* (New York: Harper and Row, 1953), 240–241, 287. Clara Cardia, *Ils ont construit New York: Histoire de la métropole au XIXe siècle* (Geneva: Georg Editeur, 1987), 85–92. Theodore Roosevelt was born in 1858 in such a brownstone at 28 East 20th Street.

37. Taylor, "Transportation System," 148–149.

38. Public Service Commission for the First District of the State of New York (hereafter abbreviated PSC), *Report 1913*, vol. 2, *Statistics of Transportation Companies*, 28.

39. Blackmar, *Manhattan for Rent*, 205–212. Richard Plunz, *A History of Housing in New York City: Dwelling Type and Social Change in the American Metropolis* (New York: Columbia University Press, 1990), 4–8.

40. Howe, *World of Our Fathers*, 151.

41. Cardia, *Ils ont construit*, 122–124. See also Jared N. Day, *Urban Castles: Tenement Housing and Landlord Activism in New York City, 1890–1943* (New York: Columbia University Press, 1999), 13–29.

42. David Rosner, "Introduction: 'Hives of Sickness and Vice,'" in Rosner, ed., *Hives of Sickness*, 7.

43. In 1860, 48 percent of New York's inhabitants were foreign born, 204,000 from Ireland and 120,000 from Germany. Bayrd Still, *Urban America: A History with Documents* (Boston: Little, Brown, 1974), 118.

44. Cardia, *Ils ont construit,* 143–149. Homberger, *Historical Atlas,* 98–99, 136–137. Frederick M. Binder and David M. Reimers, *All the Nations under Heaven: An Ethnic and Racial History of New York City* (New York: Columbia University Press, 1995), 116–135, 245.

45. Iver Bernstein, *The New York Draft Riots: Their Significance for American Society and Politics in the Age of the Civil War* (New York: Oxford University Press, 1990), 17–42.

46. Ibid., 5.

47. *Sanitary Condition of the City,* xv–xvi.

48. Ibid., lxix.

49. Ibid., cxxv–cxliii. Rosner, "Introduction," 3. Plunz, *History of Housing,* 22.

50. Robert C. Reed, *The New York Elevated* (South Brunswick and New York: A. S. Barnes, 1978), 14.

51. The area north of the Harlem River, in what is now the Bronx, was mostly scattered villages and farms. In Brooklyn, only the core areas downtown and along the river had been built up; beyond these areas, most of the land was lightly developed. What is now Queens consisted mostly of fields and farms, and distant Staten Island was a predominantly rural community. Plenty of land was available for suburban development in what are now the suburbs of Westchester and Long Island and across the Hudson River in New Jersey. Thomas Adams, Harold M. Lewis, and Theodore McCrosky, *Population, Land Values and Government: Studies of the Growth and Distribution of Population and Land Values; and of Problems of Government,* vol. 2 of the Regional Survey (New York: Regional Plan of New York and Its Environs, 1929), 65–75. Evelyn Diaz Gonzalez, "City Neighborhoods: Growth and Change in the South Bronx, 1840–1940" (Ph.D. diss., Columbia University, 1993), 64. Burrows and Wallace, *Gotham,* 660–662.

52. Forty-second Street is about four miles north of City Hall. In 1869, one author wrote that in using the horsecars, "one learns cynicism and feels suffocation in daily rides, through the sinuosities and odors of the filthiest streets. There is no monotony, some romance, much danger, and more disgust in the cars." He also noted that certain preparations were desirable before riding a streetcar: "The regular passenger should lose his sense of smell; have the capacity to shut himself up like a patent umbrella . . . hold drunken men and fat women on his lap . . . be skilled as a pugilist and a crackshot with a revolver." Junius Browne in *The Great Metropolis: A Mirror of New York,* quoted in Reed, *The New York Elevated,* 19–20.

53. Taylor, "Transportation System," 139–143. Jackson, *Crabgrass Frontier,* 94–97. Tom Nellison, *Commuter Trains to Grand Central Terminal* (New York: Quadrant Books, 1986), 3–9.

54. Robert C. Sturm, "The Sunrise Trail: A Brief History of the Long Island Rail Road," *National Railway Bulletin* 60, no. 4 (1995): 4–7. Stan Fischler, *Next Stop Grand Central: A Trip through Time on New York's Metropolitan Area Commuter Railroads* (Erin, Ontario: Boston Mills Press, 1986), 15–21. Karl Groh, "Above the Streets of Brooklyn," *Headlights* 37, nos. 9–11 (September–November 1975): 3–9.

55. Taylor, "Transportation System," 143.

56. Private railroad companies, which had built most of these rail lines mainly for long-haul intercity services, sought to attract local passenger traffic to fill up seats that might otherwise be empty, thereby increasing revenues at no increase in cost. To do this, the railroad companies offered a discount to the predominantly upper-income owners of country homes and city businesses. This discount was called a "commutation," that is, a reduced rate from the normal fare. From this comes the term "commuter." Lawrence Grow, *On the 8:02: An Informal History of Commuting by Rail in America* (New York: Mayflower Books, 1979), 25.

57. This was for a commuter ticket. Jackson, *Crabgrass Frontier*, 101.

58. Added to the rail commuter's travel time and cost in getting to work was the extra leg from the rail terminal to Lower Manhattan by ferry or horsecar. The average worker, who put in more than ten hours of labor a day, did not have time to commute by rail, even if he or she could have afforded it. Taylor, "Transportation System," 142.

59. Although the railroad lines influenced the development of the parts of the city through which they passed, the number of passengers was relatively small compared to the carrying capacity of the later rapid transit lines. One of the reasons for this was the comparatively high cost of commuter rail service. Irving M. Plant, *Population Growth of New York City by Districts, 1910–1948* (Report prepared for Consolidated Edison Company of New York, December 1948), 19.

60. Harkness, "Dual System," 225–226.

61. Ibid., 226.

62. Clifton Hood, *722 Miles: The Building of the Subways and How They Transformed New York* (New York: Simon and Schuster, 1993), 50. Benson Bobrick, *Labyrinths of Iron: A History of the World's Subways* (New York: Newsweek Books, 1982), 202–204. The city's newspapers also became enamored of the transforming power of mass transit. The editors of the *New York World* argued in 1871 that the new technology of rapid transit would allow the lateral dispersal of the city, thereby overcoming a host of social ills. "Can We Have a Model City?" *New York World*, October 20, 1871. Cited in Plunz, *History of Housing*, xxx. Similar thoughts were expressed in a fantasy article, "New York A.D. 1900," in which the slums had been broken up and the pop-

ulation dispersed throughout the region. *New York World,* March 27, 1870. Cited in Michael W. Brooks, *Subway City: Riding the Trains, Reading New York* (New Brunswick, N.J.: Rutgers University Press, 1997), 30. This vision of mass transit as a means of disbursing the population was popular in many American cities. See Joel Arthur Tarr, "From City to Suburb: the 'Moral' Influence of Transportation Technology," in Alexander B. Callow, Jr., ed., *American Urban History: An Interpretive Reader with Commentaries,* 2d ed. (New York: Oxford University Press, 1973), 202–212.

63. LeRoy T. Harkness noted with respect to the 1866 promotional literature: "The promoters of this scheme certainly had the courage of their convictions, but the results to flow from the later construction of elevated lines hardly bore out their prophecy." Harkness, "Dual System," 226.

64. Pratt, *Causes of Congestion,* 28, 35.

65. Brian J. Cudahy, *Under the Sidewalks of New York: The Story of the World's Greatest Subway System,* rev. ed. (Lexington, Mass.: Stephen Greene Press, 1988), 14–16.

66. Roth, "History of Rapid Transit Development," 6.

67. Brooks, "Rapid Transit," 188. Jackson, *Crabgrass Frontier,* 119.

68. Harkness, "Dual System," 236.

69. A number of proposals to build rapid transit lines had been made prior to the 1860s. In the 1830s, for example, a magazine called the *New Yorker* advocated a "second story" railway through Broadway. In 1847, a plan was prepared and endorsed by the Mechanic's Institute, again for an elevated railroad. None of these plans came to fruition. Brooks, "Rapid Transit," 133. Harkness, "Dual System," 222. James Blaine Walker, *Fifty Years of Rapid Transit, 1864–1917* (New York: Law Printing Company, 1918), 10, 15.

70. Walker, *Fifty Years,* 10–11. This was the world's first rapid transit line. John R. Day, *The Story of London's Underground* (London: London Transport, 1963), 1.

71. Walker, *Fifty Years,* 11–12. Until 1875, franchises to build and operate rail lines in the city were granted by the New York State Legislature and the governor through the passage of a bill for each proposal. Roth, "Rapid Transit Development," 6.

72. Brooks, "Rapid Transit," 136.

73. *New York Times,* April 11, 1864.

74. A. P. Robinson, *Report upon the Contemplated Metropolitan Railroad of the City of New York* (January 1865), 6–7.

75. Walker, *Fifty Years,* 38–39.

76. Ibid., 58–59.

77. Robert A. Hall, *New York City Rapid Transit Chronology* (Ann Arbor, Mich.: privately printed, 1945), 3.

78. Walker, *Fifty Years,* 79.

79. Joseph Cunningham and Leonard O. DeHart, *A History of the New York City Subway System,* Part I, *The Manhattan Els and the I.R.T.* (privately printed, 1976), 8.

80. Alexander B. Callow, Jr., *The Tweed Ring* (New York: Oxford University Press, 1965), 185.

81. Miller, *Fares, Please!,* 89. Stan Fischler, *Uptown, Downtown: A Trip through Time on New York's Subways* (New York: Hawthorn Books, 1976), 19–27.

82. Callow, *Tweed Ring,* 186. Hood, *722 Miles,* 42–48.

83. Walker, *Fifty Years,* 94–97.

84. Callow, *Tweed Ring,* 185, 187. William Fullerton Reeves, *The First Elevated Railroads in Manhattan and the Bronx of the City of New York* (New York: The New-York Historical Society, 1936), 9–10.

85. Brooks, "Rapid Transit," 149.

86. Walker, *Fifty Years,* 101–102.

87. Brooks, "Rapid Transit," 149.

88. Callow, *Tweed Ring,* 187.

89. Harvey himself was no longer with the company then operating the line. Corning was a politically powerful Albany merchant who had consolidated a number of upstate rail lines into the New York Central Railroad. Neither Harvey nor Corning had a financial interest in the matter—they acted to save the elevated railroad in the public interest. Walker, *Fifty Years,* 84. Reeves, *First Elevated Railroads,* 11.

90. Brooks, "Rapid Transit," 157.

91. Ibid., 154.

92. Ibid., 158. Joseph L. Weiner, "Rapid Transit: History of Rapid Transit in New York City," in New York State Constitutional Convention Committee, *New York City Government: Functions and Problems* (New York, 1938), 5:108.

93. Harkness, "Dual System," 233–235. The Sixth Avenue el also had a branch going up Sixth Avenue to 59th Street.

94. Charles W. Cheape, *Moving the Masses: Urban Public Transit in New York, Boston, and Philadelphia, 1880–1912* (Cambridge: Harvard University Press, 1980), 35.

95. Brooks, "Rapid Transit," 185. Reeves, *First Elevated Railroads,* 23.

96. Fischler, *Uptown, Downtown,* 254.

97. Reeves, *First Elevated Railroads,* 41. Brooks, "Rapid Transit," 185. Cunningham and DeHart, *Subway System* I, 12, 15.

98. The development of the Brooklyn elevated railroad network, as well as of the steam railroad lines in southern Brooklyn that connected to the els, is covered in Walker, *Fifty Years,* 274–283; and Joseph Cunningham and

Leonard DeHart, *A History of the New York City Subway System,* Part II, *Rapid Transit in Brooklyn* (privately printed, 1977). See also Karl Groh, "Above the Streets of Brooklyn," *Headlights* 37, nos. 9–11 (September–November 1975): 2–20; Alan Paul Kahn and Jack May, *The Tracks of New York, Number 2, Brooklyn Elevated Railroads* (New York: n.p., ca. 1975); and James C. Greller and Edward B. Watson, *The Brooklyn Elevated* (Hicksville, N.Y.: N.J. International, ca. 1990s).

99. PSC, *Statistics 1913,* 28.

100. Most horsecar lines were converted to electric operation in the 1890s, becoming streetcars, or "trolleys." Between 1880 and 1900, the street railways provided a basic means of transportation, mainly for short trips. The street railways carried 604 million riders in 1900. Ibid., 28.

101. Adams, Lewis, and McCrosky, *Population, Land Values, and Government,* 73, 152–153. Moehring, "Public Works Revolution," 47. Walter Laidlaw, *Population of the City of New York, 1890–1930* (New York: Cities Census Committee, 1932), 234.

102. Pratt, *Causes of Congestion,* 31–35.

103. Harkness, "Dual System," 236. Roth, "Rapid Transit Development," 7. Cheape, *Moving the Masses,* 72.

104. In the United States, improvements in electric trolley motors led to the opening of the first commercial electric street railway in Montgomery, Alabama, in 1886. Success in Montgomery was followed two years later by Frank J. Sprague's building of an extensive street railway network in Richmond, Virginia, proving conclusively that electric traction was practical. Day, *London's Underground,* 50. Miller, *Fares Please!,* 56, 63–66. Brian J. Cudahy, *Cash, Tokens, and Transfers: A History of Urban Mass Transit in North America* (New York: Fordham University Press, 1990), 39–41, 54, and *Under the Streets,* 14. Harre Demoro, "Frank Julian Sprague: A Transit Genius," *Mass Transit,* 5 (September 1978): 60–61.

105. Cudahy, *Under the Streets,* 14–15.

106. Ibid., 19.

107. Hood, *722 Miles,* 57.

108. Harkness, "Dual System," 236. All subsequent public agencies having control over rapid transit in New York City have been the successors of this first permanent commission. From 1968 on, this agency has been the Metropolitan Transportation Authority (MTA), which has jurisdiction over the subways and buses operated by MTA New York City Transit as well as commuter trains run by MTA Metro-North Railroad and MTA Long Island Rail Road.

109. Chamber of Commerce of the State of New York, *Rapid Transit in New York City and in Other Great Cities* (New York, 1905), 56.

110. Walker, *Fifty Years,* 136. Mark David Hirsch, *William C. Whitney: Modern Warwick* (New York: Dodd, Mead, 1948), 433. James Blaine Walker to George McAneny, February 5, 1925, George McAneny Papers, Princeton University. Ray Stannard Baker, "'The Subway Deal': How New York City Built Its New Underground Railroad," *McClure's Magazine* 24, no. 5 (March 1905): 457.

111. Chamber of Commerce, *Rapid Transit,* 57, 60.

112. Abram S. Hewitt, "Address before Proceedings on the Presentation of a Gold Medal," in Board of Rapid Transit Railroad Commissioners for and in the City of New York (hereafter abbreviated RTB), *Report, 1901,* 106.

113. Chamber of Commerce, *Rapid Transit,* 61.

114. Ibid., 64.

115. Ibid., 68.

116. Henry C. Wright, "Development of Transit Control in New York City," *Annals of the American Academy of Political and Social Science* 31 (May 1908): 560.

117. Chamber of Commerce, *Rapid Transit,* 72.

118. Ibid., 74, 76, 84. RTB, *Report, 1901,* 16–17.

119. Besides the ex officio members, Board members included Alexander E. Orr, William Steinway, John Claflin, John H. Starin, and Seth Low. With the exception of Low, who was president of Columbia University, these men were all prominent businessmen of New York and Brooklyn. Walker, *Fifty Years,* 106. Chamber of Commerce, *Rapid Transit,* 84.

120. An additional sum also would be paid to the City, representing not less than 1 percent of the value of the bonds, to serve as a sinking fund. Chamber of Commerce, *Rapid Transit,* 74.

121. Ibid., 74–75.

122. Ibid., 90.

123. RTB, *Report, 1901,* 26, 37.

124. Brooks, "Rapid Transit," 223.

125. Walker, *Rapid Transit,* 155.

126. RTB, *Report, 1901,* 41.

127. These included the Chamber of Commerce, the City Club, the Citizens Union, and the Reform Club. Brooks, "Rapid Transit," 223.

128. *New York Times,* January 13, 1900.

129. *New York Times,* May 27, 1898.

130. Brooks, "Rapid Transit," 229.

131. Chamber of Commerce, *Rapid Transit,* 111.

132. The City agency in charge of parks, for example, started proceedings against the elevated railroad tracks in Battery Park; the tracks had been there for more than two decades. Brooks, "Rapid Transit," 237.

133. Ibid., 231.

134. John T. Hettrick Oral History Project, Oral History Collection, Columbia University, 1949, 77.

135. RTB, *Report, 1901*, 73.

136. Chamber of Commerce, *Rapid Transit*, 106.

137. Hettrick Oral History, 78–79.

138. Chamber of Commerce, *Rapid Transit*, 119.

139. Hettrick Oral History, 76.

140. Arthur J. Waterman, Jr., "Integration of Rapid Transit Facilities of the City of New York" (Ph.D. diss., New York University, 1940), 85.

141. Baker, "The Subway Deal," 461. Walker, *Fifty Years*, 167.

142. Interborough Rapid Transit Company, *The New York Subway: Its Construction and Equipment* (New York, 1904), 13.

143. Roth, "Rapid Transit Development," 14.

144. Chamber of Commerce, *Rapid Transit*, 152.

145. Ibid., 157.

146. Ibid., 152, 154.

147. Ibid., 158.

148. Cynthia Morse Latta, "The Return on the Investment in the Interborough Rapid Transit Company" (Ph.D. diss., Columbia University, 1975), 30.

149. Walker, *Fifty Years*, 186.

150. Ibid., 186. The rapid transit lines constructed under Contracts No. 1 and No. 2 will be referred to collectively as the "first subway."

151. Latta, "Return on the Investment in the IRT," 109–112. Hood, *722 Miles*, 123.

152. In addition to the rapid transit lines, New York's street railways carried a total of 764 million riders in 1910, 428 million in Manhattan and the Bronx, 349 million in Brooklyn and Queens, and 12 million on Staten Island. PSC, *Statistics, 1913*, 28–29.

153. Boris Pushkarev, Jeffrey M. Zupan, and Robert S. Cumella, *Urban Rail in America: An Exploration of Criteria for Fixed-Guideway Transit* (Bloomington: Indiana University Press, 1982), Appendix, Table H-5.

154. The "New Law" was the New York State Tenement House Act of 1901. This law aimed to improve housing conditions in New York City.

155. Gonzalez, "City Neighborhoods," 244–252. Howe, *World of Our Fathers*, 132. Hood, *722 Miles*, 108–112.

156. New York City, Commission on Congestion of Population, *Report of the New York City Commission on Congestion of Population* (New York, February 28, 1911), 8.

157. Hood, *722 Miles*, 105–108.

158. Gilbert Osofsky, *Harlem: The Making of a Ghetto, Negro New York 1890–1930* (New York: Harper and Row, 1963), 89–93. See also James Weldon Johnson, *Black Manhattan* (New York: Alfred A. Knopf, 1930).

NOTES TO CHAPTER 2

1. Board of Rapid Transit Railroad Commissioners for and in the City of New York (hereafter abbreviated RTB), *Report, 1901,* 85, and *Report, 1903,* 207. *New York Times,* March 25, 1900. "Subway network" means subway lines—that is, underground lines—in Manhattan and connections to these lines in the outlying boroughs. Some of the connections or extensions to the Manhattan subway lines were actually elevated lines. In the southern Bronx, for example, the first "subway" in the Bronx ran as an elevated line north of 149th Street. The terms "route" and "line" are used synonymously.

2. RTB, *Report, 1905,* 12. Chamber of Commerce of the State of New York, *Rapid Transit in New York and in Other Great Cities* (New York, 1905), 177–189.

3. Public Service Commission for the First District of the State of New York (hereafter abbreviated PSC), *Combination Map of the Rapid Transit Routes in Greater New York* (New York, December 31, 1909). This map shows the status of all rapid transit routes in the City of New York at the end of 1909, including existing lines as well as proposed lines that were in various stages of planning or construction. See also PSC, "History and Description of Rapid Transit Routes in New York City," in *Annual Report 1909,* 1:251–254.

4. Brian J. Cudahy, *Under the Sidewalks of New York: The Story of the World's Greatest Subway System,* rev. ed. (Lexington, Mass.: Stephen Greene Press, 1988), 27.

5. Parsons Brinckerhoff Quade and Douglas, Inc., Historical Perspectives, Inc., and Robert A. Olmsted, P.E., *Phase I: Reconnaissance Level Historical Survey of Transit Authority Properties. Task 1 Report: The New York City Transit System—Historical Context and Evaluation Parameters* (Report to the New York City Transit Authority, June 1991), III-2.

6. Subway expansion remained one of the top issues for two decades, including the municipal elections of 1905, 1909, 1913, 1917, 1921, and 1925. Michael W. Brooks, *Subway City: Riding the Trains, Reading New York* (New Brunswick, N.J.: Rutgers University Press, 1997), 78. Clifton Hood, *722 Miles: The Building of the Subways and How They Transformed New York* (New York: Simon and Schuster, 1993), 187–189, 197. Joel Fischer, "Urban Transportation: Home Rule and the Independent Subway System in New York City, 1917–1925" (Ph.D. diss., St. Johns University, 1978), 90–92,

138–147, 299–303. Peter Derrick, "The New York City Transit Crisis of 1918–1925" (Master's thesis, Columbia University, 1967), 26–31.

7. RTB, *Report, 1903.* 211. *New York Times,* December 13, 1900.

8. RTB, *Report, 1902,* 65.

9. RTB, *Report, 1903,* 11.

10. As was discussed in Chapter 1, the reason for this illogical route was the $50 million limit on City borrowing for subways.

11. RTB, *Report, 1903,* 209–211.

12. Ibid., 209–212. *New York Times,* November 12, 1902. James Blaine Walker, *Fifty Years of Rapid Transit, 1864–1917* (New York: Law Printing Company, 1918), 186.

13. RTB, *Report, 1903,* 215.

14. Richard Stephen Skolnik, "The Crystallization of Reform in New York City, 1890–1917" (Ph.D. diss., Yale University, 1964), 273.

15. Parts of Queens were served by lines of the Long Island Rail Road, some of which connected to a ferry across the East River to 34th Street in Manhattan. From 1910 on, there was direct service to Pennsylvania Station in Manhattan. Robert C. Sturm, "The Sunrise Trail: A Brief History of the Long Island Rail Road," *National Railway Bulletin* 60, no. 4 (1995): 7, 11.

16. The Broadway (Brooklyn) elevated line was to be extended from its existing terminus near the Brooklyn-Queens border to Jamaica, Queens. The Fulton Street line was to be extended from the Brooklyn-Queens border to Richmond Hill. RTB, *Report, 1903,* 220.

17. Originally, the loop was to connect to the rail line coming across the Brooklyn Bridge, but this never happened. Instead, under later plans, the loop was extended from Chambers Street south to the Battery, connecting to a new BRT subway tunnel to Downtown Brooklyn.

18. RTB, *Report, 1903,* 218.

19. This area of Brooklyn was not served by any existing rapid transit line. Ibid., 219.

20. RTB, *Report, 1904,* 12.

21. The mayor, the comptroller and the president of the Board of Aldermen each had three votes on the Board of Estimate. The borough presidents of Manhattan and Brooklyn had two votes each, and the remaining borough presidents from the Bronx, Queens, and Richmond, one vote apiece.

22. PSC, *Annual Report, 1908,* 39. The total amount of such debt was in the hundreds of millions of dollars, but much of it had already been committed to other public works.

23. *New York Times,* May 25, 1905. This was the result of an effort by reformers and business leaders to reduce the influence of locally elected

officials, who were accused of incompetence. According to Lawrence Veiller, who lobbied for the change in Albany, control over new rapid transit lines needed to be vested in a body whose members took a citywide rather than a localistic view of the city's future development. The Board of Estimate was so constituted that it would decide on new transit routes only after lengthy discussion. As a small group whose members were in the public eye, the Board also could be easily held accountable for its actions. Lawrence Veiller Oral History Project, Oral History Collection, Columbia University, 1949, 12.

24. The appointed members were John Claflin, Woodbury Langdon, Alexander Orr, Charles Stewart Smith, and John H. Starin. Walker, *Fifty Years,* 181.

25. RTB, *Report, 1903,* 21.

26. The RTB believed that private transportation companies would be willing "to construct and operate rapid transit railroads without calling upon the city to advance its credit in the undertaking to the full extent, and perhaps not to any extent at all." RTB, *Report, 1905,* 15.

27. LeRoy T. Harkness, "The Dual System Contracts in Their Relation to the Rapid Transit History of New York City," Municipal Engineers of the City of New York, *Proceedings for 1913* (1914), 246. *New York Times,* January 13, 1905.

28. RTB, *Report, 1904,* 13–15.

29. *New York Times,* January 13, 1905.

30. John T. Hettrick Oral History Project, Oral History Collection, Columbia University, 1949, 4. *New York Times,* October 3, 1907.

31. "The 'Yellow Dog' in Rapid Transit," *Outlook* 87 (October 12, 1907): 273.

32. *New York Times,* October 28, 1904. Chamber of Commerce, *Rapid Transit,* 162–174. Hood, *722 Miles,* 91–96. Stan Fischler, *Uptown, Downtown: A Trip through Time on New York's Subways* (New York: Hawthorn Books, 1976), 41.

33. RTB, *Report, 1905,* 11.

34. *New York Times,* January 13, 1905.

35. RTB, *Report, 1905,* 12, 15.

36. Cynthia Morse Latta, "The Return on the Investment in the Interborough Rapid Transit Company" (Ph.D. diss., Columbia University, 1975), 338.

37. Chamber of Commerce, *Rapid Transit,* 177–189. *New York Times,* March 31, 1905.

38. Henry M. MacCracken to Alexander E. Orr, March 1, 1905, and Louis Rodney Berg to Henry M. MacCracken, March 3, 1905, Henry M.

MacCracken Papers, New York University Archives. This subway would connect to one of the north-south lines on the East Side of Manhattan.

39. Chamber of Commerce, *Rapid Transit,* 184–188. RTB, *Report, 1905,* 13. *New York Times,* April 7, 1905.

40. RTB, *Report, 1905,* 19, 40.

41. *New York Tribune,* December 23, 1905.

42. At one point, the company had even proposed that it be given a perpetual franchise to build and operate a subway, as opposed to municipal ownership. Hettrick Oral History, 78. Charles W. Cheape, *Moving the Masses: Urban Public Transit in New York, Boston, and Philadelphia, 1880–1912* (Cambridge: Harvard University Press, 1980), 89.

43. Burton J. Hendrick, "Great American Fortunes and Their Making: Street Railway Financiers," *McClure's Magazine* 30 (January 1, 1908): 323–325. Hettrick Oral History, 2. Walker, *Fifty Years,* 193.

44. Hettrick Oral History, 2. *New York Times,* December 24, 1905.

45. Hettrick Oral History, 3.

46. Quigg was paid $151,000 over a two-year period for his efforts in accelerating public support for the Metropolitan subway proposals. *New York Times,* October 3, 1907.

47. Hendrick, "Great American Fortunes," 335.

48. Walker, *Fifty Years,* 198.

49. Ibid. Hettrick Oral History, 8.

50. The complex financial arrangements that were made are discussed in Latta, "The Return on the Investment in the IRT," 74–82.

51. Hettrick Oral History, 125–126.

52. Walker, *Fifty Years,* 198. Latta, in "The Return on the Investment in the IRT," 74, says that before the merger Belmont did not realize how desperate the situation was with the Metropolitan Street Railway Company.

53. Quoted in "Traction Merger in New York City," *Outlook* 82 (January 6, 1906): 2.

54. According to Comptroller Grout, the municipality had only $50 million within the debt limit to spend on new subways. *New York Times,* December 27, 1905.

55. *New York Times,* January 13, 1906.

56. *New York Times,* January 17, 1906.

57. Gustavus Myers, *The History of Tammany Hall* (New York: Boni and Liveright, 1917), 388, 393. Irwin Yellowitz, *Labor and the Progressive Movement New York State, 1897–1916* (Ithaca, N.Y.: Cornell University Press, 1965), 107.

58. Augustus Cerillo, Jr., "Reform in New York City: A Study of Urban Progressivism" (Ph.D. diss., Northwestern University, 1969), 142, 145.

59. Besides being elected governor in 1906, Hughes was the Republican

presidential candidate in 1916 and later became chief justice of the U.S. Supreme Court.

60. William J. Gaynor, "New York's Subway Policy," *Municipal Affairs* 5 (1901): 434.

61. Senator Elsberg claimed that these defeats were the result of close ties between Tammany leaders and the private transportation companies. William Russell Hochman, "William J. Gaynor: The Years of Fruition" (Ph.D. diss., Columbia University, 1955), 355. City Club of New York, *Annual Report, 1905,* 31. *New York Times,* April 24, 1903, March 20, 1904, April 5, 1905.

62. *New York World,* March 13, 1905.

63. Roy Stannard Baker, "'The Subway Deal': How New York City Built Its Underground Railroad," *McClure's Magazine* 25 (March 1905): 453, 460.

64. Yellowitz, *Labor and the Progressive Movement,* 212.

65. According to Gustavus Myers, the Hearst newspapers neglected no means "to awaken popular resentment against the 'plunderbund' fattening on the people, and to arouse popular indignation against the bossism of Tammany Hall. Day after day effective articles, editorials and cartoons were published, written in a simple style, understandable by the crudest intelligence, . . . [which] produced a great effect among the voters. Nothing quite like this original kind of political journalism had ever been known in New York City." Myers, *Tammany Hall,* 309.

66. For an analysis of different interpretations of Hearst's motives, see James Allan Myatt, "William Randolph Hearst and the Progressive Era, 1900–1912" (Ph.D. diss., University of Florida, 1960), 160ff. Michael W. Brooks says that Hearst "exploited the myth of the Traction Trust demagogically, using it to advance his own political ambitions long after it had lost all correspondence with reality. . . . In the end his influence on the subway was largely destructive." Brooks, *Subway City,* 75. According to a recent Hearst biographer, other than President Theodore Roosevelt, in the first decade of the twentieth century the publisher "was arguably the best-known American, not just in the United States but in the world." Ben Proctor, *William Randolph Hearst: The Early Years, 1863–1910* (New York: Oxford University Press, 1998), 193.

67. Proctor, *Hearst,* 163–192.

68. Yellowitz, *Labor and the Progressive Movement,* 199.

69. *World's Work,* December, 1906, 8256.

70. Brooks, *Subway City,* 75. Proctor, *Hearst,* 173–177.

71. Proctor, *Hearst,* 189–192.

72. Yellowitz, *Labor and the Progressive Movement,* 188. Brooks, *Subway City,* 76.

73. Hood, *722 Miles,* 128–129.

74. George B. McClellan, Jr., *The Gentleman and the Tiger: The Autobiography of George B. McClellan, Jr.*, ed. Harold C. Syrett (Philadelphia: Lippincott, 1956), 237. Myers, *Tammany Hall,* 322.

75. Herbert Mitgang, *The Man Who Rode the Tiger: The Life and Times of Judge Samuel Seabury and the Story of the Greatest Investigation of City Corruption in This Century* (New York: Viking Press, 1963), 84.

76. *New York Times,* November 1, 1905.

77. Mitgang, *The Man Who Rode the Tiger,* 85. Proctor, *Hearst,* 210. The final tally was determined by the New York State Supreme Court in 1908, after years of litigation by Hearst, who claimed that the election had been stolen from him. Myatt, "Hearst," 75.

78. *New York Times,* February 7, 1906, August 27, 1906. Walker, *Fifty Years,* 199.

79. Hood, *722 Miles,* 130.

80. RTB, *Report, 1906,* 266–267.

81. Interborough Rapid Transit Company, *Annual Report for Year Ended June 30, 1910* (New York, 1911), 31–32. Latta, "The Return on the Investment in the IRT," 253.

82. RTB, *Report, 1906,* 55–59. *New York Times,* June 23, 1906, October 14, 1906.

83. *New York Times,* January 8, 1907.

84. RTB, *Report, 1906,* 266.

85. PSC, "Report of George S. Rice," *Annual Report, 1907,* 1:232–233.

86. Ibid.

87. *New York Times,* April 12, 1906.

88. PSC, *Annual Report, 1907,* 1:233.

89. Robert H. Wiebe, *The Search for Order, 1877–1920* (New York: Hill and Wang, 1967), 168.

90. Myatt, "Hearst," 84.

91. Robert F. Wesser, *Charles Evans Hughes and Reform in New York, 1905–1910* (Ithaca, N.Y.: Cornell University Press, 1967), 87–88.

92. Proctor, *Hearst,* 221–226.

93. Ibid., 225–226.

94. Wesser, *Hughes,* 98.

95. Hughes's proposal, known as the Page-Merritt bill, had the active support of New York civic groups and taxpayers' organizations. In turn, Hughes actively sought the advice of the leaders of such groups and incorporated their recommendations into legislation that was being prepared. Leaders of the City Club, for example, met with Hughes in January to discuss rapid transit matters. They urged him to give the PSC the authority to

study the transit problems of all the boroughs and to make detailed studies of population movements in order to determine the best areas for new lines. Hughes accepted these recommendations. Cerillo, "Reform in New York City," 153. Wesser, *Hughes*, 154. David I. Aronson, "The City Club of New York, 1892–1912" (Ph.D. diss., New York University, 1975), 525.

96. Testimony of William M. Ivins, in State of New York Joint Legislative Committee to Investigate the Public Service Commissions, *Final Report* (Albany, 1915), 2:1393. At the instigation of William Randolph Hearst, the State Legislature established two committees to investigate the two Public Service Commissions, one in 1915, the second in 1916. Both of these committees were chaired by Senator George F. Thompson of Niagara County and were referred to as the Thompson Committees. These committees tried to find evidence of corruption in the events leading up to the approval of the Dual System in 1913, but came away empty handed.

97. Wesser, *Hughes*, 155, 167.

98. Cerillo, "Reform in New York City," 157.

99. Milo R. Maltbie, "Fruits of Public Regulation in New York," *Annals of the American Academy of Political and Social Science* 37, no. 1 (January 1911): 170–171. PSC, *Annual Report, 1907*, 9–10.

100. Harkness, "Dual System," 250.

101. Walker, *Fifty Years*, 201. Hood, *722 Miles*, 287.

102. Maltbie was an economist who, together with Calvin Tomkins and John Martin, had written the Municipal Art Society's *Report on Rapid Transit in New York City* (Bulletin No. 14, 1904). He had also authored "Rapid Transit Subways in Metropolitan Cities," *Municipal Affairs* 4, no. 3 (September 1900): 458–480. Hood, *722 Miles*, 287.

103. Hood, *722 Miles*, 287. Edward M. Bassett, *Autobiography of Edward M. Bassett* (New York: Harbor Press, 1939), 108–110. *New York Times*, June 29, 1907.

104. *New York Times*, June 29, 1907.

105. Ibid.

106. Walker, *Fifty Years*, 209.

107. Ibid., 209. Inflated using the Consumer Price Index, $15,000 in 1907 dollars amounts to about $273,000 in year 2000 dollars. Calculations by Emanuel Tobier from U.S. Department of Commerce, *Historical Statistics of the United States* (Washington, D.C., 1975), and Bureau of Labor Statistics data from various issues of the *Statistical Abstract of the United States.*

108. Richard S. Skolnik, "Civic Group Progressives in New York City," *New York History*, 51, no. 4 (July 1970): 430.

109. Aronson, "City Club," 494. City Club, *Annual Report, 1909*, 8. The City Club was supported financially by many of the top business, banking,

and commercial leaders of the time. The major contributors to the City Club's civic fund between October 1908 and November 1909, for example, included I. N. Seligman, Andrew Carnegie, Felix M. Warburg, Paul M. Warburg, and Jacob H. Schiff. Typewritten list of contributors, George McAneny Papers, Princeton University.

110. City Club, Board of Trustees, *Minutes*, June 18, 1907. City Club, "New York City Transit: A Memorandum to the Public Service Commission of the First District" (July 22, 1907).

111. City Club, "New York City Transit," 46.

112. Ibid., 48.

113. Ibid., 50. Until this time, rapid transit planning had not addressed such issues. From the perspective of current American transportation planning practice, however, such questions must be addressed before any new lines are built. Transportation planners are expected to carefully assess the mobility needs of a community and then come up with proposals to meet these needs as cost-effectively as possible. The planners are also supposed to analyze the future ridership of new transportation services and their impact on urban development. In addition, they are expected to determine the capital costs of constructing new lines and equipment. Planners must also calculate future operating costs and revenues. See, for example, Michael D. Meyer and Eric. J. Miller, *Urban Transportation Planning: A Decision-Oriented Approach* (New York: McGraw-Hill, 1984).

114. *New York Times*, January 1, 1908.

115. Walker, *Fifty Years*, 213. *New York Times*, February 28, 1908.

116. *New York Times*, February 28, 1908.

117. *New York Times*, September 6, 1907.

118. Bion J. Arnold, *The Traffic of the Subway of the Interborough Rapid Transit Company* (December 31, 1908).

119. Bion J. Arnold, *The Return on the Investment of the Subway of the Interborough Rapid Transit Company* (February 21, 1909).

120. Ibid. Latta, "The Return on the Investment in the IRT," 116–118.

121. PSC, *Annual Report, 1908*, 1:28. According to Commissioner Bassett, in 1908 there was no doubt that the City of New York did not have the means, within the limits of its borrowing capacity, to build an extensive new rapid transit system by itself, and that private capital was not interested in investing in a large number of new lines simultaneously because it would not be profitable. After making this point, Bassett stated: "That is the plain, definite, unquestioned situation at this time. Discussion cannot make it clearer, but discussion by competent and authoritative persons such as the Public Service Commissioners may make it more widely understood." *New York Times*, March 22, 1908.

122. Latta, "The Return on the Investment in the IRT," 113–115. Chapter 7 of Latta's dissertation is titled "Subway Operation Proves Less Profitable Than Supposed."

123. Cyrus Adler, *Jacob H. Schiff: His Life and Letters* (New York: Doubleday Doran, 1928), 1:343–344.

124. Walker, *Fifty Years*, 214. *New York Times*, April 12, 1907. McClellan was a conservative Democrat who believed that the government should not be involved in the regulation or operation of public utilities. He attacked the PSC as "government by inquisition." *New York Times*, April 6, 1908.

125. *New York Times*, May 6, 1909.

126. *New York Times*, July 18, 1907.

127. Roth, "Rapid Transit Development," 10, 16, 17. PSC, *Annual Report, 1907*, 14.

128. Chamber of Commerce of the State of New York, *Report on Rapid Transit Conditions* (New York, February 25, 1909) 24. Adler, *Jacob Schiff*, 1:343. This limitation on New York City's borrowing capacity was still in effect in the year 2000. *New York Times*, January 29, 2000.

129. Walker, *Fifty Years*, 216. This amendment to the State Constitution had to be approved by the voters. Final approval was given in 1909.

130. Ibid., 217. Roth, "Rapid Transit Development," 16–17.

131. Milo R. Maltbie, "A Rapid Transit Policy for Greater New York," in Clyde Lyndon King, ed., *The Regulation of Municipal Utilities* (New York: D. Appleton, 1909), 125–127. George McAneny to C. H. Strong, January 18, 1908, George McAneny Papers, Princeton University. PSC, *Annual Report, 1909*, 1:59. Chamber of Commerce, *Report on Rapid Transit Conditions*, 19. Roth, "Rapid Transit Development," 21.

132. This controversy was summarized in a series of public letters between Calvin Tomkins and Allen Robinson, which were published as *The Subway Policy of the City of New York* by the Municipal Affairs Committee of the Reform Club in March 1909.

133. The assessment plan was one of the products of the City Club's ongoing studies of New York's transit situation. The club had determined that property values along the route of the first subway had shown marked increases between 1893 and 1900. The area one-half mile wide on each side of Broadway between 135th Street and 230th Street, for example, had shown a 104 percent increase in value, amounting to more than $49 million. The construction cost of the subway between 135th Street and 230th Street had been about $7 million. Calculations showed that debt service on the bonds sold to build the subway could have been paid for out of just a small portion of the increase in tax revenues resulting from the higher property values. City Club, *Building of Rapid Transit Lines in New York City by*

Assessment upon Property Benefitted: Memorandum to the Board of Estimate and Apportionment and the Public Service Commission of the First District (October 2, 1908), 5.

134. Ibid., 9.

135. "Rapid Transit Relief for New York City," *Outlook* 92 (May 1, 1909): 6.

136. PSC, *Annual Report, 1908,* 1:29–30.

137. Roth, "Rapid Transit Development," 17.

138. Harkness, "Dual System," 256.

139. *New York Times,* March 28, 1908. Roth, "Rapid Transit Development," 19.

140. *New York Times,* April 7, 1908.

141. This injunction had been obtained by Jefferson M. Levy, a lawyer, on the representation of Comptroller Metz. PSC, *Annual Report, 1909,* 1:65.

142. *New York Times,* June 13, 1908.

143. *New York Times,* April 9, 1909.

144. For the fiscal year ending June 30, 1906, the IRT paid a dividend of 8.25 percent on its capital stock. From 1907 to 1910, the company paid a yearly dividend of 9 percent. Interborough Rapid Transit Company, *Annual Report for Year Ended June 30, 1910,* 31–32. The return on the IRT's own investment in constructing the subway and providing the subway cars was 11.4 percent in 1908, 15.9 percent in 1909, and 18.2 percent in 1910. This figure is misleading with respect to the potential return on new investment, however, since most of the investment in the construction of the first subway was made by the City of New York. The return for the total investment of the City and the IRT in the subway constructed under Contracts No. 1 and No. 2 was 7.1 percent in 1908, 8.8 percent in 1909, and 10 percent in 1911. Latta, "The Return on the Investment in the IRT," 253.

145. PSC, *Report, 1913,* 2:29.

146. Latta, "The Return on the Investment in the IRT," 94–97.

147. Ibid., 116.

148. In a speech before a group of real estate men in January, 1908, August Belmont, chairman of the IRT's board of directors, criticized the PSC's development of the Triborough System as a financial impossibility. Belmont said that not another foot of new transportation lines would be built in New York unless some arrangement was made with those whose capital was already invested in transportation lines. *New York Times,* January 12, 1908.

149. William R. Willcox, "The Transportation Problem in New York City," *Harper's Weekly* 54, no. 13 (March 5, 1910): 13.

150. *New York Times,* April 15, 1909. Interborough Rapid Transit Company, *We Are Ready to Act* (pamphlet, ca. April 1909), New York Public Library.

151. *New York Times,* March 19, 1909.

152. The company did say it would equip and operate the Fourth Avenue subsystem, provided the City guaranteed to cover any losses. The cost of the Triborough System was estimated at $127 million, of which $101 million would be provided by the company and the balance by the City. Roth, "Rapid Transit Development," 28–29. *New York Times,* June 19, 1909.

153. The company believed that a four-track subway up Lexington Avenue would be too expensive to build.

154. Roth, "Rapid Transit Development," 27–28.

155. Ibid., 28.

156. Ibid.

157. *New York Times,* July 20, 1909.

158. *New York Times,* August 16, 1909.

159. PSC, *Annual Report, 1909,* 1:31.

160. Ibid., 1:33.

161. Ibid., 1:35.

162. Ibid., 1:36–37.

163. The Civic Alliance stood for municipal ownership and operation of rapid transit lines in the same manner as the Municipal Ownership League of 1905. It was organized specifically for the 1909 election.

164. The details of the 1909 election are discussed in Hochman, "Gaynor," 62–116, 387–393.

165. William Jay Schieffelin of the Citizen's Union, for example, had written to George McAneny suggesting an anti-Tammany campaign, the key issue of which would be "the failure to provide for adequate interborough transit facilities." McAneny replied to Schieffelin that he agreed that subways were the main issue. William Jay Schieffelin to George McAneny, March 11, 1909, and George McAneny to William Jay Schieffelin, March 14, 1909, George McAneny Papers, Princeton University.

166. *New York Telegram,* May 9, 1909. *New York Press,* May 10, 1909.

167. Bannard Fusion Campaign, *New York's Opportunity* (campaign pamphlet, 1909), George McAneny Papers, Princeton University.

168. The Fusionists were willing to accept the Republican nominees because the Republicans had selected a ticket composed of both Republicans and independent Democrats. Hochman, "Gaynor," 77.

169. Ibid., 76.

170. Edwin R. Lewinson, *John Purroy Mitchel: The Boy Mayor of New York* (New York: Astra Books, 1965), 35–36.

171. *New York Times,* September 24, 1909.

172. Hochman, "Gaynor," 77.
173. Ibid, 84–85.
174. Ibid., 22.
175. Ibid., 79.
176. William J. Gaynor, "The Looting of New York," *Pearson's Magazine* 21 (May 1909): 461–473. One contemporary observer believed that this article had contributed more to Gaynor's election than anything he had said or done during the campaign. William Lustgarten to William J. Gaynor, August 1, 1910, cited in Hochman, "Gaynor," 389.
177. *Our City: The Story of a Progressive People* (Democratic campaign pamphlet, 1909), George McAneny papers, Princeton University.
178. Hochman, "Gaynor," 98–101.
179. Had the Republican-Fusionists selected a candidate more acceptable to Hearst, they probably also would have won the mayoral race, because Bannard and Hearst together polled 57 percent of the vote. Prendergast and Mitchel, the only other candidates running for citywide office, polled 57 percent and 56 percent of the vote, respectively. Ibid., 108.
180. PSC, *Annual Report, 1909,* 1:70.
181. *New York Times,* October 30, 1909. After the election, the PSC proceeded to let the contracts to the bidders it had chosen in 1908. PSC, *Annual Report, 1909,* 1:11.
182. Roth, "Rapid Transit Development," 30.
183. *New York Times,* November 14, 1909.
184. These prospects had been reinforced by voter approval in the 1909 elections of an amendment to the State Constitution allowing self-supporting subway and dock bonds to be exempt from the calculation of the City's debt limit. The Legislature had approved this proposal in both 1908 and 1909. *New York Times,* November 14, 1909.
185. Hochman, "Gaynor," 394.

NOTES TO CHAPTER 3

1. New York City, Commission on Congestion of Population, *Report of the New York City Commission on Congestion of Population* (New York, February 28, 1911), 5. This report was reprinted in *City Record* 34, no. 11500 (March 7, 1911): 1830–1902. Hereafter cited as *Congestion Commission Report.*
2. *Congestion Commission Report,* 8. Edward Ewing Pratt, *Industrial Causes of Congestion of Population in New York City* Columbia University Studies in History, Economics and Public Law 43, no. 1, Whole Number 109 (New York: Columbia University Press, 1911), 28, 35.
3. Carol Willis, *Form Follows Finance: Skyscrapers and Skylines in New York*

and Chicago (New York: Princeton Architectural Press, 1995), 18–23, 34–47. Sarah Bradford Landau and Carl W. Condit, *Rise of the New York Skyscraper, 1865–1913* (New Haven: Yale University Press, 1996), 298–330, 347–397.

4. Landau and Condit, *Rise of the New York Skyscraper,* 382. The bird's-eye view is on 396–397. The architecture of New York during this period is discussed in detail in Robert A. M. Stern, Gregory Gilmartin, and John Montague Massengale, *New York 1900: Metropolitan Architecture and Urbanism, 1890–1915* (New York: Rizzoli, 1983). This book has numerous photographs and illustrations.

5. The amount of each lot these factories occupied can be seen in real estate atlases from the period. See, for example, George W. Bromley and Walter S. Bromley, *Atlas of the City of New York, Borough of Manhattan* (Philadelphia: G. W. Bromley and Co., 1911). Pratt, *Causes of Congestion,* 45. Emanuel Tobier, "Manhattan's Business District in the Industrial Age," in John Hull Mollenkopf, ed., *Power, Culture and Place: Essays on New York City* (New York: Russell Sage Foundation, 1988), 83–84, 87–88. U.S. Census, *Census of Manufactures* (Washington, D.C., 1905).

6. Clifton Hood, *722 Miles: The Building of the Subways and How They Transformed New York* (New York: Simon and Schuster, 1993), 113–119.

7. For the density of the blocks and heights of the tenements, see Bromley and Bromley, *Atlas of the City of New York, Borough of Manhattan.* Pratt, *Causes of Congestion,* 31–35. Clara Cardia, *Ils ont construit New York: Histoire de la métropole au XIXe siècle* (Geneva: Georg Editeur, 1987), 199–202. Norval White, *New York: A Physical History* (New York: Atheneum, 1987), 113–117.

8. Frederick M. Binder and David M. Reimers, *All the Nations under Heaven: An Ethnic and Racial History of New York City* (New York: Columbia University Press, 1995), 117, 137.

9. Reformer Lawrence Veiller argued: "So congested have become the conditions of some of the quarters of this City that it is not an exaggeration to say that there are more people living there than the land or the atmosphere can with safety sustain. The limits have not only been reached, they have long been passed." *Congestion Commission Report,* 5.

10. See Allen F. Davis, *Spearheads for Reform: The Social Settlements and the Progressive Movement, 1890–1914* (New York: Oxford University Press, 1967), and Roy Lubove, *The Progressives and the Slums: Tenement House Reform in New York City, 1890–1917* (Pittsburgh: University of Pittsburgh Press, 1962). For the impact of educational efforts, see Selma Berrol, *East Side/East End: Eastern European Jews in London and New York, 1870–1920* (Westport, Conn.: Praeger, 1994), and Gary Hermalyn, *Morris High School and the Creation of the New York City Public School System* (The Bronx, N.Y.: The Bronx County Historical Society, 1995), 9–16.

11. In pre–automobile age New York, improving transportation largely meant building more rapid transit lines. Before World War I, only heavy rail technology, meaning rapid transit and commuter rail, could move large numbers of people—hundreds of thousands per hour—to and from the Manhattan Central Business District. The automobile and its cousin, the limited access highway, were not seen as a potential means of mass commutation anywhere in the United States until the 1920s. See John R. Meyer and José A. Gómez-Ibáñez, *Autos, Transit and Cities* (Cambridge: Harvard University Press, 1981), 4–5. See also Scott Bottles, *Los Angeles and the Automobile: The Making of the Modern City* (Berkeley and Los Angeles: University of California Press, 1987), 55.

12. The reformers' analyses of the costs and financing of new rapid transit lines are discussed in Chapter 2.

13. Anthony Sutcliffe, "Introduction: Urbanization, Planning and the Giant City," in Anthony Sutcliffe, ed., *Metropolis 1890–1940* (Chicago: University of Chicago Press, 1984), 7.

14. New York City, *The 1998–1999 Green Book: Official Directory of the City of New York* (New York, 1998), 608.

15. Statistics from a population table prepared in 1971 from U.S. Census data by Bayrd Still of New York University. Donna Gabaccia estimates that three-quarters of all New Yorkers in the Progressive Era were immigrants and their children. Donna Gabaccia, "Little Italy's Decline: Immigrant Renters and Investors in a Changing City," in David Ward and Olivier Zunz, eds., *The Landscape of Modernity: New York City, 1900–1940* (Baltimore: Johns Hopkins University Press, 1992), 235.

16. Walter Laidlaw, *Population of the City of New York, 1890–1930* (New York: Cities Census Committee, 1932), 245, 247. Ira Rosenwaike, *Population History of New York City* (Syracuse, N.Y.: Syracuse University Press, 1972), 67–70, 95–96. Binder and Reimers, *All the Nations under Heaven,* 114–148. Kate Holladay Claghorn, "Foreign Immigrants and the Tenement House Problem," in Robert W. DeForest and Lawrence Veiller, eds., *The Tenement House Problem* (New York: Macmillan, 1903), 2:80–84. Hereafter cited as *The Tenement House Problem.*

17. In 1880, there were 80,000 Jews in New York, mostly from Germany; by 1910, there were 1.1 million, mostly from eastern Europe. In 1910, there were 338,000 residents who had been born in Italy. The next largest groups were the Germans (276,000 born overseas), followed by the Irish (253,000). At this time, few African-Americans lived in New York, their relative numbers having declined throughout the nineteenth century as a result, in part, of job competition from European immigrants. In 1910, there were 92,000 thousand blacks in New York City, comprising 2 percent of the population.

Statistics on foreign-born residents in New York City in 1910 from a population table prepared in 1971 from U.S. Census data by Bayrd Still of New York University. Jewish population statistics from Irving Howe, *World of Our Fathers* (New York: Harcourt Brace Jovanovich, 1976), xix. Statistics on the black population from Bayrd Still, *Urban America: A History with Documents* (Boston: Little, Brown, 1974), 406.

18. Thomas Kessner, *The Golden Door: Italian and Jewish Immigrant Mobility in New York City, 1880–1915* (New York: Oxford University Press, 1977), 13–15. Howe, *World of Our Fathers,* 87–90, 148–154.

19. Tobier, "Manhattan's Business District," 77–78, 81–88.

20. David C. Hammack, *Power and Society: Greater New York at the Turn of the Century* (New York: Russell Sage Foundation, 1982), 51. The New York banking houses are discussed in Jean Strouse, *Morgan: American Financier* (New York: Random House, 1999); Vincent P. Carosso, *The Morgans: Private International Bankers, 1854–1917* (Cambridge: Harvard University Press, 1987), and *Investment Banking in America* (Cambridge: Harvard University Press, 1970); and Cyrus Adler, *Jacob H. Schiff: His Life and Letters,* 2 vols. (New York: Doubleday Doran, 1928).

21. Louis Galambos and Joseph Pratt, *The Rise of the Corporate Commonwealth: United States Business and Public Policy in the 20th Century* (New York: Basic Books, 1988), chaps. 1 and 2. Albro Martin, *Railroads Triumphant: The Growth, Rejection and Rebirth of a Vital American Force* (New York: Oxford University Press, 1992), 333–336. Ron Chernow, *The House of Morgan: An American Banking Dynasty and the Rise of Modern Finance* (New York: Atlantic Monthly Press, 1990), chaps. 5–8.

22. Kenneth T. Jackson, "The Capital of Capitalism: The New York Metropolitan Region, 1890–1840," in Anthony Sutcliffe, ed., *Metropolis 1890–1940* (Chicago: University of Chicago Press, 1984), 322. Hammack, *Power and Society,* 52–55.

23. Eugene P. Moehring, "Space, Economic Growth, and the Public Works Revolution in New York," in Public Works Historical Society, *Infrastructure and Urban Growth in the Nineteenth Century,* Essays in Public Works History no. 14 (Chicago: Public Works Historical Society, 1985), 52.

24. Hammack, *Power and Society,* 81, 83.

25. Tobier, "Manhattan's Business District," 78.

26. Pratt, *Causes of Congestion,* 42. Another 160,000 factory jobs were in Manhattan north of 14th Street. There were also 54,000 manufacturing jobs in Brooklyn, 18,000 in the Bronx, 22,000 in Queens, and 8,000 on Staten Island.

27. Most of the buildings were five to seven stories high, although many of them had ten or more stories. Bromley and Bromley, *Atlas of the*

City of New York, Borough of Manhattan. As manufacturing declined in New York City after World War II, most of the factory jobs left the area south of 14th Street. From the 1960s on, artists moved into the area, seeking space to work. Various parts of the loft area were soon given names: The area south of Houston Street became SoHo, and the area to the north NoHo; and the triangle below Canal Street became TriBeCa. The loft areas are now expensive residential districts and are among New York's major tourist centers.

28. Tobier, "Manhattan's Business District," 89–90.

29. The second largest was metals and machinery, with 100,000 employees, followed by printing and paper goods with 71,000. Food and tobacco had 65,000 workers and leather and rubber goods had 37,000. There were also thousands of blue-collar workers employed in construction, transportation, and the skilled trades. Pratt, *Causes of Congestion,* 40.

30. Laidlaw, *Population of New York,* 233–234. Only in northern Manhattan and the southern Bronx had the first subway and an extension of the Third Avenue el pushed the reach of rapid transit up to twelve miles from City Hall.

31. Jackson, "Capital of Capitalism," 325. Cardia, *Ils ont construit,* 169,172, 174, 177, 181, 182, 197, 200, 201, 203, 210, 211. Atlases produced for the real estate industry show the density of housing on each block. See, for example, Bromley and Bromley, *Atlas of the City of New York, Borough of Manhattan.*

32. Between 1860 and 1910, Manhattan's density of population per acre rose from 37 to 166. By the latter year, residential districts along the elevated lines on the East Side had average densities of more than 200 people per acre; on the West Side, densities varied between 100 and 200. Several central Brooklyn neighborhoods that were served by elevated lines had densities between 100 and 150 people per acre. The first subway had not helped matters. In northern Manhattan and the South Bronx, mile after mile had been totally built up with dense apartment houses. In these neighborhoods, population densities were increasing rapidly. According to Pratt, the underlying causes of the increasing congestion of population in the older areas of New York were related to the growth and concentration of industry and commerce, the income levels of workers, and the need for employees to be near their jobs. The first direct consequence of congestion was the intensive use of land, evident in high land values and rents, tall buildings, and buildings occupying most of their lots. In residential areas, land was limited and demand high, as more people moved to New York, resulting in a steady rise in population density. Pratt, *Causes of Congestion,* 14–23, 28, 35. Irving M. Plant, *Population Growth of New York City by Districts,*

1910–1948 (Report prepared for Consolidated Edison Company of New York, December 1948), 11. Howe, *World of Our Fathers,* 132–133. Evelyn Diaz Gonzalez, "City Neighborhoods: Growth and Change in the South Bronx, 1840–1940" (Ph.D. diss., Columbia University, 1993), 246–250. Along the route of the Third Avenue el in the southern Bronx, some neighborhoods had more that 600 people per acre by 1905. *Congestion Commission Report,* 8.

33. Pratt, *Causes of Congestion,* 31–32. Eric Homberger, *The Historical Atlas of New York City: A Visual Celebration of Nearly 400 Years of New York City's History* (New York: Henry Holt, 1994), 136–137.

34. Plant, *Population Growth of New York City,* 12. Pratt, *Causes of Congestion,* 33. Brownsville, at the end of the elevated line from Williamsburg, grew from a population of 10,000 in 1899 to 60,000 in 1904. Moses Rischin, *The Promised City: New York's Jews, 1870–1914* (New York: Harper and Row, 1970), 92. See also Alter F. Landesman, *Brownsville: The Birth, Development and Passing of a Jewish Community in New York* (New York: Bloch Publishing, 1969).

35. One block had nearly 1,700 persons per acre. Pratt, *Causes of Congestion,* 31, 35. *Congestion Commission Report,* 6.

36. In comparison, at the time the most densely crowded parts of Bombay had 759 persons per acre; in Europe, the highest densities per acre were in Prague (481), Paris (434), and London (365). *Congestion Commission Report,* 5. An acre is 43,650 square feet. The standard block on the Manhattan grid is 200 by 800 feet, or 3.7 acres. At population densities of 600+ per acre, one block would have more that 2,200 people; at 1,000 per acre, a block would have almost 3,700 inhabitants. In 1910, there were fifty blocks on the Lower East Side that had more than 3,000 inhabitants. Ibid., 4.

37. Pratt, *Causes of Congestion,* 31. Pratt defined the Lower East Side as extending from what is now Chinatown, just northeast of City Hall, to 14th Street, and from Lafayette Street (just east of Broadway) to the East River. Under this definition, the area was 1,092 acres in size. Pratt, *Causes of Congestion,* 34.

38. Still, *Urban America,* 210–211.

39. Pratt, *Causes of Congestion,* 33–35.

40. These included the far northern tip of Manhattan; most of the West, North Central, and East Bronx; almost all of Queens; a swath of Brooklyn running west from Canarsie through Flatbush to Bensonhurst and Bay Ridge; and most of Staten Island.

41. Laidlaw, *Population of New York,* 234. Plant, *Population Growth of New York City,* 17. Most of the people living in these areas worked nearby. Emanuel Tobier, "The Bronx in the Twentieth Century: Dynamics of Population and Economic Change," *The Bronx County Historical Society Journal,*

35, no. 2 (Fall 1998): 72. David Ment, *The Shaping of a City: A Brief History of Brooklyn* (Brooklyn, N.Y.: Brooklyn Rediscovery and Brooklyn Educational and Cultural Alliance, 1979), 55–58.

42. Pratt, *Causes of Congestion*, 21. "Tenement Evils as Seen by the Tenants" in *The Tenement House Problem*, 1:409.

43. Cardia, *Ils ont construit*, 167, 189, 214, 220–221.

44. Richard Plunz, A *History of Housing in New York City: Dwelling Type and Social Change in the American Metropolis* (New York: Columbia University Press, 1990), 58–87. White, *A Physical History*, 118–119. The development of the apartment house as a multiple dwelling for affluent New Yorkers is covered in Stern, Gilmartin, and Massengale, *New York 1900*, 279–305. See also Elizabeth Hawes, *New York, New York: How the Apartment House Transformed the Life of a City (1869–1930)* (New York: Alfred A. Knopf, 1993), and Elizabeth Collins Cromley, *Alone Together: A History of New York's Early Apartments* (Ithaca, N.Y.: Cornell University Press, 1990).

45. Cardia, *Ils ont construit*, 167–168, 221.

46. New York State law defined a tenement house as any building rented or leased and occupied as "the home or residence of three families or more living independently of each other, and doing their own cooking on the premises . . . [and] having a common right in the halls, stairways, yards, water closets and privies." Tenement House Act as amended as of April 12, 1901, quoted in *The Tenement House Problem*, 2:167.

47. At the turn of the century, there were more than 82,652 tenement buildings in the city, of which 42,700 were in Manhattan, 33,771 in Brooklyn, 4,365 in the Bronx, 1,398 in Queens, and 418 on Staten Island. Robert W. DeForest and Lawrence Veiller, "The Tenement House Problem," in *The Tenement House Problem*, 1:4–5.

48. Thomas Adams, "The Peculiar Social and Economic Conditions of New York and the Need for a City Plan," *Town Planning Review*, 2, no. 3 (October 1911): 190.

49. Better quality tenement buildings constructed before 1901 had toilets and baths in each apartment and hot and cold running water. The market for these buildings was mainly second- and third-generation New Yorkers of Irish, German, and Scandinavian descent, who had higher incomes than most of the new immigrants. After 1901, all new tenement buildings had to meet the higher standards of a new State Tenement House Act, which defined the parameters of what came to be called a "New Law" tenement. The new apartment houses constructed along the route of the first subway in northern Manhattan and the Bronx, although densely packed together, were of better quality than the "Old Law" tenements in districts such as the Lower East Side and East Harlem. Many of the inhabitants of

the areas that grew up along the first subway in the South Bronx were lower-middle-class Jews, seeking better housing than was available to them in Manhattan. Howe, *World of Our Fathers,* 132–133. The same was true of the many Jews who migrated to Brownsville from 1900 on. Rischin, *The Promised City,* 93.

50. DeForest and Veiller, "The Tenement House Problem," 8–10, 42–43. See also Jared N. Day, *Urban Castles: Tenement Housing and Landlord Activism in New York City, 1890–1943* (New York: Columbia University Press, 1999), 31–56.

51. Jacob A. Riis, *How the Other Half Lives: Studies among the Tenements of New York* (1890; reprint, New York: Penguin Books, 1997), 19. Thanks to the efforts of New York's Lower East Side Tenement Museum, it is now possible to visit a pre–Old Law tenement building at 97 Orchard Street, built in 1863. The museum has undertaken period restoration of several apartments of families who lived in the building from the 1870s on.

52. Multiple dwellings constructed in Manhattan before 1879 came to be called "pre–Old Law" tenements. These buildings did not have to have windows for every room, or indoor plumbing. See Lawrence Veiller, "Tenement House Reform in New York City, 1834–1900," in *The Tenement House Problem,* 1:71–118.

53. DeForest and Veiller, "The Tenement House Problem," 7–9.

54. Howe, *World of Our Fathers,* 72.

55. The absence of parks and shortage of playgrounds is covered in Lawrence Veiller, "Parks and Playgrounds for Tenement Districts," in *The Tenement House Problem,* 2:3–13. Almost all of the parks on the Lower East Side date from the twentieth century, many on blocks that once were covered with tenements. The major park at the time was Tompkins Square Park. See also Robert A. Caro, *The Power Broker: Robert Moses and the Fall of New York* (New York: Alfred A. Knopf, 1974), 337.

56. Tobier, "Manhattan's Business District," 90.

57. Kessner, *The Golden Door,* 99–103. Howe, *World of Our Fathers,* 142, 177. See also Abraham Cahan, *The Rise of David Levinsky* (New York: Harper and Bros., 1917).

58. John Martin, *Rapid Transit: Its Effects on Rents and Living Conditions, and How to Get It* (New York: Committee on Congestion of Population, 1909), 3.

59. A 1908 survey of 250 typical families on the Lower East Side indicated that fewer than a quarter of them slept two or less in a room; 50 percent slept three or four in a room; and nearly 25 percent slept five or more in a room. Howe, *World of Our Fathers,* 171.

60. *Congestion Commission Report,* 5. At an exhibit on conditions in the

tenement districts, Veiller showed a model of an actual tenement block on the Lower East Side that contained 39 tenements, 2,781 residents, 264 toilets, and not one bathtub. Only forty apartments had hot running water. He claimed that this block was not atypical. Howe, *World of Our Fathers*, 89. Rents were high in proportion to the average worker's salary. In the areas with the worst buildings, the poorest families paid up to one half of their income in rent. Martin, *Rapid Transit*, 3.

61. Howe, *World of Our Fathers*, 70.

62. Hugh Bonner and Lawrence Veiller, "Tenement House Fires in New York," in *The Tenement House Problem*, 1:275–292. Of the 250 recorded deaths from fire in Manhattan 1902–1909, one-third were on the Lower East Side. Alan M. Kraut, *Silent Travelers: Germs, Genes, and the "Immigrant Menace"* (Baltimore: Johns Hopkins University Press, 1994), 144. For petty crime, see James B. Reynolds, "Prostitution as a Tenement House Evil," in *The Tenement House Problem*, 2:15–24, and F. Norton Goddard, "Policy—A Tenement House Evil," in *The Tenement House Problem*, 2:25–31.

63. See New York City, Board of Estimate and Apportionment, *Commission on Building Districts and Restrictions, Final Report* (New York, June 2, 1916), Appendix V, for numerous photographs of the mix of noxious activities and tenement housing.

64. "Tenement House Evils as Seen by the Tenants," and "Tenement House Evils as Seen by an Inspector," in *The Tenement House Problem*, 1:385–417 and 419–443, respectively. Quotes from pages 1:385, 386, 415, 418, 431.

65. Ibid., 1:387, 397, 410, 413, 422, 427.

66. Howe, *World of Our Fathers*, 154–159.

67. Pratt, *Causes of Congestion*, 23.

68. *New York Times*, March 9, 1908.

69. Stephen Birmingham, *"Our Crowd": The Great Jewish Families of New York* (New York: Harper and Row, 1967), 289–297. Jenna Weissman Joselit, *Our Gang: Jewish Crime and the New York Jewish Community, 1900–1940* (Bloomington: Indiana University Press, 1983), 5–11. Kraut, *Silent Travelers*, 139–140.

70. Quoted in the *New York Times*, March 9, 1908.

71. Pratt, *Causes of Congestion*, 23.

72. Frederick C. Howe, *The City: The Hope of Democracy* (New York: Charles Scribner's Sons, 1906), 212.

73. Charles A Beard, *American City Government: A Survey of Newer Tendencies* (New York: Century Co., 1912), 14. Claude H. Miller, "The Menace of Crowded Cities," *World's Work* 16 (May 1908): 10269.

74. David Rosner, "Introduction: 'Hives of Sickness and Vice,'" in David

Rosner, ed., *Hives of Sickness: Public Health and Epidemics in New York City* (New Brunswick, N.J.: Rutgers University Press, 1995), 12–14. Gretchen A. Condran, "Changing Patterns of Epidemic Disease in New York City," in *Hives of Sickness,* 29–35. Kraut, *Silent Travelers,* 143–144, 155–157.

75. Until this time, it was believed that many diseases were caused directly by dirt or other environmental factors. The decline in death rates was due in part to the development of vaccines for many contagious diseases. Attempts to develop a vaccine for tuberculosis, however, were unsuccessful. Rosner, "Introduction: 'Hives of Sickness,'" 11–16. Condran, "Changing Patterns," 29, 34.

76. Before 1882, when the tubercule bacillus was discovered, susceptibility to tuberculosis and other contagious diseases was believed to depend in large part on a person's constitution and temperament, as well as circumstance. Many doctors believed that tuberculosis was the direct result of environmental toxins, not germs. By the 1890s, it was clear that tuberculosis was a contagious disease that all persons exposed to the germ could pick up, regardless of their "constitution." Once this was known, the focus of medicine and public health shifted to preventing any healthy person from being infected by a person with the disease. Barbara Gutmann Rosenkrantz, "Introductory Essay," in Réne Dubos and Jean Dubos, *The White Plague: Tuberculosis, Man and Society,* rev. ed. (New Brunswick, N.J.: Rutgers University Press, 1996), xiii–xiv, xix–xxi. Katherine Ott, *Fevered Lives: Tuberculosis in American Culture since 1870* (Cambridge: Harvard University Press, 1996), 67–68 and illustration following 116. Thomas M. Daniel, *Captain of Death: The Story of Tuberculosis* (Rochester, N.Y.: University of Rochester Press, 1997), 87–92. Kraut, *Silent Travelers,* 155–156. Dubos and Dubos, *The White Plague,* 96.

77. Rosner, "Introduction: 'Hives of Sickness,'" 16. Known as "The Captain of Death of All the Men of Death" and "The Great White Plague," tuberculosis was foremost among infectious diseases as a cause of death. Alan M. Kraut, "Plagues and Prejudice: Nativism's Construction of Disease in Nineteenth- and Twentieth-Century New York City," in Rosner, ed., *Hives of Sickness,* 75. Death rates from tuberculosis were 210 per 100,000 in New York City in 1900. The only disease with a higher rate was pneumonia. Condran, "Changing Patterns of Epidemic Disease," 34.

78. Howard Markel, "Tuberculosis," in Kenneth T. Jackson, ed., *The Encyclopedia of New York City* (New Haven: Yale University Press, 1995), 1202. (Hereafter cited as *Encyclopedia of New York City.*) In 1899, 8,015 people died of tuberculosis in New York City, 5,238 of them in Manhattan and The Bronx. Arthur R. Guerard, "The Relation of Tuberculosis to the Tenement House Problem," in *The Tenement House Problem,* 1:470. It was the most fre-

quent cause of death among people ages fifteen to forty-five. Rosenkrantz, "Introductory Essay," xv.

79. By 1904, the number of cases had tripled. Howard Markel, "Tuberculosis," in *Encyclopedia of New York City*, 1202. George J. Lankevich, *American Metropolis: A History of New York City* (New York: New York University Press, 1998), 128. Rischin, *The Promised City*, 87–88.

80. Kraut, *Silent Travelers*, 155. Not until 1947 were antibiotics used to cure tuberculosis. Ibid., 159. Daniel, *Captain of Death*, 207–218.

81. Kraut, *Silent Travelers*, 180–183.

82. Daniel, *The Captain of Death*, 87–92. Dr. Hermann Biggs, chief medical officer of the New York City Health Department, called for improving sanitary conditions in homes and workplaces, including using strong disinfectants. Spitting in homes, workshops, and public conveyances was to be forbidden. Hermann M. Biggs, "Tuberculosis and the Tenement House Problem," in *The Tenement House Problem*, 1:453–457.

83. In fact, tuberculosis is almost always spread through the air directly from the breath of infected patients, but this was not known until thirty years later. Ott, *Fevered Lives*, 117. Daniel, *The Captain of Death*, 92–94.

84. Biggs, "Tuberculosis and the Tenement House Problem," 448. Kraut, "Plagues and Prejudice," 77. Kraut, *Silent Travelers*, 178–191. See also Arthur R. Guerard, "The Relation of Tuberculosis to the Tenement House Problem," 1:459–470. Physicians at the turn of the century correctly believed that the tuberculosis bacillus is killed by direct sunlight and that adequate ventilation is essential to disperse the germs. Daniel, *The Captain of Death*, 93.

85. Mary Van Kleeck, talk on "Children of Congested Districts" at *Exhibit on Congestion of Population in New York*, reported in the *New York Times*, March 12, 1908.

86. Ott, *Fevered Lives*, 127.

87. Howe, *World of Our Fathers*, 149.

88. The older name for tuberculosis, phthisis, in fact, means to waste away; a common name was consumption.

89. Maps of the incidence of tuberculosis on the Lower East Side show that almost every block had cases of the disease; several blocks had at least one case in every building. Ott, *Fevered Lives*, map opposite page 116. Biggs, "Tuberculosis and the Tenement House Problem," 449. Jacob H. Schiff and others helped to establish a sanitarium for poor patients run by Montefiore Hospital in Bedford Hills, New York. Kraut, "Plagues and Prejudice," 78. The public sanitarium on Blackwell's Island, now Roosevelt Island, was abysmal; Dr. Abraham Jacobi, for instance, attacked it for its lack of proper ventilation and sunlight. *New York Times*, March 13, 1908. Poor families were

reluctant, in any event, to send family members to hospitals. Rosenkrantz, "Introductory Essay," xxii.

90. Rosenkrantz, "Introductory Essay," xv.

91. *New York Times*, March 9, 1908. The fear of the spread of the disease led Dr. Biggs to begin a sustained public health campaign in the city, followed by a statewide campaign and then a national effort. The national campaign became the Tuberculosis League (now the American Lung Association), which directly linked tuberculosis rates with overcrowding in homes and workplaces, inadequate ventilation, exposure to toxicants, and poor infant nutrition. C. E. A. Winslow, *The Life of Hermann M. Biggs* (Philadelphia: Lea and Febiger, 1929), 200–213. Deborah Wallace and Roderick Wallace, *A Plague on Your Houses* (New York: Verso, 1918), 87. Markel, "Tuberculosis," 1202. Commenting on tuberculosis, Governor Charles Evans Hughes said: "If we had through the misfortune of war, or the sudden rise of pestilence, or through some awful calamity, the destruction of life that annually takes place on account of this disease, we should be appalled and mass meetings would be held in every community and demand would be made that the most urgent measures be adopted." Untitled brochure, Committee on the Prevention of Tuberculosis of the Charity Organization Society (1908), in Congestion Exhibit Material, New York Public Library. The Wallaces note that once an epicenter of tuberculosis is established, such as on the Lower East Side, the disease will spread to outlying areas, such as the Bronx and Brooklyn, along commuting paths. The authors call this spread "the Manhattan dispersion effect." Wallace and Wallace, *A Plague on Your Houses*, xvi–xvii.

92. This is the theme of Kraut's *Silent Travelers*. Howard Markel has shown how the city's typhus fever and cholera epidemics of 1892 led to fear of Eastern European Jews as vectors of the disease, with a corollary that poor immigrants were also somehow responsible for the social upheavals that were then transforming American society. Howard Markel, *Quarantine! East European Jewish Immigrants and the New York City Epidemics of 1892* (Baltimore: Johns Hopkins University Press, 1997), 5.

93. Howe, *World of Our Fathers*, 149.

94. Kraut, *Silent Travelers*, 108–109. Naomi Rodgers, "A Disease of Cleanliness: Polio in New York City, 1900–1990," in Rosner, ed., *Hives of Sickness*, 115–118. In New York, the smears on the new immigrants led physicians in both the Jewish and Italian communities to defend their compatriots. Dr. Maurice Fishberg proved statistically that the death rate from pulmonary tuberculosis among Jews was lower than that of the general population. Fishberg noted, however, that the incidence of tuberculosis among Jews depended upon their social and economic conditions, including living and

working in clean, well-ventilated and uncrowded rooms. Kraut, *Silent Travelers,* 157–158. Dr. Antonio Stella argued that rates of tuberculosis among Italians had nothing to do with any innate inferiorities. Instead, Stella blamed New York's congested housing and dark, unventilated sweatshops for tuberculosis among recent Italian immigrants. Kraut, *Silent Travelers,* 125. See also David Ward, "The Making of Immigrant Ghettoes," in Alexander B. Callow, Jr., ed., *American Urban History: An Interpretive Reader with Commentaries,* 3d ed. (New York: Oxford University Press, 1982), 271–275.

95. Hermann M. Biggs to Governor-Elect John A. Dix, November 14, 1910, quoted in Winslow, *Life of Biggs,* 231–232. Linking diseases to specific groups was part of an effort to show that the new immigrants were carriers of diseases and were inferior physically to native Americans. On a national level, this was part of a campaign to restrict immigration from southern and eastern Europe, which succeeded in the 1924 Federal Immigration Act. Kraut, *Silent Travelers,* 145–147. Kessner, *The Golden Door,* 24–26.

96. For a discussion of AIDS, see Ronald Bayor, "The Dependent Center: The First Decade of the AIDS Epidemic in New York City," in Rosner, ed., *Hives of Sickness,* 131–154.

97. Ott, *Fevered Lives,* 123. AIDS also has had a major impact on the poor, similar to that of tuberculosis for the new immigrants. During the 1980s and 1990s, there was a high rate of AIDS among poor minority groups, whose conditions of daily life rivaled those of the "new immigrants" of the turn of the century. By 1992, 64 percent of the AIDS cases in New York City were among African-Americans and Latinos. Bayor, "The Dependent Center," 132. At the end of the twentieth century, both AIDS and new virulent strains of tuberculosis were wreaking havoc among poor people in less developed countries, with tuberculosis killing two million people annually. As of summer 1999, vaccines had still not been developed for either disease. Jeffrey Sachs, "Helping the World's Poorest," *The Economist* 352, no. 6132 (August 14, 1999): 19. The reaction in the United States was similar to that a century ago. "U.S. Increases Screening of Immigrants for Tuberculosis," *New York Times,* January 3, 2000.

98. Kraut, *Silent Travelers,* 126–127. Kraut cites Antonio Stella, "The Effect of Urban Congestion on Italian Women and Children," *Medical Record* 74 (May 2, 1908): 732.

99. Howe, *World of Our Fathers,* 91.

100. Ibid., 165. Howard Markel, "Smallpox," in *Encyclopedia of New York City,* 1078–1079.

101. Howe, *World of Our Fathers,* 91.

102. *Congestion Commission Report,* 35.

103. According to Binder and Reimers, "Poverty, despair and dislocation

ever breed crime, and the Jewish Lower East Side was no exception." Binder and Reimers, *All the Nations,* 119.

104. Ibid., 119, 139.

105. Joselit, *Our Gang,* 23–53. Binder and Reimers, *All the Nations,* 119.

106. Binder and Reimers, *All the Nations,* 119. Reynolds, "Prostitution as a Tenement House Evil," 15–24. Goddard, "Policy—A Tenement House Evil," 25–31. For a comprehensive description of life in Manhattan's tenement districts, including crime, see Luc Sante, *Low Life: Lures and Snares of Old New York* (New York: Vintage Books, 1992).

107. Joselit, *Our Gang,* 1.

108. According to Joselit, to the minds of this affluent group, the herding of immigrant Jews into "accommodations which seemed to be entire villages of people . . . attacked their moral fiber . . . for the natural concomitants of overcrowding are disease, vice and crime. Just as congestion bred TB and consumption, it bred promiscuity and immorality." Ibid., 18.

109. Planner Peter Hall places the New York reaction to problems in the tenement house districts in an international context, comparing it to efforts in London, Paris, and Berlin. One thing that did not happen in New York at the turn of the century, as compared to the European cities, was an attempt to build public housing. Instead, efforts in New York focused on upgrading the regulation of privately constructed housing and on attempts to socialize the immigrants to American customs, so that they might better adjust to urban life. Peter Hall, *Cities of Tomorrow: An Intellectual History of Urban Planning and Design in the Twentieth Century* (London and New York: Basil Blackwell, 1988), chap. 2, "The City of Dreadful Night. Reactions to the Nineteenth-Century Slum City: London, Paris, Berlin, New York, 1880–1900." See also Davis, *Spearheads for Reform.* A very different situation than in New York, London, Paris, or Berlin existed in Chicago, America's second largest city in 1900. Although there were some neighborhoods with overcrowded housing and high poverty rates, most working families were able to live in low-density housing. Few natural barriers, an extensive streetcar network, the availability of cheap land, and a value system that encouraged single-family homes resulted in a relatively uncongested metropolis. Donald L. Miller, *City of the Century: The Epic of Chicago and the Making of America* (New York: Simon and Schuster, 1996), 265–281.

110. Howe, *World of Our Fathers,* 225–255. Hermalyn, *Morris High School,* 9–16. Berrol, in *East Side/East End,* argues that the importance of public schools in the upward mobility of Jewish immigrants has been exaggerated.

111. Elizabeth Fee and Evelynn M. Hammonds, "Science, Politics, and the Art of Persuasion: Promoting the New Scientific Medicine in New York City," in Rosner, ed., *Hives of Sickness,* 163–164.

112. After 1901, all new apartment buildings had to meet the requirements of the "New Law" Tenement House Act, which made it almost impossible to construct buildings on twenty-five by one hundred foot lots, mandated more space between buildings to let in light and air to each apartment, and required that each apartment have its own toilet. Plunz, *History of Housing*, 47–49.

113. Lubove, *The Progressives and the Slums*, 117–149.

114. Charles Cooley, "The Theory of Transportation," *Publications of the American Economic Association* 60, no. 3 (May 1894): 1–148. One geographer has commented about this paper that for the next seventy years, nothing was published about the theory of transportation "that came even close to superseding it." Roy I. Wolfe, *Transportation and Politics* (Princeton, N.J.: Van Nostrand, 1963), 3.

115. Cooley, "The Theory of Transportation," 42, 74.

116. Ibid., 76–77.

117. Ibid., 76.

118. Ibid., 127–130.

119. Ibid., 137.

120. Ibid., 143. Cooley's ideas found expression in the creation of the New York State Public Service Commission in 1907.

121. Ibid., 124. A 1905 report on the effects of street railways and rapid transit, based on the Census of 1900, supported Cooley's thinking. The Census Bureau asserted that the more transit lines, the better for the people, because transit tended to distribute and equalize land values in residential areas and thus prevented excessive rents. U.S. Census Bureau, *Street and Electric Railways* (Washington, D.C., 1905), 30.

122. Adna Ferrin Weber, *The Growth of Cities in the Nineteenth Century: A Study in Statistics* (New York, 1899; reprint, Ithaca, N.Y.: Cornell University Press, 1963), 471.

123. T. C. Barker, "Urban Transport," in Michael J. Freeman and Derek H. Aldcroft, eds., *Transport in Victorian Britain* (Manchester and New York: Manchester University Press, 1988), 149. Asa Briggs, *Victorian Cities* (New York: Harper and Row, 1963), 15.

124. Edward T. Higgins, "Some of the Larger Transportation Problems in Cities," *Municipal Affairs* 3 (June 1899): 247. Bion J. Arnold, "The Urban Transportation Problem: A General Discussion," *Annals of the American Academy of Political and Social Science* 37, no. 1 (January 1911): 5.

125. Adna Ferrin Weber, "Growth of Cities in the United States: 1890–1900," *Municipal Affairs* 5, no. 2 (June 1901): 375.

126. The reform movement in New York during the Progressive Era is

covered in detail in Richard S. Skolnick, "The Crystallization of Reform in New York City, 1890–1917" (Ph.D. diss., Yale University, 1964).

127. Calvin Tomkins, "The Desirability of Comprehensive Municipal Planning in Advance of Development," in Municipal Engineers of the City of New York, *Proceedings for 1905* (1906), 226. Tomkins was chairman of the City Plan Committee of the Municipal Art Society. Harvey A. Kantor, "Modern Urban Planning in New York City: Origins and Evolution, 1890–1933" (Ph.D. diss., New York University, 1971), 108.

128. Tomkins, "The Desirability of Comprehensive Municipal Planning," 227, 233.

129. This group included Florence Kelley; Mary Simkhovitch, director of Greenwich House; Lillian Wald, head of Nurses Settlement; Dr. Gaylord S. White of Union Settlement; and Public Service Commissioner Edward M. Bassett. Davis, *Spearheads for Reform,* 70. Susan Marie Wirka, "The City Social Movement: Progressive Women Reformers and Early Social Planning," in Mary Corbin Sies and Christopher Silver, eds., *Planning the Twentieth-Century City* (Baltimore: Johns Hopkins University Press, 1996), 64–67. Simkhovitch was the chair of the Congestion Committee. Wald, who also was active on the Congestion Committee, had worked in tenements as a nurse from 1892 on, funded secretly by Jacob H. Schiff, before going on to found Nurses Settlement House, later called Henry Street Settlement House. Howe, *World of Our Fathers,* 90–94.

130. Members of the Congestion Committee included civic group leaders such as George McAneny, Calvin Tomkins, Charles Sprague Smith, Lawrence Veiller, Richard Watson Gilder, and Homer Folks. Men of wealth, such as Jacob H. Schiff, Paul M. Warburg, Isaac N. Seligman, and Henry Morgenthau, were members, as well as Socialist Morris Hillquit. Workers were represented, among others, by Mary E. Drier of the Woman's Trade Union League and Herman Robinson of the Central Federated Union. The churches sent Dr. Walter Laidlaw of the Federation of Churches and a number of other clergymen. City planner Charles Mulford Robinson served on the committee along with President John H. Finley of the City College of New York, Jacob Riis, Dr. Antonio Stella of the Society for Italian Immigrants, Dr. Abraham Jacobi, Dr. E. R. L. Gould of the City and Suburban Homes Company, John Martin of the Public Education Association, and William Barclay Parsons, the planner of the first subway. Benjamin C. Marsh to George McAneny, March 20, 1908, George McAneny Papers, Princeton University.

131. Morgenthau quoted in Richard E. Foglesong, *Planning the Capitalist City: The Colonial Era to the 1920s* (Princeton: Princeton University Press, 1986), 204.

132. Simkhovitch quoted in ibid., 168.

133. Wirka, "The City Social Movement," 64–66.

134. N. O. Nelson, "The Remedy for City Congestion," *Independent* 65 (September 24, 1908): 703. See also Florence Kelley, "The Settlements: Their Lost Opportunity," *Charities and the Commons*, April 7, 1906, 79–81. According to Richard E. Foglesong, the members of the Congestion Committee "had come to recognize that their multifarious efforts in combating bad housing, insufficient schools, the dearth of parks and playgrounds, juvenile crime, and tuberculosis and other health problems only dealt with the effects of congestion; what was needed was an attack on congestion itself." Foglesong, *Planning the Capitalist City*, 168.

135. Davis, *Spearheads*, 70. The stated objective was "to depict some of the causes, conditions and the evils of the massing of people in New York and in limited areas" and to discuss methods needed "to remedy such congestion." Committee on Congestion of Population in New York, "Announcement for an Exhibit on Congestion of Population in New York" (1908), in Congestion Exhibit Material, New York Public Library.

136. Wirka, "The City Social Movement," 68.

137. Congestion Committee, *Catalogue: Exhibit Held in the American Museum of Natural History, March 9th to 22nd, 1908*, and *Exhibit of Congestion of Population, Brooklyn Institute Art Rooms, April 6th to 19th, 1908*. Congestion Exhibit Material, New York Public Library.

138. Congestion Committee, *Catalogue for Exhibit at Museum of Natural History*. See also Anthony Sutcliffe, *Toward the Planned City: Germany, Britain, the United States and France, 1780–1914* (New York: St. Martin's Press, 1981), 112–113.

139. Congestion Committee, *Exhibit of Congestion of Population at Brooklyn Institute.*

140. Printed speech, "Address of Governor Charles E. Hughes at the Opening of the Exhibit of Congestion of Population in New York," March 9, 1908, in Congestion Committee Material, New York Public Library. The *New York Times* lead on this was "Congestion Menaces City, Says Hughes." *New York Times*, March 10, 1908.

141. "Address of Governor Hughes at Congestion Exhibit."

142. Ibid.

143. Commissioner Edward M. Bassett said that he was most impressed by exhibits showing conditions in the congested areas of the Lower East Side. Commissioner Bassett cited the necessity for new subways as well as for restrictions on building heights and zoning, which together would allow New York to avoid past mistakes in urban development. *New York Times*, March 14, 1908.

144. Congestion Committee, catalogs, *Addresses, Lectures and Conferences Relating to the Exhibit* and *Meetings and Functions to be Held in Connection with the Exhibit of Congestion of Population in New York*, Congestion Committee Material, New York Public Library. The lectures covered a wide variety of topics relating to conditions in the congested districts and potential ways of alleviating the congestion problem.

145. Edward M. Bassett, "Brooklyn's Needs in Transportation," address given in conjunction with the *Exhibit of Congestion of Population in Brooklyn*, in Congestion Exhibit Material, New York Public Library.

146. This was in contrast to the first subway, operated by the IRT, which had only two branch lines to the north, the feeder territories of which had soon been densely built up. Hood, *722 Miles*, 138–139.

147. Benjamin C. Marsh, *An Introduction to City Planning: Democracy's Challenge to the American City* (New York, 1909). Martin, *Rapid Transit*. Pratt, *Causes of Congestion*.

148. Marsh, *Introduction to City Planning*, 5. Benjamin Marsh served as executive secretary of the Congestion Committee from February 1907 on. He later became secretary of the New York City Commission on Congestion of Population. Marsh was a dedicated reformer who had studied economics at both the University of Chicago and the University of Pennsylvania. Benjamin C. Marsh, *Lobbyist for the People: A Record of Forty Years* (Washington, D.C.: Public Affairs Press, 1953), viii.

149. Marsh, *Introduction to City Planning*, 28–29. German city planning had a major influence in the United States at this time, and Marsh and many other planners visited German cities. See Frank B. Williams, *The Lessons of Germany* (Report of the Chairman of the City Planning Committee of the City Club of New York, December 16, 1913), and John R. Mullin, "American Perceptions of German City Planning at the Turn of the Century," *Urbanism Past and Present* 3 (Winter 1976–1977): 5–15. The influence of European city planning on Marsh and other members of the Congestion Committee is discussed in Daniel T. Rodgers, *Atlantic Crossings: Social Politics in a Progressive Age* (Cambridge: Harvard University Press, 1998), 181–186. See also Brian Ladd, *Urban Planning and Civic Order in Germany, 1860–1914* (Cambridge: Harvard University Press, 1990).

150. Marsh, *Introduction to City Planning*, 37. See also Harvey A. Kantor, "Benjamin C. Marsh and the Fight over Population Congestion," *Journal of the American Institute of Planners* 40 (November 1974): 422–429.

151. Martin, *Rapid Transit*, 3–10.

152. This work was published by Columbia University in 1911. The research for it, however, had been conducted for the Congestion Committee in the spring of 1908. Pratt, *Causes of Congestion*, 6.

153. Ibid., 209.

154. Ibid., 194.

155. Ibid., 204–206.

156. Ibid., 211–212.

157. The Congestion Show was well publicized—including extensive coverage in the *New York Times*—and was very popular, both in Manhattan and Brooklyn, with thousands of attendees coming from the tenement districts. *New York Times,* March 16, 1908. See also Wirka, "The City Social Movement," 67, and Gregory F. Gilmartin, *Shaping the City: New York and the Municipal Art Society* (New York: Clarkson Potter, 1995), 165–168.

158. Similar points are made by Gilmartin in *Shaping the City*, 164–168. Rosner, "Introduction: 'Hives of Sickness,'" 4, says that it was believed that disease rates could not be reduced substantially because of the conditions of daily life in the tenement districts.

159. Homberger, *Historical Atlas of New York City*, 110.

160. George McAneny Oral History Project, Oral History Collection, Columbia University, 1949, 37.

161. George McAneny, "Response to Address of Welcome by the Duke of Connaught," *Proceedings of the Sixth National Conference on City Planning* (1914), 3. According to McAneny, coordination of urban growth was essential to the well-being of the city's citizens. "On the face of it," said McAneny, city planning "has to do with things physical—the laying out of streets and parks and rapid transit lines. But its real significance is far deeper; a proper city plan has a powerful influence for good upon the mental and moral development of the people. It is the firm basis for a healthy and happy community." McAneny quoted in Nelson P. Lewis, *The Planning of the Modern City: A Review of the Principles Governing City Planning* (New York: John Wiley and Sons, 1916), 50.

162. *New York Evening Journal,* November 15, 1909.

163. Hood, *722 Miles*, 150–154. Gilmartin, *Shaping the City*, 181–202.

164. This is perhaps because his daughter, Ruth McAneny Loud, restricted access to his papers. Gilmartin, *Shaping the City*, 380.

165. *New York Times,* George McAneny obituary, July 30, 1953.

166. Gilmartin, *Shaping the City*, 181.

167. *New York Times,* July 30, 1953.

168. George McAneny Oral History, 1–2.

169. Edward T. O'Donnell, "Carl Schurz," in *Encyclopedia of New York City*, 1049.

170. Gilmartin, *Shaping the City*, 181.

171. *New York Times,* July 30, 1953.

172. George McAneny Oral History, 1.

173. Ibid., 18.

174. Rhoda Truax, *The Doctors Jacobi* (Boston: Little, Brown, 1952), 221.

175. Ibid.

176. Ibid., 155, 157, 160, 227.

177. Ibid., 145, 225.

178. Ibid., 232. Winslow, *Life of Biggs,* 201.

179. Truax, *The Doctors Jacobi,* 234.

180. *New York Times,* March 13, 1908.

181. Ibid.

182. Abraham Jacobi had had two previous wives, both of whom died in childbirth. Truax, *The Doctors Jacobi,* 2, 12, 32–38, 62–68, 137, 160.

183. Ibid., 197–198. This was all the more tragic because Jacobi was an expert on diphtheria among children.

184. Ibid., 198.

185. Katherine Kish Sklar, "Mary Putnam Jacobi," in *The Encyclopedia of New York City,* 607.

186. Truax, *The Doctors Jacobi,* 206.

187. Ibid., 241.

188. *Who's Who in New York City and State* (New York: W. F. Brainard, 1909), 810.

189. *New York Times,* July 30, 1953.

190. Truax, *The Doctors Jacobi,* 214.

191. Draft of a lecture dated May 1, 1914, one of six McAneny gave at Yale University. George McAneny Papers, Columbia University. Cited in Lubove, *The Progressives and the Slums,* 239.

192. Louis E. Van Norman, "A New Transportation Era for New York," *Review of Reviews* 52, no. 4 (October 1910): 434.

NOTES TO CHAPTER 4

1. When Mayor William J. Gaynor came into office, he believed that the whole rapid transit problem would be solved in three months. Press release, "Mayor's Remarks to the Delegations of the Building Trades of Brooklyn and Queens," January 4, 1910, Clippings and Correspondence from the Office of the Mayor of the City of New York, 1904–1916, Newspaper Division, New York Public Library. Chairman Willcox and the other members of the Public Service Commission also thought that a solution would be found quickly. *New York Times,* November 5, 1909.

2. The Fusion members were Comptroller William A. Prendergast, with three votes; President of the Board of Aldermen John Purroy Mitchel, with three votes; Manhattan Borough President George McAneny, with two

votes; Brooklyn Borough President Alfred Steers; with two votes; Bronx Borough President Cyrus L. Miller, with one vote; and Richmond Borough President George Cromwell, with one vote. The two members of the Board elected as Democrats were Mayor Gaynor, with three votes, and Queens Borough President Lawrence Gresser, with one vote. Gresser was the only holdover on the Board.

3. George McAneny, "The Responsibility of the City Administration in Regard to Subway Construction," address given at the City Club of Philadelphia, January 27, 1912, George McAneny Papers, Columbia University, and "What I Am Trying to Do: Helping to Make New York a Cleaner, More Healthful, More Beautiful, and Greater City," *World's Work* 26 (June 1913): 172–181.

4. The comptroller was responsible for City finances. The presidency of the Board of Aldermen was a curious position, in that the person in office was first in line to succeed the mayor if a vacancy occurred. The main power of this office was the votes the president had on the Board of Estimate. The borough presidents were elected within each of the boroughs. Together with the mayor, the Board of Estimate controlled finances and franchises in the City of New York until it was abolished in 1989. See Wallace S. Sayre and Herbert Kaufman, *Governing New York City: Politics in the Metropolis* (New York: W. W. Norton, 1965), 626–656, for a discussion of the functions and powers of the Board of Estimate.

5. William A. Prendergast Oral History Project, Oral History Collection, Columbia University, 1951, 335. During the 1909 election campaign, Prendergast had given a speech, "Transit Development," in which he said that new subways were necessary not just to relieve overcrowding on existing lines, but also to properly distribute the city's rapidly growing population. Testimony of William A. Prendergast in State of New York, Joint Legislative Committee to Investigate the Public Service Commission, *Minutes and Testimony* (1917), 5:487. At the instigation of William Randolph Hearst, the New York State Legislature established two temporary committees to investigate the Public Service Commission. These committees will be cited in these notes as the First Thompson Committee and the Second Thompson Committee. The First Thompson Committee held hearings in 1915 and issued a two-volume *Final Report,* which included minutes of the testimony it had taken. The Second Thompson Committee held public hearings in 1916 and published its findings in a volume titled *Complete Report* in 1917, as well as the *Minutes and Testimony* of the hearings, which ran to six volumes. Subsequent references to testimony taken during the Thompson Committee hearings will be cited by the speaker's name, followed by 1TC or 2TC (for the First and Second Thompson Committees, respectively) and the volume and page number, for example, Prendergast, 2TC, 5:487.

6. Mitchel believed in competition among transit operators. He thought that a new Triborough Subway System that could be operated independently of existing services was the best way to proceed. Undated typescript, "Subway Record of the President of the Board of Aldermen, John Purroy Mitchel," John Purroy Mitchel Papers, the Library of Congress. Mitchel succeeded in his goal of achieving higher office by being elected mayor in 1913, with the support of Hearst.

7. Edwin R. Lewinson, *John Purroy Mitchel: The Boy Mayor of New York* (New York: Astra Books, 1965). Michael W. Brooks, *Subway City: Riding the Trains, Reading New York* (New Brunswick, N.J.: Rutgers University Press, 1997), 83.

8. William J. Gaynor, "The Looting of New York," *Pearson's Magazine* 21 (May 1908): 461–473.

9. George J. Lankevich, *American Metropolis: A History of New York City* (New York: New York University Press, 1998), 148.

10. Willcox argued that new rapid transit lines, built as part of a larger planning effort, could be used to channel future growth rationally. For the City to develop its outlying areas under a comprehensive plan, however, many more subway lines were needed. Willcox stated his views on rapid transit expansion and its relationship to city planning in a symposium, "New York City Twenty Years Hence," *New York Times Magazine*, February 6, 1910. In 1909, at a planning meeting chaired by McAneny, Bassett had argued that the solution to the problem of congestion of population was to construct a great number of subway lines in every borough, each leading from one residential district to another and then into the centers of business in Manhattan and Downtown Brooklyn. He made these remarks at the First National Conference on City Planning and the Problems of Congestion, held in Washington, D.C. *New York Times*, March 20, 1909. In an academic article, Maltbie said that if all the plans for new subways then under consideration could be carried out, "congestion of population would be relieved, transit conditions would greatly improve, and new areas would be opened for development." Even then, however, transit facilities would not exceed demand, because the population was growing rapidly, "and the problem is not only to provide for transportation already necessary, but how to prevent the recurrence of indecent conditions and to meet the demands of the immediate future." Milo R. Maltbie, "The Fruits of Public Regulation in New York," *Annals of the American Academy of Political and Social Science* 48, no. 1 (January 1911): 190.

11. Testimony of Milo R. Maltbie, 1TC, 1:1300.

12. New York City, Board of Estimate and Apportionment, *Minutes*, January 7, 1910.

13. *New York Times*, January 15, 1910.

14. The estimated cost of the Triborough System is given in Public Service Commission (hereafter abbreviated PSC), *Annual Report, 1912*, 1:61. The cost of the proposed IRT subway lines is cited in the testimony of IRT president Theodore P. Shonts, 2TC, 3:675. The estimated cost of the elevated extensions is in PSC, *Proceedings*, vol. 5 (1910), 460. Using the Construction Cost Index History (1910–1999) of *Engineering New Record*, the total estimated cost of $210 to $250 million equals $13.1 to $15.6 billion in year 1999 dollars. *Engineering News Record*, March 22–29, 1999, 100.

15. Cynthia Morse Latta, "The Return on the Investment in the Interborough Rapid Transit Company" (Ph.D. diss., Columbia University, 1975), 338.

16. PSC, *Combination Map of the Rapid Transit Routes in Greater New York* (New York, December 31, 1909).

17. As discussed in Chapter 2, the indeterminate franchise plan was approved by the New York State Legislature in 1909 as a way of attracting private companies to invest in new rapid transit.

18. This was due largely to the economics of building new rapid transit lines to outlying areas of the city that were as yet largely undeveloped. It was universally agreed that a five-cent fare would be charged on any new lines, yet, at this rate the new lines would not be profitable for many years. The result was that private capital had so far been hesitant to invest in such lines. *New York Times*, October 11 and 26, 1909. See also William S. Twinning, "The Investigation of the Traffic Possibilities of Proposed Subway Lines," *Annals of the American Academy of Political and Social Science* 48, no. 1 (January 1911): 56–67.

19. PSC, "History and Description of Rapid Transit Routes in New York City," in *Annual Report, 1909*, 1:251–254. PSC, *Annual Report, 1912*, 1:63, 71–72.

20. Between January 1, 1898, and January 1, 1913, the City of New York appropriated more than $797 million in capital improvements, paid for by the sale of bonds. Of this amount, $93.1 million was for subways. The rest was for other "permanent improvements," such as new schools, water supply projects, docks, bridges, streets, and sewers. The expense budget for ongoing operations (police, fire, teachers' salaries, etc.) in 1913 was $192,711,000. McAneny, "What I Am Trying to Do," 174, 176.

21. New York City, "Financial Statement of Funded Debt, City of New York," *New York Times*, March 14, 1910.

22. William Russell Hochman, "William J. Gaynor: The Years of Fruition" (Ph.D. diss., Columbia University, 1955), 328.

23. *New York Herald*, April 2, 1910.

24. Not surprisingly, McAneny, who wrote the assessment bill and had lobbied for its passage in the State Legislature, was the major public official backing the plan. President Mitchel also favored using the assessment plan. In the PSC, Commissioner Bassett, who also had helped draft the assessment bill, was a strong supporter of the plan. Commissioner Maltbie also favored the idea. *New York Times,* January 11, 1910. *New York Tribune,* February 17, 1910.

25. *New York Evening World,* April 4, 1910. *New York Times,* April 5, 1910.

26. According to PSC Commissioner Bassett, the major problem with the assessment plan was that although it strongly appealed to many members of the Board of Estimate and PSC, it was opposed by many property owners in outlying areas. Edward M. Bassett, "Remarks," *Proceedings of the Sixth National Conference on City Planning* (1914), 253.

27. Of this amount, $13 million was to come from funds available within the debt limit; the balance was to be from the $47 million in increased borrowing made possible by the exemption of current self-supporting bonds from the calculation of the debt limit. These funds were to be appropriated over a three-year period. *New York Times,* April 7, 1910.

28. Testimony of Cornelius Vanderbilt, 2TC, 5:574. Shonts, 2TC, 3:706.

29. Jean Strouse, *Morgan: American Financier* (New York: Random House, 1999). Ron Chernow, *The House of Morgan: An American Banking Dynasty and the Rise of Modern Finance* (New York: Atlantic Monthly Press, 1990), chaps. 5–8. Robert Sanger Steel, "J(ohn) P(ierpont) Morgan," in Kenneth T. Jackson, ed., *The Encyclopedia of New York City* (New Haven: Yale University Press, 1995), 769.

30. In early 1909, Shonts had suggested to J. P. Morgan, Jr., that the Morgan bank provide financial backing for the IRT in its plans to build new subway and elevated lines. (J. P. Morgan, Jr., or Jack, was the son of the elder J. P. Morgan. He took over direction of J. P. Morgan and Company when the elder Morgan died in 1913.) Shonts told Morgan that he was not talking with any other banker at the time and that the IRT's board of directors had authorized him to deal with the Morgan bank. He showed Morgan figures and calculations he had made indicating that an agreement might be made with the PSC for transit extensions that would be of advantage to the IRT. Morgan wrote back to Shonts advising him that the bank would be willing to finance expansion of the IRT system if a suitable arrangement could be made with the PSC. Shonts, 2TC, 3:697–699. Testimony of J. P. Morgan, Jr., 2TC, 5:1146–1150.

31. From June 1909 on, Shonts dealt only with the House of Morgan. He kept the bank informed, either through Morgan, Jr., or Henry P. Davison, of his negotiations with the PSC, believing that the bank had the right to set

the terms on which it would lend its money. This was a matter of sound investment practices for an underwriter. Morgan himself stated that his primary interest in the matter, from June 1909 on, was to make sure that any proposition for financing transit extensions would ensure the payment of interest on any bonds that were issued for such improvements. Shonts, 2TC, 3:567, 701. Morgan, 2TC, 5:1158.

32. Testimony of William R. Willcox, 2TC, 5:537.

33. *New York Times*, March 8, 1910. Shonts, 2TC, 4:516. Theodore P. Shonts to William R. Willcox (draft agreement), March 12, 1910, 2TC, 4:435–455.

34. Morgan, 2TC, 5:1151.

35. Ibid.

36. *New York Times*, April 5, 1910. *Brooklyn Citizen*, April 5, 1910.

37. *New York Times*, October 26, 1909. The *Times* was hesitant to see lines put under construction unless it was certain that they would be financially viable, but admitted that "there are those who heartily support them as part of the city's duty to incur expense for the sake of relieving congestion of population. If New York's credit was better, and its finances were stronger, philanthropic subways might be defensible."

38. Testimony of Mirabeau Towns, 2TC, 3:953. Shonts, 2TC, 3:675. According to one of its directors, the IRT thought that Gaynor's rhetoric during the 1909 campaign was not "anything more than just talk." Testimony of Francis De C. Sullivan, 2TC, 5:467.

39. Towns, 2TC, 4:235.

40. Gaynor Press Release, January 26, 1910, Clippings and Correspondence from the Office of the Mayor of the City of New York, 1904–1916, Newspaper Division, New York Public Library.

41. Shonts, 2TC, 4:470.

42. Shonts, 2TC, 4:472. Testimony of E. J. Berwind, 2TC, 4:1058.

43. In addition to his vote on the Board of Estimate, the mayor also had considerable powers over the use of the public streets that could effectively block actual construction of the Triborough System. *New York Post*, July 20, 1910.

44. Shonts told Gaynor that the Triborough System would compete with the IRT subway, raising the risk that any private capital invested in new lines by the IRT would not make a satisfactory profit. Towns, 2TC, 4:231. Shonts, 2TC, 3:674–685, 704–706.

45. Shonts, 2TC, 3:676, and 4:225.

46. Testimony of Kingsley Martin, 2TC, 4:252, 257.

47. George McAneny Oral History Project, Oral History Collection, Columbia University, 1949, 4.

48. Shonts, 2TC, 4:544. William J. Gaynor to William R, Willcox, July 6, 1910, in PSC, *Proceedings,* vol. 5 (1910), 507–508.

49. The IRT justified asking that City money be used by saying that, "since the Legislature eliminated subway bonds from the debt limit of the City," it was impossible to enlist private capital for subway construction out of fear of possible competition. Theodore P. Shonts to William R. Willcox, July 5, 1910, PSC, *Proceedings,* vol. 5 (1910), 505–507.

50. In the Bronx, the Jerome Avenue and White Plains Road lines would be built, the former connecting to the Lexington Avenue trunk line. In Brooklyn, the existing IRT subway would be extended to and along Eastern Parkway. For Queens, a new line would pass from 42nd Street in Manhattan to Long Island City, just across the East River.

51. William R. Willcox to William J. Gaynor, PSC, *Proceedings,* vol. 5 (1910), 508–510. "Equipping" means providing the subway cars.

52. William J. Gaynor, "The New York Subway Situation," *Outlook* 95 (July 30, 1910): 713–714, 726.

53. Hochman, "Gaynor," 216.

54. *New York World,* April 29, 1910.

55. John Purroy Mitchel's biographer has noted that "no political leader of any party could afford to ignore William Randolph Hearst." Lewinson, *Mitchel,* 51.

56. Lately Thomas, *The Mayor Who Mastered New York: The Life and Opinions of William J. Gaynor* (New York: William Morrow, 1969), 334–335. Brooks, *Subway City,* 81.

57. *Brooklyn Citizen,* July 7, 1910. *New York Times,* July 9, 1910.

58. Ideally for these officials, a private operator would build the Triborough System with its own funds, but the prospects for this seemed to diminish as the realities of subway economics became even more apparent. Hochman, "Gaynor," 424.

59. Morgan, 2TC, 5:1154.

60. *New York World,* November 14, 1910. The assassination attempt is described in Thomas, *Gaynor,* 290–292.

61. Thomas, *Gaynor,* 290–292. Morgan was uncertain about the exact date of this meeting.

62. Morgan, 2TC, 5:1154.

63. PSC, "Subway Construction" (September 1, 1910), *Proceedings,* vol. 5 (1910), 517–518, and *Annual Report, 1910,* 1:585–586. *New York Times,* September 2, 1910. William A. Prendergast, "Statement of William A. Prendergast in Regard to the Negotiations Leading up to the Signing of the Rapid Transit Contracts Nos. 3 and 4 by the Board of Estimate and Apportionment. Read into the Record of the Legislative Investigating Committee

Known as the Thompson Committee, June 19, 1916," 5, in William A, Prendergast Oral History Project, Oral History Collection, Columbia University, Appendix 3. (Hereafter cited as Prendergast Statement.)

64. PSC, *Proceedings*, vol. 5 (1910), 517–518, and *Annual Report, 1910*, 1:585–586.

65. Louis Roth, "History of Rapid Transit Development in the City of New York" (Memorandum for Commissioner Whitney, April 3, 1917), 30.

66. *Brooklyn Eagle*, November 2, 1910.

67. The Triborough System plan was attacked in Chamber of Commerce of the State of New York, Special Committee on Rapid Transit, *Report on the "Tri-Borough Route"* (New York, November 3, 1910). It was also attacked by other business groups, by railroad groups, and by some local citizens' associations. *New York Press*, October 11, 1910. *New York American*, October 14, 1910. *Brooklyn Eagle*, November 4, 1910. *New York American*, November 17, 1910. The PSC received communications opposing the Triborough System plan from a few local organizations, including the Bedford Park Taxpayers Association (Bronx), the East Flatbush Taxpayers Association (Brooklyn), and the Taxpayers Association of the Thirty-second Ward of Brooklyn. PSC, *Proceedings*, vol. 5 (1910), 703, 774.

68. The proponents of the Triborough System plan included a number of citizens' organizations as well as the Hearst press. *Brooklyn Times*, November 2, 1910. *Brooklyn Eagle*, November 4, 1910. *New York Evening Journal*, November 16, 1910. *New York American*, November 17, 1910. The PSC received communications from groups as diverse as the South Bronx Property Owners Association, the Citizens Association of Bay Ridge and Ft. Hamilton (Brooklyn), the Brooklyn Board of Real Estate Brokers, and the Italian-American Improvement League of New Utrecht (Brooklyn). PSC, *Proceedings*, vol. 5 (1910), 691, 703, 748, 768. It is impossible to determine the relative strength of public support for and opposition to the Triborough System. A number of groups, such as the Fordham Club of the Borough of the Bronx, wanted to see the IRT System extended, but also wanted the Triborough System put under construction. Ibid., 703.

69. *New York American*, November 17, 1910.

70. "Statement by Mr. Willcox," November 16, 1910, 2TC, 6:192.

71. Favoring immediate construction were Prendergast, Mitchel, and Richmond Borough President George Cromwell, who hoped to see the Fourth Avenue line extended to Staten Island. Together the three had seven votes on the Board of Estimate. Against the Triborough were Gaynor and Queens Borough President Lawrence Gresser, with four votes. These two men were the only non-Fusionists on the Board of Estimate. Borough President Cyrus L. Miller of the Bronx was thought to be

in favor of the Triborough, but his one vote was likely to change if the IRT agreed to build the Pelham line. In the middle were McAneny and Brooklyn Borough President Alfred Steers, with two votes apiece. Steers, however, was thought to support any plan that would be most favorable to Brooklyn. *Brooklyn Times,* November 2, 1910. *New York Times,* November 11, 1910. *New York American,* November 14, 1910.

72. *New York Times,* November 11, 1910. *New York Sun,* November 11, 1910. *New York American,* November 12, 1910.

73. *New York Press,* November 11, 1910.

74. Ibid. *New York American,* November 12, 1910.

75. *Brooklyn Times,* November 11, 1910. *New York American,* November 15, 1910.

76. Gaynor speech to Chamber of Commerce, November 17, 1910, Clippings and Correspondence, New York Public Library.

77. Chamber of Commerce, *Report on the "Tri-Borough Route,"* 7.

78. This system is now operated by the Port Authority of New York and New Jersey as PATH (an acronym for Port Authority Trans Hudson). Robert A. Olmsted, "PATH," in Jackson, ed., *The Encyclopedia of New York City,* 885.

79. Prendergast Statement, 6. William G. McAdoo to William R. Willcox, PSC, *Proceedings,* vol. 5 (1910), 759–762.

80. Testimony of George V. S. Williams, 1TC, 1:931.

81. *New York Times,* November 17, 1910.

82. *New York Times,* November 23, 1910.

83. *Brooklyn Eagle,* November 30, 1910.

84. *New York Times,* December 5, 1905.

85. On September 13, 1910, Shonts had informed IRT director Andrew Freedman that J. P. Morgan and Company had announced that it, the National City Bank, and the First National Bank, as a syndicate, "were prepared to get under the Interborough securities, and put representatives of each institution on our board, and become publicly identified with the property." On September 15, 1910, Morgan and Company wrote to Shonts confirming conversations the company had held about the plan for financing the IRT. The basis of the plan would be "a new first and refunding mortgage securing an authorized issue of $150,000,000, fifty-year five per cent coupons and registered form bonds due in 1960." This money was to be used for the construction and equipping of new subway lines, to build elevated railroad extensions and third-track the elevated lines, and to refund maturing IRT notes. The $150 million would be loaned in whole or in part at any time before May 1, 1911. Theodore P. Shonts to Andrew Freedman, September 13, 1910, 2TC, 3:703–704. J. P. Morgan and Co. to Theodore P. Shonts, September 15, 1910, 2TC, 3:461–464.

86. Morgan, 2TC, 5:1225.

87. In a letter to the presidents of the Chamber of Commerce and the Merchants Association, Gaynor said that he believed that the subway difficulty would be solved if some company, namely the IRT, would put in all the capital that was needed over and above the $57 million that the mayor believed the City had available for new subways. Construction could go on in all boroughs simultaneously, instead of piecemeal. William J. Gaynor to A. B. Hepburn and H. R. Towne, November 23, 1910, in Citizens' Committee Appointed by the Presidents of the Chamber of Commerce and the Merchants Association, *The Rapid Transit Problem of New York* (December 1910), 3–4. This message had undoubtedly been conveyed to the IRT.

88. PSC, *Proceedings*, vol. 5 (1910), 792–793.

89. Ibid., 793.

90. Irving M. Plant, *Population Growth of New York City by Districts, 1910–1948* (Report prepared for Consolidated Edison Company of New York, New York, 1948), 17.

91. PSC, *Proceedings*, vol. 5 (1910), 795.

92. In addition, the IRT would pay $8.5 million of the estimated $10 million needed to complete the Steinway Tunnel if the City would provide the balance. Ibid., 792, 795.

93. Ibid., 793.

94. Prendergast, 2TC, 6:170.

95. LeRoy T. Harkness, speech at Central Citizens' League (Brooklyn), *New York Times*, December 15, 1910.

96. Commissioner John E. Eustis expressed the opinion of the majority of the PSC when he said that if he thought that the money to finish the Triborough System were available, then he would prefer to see work on it begin. Yet, he said, there was no assurance that enough money would be available. Meanwhile, the IRT proposition "offered something that would be very complete, and at the same time furnish more to the three boroughs than the Triborough does." *New York Times*, December 22, 1910.

97. Prendergast Statement, 6.

98. PSC, *Proceedings*, vol. 5 (1910), 822–825.

99. William J. Gaynor to J. Edward Swanstrom, December 20, 1910, Clippings and Correspondence, New York Public Library.

100. Ibid.

101. *Brooklyn Eagle*, December 21, 1910. *New York Tribune*, December 22, 1910.

102. *Brooklyn Eagle*, December 21, 1910. *New York Post*, December 22 and 23, 1910. *New York Tribune*, December 23, 1910. *New York Times*, December 31, 1910.

103. *New York Times,* December 25, 1910. The total borrowing capacity of the City of New York was expected to increase by $172 million between 1911 and 1915, of which $60 million would be for new subways. *Brooklyn Eagle,* December 1, 1910. The total subway investment of the City up to December 31, 1910, including the costs of the Centre Street loop, portions of the Fourth Avenue line, and the subway operated by the IRT, was $63,740,737. *New York Times,* January 10, 1911.

104. *New York Tribune,* December 23, 1910.

105. Ibid.

106. Prendergast Statement, 6.

107. *Brooklyn Eagle,* December 28, 1910.

108. *Brooklyn Eagle,* January 6, 1911.

109. Board of Estimate, *Minutes,* January 5, 1911. *New York Times,* January 6, 1911.

110. McAneny summarized the issues with respect to the IRT proposal in a press release, "For the Press—On the Subway Situation," January 18, 1911, John Purroy Mitchel Papers, Library of Congress.

111. Ibid.

112. The PSC had this route under serious consideration in 1910 largely because of constant demands from citizens and politicians from this densely populated area. *Brooklyn Citizen,* December 29, 1910.

113. William R. Willcox to William J. Gaynor, June 10, 1910, 2TC, 5:478. *Brooklyn Times,* December 17, 1910. *Brooklyn Eagle,* January 10, 1911.

114. PSC, *Proceedings,* vol. 6 (1911), 10–12. *Brooklyn Eagle,* January 10, 1911.

115. *Brooklyn Eagle,* January 11, 1911.

116. *New York American,* January 6, 1911.

NOTES TO CHAPTER 5

1. According to McAneny, the determination of which routes needed to be built and where they should be located belonged "to the City alone" and not to any private company. George McAneny, "For the Press—On the Subway Situation," January 18, 1911. McAneny's conception was the modern one. Currently, decisions on building new subways and other mass transportation lines are based almost solely on whether proposed new lines will achieve public goals. In McAneny's time, however, local rail systems were regarded largely as private-sector activities, to be operated at a profit.

2. According to Homer Folks, who was chairman of the Transit Committee of the City Club and shared McAneny's ideas: "The principal thing the New Yorker wants is to go where he wants to and when he wants to. He

cares little about the financial aspects of the matter, and I believe we have been putting emphasis on the wrong thing." *New York Times*, January 23, 1910. In 1912, McAneny himself argued that how new subways were financed was not the main issue. George McAneny, "The Responsibility of the City Administration in Regard to Subway Construction," address given at the City Club of Philadelphia, January 27, 1912, George McAneny Papers, Columbia University.

3. New York City, Commission on Congestion of Population, *Report of the New York City Commission on Congestion of Population* (New York, February 28, 1911). This report was reprinted in *City Record* 34, no. 11500 (March 7, 1911): 1830–1902. Hereafter cited as *Congestion Commission Report*. McAneny had strongly urged Gaynor to appoint the Commission. George McAneny, "Bulletin for Press Release on Congestion," February 26, 1910, George McAneny Papers, Princeton University. In December 1910, in part to follow up on the recommendations of the Congestion Commission, McAneny announced that the Board of Estimate would appoint a new Committee on the City Plan to "study conditions that obtain in the city and lay out projects for future development, especially in the outlying boroughs." "The Metropolis to Be," *New York Evening Mail*, December 20, 1910. *New York Tribune*, December 23, 1911. *New York Times*, December 31, 1910.

4. Gregory F. Gilmartin, *Shaping the City: New York and the Municipal Art Society* (New York: Clarkson Potter, 1995), 185.

5. *Congestion Commission Report*, 80.

6. George McAneny, "For the Press—On the Subway Situation," January 18, 1911.

7. Ibid.

8. Ibid.

9. Ibid.

10. *New York Evening Mail*, January 18, 1911.

11. *New York Post*, January 18, 1911.

12. *New York Times*, January 20, 1911.

13. George McAneny, "Memorandum of Modifications in the Pending Proposition of the Interborough Rapid Transit Company Suggested by Members of the Board of Estimate and Apportionment," January 23, 1911, John Purroy Mitchel Papers, Library of Congress.

14. Ibid.

15. Ibid.

16. New York City, Board of Estimate and Apportionment, *Minutes*, January 19, 1911.

17. *Brooklyn Eagle*, January 23, 1911.

18. Testimony of Theodore P. Shonts, Joint Legislative Committee to

Investigate the Public Service Commission, *Minutes and Testimony* (1917), 4:320. Subsequent references to testimony taken during the Second Thompson Committee hearings will be cited by the speaker's name, followed by 2TC and the volume and page number, for example, Shonts, 2TC, 4:320.

19. William A. Prendergast Oral History Project, Oral History Collection, Columbia University, 1951, 471. The debt limit remained as a restriction on New York City's capacity to borrow for public works in the year 2000. The *New York Times* on January 29, 2000, noted that Mayor Rudolph W. Giuliani's plans to spend billions of dollars on construction projects might be limited by the provision in the State Constitution capping the amount of debt at any one time to ten percent of the assessed value of taxable real estate in New York.

20. Members of the Board of Estimate and PSC realized, as one unidentified Board member told a reporter, that if private capital were to be recruited for the building of subways, "we cannot deal with this capital in any vague way. The bankers handling the money cannot allow this." *Brooklyn Eagle*, February 15, 1911.

21. Prendergast Oral History, 330.

22. *New York Times*, January 20, 1911.

23. George McAneny to Governor John A. Dix, June 2, 1911, George McAneny Papers, Princeton University.

24. *New York American*, February 8, 1911. *New York Times*, April 14, 1911.

25. New York State, Public Service Commission for the First District (hereafter abbreviated PSC), *Proceedings*, vol. 6 (1911), 298. E. P. Goodrich, "Remarks," in *Proceedings of the Fifth National Conference on City Planning* (1913), 123. City Club of New York, *Bulletin*, June 1911.

26. George McAneny, "Memorandum of Modifications," January 23, 1911. John Purroy Mitchel and William A. Prendergast to William R. Willcox, February 4, 1911, in PSC, *Proceedings*, vol. 6 (1911), 71–73.

27. *New York Post*, January 26, 1911. *New York Globe*, January 26, 1911. Testimony of E. J. Berwind, 2TC, 4:1050.

28. *New York Times*, February 8, 1911. *Brooklyn Eagle*, March 15, 1911. *New York Press*, March 17, 1911.

29. PSC, *Annual Report, 1912*, 1:76.

30. Testimony of Timothy S. Williams, 2TC, 4:310. *Brooklyn Eagle*, February 28, 1911.

31. Williams, 2TC, 4:310.

32. Testimony of LeRoy T. Harkness, 2TC, 5:750.

33. Brooklyn Rapid Transit Company to George McAneny and William R. Willcox, March 2, 1911, in PSC, *Proceedings*, vol. 6 (1911), 121–124.

34. Ibid.

35. Ibid.

36. At the time, the Sea Beach, West End, and Culver lines had all been converted to electric operation. They connected with the BRT's Fifth Avenue el at a station at Ninth Avenue and 39th Street. The Fifth Avenue el ran from Downtown Brooklyn to 36th Street, where one branch went east to the Ninth Avenue station. Another branch went west and down Third Avenue to 65th Street. Brian Cudahy, *Under the Sidewalks of New York: The Story of the Greatest Subway System in the World,* rev. ed. (Lexington, Mass.: Stephen Greene Press, 1988), 60.

37. The Brighton line had opened as a steam railroad in 1878. In 1899, the line was electrified and connected to the BRT's Fulton Street el. Through el service between the Park Row terminal over the Brooklyn Bridge and Brighton Beach had begun in 1900. Between 1905 and 1907, the company had rebuilt the at-grade line, partly as an open cut viaduct and partly on an embankment. Parsons Brinckerhoff Quade and Douglas, Inc., Historical Perspectives, Inc., and Robert A. Olmsted, P.E., *Phase I: Reconnaissance Level Historical Survey of Transit Authority Properties. Task 1 Report: The New York City Transit System—Historical Context and Evaluation Parameters* (Report to the New York City Transit Authority, June 1991), Appendix C, C-1.

38. Brooklyn Rapid Transit Company to McAneny and Willcox, March 2, 1911.

39. Ibid.

40. Ibid. This northern part of Brooklyn was called the "Eastern District."

41. Ibid.

42. Ibid.

43. Ibid.

44. Ibid. *New York Times,* April 17, 1911.

45. *Brooklyn Times,* March 2, 1911. Comptroller Prendergast later said that the struggle between the IRT and the BRT during the spring of 1911 was a real battle: "Each road was striving in a most energetic way to secure for itself the advantage that it believed belonged to it." Prendergast, 2TC, 6:236.

46. *Brooklyn Eagle,* March 3, 1911.

47. *Brooklyn Citizen,* March 3, 1911. *New York Sun,* March 3, 1911. At the end of 1910, the City of New York would have an estimated $116 million available within the debt limit for subway construction. Even if the total cost turned out to be slightly higher, the difference could be made up by spending less on other capital projects. The key point was to leverage City funds as much as possible, by using them to attract private capital to invest in new lines.

48. *Brooklyn Citizen,* March 15, 1911.

49. *New York Times,* April 13 and 18, 1911.

50. *New York Press,* March 10, 1911. *Brooklyn Times,* April 8, 1911. John Purroy Mitchel, "A Short History of the Transit Situation with Special Reference to Queens," March 25, 1912, John Purroy Mitchel Papers, Library of Congress.

51. *Brooklyn Eagle,* March 15 and 17, 1911. *Brooklyn Times,* March 17, 1911. *New York Globe,* March 20, 1911.

52. *New York Press,* March 17, 1911. *Brooklyn Times,* April 8, 1911.

53. *Brooklyn Eagle,* March 15, 1917. *New York Press,* March 17, 1911.

54. *New York Times,* April 13, 1911.

55. *New York Standard Union,* March 21, 1911. *Brooklyn Citizen,* March 22, 1911.

56. *New York Times,* April 13, 1911. Brooklyn Rapid Transit Company to George McAneny and William R. Willcox, April 25, 1911, in PSC, *Proceedings,* vol. 6 (1911), 251–257. New York City, Board of Estimate and Apportionment, Transit Committee, and Public Service Commission, "Report of the Conferees" (to the Board of Estimate and Apportionment, June 5, 1911), in PSC, *Annual Report, 1911,* 1:438–474. This report is hereafter cited simply as "Report of the Conferees." Although the date of the report was given as June 5, it was actually ready on June 13. It was given the earlier date in order to allow Commissioner Bassett, whose term expired on June 8, to sign it.

57. "Report of the Conferees."

58. Brooklyn Rapid Transit Company to George McAneny and William R. Willcox, April 25, 1911, in PSC, *Proceedings,* vol. 6 (1911), 256.

59. *New York American,* April 27, 1911.

60. *New York American,* April 28, 1911.

61. *New York Standard Union,* April 30, 1911. There was a close connection between the IRT stockholders and real estate interests in northern Manhattan and the Bronx. Andrew Freedman, one of the IRT directors, was "an owner of a great deal of property in The Bronx." Andrew Freedman to A. J. County, July 26, 1911, 2TC, 4:496. Another IRT director, Charles T. Barney, had made large profits from real estate investments in northern Manhattan and the Bronx, along the route of the first subway. Clifton Hood, *722 Miles: The Building of the Subways and How They Transformed New York* (New York: Simon and Schuster, 1993), 110.

62. *New York Standard Union,* April 30, 1911.

63. *New York Tribune,* May 5, 1911.

64. Interborough Rapid Transit Company to William R. Willcox and George McAneny, May 9, 1911, in PSC, *Proceedings,* vol. 6 (1911), 281–284.

65. Ibid.

66. Ibid.

67. Ibid.

68. Prendergast, 2TC, , 6:236. *Brooklyn Citizen*, May 3, 1911. *New York Press*, May 12, 1911. *New York Times*, May 16, 1911.

69. *New York Times*, May 15, 1911.

70. *Brooklyn Citizen*, May 3, 1911.

71. Williams, 2TC, 4:312. *New York World*, May 16, 1911. *New York Times*, May 17, 1911.

72. Timothy S. Williams to William G. Morrissey, May 16, 1911, in *New York Times*, May 24, 1911.

73. *Brooklyn Eagle*, June 2, 1911.

74. PSC, *Proceedings*, vol. 6 (1911), 272.

75. City Club of New York, *Bulletin*, June 1911.

76. George McAneny to Governor John A. Dix, June 2, 1911, George McAneny Papers, Princeton University.

77. "Report of the Conferees." The report was called the "McAneny Report" in several newspapers: *Sun*, June 13, 1911. *Evening Mail*, June 13, 1911. *Globe*, June 13, 1911. *Brooklyn Eagle*, June 13, 1911. *Post*, June 14, 1911.

78. Ibid.

79. The reformers' ideal was depicted in a series of drawings showing small single-family detached houses in the outlying districts that were to be opened for development by the Dual System lines. These drawings are in the George McAneny Papers, Princeton University. Henry Wright, who had prepared the City Club displays at the *Exhibit of Congestion of Population in New York*, believed that the City of New York should aid its citizens to live in single- and two-family homes, because living in apartments tended, he believed, "to destroy the sense of individual responsibility and loyalty to the community." Henry Wright, "The Interrelation of Housing and Transit," *American City* 10 (January 1914): 51. Willcox, Bassett, McAneny, and their allies, however, understood the economics of subway costs and revenues. For passenger revenues to cover all capital and operating costs, at a five-cent fare, then population densities in many of the new residential areas would have to be higher than those in neighborhoods built up exclusively with single-family homes. This meant neighborhoods with a mix of one- and two-family homes and apartment houses.

80. Ibid.

81. The description of proposed routes is from the "Report of the Conferees."

82. Ibid.

83. Ibid. The IRT had not wanted to build these extensions. Their inclusion in the plan was the result of a decision by the conferees that these

extensions were imperative. Commissioner Bassett had done a survey of the area along Nostrand Avenue and concluded that it was well suited for the construction of two- to six-family homes. This was revealed in a speech given by Bassett on May 2, in which he also said that outlying areas of Brooklyn and Queens should not "grow up to six-story apartment houses" as had happened along the route of the first IRT subway in Harlem and the southern Bronx. Bassett contended that New York would be a better city "when its families live in small housing units." *Brooklyn Eagle,* May 3, 1911.

84. "Report of the Conferees."

85. Ibid. The conferees calculated that the City then had available $140 million for additional subway construction. At the end of 1910, the Board of Estimate had determined that at least $116 million in borrowing capacity would be available, based on expected increases in real estate assessments and $43 million from the exemption of self-supporting bonds from the calculation of the debt limit. *New York Times,* December 25, 1910. The additional $24 million was available within the expected increases in real estate assessments, but meant having to put off other, non-transit-related, capital projects.

86. "Report of the Conferees."

87. Ibid.

88. This did not include the Manhattan Railway elevated lines, which would retain a separate fare system.

89. "Report of the Conferees."

90. Ibid.

91. Ibid.

92. Ibid.

93. Ibid.

94. John Vipond Davies, "Provision for Future Rapid Transit: Subway, Elevated or Open Cut, and Their Influence on the City Plan," in *Proceedings of the Sixth National Conference on City Planning* (1914), 197.

95. George McAneny, "Remarks," in *Proceedings of the Sixth National Conference on City Planning* (1914), 228. The planners had calculated that the average cost of one mile of elevated line in New York was between $125,000 and $175,000. The cost of one mile of the Fourth Avenue subway in Brooklyn was $402,000. Thus, about three miles of elevated line could be constructed for the same price as the cheapest form of subway construction. Davies, "Provision for Future Rapid Transit," 202. One mile of a subway under Broadway was expected to cost $1,190,000.

96. Edward M. Bassett, "Remarks," in *Proceedings of the Sixth National Conference on City Planning* (1914), 236. McAneny, "Remarks," 254. Harkness, "Dual System," 258.

97. *New York Post,* June 22, 1911.
98. *New York Post,* June 13, 1911.
99. *New York Times,* June 14, 1911.
100. Seth Low, *Report to the Citizens' Committee on Rapid Transit* (June 20, 1911).

NOTES TO CHAPTER 6

1. New York City, Board of Estimate and Apportionment, Transit Committee, and Public Service Commission, "Report of the Conferees" (to the Board of Estimate and Apportionment, June 5, 1911), in State of New York, Public Service Commission for the First District, *Annual Report, 1911,* 1:438–474. Hereafter cited as "Report of the Conferees."

2. Most public officials had accepted this proposed arrangement, regarding it as sort of an annual rent to be paid to the company for merging the existing BRT lines with the new lines, and for agreeing to operate all the lines together as a unified BRT system.

3. Comptroller William A. Prendergast noted in 1916 that by the middle of 1911, "it was completely demonstrated that the city could not with its own means create a system as is now in course of construction." He was referring to the Dual System. William A. Prendergast, "Statement of William A. Prendergast, Comptroller of the City of New York, in regard to the negotiations leading up to the signing of the Rapid Transit Contracts Nos. 3 and 4 by the Board of Estimate and Apportionment, Read into the Record of the Legislative Investigating Committee known as the Thompson Committee, June 19, 1916," in William A. Prendergast Oral History Project, Oral History Collection, Columbia University, Appendix 3. Hereafter cited as Prendergast Statement.

4. Sworn public testimony of employees and directors of the IRT reveals that the company was actively hostile to the Dual System plan between June 1911 and January 1912, belying assertions by the Hearst newspapers and others that the plan was the result of an arrangement between the IRT and the BRT. Testimony of Theodore P. Shonts, State of New York, Joint Legislative Committee to Investigate the Public Service Commission, *Minutes and Testimony* (1917), 3:685. Subsequent references to testimony taken during the Second Thompson Committee hearings will be cited by the speaker's name, followed by 2TC and the volume and page number, for example, Shonts, 2TC, 3:685. Testimony of James L. Quackenbush (IRT counsel), 2TC, 3:918. Testimony of E. J. Berwind (IRT director), 2TC, 4:1051. Testimony of Delaney Nicoll (IRT counsel), 2TC, 3:834. Testimony of Francis De C. Sullivan (IRT director), 2TC, 5:432.

5. *New York Standard Union,* June 14, 1911. Shonts, 2TC, 3:726.

6. IRT counsel James L. Quackenbush reported that when he contended that the Dual System could not operate at a profit, the conferees had replied "that they were not engaged in looking for profits, but in the building of the city and that they would take care of it all out of taxation." Quackenbush contended that the conferees were well aware that the new lines might have to be subsidized for a number of years, but that they believed they could justify taxing property to do so in view of "the sociological advantages" that would result from "the dispersal of the congested population . . . [and] the building up of the outlying districts." Quackenbush, 2TC, 5:576, 578.

7. The contract with the BRT was to run for forty-nine years.

8. This was a developed residential area already served by several BRT elevated lines. It was one of the few areas of the city where there was opposition to the route structure of the plan. *New York Press,* June 15, 1911. *Brooklyn Times,* June 15, 1911. *New York Standard Union,* June 16, 1911.

9. Quackenbush, 2TC, 5:578. *New York Press,* June 15, 1911. *New York Globe,* June 16, 1911. *New York Times,* June 16, 1911.

10. The IRT estimated that the "Broadway competitive route" would reduce its own revenues by not less than $5 million a year. Interborough Rapid Transit Company to William R. Willcox and George McAneny, June 27, 1911, Public Service Commission (hereafter abbreviated PSC), *Proceedings,* vol. 6 (1911), 399–404. In 1910, the return on the IRT's investment in the subway was 18.2 percent; in 1911, it was 14.1 percent. If both the IRT's and the City's investment are used in the calculations, the return on investment was 10.0 percent in 1910 and 8.5 percent in 1911. Cynthia Morse Latta, "The Return on the Investment in the Interborough Rapid Transit Company" (Ph.D. diss., Columbia University, 1975), 253. Comptroller Prendergast said that the net profits of the IRT averaged 13.5 percent annually for the two years ending June 30, 1911. Prendergast Statement, 16.

11. Interborough Rapid Transit Company to Willcox and McAneny, June 27, 1911, 399–404.

12. The BRT agreed to the Dual System plan after the conferees had gained the consent of the Board of Estimate to certain modifications desired by the company. Brooklyn Rapid Transit Company to George McAneny and William R. Willcox, June 27, 1911, PSC, *Proceedings,* vol. 6 (1911), 404–412.

13. Testimony of William Bullock (BRT secretary), 2TC, 5:1125.

14. Testimony of Edward M. Grout, 2TC, 4:626.

15. According to Comptroller Prendergast, Low "followed these negotiations solely from the standpoint of a citizen, and always in the public in-

terest." Prendergast also said that Low argued in favor of the preferentials to both companies "not on the theory that the city should deal overgenerously with the transit companies, but solely on the ground that where a bargain was to be made involving the interests of millions of people and the expenditure of hundreds of millions of dollars, the question should be decided upon broad lines." Prendergast Statement, 17.

16. Grout stated the dilemma when he said that the City wanted to construct, within the next five years, a transit network that in his opinion ought to have been spread out over twenty-five years. To do this, the City needed private capital that the IRT would not provide "unless it was assured of repayment and revenue." Grout, 2TC, 4:642–643.

17. Ibid., 626.

18. Shonts proposed that this payment be based upon the average net profits of the IRT for the four years previous to June 30, 1911. This would amount to between 14 and 15 percent, if calculated upon the actual amount of capital invested by the IRT in the existing subway system. *New York Evening Mail*, July 5, 1911.

19. Grout, 2TC, 4:646.

20. *New York Press*, July 11, 1911. *New York Evening World*, July 11, 1911. *New York Globe*, July 18, 1911.

21. *New York Globe*, July 18, 1911. *New York Evening Mail*, July 18, 1911. The IRT calculated its investment in the old lines as $50 million; the new money to be invested by the IRT was $75 million, for a total of $125 million, 8 percent of which came to $10 million. *New York Times*, July 12, 1911.

22. *New York Evening Mail*, July 12, 1911. *New York Times*, July 13, 1911.

23. Berwind, 2TC, 4:1052.

24. Seth Low to Board of Estimate and Apportionment, untitled memorandum (July 1911), Seth Low Papers, Columbia University.

25. Although it was never clearly spelled out publicly how a plan for a guarantee would work, any such plan would have had to provide that, if the earnings from the expanded IRT system were insufficient to meet the specified amount of the guarantee, then the IRT's return on its investment would be subsidized by tax revenues or the sale of City bonds. If, however, the IRT was only to receive a preferential payment from the operating revenues of the expanded system, then City tax revenues would never be used directly to subsidize IRT profits. Grout, 2TC, 4:646–648. *New York Evening Mail*, July 18, 1911.

26. *Brooklyn Eagle*, July 18, 1911.

27. This preferential of $11.25 million annually would be made before the City of New York received any payment from operating revenues on the bonds it would sell to construct the IRT's portion of the new Dual System

lines. If revenues from the expanded system in any given year did not meet the specified deductions to be made to the company and the City, then such deficiencies were to be cumulative and would be made up in future years out of operating revenue. According to estimates prepared by the IRT, which the conferees believed were very conservative, any cumulative deficits would be discharged thirteen years after the beginning of operation of the new lines. After this, the expanded system would begin to produce an annual profit, to be split by the company and the City. Public Service Commission for the First District and Special Committee of the Board of Estimate and Apportionment to Board of Estimate and Apportionment, "Rapid Transit System: Report of Conferees to Board of Estimate and Apportionment," PSC, *Proceedings,* vol. 6 (July 20, 1911), 490–495.

28. Ibid.

29. Though Willcox signed the report, he later testified that he had not liked the proposed compromise reached with the IRT in July 1911, but had felt that it was justified because the Dual System plan would connect "all of the outlying districts by rapid transit to the center of the city." This would be accomplished at a time when "the City's financial strength was not great enough to pay for this large system." Testimony of William R. Willcox, 2TC, 4:539. The new PSC commissioner, J. Sergeant Cram, disliked the Dual System plan and the proposal for preferential payments for much the same reason as Mayor Gaynor and refused to sign the report. Ibid. Cram's views were outlined in the *Brooklyn Citizen,* July 14, 1911.

30. According to Maltbie, under this proposal the City practically guaranteed the IRT 9 percent on all the money it was to provide for the entire life of the proposed contract. He believed that the distinction that had been drawn between a preferential and a guarantee was fictitious, because the City was not to have any interest paid on its investment of new money until the company had received 9 percent cumulative. Milo R. Maltbie, "Statement by Commissioner Maltbie," PSC, *Proceedings,* vol. 6 (1911), 495–499.

31. *New York Press,* July 19, 1911. *New York Tribune,* July 19, 1911. *New York Globe,* July 19, 1911. *New York World,* July 19, 1911. *New York Times,* July 19, 1911. Grout said that Prendergast had agreed in conference to vote in favor of the compromise reached with the IRT. Grout, 2TC, 4:648.

32. New York City, Board of Estimate, *Minutes,* July 21, 1911. *Brooklyn Citizen,* July 21, 1911. *Brooklyn Eagle,* July 21, 1911. *New York Times,* July 22, 1911.

33. William J. Gaynor, press release, "To the People of New York City Relative to Subways," July 13, 1911, Clippings and Correspondence from the Office of the Mayor of the City of New York, New York Public Library. Grout, 2TC, 4:1052.

34. Gaynor alleged that the plan to grant the IRT a preferential was "a wrong and a humiliation" that had been foreseen just a few months before. The City, he said, was "being overreached by a few financiers of great ability," who had actually induced public officials to agree to subsidize the private companies to equip and operate new rapid transit facilities, "as though the City were in such evil case as to require that to be done in order to get necessary subways." Gaynor, press release, "To the People of New York City Relative to Subways," July 19, 1911. Andrew Freedman to A. J. County, July 26, 1911, 2TC, 4:495. Testimony of Bradford Merrill, 2TC, 6:704.

35. In 1910, Governor Charles Evans Hughes, who had created the PSC, decided not to run for reelection because of his "abiding distaste for politics and politicians." He was appointed to the U.S. Supreme Court in 1910 but resigned to make an unsuccessful bid for president in 1916 against the incumbent Woodrow Wilson. (Former PSC Chairman William R. Willcox was his campaign manager.) He was later reappointed to the Supreme Court and served as Chief Justice from 1930 to 1941. Robert F. Wesser, *Charles Evans Hughes: Politics and Reform in New York, 1905–1910* (Ithaca, N.Y.: Cornell University Press, 1967), 280, 290. Frederick S. Voss, "Charles Evans Hughes," in Kenneth T. Jackson, ed., *The Encyclopedia of New York City* (New Haven: Yale University Press, 1995), 572–573. In the 1910 gubernatorial election, Democrat John A. Dix, from upstate New York, beat Republican Henry L. Stimson. Dix had the support of Tammany Boss Charles F. Murphy. J. Sergeant Cram, appointed to the PSC by Dix to replace Edward M. Bassett, was Boss Murphy's social mentor. Robert F. Wesser, *A Response to Progressivism: The Democratic Party and New York Politics, 1902–1918* (New York: New York University Press, 1986), 37–39, 53.

36. *New York Tribune,* July 12, 1911. *New York Times,* July 12, 1911. *New York Post,* July 20, 1911.

37. Undated typescript, "Subway Record of the President of the Board of Aldermen, John Purroy Mitchel," John Purroy Mitchel Papers, Library of Congress. Edwin R. Lewinson, *John Purroy Mitchel: The Boy Mayor of New York* (New York: Astra Books, 1965), 95. Lately Thomas, *The Mayor Who Mastered New York: The Life and Opinions of William J. Gaynor* (New York: William Morrow, 1969), 461–462. Mitchel also appears to have sincerely believed that competition between transit companies was the best way for the City to proceed with subway expansion. He had been a consistent supporter of the Triborough System plan. From July 1911 on, he was willing to come to arrangements with the BRT to construct most of the lines that had been part of the Triborough System.

38. *New York American,* July 20, 1911.

39. Testimony of Bradford Merrill, 2TC, 6:797–799. Testimony of William R. Prendergast, 2TC, 6:165.

40. Board of Estimate, *Minutes*, July 20, 1911. *New York Post*, July 20, 1911. *New York Tribune*, July 21, 1911. *New York Times*, July 21, 1911. The Bronx representative was opposed to the solution because he did not believe that the alternative plan, in which the BRT would operate the Lexington Avenue line and the Jerome Avenue and Pelham lines in the Bronx, would benefit his area as much as the expansion of the IRT system. *New York Journal*, July 20, 1911. *New York Times*, July 21, 1911.

41. On July 26, J. P. Morgan, Jr., wrote to President Shonts: "I feel sure that it would be wiser for your company not to appear to be subway hunting for a little while." J. P. Morgan, Jr., to Theodore P. Shonts, July 26, 1911, 2TC, 5:1176. In a letter to Seth Low, Morgan said: "It does seem as though your work and ours had gone for nothing, but I don't believe it has, for, in the long last, it seems to me that the City must come back to the Interborough." J. P. Morgan, Jr., to Seth Low, July 24, 1911, Seth Low Papers, Columbia University.

42. Andrew Freedman to A. J. County, July 26, 1911, 2TC, 4:495.

43. *Brooklyn Citizen*, July 31, 1911.

44. *New York Tribune*, August 3, 1911. *Brooklyn Eagle*, August 21, 1911. The scheme to increase the mayor's power over transit development was only part of a plan for a revision of the City Charter that was under consideration by the State Legislature. The portions of the proposed revised charter having to do with rapid transit had been included at the specific request of Mayor Gaynor. According to Henry Bruère of the Bureau of Municipal Research, Gaynor did not want any new charter unless the rapid transit provisions were included because "the crux of the whole business" was the mayor's desire to get control over subways. Henry Bruere to John Purroy Mitchel, September 11, 1911, John Purroy Mitchel Papers, Library of Congress.

45. *Brooklyn Times*, August 3, 1911. *New York Globe*, August 3, 1911. *New York Standard Union*, August 3, 1911.

46. *Brooklyn Times*, September 11, 1911. *Brooklyn Eagle*, September 11, 1911.

47. *New York Evening World*, September 20, 1911.

48. *Brooklyn Eagle*, October 1, 1911.

49. *New York Times*, October 12, 1911.

50. *New York Times*, November 16, 1911. John Purroy Mitchel, "A Short History of the Transit Situation with Special Reference to Queens," John Purroy Mitchel Papers, Library of Congress.

51. Prendergast Statement, 14. Brian J. Cudahy, *Under the Sidewalks of*

New York: The Story of the World's Greatest Subway System, rev. ed. (Lexington, Mass.: Stephen Greene Press, 1988), 54.

52. Samuel Rea to John Purroy Mitchel, October 27, 1911, in Prendergast Statement, 11–13.

53. Prendergast Statement, 13–14.

54. Prendergast said that his relations with Mayor Gaynor for more than a year "had been very unpleasant." Prendergast Statement, 3.

55. Prendergast, 2TC, 6:248.

56. Prendergast Statement, 15.

57. Ibid., 14.

58. Ibid., 17–18. McAneny probably also was instrumental in convincing Prendergast that the Dual System plan should move forward. He and Prendergast were political allies within the Fusion movement. The two went to various political events together, at which McAneny made his usual arguments about breaking up congestion of population and so on. Ibid., 15. In the 1913 municipal elections, under the Fusion ticket, McAneny was elected president of the Board of Aldermen, Comptroller Prendergast was reelected, and John Purroy Mitchel was elected mayor.

59. Willcox, 2TC, 6:248. The only member of the Board of Estimate who opposed the financial arrangements with the IRT was President Mitchel.

60. *Brooklyn Eagle*, November 16, 1911. Chairman Willcox and two other commissioners, Eustis and McCarroll, constituting a majority of the Commission, said they were in favor of such an arrangement with the IRT. Commissioners Maltbie and Cram were still opposed.

61. McAneny, PSC Chairman William R. Willcox, and Comptroller Prendergast were the only public officials directly involved in the negotiations at this time. Prendergast Statement, 14–15. The presence of a representative of the Morgan bank at this meeting, and the participation of Davison and J. P. Morgan, Jr., at later conferences, are significant. Morgan later insisted that the Pennsylvania Railroad alone was responsible for the resumption of negotiations with the IRT. Morgan, 2TC, 5:1207. Nonetheless, the bank, which had an understanding with the IRT that it would handle all of the company's financial arrangements with respect to the money the IRT would need to participate in the Dual System plan, clearly was interested in this matter and played a prominent role in the negotiations. Indeed, the Morgan bank wanted a resumption of negotiations more than the IRT itself did. Testimony of August Belmont, 2TC, 6:508. Quackenbush, 2TC, 3:466.

62. Testimony of Milo R. Maltbie in State of New York Joint Legislative Committee to Investigate the Public Service Commissions, *Final Report* (1915), 1:1121.

63. Prendergast Statement, 15.

64. Ibid. Testimony of Duncan MacInness, 2TC, 3:594, 598–602.

65. MacInness, 2TC, 3:602.

66. This meant that the new lines would become self-sustaining sooner. LeRoy T. Harkness, "The Dual System Contracts in Their Relation to the Rapid Transit History of New York City," Municipal Engineers of the City of New York, *Proceedings for 1913* (1914), 264.

67. MacInness, 2TC, 3:629.

68. Ibid., 631.

69. *New York Sun*, January 22, 1912. *New York Times*, January 23, 1912. Prendergast, when asked why he had agreed to accept a plan amounting to a preferential to the IRT equivalent to 8.76 percent of the money it invested in old and new lines, while he had refused to accept the plan allowing the company a 9 percent preferential in July 1911, said that he and the other public negotiators had come to the conclusion that the bankers would accept no less. Since the City wanted the Dual System lines, it "was compelled to meet the terms." Prendergast, 2TC, 6:265. As for the attitude of the Morgan bank, Belmont said: "This matter of dealing with subways was based upon what would make a lasting and sound business enterprise. It is a banker's business to see to that, and that was the controlling element in it." Belmont, 2TC, 6:507.

70. *New York Times*, January 24, 1912.

71. *New York Times*, December 22, 1911. *New York Tribune*, December 28, 1911. *Brooklyn Eagle*, December 29, 1911. *New York Sun*, January 1, 1912.

72. *New York Times*, January 24, 1912. Thomas, *Gaynor*, 335.

73. *New York Sun*, August 5, 1913. *New York American*, August 25, 1913. Mitchel, the only member of the Board of Estimate to vote against the final Dual System contracts, was elected mayor on the Fusion ticket in 1913 after receiving strong support from Hearst and his allies. By 1917, however, Hearst and Mitchel were no longer cooperating and Hearst was influential in obtaining the Democratic mayoral nomination for John F. Hylan, a vigorous opponent of the Dual System plan. Hylan was elected mayor in 1917 and 1921. See Lewinson, *Mitchel*, 91–95, and Peter Derrick, "The New York City Transit Crisis of 1918–1925," (Master's thesis, Columbia University, 1967), 29–30.

74. *New York American*, January 24, 1912.

75. *New York American*, January 27, 1912.

76. *New York Evening Journal*, January 30, 1912.

77. McAneny and former Public Service Commissioner Edward M. Bassett gave speeches at the Central Citizens League on January 22. Bassett saw the Dual System as the first step toward "the rational development of the city" using city planning techniques. *Brooklyn Eagle*, January 23, 1912. In an-

other series of speeches at the City Club, Chief Engineer Nelson Lewis of the Board of Estimate gave a speech titled "The Relation of Adequate Planning to the Distribution of Population." Lewis argued that the purpose of the Dual System plan was to distribute the population by direct lines of transportation at a low fare. *New York Times*, January 28, 1912.

78. George McAneny, "The Responsibility of the City Administration in Regard to Subway Construction," address given at the City Club of Philadelphia, January 27, 1912, George McAneny Papers, Columbia University. This speech was reported in New York newspapers. *New York American*, January 28, 1912. *New York Times*, January 28, 1912. *New York Post*, February 10, 1912.

79. McAneny, "The Responsibility of the City Administration."

80. Ibid.

81. Ibid.

82. McAneny's ridership estimates were essentially correct. In 1917, when several of the Dual System lines opened for operation, 990 million trips were made annually on New York's rapid transit lines. In 1927, the figure was 1.83 billion; by 1930, there were more than 2 billion riders. See Table 2.

83. McAneny, "The Responsibility of the City Administration."

84. "Letter from Interborough Company to Commission," February 27, 1912, PSC, *Annual Report, 1912*, 1:683–692.

85. Ibid.

86. Ibid.

87. The IRT would pay the construction costs of these improvements as well as the cost of new equipment. For the elevated extensions, the IRT was to receive a certificate from the PSC allowing the company an eighty-five-year franchise. As compensation, the City was to share equally with the IRT any increased profits from the Manhattan Railway lines after the extensions were put in operation. Ibid.

88. Theodore P. Shonts to William R. Willcox, February 27, 1912, PSC, *Annual Report, 1912*, 1:692.

89. *New York Times*, January 24, 1912.

90. Shonts, 2TC, 3:734.

91. PSC, *Annual Report, 1912*, 1:84.

92. Timothy S. Williams to Thomas E. Clark, December 10, 1912, 2TC, 5:1037–1043.

93. Specifically, the PSC wanted the power, which it did not have under existing law, to make contracts under which existing transit lines could be operated in conjunction with new City-owned lines. Such a contract could allow a private operator to retain, from the combined revenues of the City-owned and privately owned lines, an amount equal to its average annual

income from its existing system. These provisions were applicable to the proposed contract with the BRT. *Brooklyn Eagle,* March 19, 1912.

94. The proposed legislation also would permit the Commission, in exchange for the pooling of receipts on old and new subway lines, to enter into a contract under which a private operator (i.e., the IRT) could retain annually from operating revenue a sum equal to its annual profits from existing subway lines plus a sum not exceeding 6 percent on its new investment in new subway lines. *Brooklyn Eagle,* March 19, 1912.

95. Ibid.

96. J. Joseph Huthmacher, *Senator Robert F. Wagner and the Rise of Urban Liberalism* (New York: Atheneum, 1971), 24.

97. *Brooklyn Citizen,* March 27, 1912.

98. *New York Post,* March 26, 1912.

99. *Brooklyn Citizen,* March 27, 1912.

100. *New York Times,* March 25, 1912.

101. *Brooklyn Eagle,* March 27 and 28, 1912. *New York World,* March 28, 1912.

102. The Wagner Act is Chapter 226, Laws of New York, 1912. *Brooklyn Eagle,* April 8, 1912. *New York Times,* April 11, 1912.

103. The two were Maltbie and Cram. If Williams had sided with these men, the Dual System plan would not have proceeded with IRT participation at this time. After discussing the matter with Willcox and McAneny, Williams told them he thought that the Dual System plan "was the best thing that could be done for the city" and that he was "ready to stand for it." Testimony of George V. S. Williams, 1TC, 1:1038–1041.

104. The Morgan bank's understanding was that the IRT wanted to borrow $157,656,950, of which $50,656,950 was needed for refunding the IRT's present debt; $56 million was to be used for new subway construction, $21 million for new subway equipment, and $30 million for improvements on the Manhattan Railway Company's lines. In order to procure this money, the IRT would authorize and issue new, first-mortgage, 5 percent, thirty-three-year bonds to an aggregate amount of about $170 million, to be secured by a first mortgage on all the property, leasehold and freehold, of the IRT. The IRT was to sell the bonds to the Morgan bank at 93.5 cents on the dollar, which would yield the $157,656,000 it needed. The Morgan bank notified the IRT that it intended to form a syndicate to take those bonds, in which the firm itself was to have a share. It was understood that the entire transaction depended upon confirmation of the legality and constitutionality of the proposed contract between the City and the IRT. J. P. Morgan and Company to Theodore P. Shonts, April 9, 1912, 2TC, 3:343–345.

105. Theodore P. Shonts to J. P. Morgan and Company, April 12, 1912, 2TC, 3:484. Three days later, Shonts informed the bank that the PSC would allow a brokerage charge of only 3 percent upon the $77 million to be used for new subway construction and equipment. Theodore P. Shonts to J. P. Morgan and Company, April 15, 1912, 2TC, 3:514. According to IRT secretary Horace Fisher, it was understood that the difference between this 3 percent and the 6.5 percent discount at which the bonds were actually sold would be made up by the IRT out of its own funds and would not be charged to the cost of construction or equipment. Testimony of Horace Fisher, 2TC, 3:516.

106. *Brooklyn Eagle*, April 12, 1912. Shonts, 2TC, 3:730. "Opinion of Supreme Court In Re Subway Contracts," *The Admiral Realty Company, Plaintiff, v. The City of New York*, in PSC, *Annual Report, 1912*, 1:698–704.

107. Ibid.

108. Testimony of BRT Counsel George Yeomans, 2TC, 3:845. Testimony of IRT counsel Delancey Nicoll, 2TC, 3:734. The Court of Appeals upheld Blackmar's decision in a four-to-two decision on June 29, 1912. *Admiral Realty Company v. City of New York*, 206 New York Reports (1912), 110–162.

109. PSC, *Annual Report, 1912*, 1:94.

110. New York City, Board of Estimate and Apportionment, Special Committee on Pending Transit Proposals, "Supplementary Report of a Committee of the Board of Estimate and Apportionment with Relation to Pending Proposals for the Construction, Equipment and Operation of Rapid Transit Lines in the City of New York," May 22, 1912, in PSC, *Annual Report, 1912*, 1:704–731. (This report was supplementary to the "Report of the Conferees" of June 5, 1911).

111. Ibid.

112. McAneny defended the terms of the proposed contracts, saying that the companies had conceded "the utmost that they can afford to give." *New York Post*, May 24, 1912.

113. *Brooklyn Citizen*, May 25, 1912.

114. Board of Estimate, *Minutes*, May 24, 1912. At the May 24 meeting, Mitchel filed a brief with the Board stating the reasons he opposed the proposed contracts. Mitchel's brief contained no criticism of the route structure of the Dual System plan; his comments were devoted solely to the proposed financial terms and their possible results. His main argument against the IRT contract was that it would capitalize for fifty years the company's present earnings and would do so under a formula for distributing subway earnings by which the City might never be able to recoup the money it had invested in new subway construction. John Purroy Mitchel, "Defects of the Offer of the Interborough Rapid Transit Company of February 27, 1912"

(to the Board of Estimate and Apportionment), May 24, 1912, John Purroy Mitchel Papers, Library of Congress.

115. PSC, *Annual Report, 1912,* 1:98. *Brooklyn Eagle,* October 29, 1912. Timothy S. Williams to Thomas E. Clark, December 10, 1912, 2TC, 5:1037–1043.

116. Albert Rathbone, Counsel to the Central Trust Company, Memorandum to the Public Service Commission for the First District, June 13, 1910, in 2TC, 5:1024–1025. Yeomans, 2TC, 5:1007. Testimony of BRT Auditor Howard Abel, 2TC, 5:1022.

117. Existing BRT subsidiaries could not enter into the contract because none was in a position to accept a first mortgage. Testimony of LeRoy T. Harkness, 2TC, 5:738.

118. Rathbone Memorandum, 2TC, 5:1024–1025. Abel, 2TC, 5:1034. Testimony of Timothy S. Williams, 2TC, 5:1055.

119. The notes were secured by an agreement of trust running to the Central Trust Company, as trustee. Abel, 2TC, 5:992. The additional $20 million was to be sold later.

120. Until this time, the public negotiators had not realized that the BRT plan was to charge up interest on the whole $40 million from October 1, 1912, on. The Commission was concerned that if this interest were added to the cost of construction, then the preferential payment that the New York Municipal Railway would be allowed to deduct out of future earnings would be increased and, as a result, the City would begin to receive its preferential later. Harkness, 2TC, 5:748. Timothy S. Williams to Thomas E. Clark, December 10, 1912, in 2TC, 5:1037–1043.

121. Williams to Clark, December 10, 1912. Prendergast, 2TC, 6:271.

122. Harkness, 2TC, 5:749.

123. Under this agreement, the BRT agreed to spend $16 million of the $40 million in the first year after the contract was signed, and interest on this $16 million would be allowed toward the cost of construction. Interest on the other $24 million would also be charged to the cost of construction, but the final contract would specify that the New York Municipal Railway was committed to pay back this interest sometime in the future when the new lines were earning a profit. In other words, the BRT, via its subsidiary, would eventually absorb $1.33 million, representing the excess interest on the $24 million. Harkness, 2TC, 1:350 and 5:743. *New York American,* December 24, 1912.

124. *Brooklyn Citizen,* December 24, 1912.

125. *New York World,* December 31, 1912. *Brooklyn Citizen,* January 4, 1913.

126. *New York World,* January 30, 1913.

127. *New York Globe,* January 30, 1913.

128. Irving M. Plant, *Population Growth of New York City by Districts, 1910–1948* (Report prepared for Consolidated Edison Company of New York, December 1948), 4. Edward Ewing Pratt, *Industrial Causes of Congestion of Population in New York City*, Columbia University Studies in History, Economics and Public Law, 43 no. 1, Whole Number 109 (New York: Columbia University Press, 1911), 33.

129. Testimony of George McAneny, 1TC, 1:1450.

130. *New York World*, December 4, 1912.

131. Pratt, *Causes of Congestion*, 33.

132. *Brooklyn Eagle*, December 4, 1912. Willcox, in a letter to Hylan, criticized him for his narrow point of view, saying that his only concern seemed to be with the Eastern District and that Hylan did "not comprehend the full significance" of the Dual System. *New York World*, December 4, 1912.

133. *New York Journal*, January 6, 1913.

134. *Brooklyn Eagle*, January 14, 1913. *New York World*, January 15, 1913. Although it is impossible to determine just what "public opinion" thought of the proposed Dual System contracts at the time, even the *World*, which strongly opposed the contracts, admitted that "we do not flatter ourselves that the people, now, generally oppose the contracts. They, too, are tired . . . they want to see rapid transit upon some terms—almost any terms." *New York World*, January 20, 1913.

135. *Brooklyn Times*, January 18, 1913.

136. *New York Times*, January 21, 1913.

137. Ibid. John Purroy Mitchel, "Subway Record of the President of the Board of Aldermen, John Purroy Mitchel" (undated, 1913), John Purroy Mitchel Papers, Library of Congress.

138. *New York Post*, January 23, 1913.

139. *New York Tribune*, January 22, 1913.

140. Ibid. *New York Sun*, January 21, 1913. Later in 1913, Governor Sulzer would break with Tammany, which then sought to destroy him politically. After a fierce struggle during which it was shown that Sulzer had pocketed some campaign contributions for his personal use, he was impeached and removed from office. Wesser, *A Response to Progressivism*, 118–124.

141. *New York Mail*, January 21, 1913. The State Senate had the responsibility of approving gubernatorial nominations to the PSC.

142. Ibid.

143. *New York American*, January 21, 1913.

144. *New York American*, January 23, 1913.

145. *New York Evening Journal*, January 28, 1913.

146. *New York Post*, January 31, 1913.

147. *New York Globe*, January 29, 1913.

148. Essentially, all these statements were variations of the arguments made in McAneny's January 1912 speech, "The Responsibility of the City Administration." A speech by Willcox defending the Dual System was reported in the *New York Herald*, January 27, 1913. On January 30, 1913, Prendergast made a speech, "The Dual Subway Plan," Seth Low Papers, Columbia University. McAneny gave a speech to the Real Estate Board of Brokers on February 1, "Speech to Real Estate Board of Brokers," George McAneny Papers, Princeton University. This was reported in the *New York Times* on February 2, 1913.

149. Sulzer told Low that he had decided in favor of the plan as a result of the letter. William Sulzer to Seth Low, March 20, 1913, Seth Low Papers, Columbia University.

150. Seth Low to William Sulzer, January 22, 1913, Seth Low Papers, Columbia University. *New York Times*, January 23, 1913. Sulzer had represented a district on the Lower East Side for many years in the State Legislature and the U.S. Congress. Wesser, *A Response to Progressivism*, 101–102.

151. The *Times* noted that this letter was the bank's response to the "sharp criticism" of the proposed financial arrangements in the proposed Dual System contract between the City and the IRT. *New York Times*, January 28, 1913.

152. The bank said that it had told the IRT that "we and our immediate associates would buy the issue at 93½, being on a basis to net 5⅝ percent per annum." The amount of the debt discount and expense was the subject of discussion between the conferees and the IRT and its banker. It was agreed that the final contract with the IRT would specifically say that the debt discount and expense allowed to the IRT would not exceed 3 percent. Any discount above 3 percent would have to be paid by the IRT out of its own funds. This provision was included in Contract No. 3. Ibid.

153. J. P. Morgan and Company would form a syndicate to take the bonds at ninety-six cents on the dollar, reserving to itself and its associates "a compensation of 2½ percent, in return for our original undertaking to purchase the bonds, for our work in forming and managing the syndicate, and for the general services rendered in a transaction of such magnitude and complexity." The bank also said that throughout the transaction, "our idea had been to serve the Interborough Company upon the best terms at which it could reasonably expect to secure its fund here and elsewhere, and at the same time to safeguard the terms of the bond issue in such a way that, for the investment, no question can properly arise as to the soundness of this security." According to the House of Morgan: "Unless the likelihood of a reasonable and substantial profit were held out, no group could have been found to undertake a contract of this size and importance." Of the

proceeds to the IRT, $50 million was to be used to refund existing debt of the company. Ibid.

154. Ibid.

155. In 1916, J. P. Morgan, Jr., made it clear that the preferential arrangement with the IRT was the price the City had to pay to have the company's help in achieving the extensive subway system that the public negotiators wanted. There was nothing more to it than that, Morgan said, and certainly nothing underhanded about it. Morgan called his firm "the Interborough bank" and admitted that the stand taken by his bank had strengthened the IRT in its negotiations with the conferees. He said that he would not have considered financing the plan for the expansion of the IRT subway system unless he had felt that the investment was "really safe." The conferees had wanted a new system that went far beyond previous offers of the IRT in scope, with lines running out "into the Bronx and the wilds of the Parkway" (that is, Eastern Parkway in Brooklyn). He defended the amount of the preferential payment by saying that it was based on the amount of profit the IRT was making from the existing subway. Testimony of J. P. Morgan, Jr., 2TC, 4:1163, 1179, 1221, 1225.

156. *New York Times,* January 28, 1913.

157. *New York Tribune,* February 4, 1913. The *Times* immediately observed that, with McCall's appointment, Tammany was setting up for the mayoral election of 1913, a prediction that proved to be entirely accurate. McCall was the Democratic candidate for mayor in 1913, but was defeated by Mitchel. *New York Times,* February 4, 1913. Lewinson, *Mitchel,* 94.

158. *New York World,* February 6, 1913. *New York Herald,* February 6, 1913. *New York Times,* February 6, 1913.

159. *New York Herald,* February 15, 1913. *New York World,* February 17, 1913. *New York Sun,* February 18, 1913.

160. *New York World,* February 17, 1913.

161. *New York Sun,* February 18, 1913.

162. PSC, *Annual Report, 1913,* 1:41.

163. Maltbie and Mitchel said they opposed the contracts because they believed that the financial concessions embodied in them were too high a price to pay for the benefits the City expected to derive from the realization of the Dual System plan. They made no criticism of the route structure of the Dual System plan. As an alternative to the Dual System plan, Maltbie and Mitchel urged consideration of the plan they had prepared in February. Milo R. Maltbie, "Analysis of the Rapid Transit Contracts between the City of New York and the Interborough Rapid Transit Company and New York Municipal Railway Corporation," in PSC, *Proceedings,* vol. 8 (1913), 189–214. John Purroy Mitchel, untitled memorandum to the Board of

Estimate and Apportionment, March 11, 1913, John Purroy Mitchel Papers, Library of Congress.

164. Board of Estimate, *Minutes*, March 18, 1913. *New York Times*, March 19, 1913.

165. PSC, *Annual Report, 1913*, 1:44.

166. *City of New York, by the Public Service Commission for the First District with Interborough Rapid Transit Company, Contract No. 3: Contract for Additional Rapid Transit Railroads*, March 19, 1913. *City of New York, by the Public Service Commission for the First District with New York Municipal Railway Corporation, Contract No. 4: Contract for New Rapid Transit Railroads*, March 19, 1913. (These were the Dual System contracts.) *Public Service Commission for the First District to Manhattan Railway Company, Certificate: Second Avenue, Third Avenue and Ninth Avenue Additional Tracks*, March 19, 1913. *Public Service Commission for the First District to Interborough Rapid Transit Company, Certificate: Webster Avenue Line, Eighth Avenue and 162nd Street Connection, Queensboro Bridge Line, West Farms Subway Connection*, March 19, 1913. (These were certificates for improvements to the elevated lines of the Manhattan Railway Company, leased to the IRT.) *Public Service Commission for the First District to New York Municipal Railway Corporation, Certificate: Jamaica Avenue Line, Liberty Avenue Line*, March 19, 1913. *Public Service Commission for the First District to New York Municipal Railway Corporation, Certificate: Broadway, Fulton Street and Myrtle Avenue Additional Tracks*, March 19, 1913. (These were the certificates for improvements on the existing BRT lines.) *City of New York, by the Public Service Commission for the First District, Supplementary Agreement: Trackage Rights, Seventh Avenue–Lexington Avenue Line, White Plains Road Line, Steinway Tunnel Line*, March 19, 1913. *City of New York by the Public Service Commission for the First District, Interborough Rapid Transit Company and New York Municipal Railway Corporation, Supplementary Agreement: Trackage Rights over Steinway Tunnel Line*, March 19, 1913. (These were the agreements for trackage rights for Manhattan Railway Company elevated trains on the Jerome Avenue line, the White Plains Road line, and the IRT's lines in Queens and for trackage rights for New York Municipal Railway Corporation [BRT] trains on the IRT lines in Queens to Astoria and Woodside-Corona.) All of these documents are in PSC, *Annual Report, 1913*, vol. 4. On March 20, 1913, the PSC approved mortgages filed by the IRT and the New York Municipal Railway Corporation and issued orders granting each company permission to issue bonds from which the funds necessary for carrying out the agreements formalized the previous day were to be derived. PSC, *Annual Report, 1913*, 1:45.

167. This fare could only be changed by mutual agreement between the respective company and the City of New York. Thus, unless the City agreed

to allow a fare increase, the fare on each system would be five cents for the entire forty-nine-year life of the lease.

168. Passengers using services originating at a station on one of the IRT subway lines, but feeding into the Manhattan elevated lines, would pay five cents for one continuous trip. For example, a West Bronx passenger boarding a station on the Jerome Avenue line using the new service feeding into the Ninth Avenue el would pay five cents for a trip. These provisions were in the contracts and the related certificates and are summarized in PSC, *New Subways for New York: The Dual System of Rapid Transit* (New York: Public Service Commission for the First District, December 1913), 62–63. This was an updated version of a report of the same title published in June 1911.

169. Statistical data on the route mileage of every expansion, and contraction, of New York's subway is in Boris Pushkarev, Jeffrey M. Zupan, and Robert S. Cumella, *Urban Rail in America: An Exploration of Criteria for Fixed-Guideway Transit* (Bloomington: Indiana University Press, 1982), Appendix, table H-5.

170. PSC, *New Subways for New York* (December 1913), 1–2. The figures in this report are the best baseline numbers for the Dual System. The extension of the Corona line to Flushing, agreed to after the signing of the contracts, added two track miles to previous estimates. As of December 1913, the IRT subway had 73 track miles, the Manhattan elevated lines had 118, and the BRT system had 105, for a total of 296 miles. The December 1913 figures indicated that the Dual System and related improvements would add 149 track miles to the IRT subway, 21 track miles to the Manhattan elevated lines, and 155 track miles to the BRT system, for a total of 325 track miles added. A track mile is one mile of single track. A route mile is one mile of a line, no matter how many tracks. Thus one route mile with four tracks is four track miles.

171. D. L. Turner, "The New Municipal Transportation System for New York City, and Its Relation to the City Plan," *Landscape Architecture*, 3, no. 4 (July 1913): 193–194. Turner's July 1913 figure was 232 route miles. To this, the one additional route mile of the extension to Flushing must be added.

172. Remarks of J. N. Dodd, Assistant Electrical Engineer, Public Service Commission, during discussion of a lecture by LeRoy T. Harkness on the Dual System, Municipal Engineers of the City of New York, *Proceedings* (1913), 280–281.

173. Brian J. Cudahy notes that the Dual System "would account for the building of the major portion of today's subway network." Cudahy, *Under the Sidewalks of New York*, 39. The only major existing lines not part of the Dual System are those of the Independent Subway System and the Dyre Avenue and Rockaway lines. A few connections between lines have also been

added since the 1940s. In addition, minor portions of the MTA expansion plan of 1968 have been put in service, including the 63rd Street and Archer Avenue lines. Meanwhile, some of the Dual System's elevated lines were torn down. Calculations from statistical tables listing the route mileage of the different segments of the New York subway show that, as of 1980, 151 of the system's 230 route miles were those of the Dual System. Pushkarev, Zupan, and Cumella, *Urban Rail in America,* Appendix, tables H-3 and H-5.

174. Turner, "The New Municipal Transportation System," 194. McAneny made this same point years later. McAneny quoted in Cyrus Adler, *Jacob H. Schiff: His Life and Letters* (New York: Doubleday Doran, 1928), 1:334.

175. Turner, "The New Municipal Transportation System," 194. "Seats" is the measure used by Turner. McAneny also noted that through the Dual System contracts "the mileage of the rapid transit lines was doubled and their carrying capacity trebled." McAneny quoted in Adler, *Jacob H. Schiff,* 1:334.

176. The Dual System quadrupled the rapid transit track mileage in the Bronx. PSC, *New Subways for New York* (December 1913), 15.

177. Ibid., 14. In 1913, there were only four stations outside of Manhattan and the Bronx—on the existing IRT subway in Brooklyn—at which a person could board a train and travel through Manhattan for a single fare. The Dual System would increase the number of such stations in Brooklyn from 4 to 193; in Queens, from none to 41; in Manhattan, from 146 to 202; and in the Bronx, from 29 to 75. Turner, "The New Municipal Transportation System," 194–195.

178. For the track configurations of the Dual System lines, as modified through the 1990s, see Peter Dougherty, *Tracks of the New York City Subway* (privately printed, 1997).

179. A few outlying districts with direct service were as much as sixty minutes away. "Time Zone Map of New York City Giving Times of Travel on Completion of the Dual System from 14th Street Manhattan by Subway, Elevated and Surface Lines to All Places Reached by a 5 Cent Fare," in New York City, Board of Estimate and Apportionment, Committee on City Plan, *Commission on Building Heights and Restrictions, Final Report* (New York: June 2, 1916), map following 48. Distances from City Hall are shown on a map, "Persons per Acre, 1930, in Statistical Areas of New York City Mapped in Five Four-Mile Zones of Radius Distance from City Hall," in Walter Laidlaw, *Population of the City of New York, 1890–1930* (New York: Cities Census Committee, 1932), 235.

180. Turner, "The New Municipal Transportation System," 196. The impact of the Dual System lines is discussed in Chapter 7.

181. The only line that was not included in the final plan was the proposed Brooklyn-Queens crosstown elevated line. The PSC also had plans for a later extension of the Fourth Avenue subway to Staten Island via a tunnel from 65th Street in Brooklyn. PSC, *New Subways for New York* (December 1913), 15. This line, however, was not included in the Dual System contracts and was never built.

182. Although the contract specified that BRT services would use the Queensboro Bridge to pass into Queens, it was later decided that the rail connection from 60th Street to this station would be via a new tunnel under the East River. According to Brian J. Cudahy, this was done "when concern developed over whether the bridge could bear up under the weight of all-steel subway trains." Cudahy, *Under the Sidewalks of New York,* 62.

183. *New York Times,* May 25, 1913. PSC, *Annual Report, 1913,* 1:48–49. Although this was technically the first extension under the contracts, the extension to Flushing is best regarded as an integral part of the original Dual System plan.

184. *City of New York by the Public Service Commission for the First District, Interborough Rapid Transit Company and New York Municipal Railway Corporation, Supplementary Agreement: Trackage Rights over Steinway Tunnel Line,* March 19, 1913.

185. This line was to begin in Manhattan at Sixth Avenue, but was later extended to Eighth Avenue. The line in Brooklyn was not completely defined when the Dual Contracts were signed. This line was eventually connected to the old Canarsie BRT elevated line.

186. *New York Times,* March 19, 1913.

187. Ibid. The estimated costs and funding responsibilities, as of March 19, 1913, broke down as follows:

For the Expanded IRT System	
City funds—construction	$63,335,637
IRT funds—construction	$56,260,000
IRT funds—equipment	$21,000,000
Subtotal, IRT	$140,595,637
For the Expanded BRT System	
City funds—new construction	$72,005,991
City funds—already committed	$28,496,000
New York Municipal Railway funds—construction of City-owned lines	$13,695,000
New York Municipal Railway funds—reconstruction, extending and	

improving existing lines	$21,000,000
New York Municipal	
Railway—equipment	$26,000,000
Subtotal, BRT	$161,196,991
Total, Dual System	$301,792,628
Improvements to Manhattan Railway lines	
IRT funds	$25,000,000
Grand Total	$326,792,628

188. Comptroller Prendergast made this comment in a speech given on January 30, 1913, at which time the estimated cost was slightly lower than $327 million. Prendergast Oral History Project, 471.

189. Ibid. The numbers had been increasing as more detailed estimates were made. On February 23, 1913, for example, it had been reported that the costs were $314 million. *New York Times,* February 23, 1913. When the Dual System contracts were signed on March 19, 1913, only preliminary engineering estimates had been made for the costs of constructing many of the new lines.

190. PSC, *New Subways for New York* (December 1913), 3.

191. Ibid.

192. The revised estimate is in PSC, *New Subways for New York: The Dual System of Rapid Transit* (New York: Public Service Commission for the First District, June 1913), 3. This is the earlier version of the December report of the same title.

193. This further revised estimate is in PSC, *New Subways for New York* (December 1913), 3. In the end, the costs of the Dual System and related improvements to the elevated lines, including equipment, was $595,844,000. Of this, $310,341,000 was paid by the City of New York; $170,714,000 by the IRT; and $114,789,000 by the New York Municipal Railway Corp. (i.e., the BRT) or its successor company, the Brooklyn Manhattan Transit Corporation (BMT). "Existing Transit Arrangements," in Citizens Budget Commission, *Studies on Transit Unification in the City of New York* (New York, September 1936), 5–7 (the pages of the articles in this collection are separately numbered). The reasons for these cost increases are discussed in Chapter 7.

194. The PSC never made explicit the reasons for the increases in costs between March and December, but they appear to largely represent more detailed engineering estimates. In 1913, PSC engineers developed official rules for determining costs. "Rules Adopted for Chief Engineer's Determination of Costs, October 17, 1913," in PSC, *Annual Report, 1913,* 4:342–355. These rules were to be used to make more precise cost estimates and appear to have resulted in raising project cost estimates. In addition, the De-

cember estimates appear to include the cost of the extension of the Queens line to Flushing, which had been included in the plan by this time. PSC, *Annual Report, 1913,* 1:48–49. All of the increases were for the City's share of the costs, which rose from approximately $164 million in March 1913 to $200 million in December 1913.

195. "Construction Cost Index History (1910–1999)" in *Engineering News Record,* March 22 to 29, 1999, 100. One dollar in 1913 is equal to sixty dollars in 1999. Thus, $366 million in 1913 dollars equaled $21.96 billion in 1999. The actual cost of building the entire system today, including the tunnels, would undoubtedly be much higher, given the constraints of constructing major public works in New York's dense urban environment.

196. According to an engineering report on the Dual System, comparing it to other large-scale projects: "The total cost of building and equipping New York's new rapid-transit lines will be in the neighborhood of $366,000,000. This is substantially equal to the entire cost of the Panama Canal. It is three times the cost of the New York barge canal [i.e., the Erie Canal]." The cost of the Panama Canal was $375 million. Fred Lavis, *Building the New Rapid Transit System of New York City* (1915; reprint, Belleville, N.J.: Xplorer Press, 1996), 2.

197. For the cost of any equipment over $22 million, the IRT would receive an amount equal to its actual annual payments for the cost of additional funds that would be borrowed.

198. This percentage was set by the fact that the amount the IRT was to receive as a preferential equaled 8.76 percent of the cost of the IRT's capital investments in old and new lines and in equipment.

199. The contracts are summarized in PSC, *New Subways for New York* (December 1913), 64–66.

200. For the cost of any equipment in addition to that required for initial operation of the new lines, the BRT subsidiary would receive an amount equal to its actual annual payments for the cost of additional funds that would be borrowed.

201. This included 1 percent for amortization.

202. George McAneny, "What I Am Trying to Do: Helping to Make New York a Cleaner, More Healthful, More Beautiful, and Greater City," *World's Work* 26 (June 1913): 172–181. Prendergast Statement.

203. Gaynor died on September 12, 1913. He had been denied the Democratic nomination for mayor by Tammany boss Charles F. Murphy shortly before and was planning to run for reelection as an independent candidate. Tammany nominated PSC chairman Edward McCall as its mayoral candidate. Thomas, *Gaynor,* 481, 486, 491. After Gaynor died, McAneny

was asked to stand in for him on an independent ticket. McAneny, however, had already accepted the Fusion nomination as president as the Board of Aldermen, along with John Purroy Mitchel as the mayoral candidate and Prendergast running for reelection as Comptroller. He therefore felt he could not honorably accept this offer. The Fusion ticket won the election. McAneny quoted in Adler, *Jacob H. Schiff*, 1:334–335.

204. Gaynor press release, March 18, 1913, Clippings and Correspondence, New York Public Library.

NOTES TO CHAPTER 7

1. Robert A. Hall, Jr., *New York City Rapid Transit Chronology* (Ann Arbor, Mich.: privately printed, 1945), 6–8. Stan Fischler, *Uptown, Downtown: A Trip through Time on New York's Subways* (New York: Hawthorn Books, 1976), 236–237, 240–241. *New York Times*, September 9, 1932.

2. Irving M. Plant, *Population Growth of New York City by District, 1910–1948* (Report prepared for Consolidated Edison Company of New York, December 1948), 4–8.

3. The amount of land in the districts served by the new rapid transit lines was twice that of existing residential areas. Calculations from statistics in Plant, *Population Growth of New York City*, 17. Plant divided New York City into twenty-six districts for this report. Manhattan plus the older areas of the Bronx and Brooklyn have 28,102 acres. (This includes all districts in Manhattan plus Districts 10 and 18–21.) The districts served by the Dual System lines (Districts 11–14, 22–25, and half of 16b) have 59,515 acres. Plant's calculation of acreage excluded parks, cemeteries, and large commercial areas. Plant also has districts that are not included in this definition of the older developed areas or the subway suburbs. These districts consist of the outer portions of Queens and all of Staten Island. In 1940, the population of these districts was 664,237, including the 174,441 people living on Staten Island.

4. Statistics on the mix of housing types for each neighborhood are in News Syndicate Co., the New York Times, Daily Mirror, and Hearst Consolidated Publications, *New York City Market Analysis* (New York: printed by the newspaper group, 1943).

5. Consolidated Edison Company of New York, *Survey of the New York City Market: Manhattan, Bronx, Brooklyn, Queens* (New York: Consolidated Edison, 1945), contains detailed information on housing quality.

6. By 1948, most of the Dual System's subway suburbs had been built up. For this year, one study has estimated that 1,930,000 people traveled to jobs in the Manhattan CBD from 6 to 10 A.M. on an average business day. Of that

total, 1,025,000 traveled from homes in the Bronx, Brooklyn, and Queens. Of these, 854,000, or 83 percent, took the subway to work, most of them on the lines of the Dual System. Another 575,000 people lived in Manhattan and worked in the Manhattan CBD, 418,000 of them using the subway. Joseph M. Leiper, "Analyze Transit Travel Trends," *Interim Technical Report, Preliminary Summary Tables*, of the Transit Service Demand and Supply Evaluation Study (New York, May 1, 1984). The Brooklyn subway ridership figures in this report have been adjusted downward.

7. George McAneny, "Zoning for Social Welfare," address delivered to the Conference on Charities and Corrections in New York City, May 26, 1916, and "Program for Comprehensive City Planning in New York City for 1917," December 21, 1916, typescript, George McAneny Papers, Princeton University. See also George McAneny, "What I Am Trying to Do: Helping to Make New York a Cleaner, More Healthful, More Beautiful, and Greater City," *World's Work* 26 (June 1913): 172–181.

8. New York City, Board of Estimate and Apportionment, *Commission on Building Districts and Restrictions, Final Report*, discusses all aspects of the zoning proposal. Appendix VII contains the full text of the Building Zone Resolution adopted by the Board of Estimate and Apportionment on July 25, 1916, followed by "Use District" maps for each borough indicating the streets that could have stores and other businesses.

9. In 1919, Transit Construction Commissioner John Delaney said: "Under existing conditions there will be in effect next year what practically amounts to a six cent fare on rapid transit lines, for the reason that the City will contribute nearly $9,000,000 of public funds to pay interest and sinking fund on the City debt of $200,000,000, incurred for rapid transit construction." Delaney quoted in "A Brief History of Transit Unification," in Citizens Budget Commission, *Studies on Transit Unification in the City of New York* (New York, September 1936), 3 (the pages of the articles in this collection are separately numbered). Since these payments continued every year for several decades, this means that since 1920 the City of New York has been subsidizing the subway from tax revenues.

10. Fred Lavis, *Building the New Rapid Transit System of New York City* (1915; reprint, Belleville, N.J.: Xplorer Press, 1996), 7–20. The Dual System contracts specified that the Public Service Commission's engineers were in charge of the contracts for City-owned facilities. Contracts for improvements to the privately owned elevated lines controlled by the IRT and BRT were to be supervised by the companies, subject to the specifications, review, and approval of the PSC.

11. See Appendix 2. Hall, *Rapid Transit Chronology*, 5–7. Fischler, *Uptown, Downtown*, 236–237, 240–241. *New York Times*, September 9, 1932. The last

section of an IRT line to open was the Brooklyn line to New Lots, which opened in 1922.

12. Report of Justice John A. McAvoy, New York State Transit Commission, *Fifth Annual Report, 1925,* 145.

13. This was the portion of the Lower Manhattan loop subway from Chambers Street south. Hall, *Rapid Transit Chronology,* 7.

14. In addition, in 1925 the Fourth Avenue subway in Brooklyn was extended to 95th Street. Ibid., 5–7.

15. New York State, Transit Commission, *Twelfth Annual Report, 1932,* 126.

16. See Table 2. The only year in which more passengers rode the system was 1947, when two million more people were carried than in 1930. (The 1947 figure includes the traffic on the Independent Subway System, which opened between 1932 and 1940.) From 1947 on, ridership declined to just under one billion trips in 1977. The number of annual passengers then started to rise again. In 1998, the New York City rapid transit system carried just over 1.2 billion passengers for the year, or nearly four million on an average weekday. 1998 Statistics from Metropolitan Transportation Authority (hereafter abbreviated MTA), *Annual Report, 1998.*

17. "Existing Transit Arrangements," in Citizens Budget Commission, *Studies on Transit Unification,* 12.

18. Ibid., 13–14.

19. Between 1913 and 1920, the cost of construction in the United States rose quickly. Construction work that would have cost $1 million in 1913 cost $2.51 million by 1920. "Construction Cost Index History (1910–1999)," in *Engineering News Record,* March 22 to 29, 1999, 100. The index number for 1913 is 100; for 1920, it is 251. Increased operating costs also affected the return on investment, since the fare was fixed at five cents. Between 1913 and 1920, operating costs increased substantially. In 1913, the ratio of operating expenses to revenues for the IRT system was 34 percent. Largely because of increased labor costs, by 1921 it was 60 percent. For the BRT, the ratio went from 50 percent to 84 percent. Citizens Budget Commission, "Existing Transit Arrangements," 13. Much of the operating cost of a rapid transit system is for the cost of labor, for which the consumer price index (CPI) is a fair indicator of trends. Between 1915 and 1920, the CPI doubled from 30.4 to 60.0. This meant that an item costing about one dollar in 1915 cost almost two dollars in 1920. "Consumer Price Index, 1915–1997," *World Almanac and Book of Facts, 1998* (Mahwah, N.J.: World Almanac Books, 1997), 128.

20. The estimated cost of the Dual System in December 1913 had been $366 million. As of 1936, the actual costs of the Dual System and related

improvements to the elevated lines, including equipment, had been $595,844,000. Of this amount, $310,341,000 was paid by the City of New York; $170,714,000 by the IRT; and $114,789,000 by the New York Municipal Railway Corp. (i.e., the BRT) or its successor company, the Brooklyn Manhattan Transit Corporation (BMT). Citizens Budget Commission, "Existing Transit Arrangements," 5–7.

21. Ibid., 5. The estimate in March 1913 had been $63,335,637. *New York Times*, March 19, 1913. By 1936, the IRT had contributed $58,158,000 toward the cost of construction of Contract No. 3 lines, plus $67,838,000 for rolling stock. The total cost of the Contract No. 3 lines was thus $246,523,000. The March 1913 estimate had been $140,595,637.

22. As of October 31, 1937, the City had received only $19,189,314 from the IRT, which was all it would ever receive. The actual cost to the City for debt service up to that time was $102,780,000. Joseph L. Weiner, "Rapid Transit: History of Rapid Transit in New York City," in New York State, Constitutional Convention Committee, *New York City Government; Functions and Problems* (New York, 1938), 114.

23. "Existing Transit Arrangements," 7. The March 1913 estimate had been $100,501,991. *New York Times*, March 19, 1913. By this time, the company had contributed $46,052,000 toward construction costs and $68,737,000 on new rolling stock. The total cost of the Contract No. 4 lines was thus $304,603,000. The March 1913 estimate had been $161,196,991.

24. The actual cost to the City up to October 31, 1937, for debt service on the bonds issued for the construction of new BRT lines was about $151,700,000. Weiner, "Rapid Transit," 114. Citizens Budget Commission, "Existing Transit Arrangements," 10.

25. Weiner, "Rapid Transit," 115. Citizens Budget Commission, "Existing Transit Arrangements," 12–14. Cynthia Morse Latta, "The Return on the Investment in the Interborough Rapid Transit Company" (Ph.D. diss., Columbia University, 1975), 243–244. Clifton Hood, *722 Miles: The Building of the Subways and How They Transformed New York* (New York: Simon and Schuster, 1993), 182–183.

26. Weiner, "Rapid Transit," 115.

27. Latta says that the Dual System contracts had been predicated on the assumption of stable prices, which is why the fare was fixed at five cents in each of the contracts. As soon as prices started to rise more quickly, however, expectations regarding the income to be derived from subway operation had to be revised downward. Latta states: "If we assume . . . that the patronage on the subway and elevated lines would not have been significantly different in the absence of inflation, we can say that divisible profits from subway operation would have arisen sooner and been larger than even the

optimists had predicted because patronage ran substantially ahead of projections." Latta, "The Return on the Investment in the IRT," 292.

28. According to Latta, the assumption of stable prices was not unreasonable in 1913. From the end of the Civil War into the late 1890s, the trend of prices had been downward. From the end of the 1890s until 1913, prices had risen, but at an average rate of 1 percent a year. She notes that the effect of such a small increase could have been made up by improvements in productivity. Latta, "The Return on the Investment in the IRT," 292.

29. A table showing transit (rapid transit and/or streetcar) fares in the nation's twenty largest cities in 1913 and 1924 reveals that New York was the only city without a fare increase during these years. Fares elsewhere ranged from six cents to ten cents. Even Cleveland, which had a three-cent fare in 1913, had a six-cent fare in 1924. Gerhard M. Dahl, *Transit Truths* (New York, 1924), 53. Clifton Hood notes: "In a single two-month period in 1918, railways in 332 towns and cities discarded the straight nickel fare and raised ticket prices. By 1920, railways in 500 cities has hiked their fares." Hood, *722 Miles,* 183.

30. Peter Derrick, "The New York City Transit Crisis of 1918–1925" (Master's thesis, Columbia University, 1967), 26–31. Michael W. Brooks, *Subway City: Riding the Trains, Reading New York* (New Brunswick, N.J.: Rutgers University Press, 1997), 93–105. Hood, *722 Miles,* 193–197.

31. Joshua B. Freeman notes that in New York City the transit fare transcended simple economics. According to Freeman, "the entire economic and social infrastructure of the city—including wage rates, residential patterns, and factory and office locations—was predicated on cheap mass transit." Joshua B. Freeman, *In Transit: The Transport Workers Union in New York City, 1933–1966* (New York: Oxford University Press, 1989), 286.

32. Peter Derrick, "The N.Y.C. Mess: Legacy of the Five-Cent Fare," *Mass Transit* 8, no. 7 (July 1981): 12–13, 26. The politicization of the subway fare also had an impact on the quality of service. In 1936, the Citizens Budget Commission noted that "[s]ervice was seriously deprecated because of reduced earnings as necessary improvements were curtailed or avoided." Citizens Budget Committee, "Existing Transit Arrangements," 15. In the year 2000, the fare on the subway was $1.50.

33. A report of the Citizens Budget Commission in 1936 noted: "Nor, contrary to popular impression, have the contracts operated entirely to the financial advantage of the Companies. For a number of years there were large deficits in the returns to the Companies under the contracts." This forced the BRT "into receivership and almost did the same for the Interborough Company in 1922." Citizens Budget Commission, "Existing Transit Arrangements," 11–12.

34. Dahl, *Transit Truths*, 19.

35. By 1936, the BRT/BMT had invested $114,768,000 of its own funds in the construction and equipment of the Dual System lines. This was up from the 1913 estimate of about $61 million. Up to 1936, the BRT/BMT had received $181,188,624 in preferential payments from operating revenues under the provisions of Contract No. 4. The company was owed an unpaid deficit of $3,127,182. Weiner, "Rapid Transit," 115. Citizens Budget Commission, "Existing Transit Arrangements," 7, 9.

36. Latta calculated the average annual rate of return available to the speculator in Interborough securities for various hypothetical investors. Depending on when an investor bought or sold, it was possible to come out ahead on an investment in IRT stock. As a general conclusion, however, Latta says that by the time the City finally took possession of the IRT in 1940, the average annual rate of return on a share of IRT stock acquired at par at the time of the company's incorporation was between -5.7 and -6.0 percent. The purchaser of a 3.5 percent rapid transit construction bond issued by the City, on the other hand, would have realized an average annual rate of 4.1 percent over the same period. Latta, "The Return on the Investment in the IRT," 284.

37. By 1936, the IRT had invested $170,714,000 in the construction and equipment of the new lines provided for under Contract No. 3 and the related certificates for the Manhattan Railway Company's lines. Up to 1936, the IRT had received $241,538,043 in preferential payments from operating revenues under the provisions of Contract No. 3. The company was owed an unpaid deficit of $446,110. The IRT had never made a profit from the improvements to the Manhattan Railway Company's elevated lines, and, in 1936, there were large deficits on this account. Citizens Budget Commission, "Existing Transit Arrangements," 3, 5, 9.

38. Latta, "The Return on the Investment in the IRT," 288, 295.

39. Joel Fischer, "Urban Transportation: Home Rule and the Independent Subway System in New York City, 1917–1925" (Ph.D. diss., St. John's University, 1978). Derrick, "The New York City Transit Crisis." Hood, *722 Miles*, 203–217. Brooks, *Subway City*, 98–105.

40. Hall, *Rapid Transit Chronology*, 8. They were operated publicly from the start by an agency created by the State of New York called the Board of Transportation of the City of New York. For details on building the IND system, see Frederick A. Kramer, *Building the Independent Subway* (New York: Quadrant Press, 1990).

41. The original IND system was all underground, except for a short section in Brooklyn. Subways were constructed under Sixth and Eighth Avenues in Manhattan to replace the els on Sixth and Ninth Avenues, and a

subway was built under Fulton Street in Brooklyn to replace a BMT el. In the West Bronx, a subway was constructed under the Grand Concourse, to compete with the Jerome Avenue line, three blocks away. There were no transfer connections between any IND station and stations of the IRT or BMT. (All of the connections that exist today were built after 1940.) The IND added 60 route miles (with 196 track miles) to the network, compared to the total of 177 route miles (with 510 track miles) for the Dual System (including the first subway), as of 1936. In addition, in 1936 the Manhattan Elevated System had 41 route miles (with 123 track miles). Citizens Budget Commission, "Existing Transit Arrangements," 1. At the end of the twentieth century, the mileage of the New York rapid transit system was considerably shorter than in 1936, since from the 1930s on, most of the oldest elevated lines were torn down. As of 1995, the subway system had 230 route miles and 656 miles of track in passenger service. MTA New York City Transit, *Facts and Figures 1995* (New York, May 1995), 20. The changes in rapid transit mileage as the elevated lines were torn down are in Boris Pushkarev, Jeffrey M. Zupan, and Robert S. Cumella, *Urban Rail in America: An Exploration of Criteria for Fixed-Guideway Transit* (Bloomington: Indiana University Press, 1982), Appendix, table H-5.

42. Arthur J. Waterman, Jr., "Integration of Rapid Transit Facilities of the City of New York" (Ph.D. diss., New York University, 1940), 324–375.

43. For the political background of unification, see Freeman, *In Transit*, 183–223, and Hood, *722 Miles*, 224–239.

44. Latta, "The Return on the Investment in the IRT," 281, 283.

45. For the New York State portion of the New York region, since 1968 the MTA's board of directors has determined policy for all passenger rail services, as well as most bus operations. Most of the members of this board are appointed by the governor of New York State, others by the mayor of New York City and officials of the various suburban counties. The MTA board approves the budgets of the New York City Transit Authority, now known as MTA New York City Transit, as well as those of the two commuter railroads under its control—MTA Metro North Railroad and MTA Long Island Rail Road. It is also the board of directors for the Triborough Bridge and Tunnel Authority, now also known as MTA Bridges and Tunnels. (This agency operates all the toll bridges and tunnels connecting the five boroughs of New York to each other.) The MTA board is also responsible for making final decisions about expanding the rail network.

46. When track, signals, stations, and other parts of the system are allowed to deteriorate and subway cars are not replaced at the end of their useful lives, on-time performance and quality of service declines. See James K. Cohen, "Capital Investment and the Decline of Mass Transit in New York

City, 1945–1981," *Urban Affairs Quarterly* 23, no. 3 (March 1988): 369–388, and MTA, *Staff Report of Capital Revitalization for the 1980's and Beyond* (New York, November 25, 1980).

47. For the impact of the pro-highway policies of Robert Moses, see Robert A. Caro, *The Power Broker: Robert Moses and the Fall of New York* (New York: Alfred A. Knopf, 1974), and H. V. Savitch, *Post-Industrial Cities: Politics and Planning in New York, Paris, and London* (Princeton: Princeton University Press, 1988), 30–33.

48. For the impact of federal policies, see Kenneth T. Jackson, *Crabgrass Frontier: The Suburbanization of the United States* (New York: Oxford University Press, 1985), 190–271.

49. For the impact of the automobile on urban areas, see Clay McShane, *Down the Asphalt Path: The Automobile and the American City* (New York: Columbia University Press, 1994).

50. Brian Cudahy, *Under the Sidewalks of New York: The Story of the Greatest Subway System in the World*, rev. ed. (Lexington, Mass.: Stephen Greene Press, 1988), 119, 130.

51. After the elevated lines were torn down, the East Side saw the construction of hundreds of high-rise apartment buildings, many replacing old tenement buildings. Meanwhile, the business districts served by the Lexington Avenue line, particularly East Midtown, grew in employment. As a result, the Lexington Avenue subway, the only line serving this area, became severely overcrowded, especially during peak periods. The original plans for the Second Avenue subway are shown on a map done by the Board of Transportation of the City of New York titled "Proposed Additional Rapid Transit Lines and Proposed Vehicular Tunnels" (August 25, 1929). The last portion of the Second Avenue el was closed in 1942; the Third Avenue el was closed in Manhattan in 1955 and in the Bronx in 1973. Pushkarev, Zupan, and Cumella, *Urban Rail in America*, Appendix, table H-5.

52. MTA, *Staff Report of Capital Revitalization.*

53. The efforts of MTA chairman Richard Ravitch to win support of the first capital plan in Albany are discussed in James Lardner, "Painting the Elephant," *The New Yorker*, June 25, 1984, 41–72.

54. MTA, *Submission to the MTA Capital Program Review Board* (New York, September 25, 1981); *MTA Capital Program, 1982–1991* (New York, May 1992); *MTA Capital Program, 1992–1996* (New York, October 1992); *MTA Capital Program Needs and Opportunities, 1991–2001* (New York, March 25, 1990), 18–21.

55. Urbanomics, *The Future of the Extended Core in the Global Economy* (Draft report to Access to the Region's Core, a joint transportation study of the

Metropolitan Transportation Authority, the Port Authority of New York and New Jersey, and New Jersey Transit, New York, June 16, 1995).

56. MTA, *Annual Report, 1998,* 104.

57. MTA, *MTA Capital Needs and Opportunities, 1992–2011* (New York, May 25, 1990) and *Capital Program, 2000–2004* (New York, October 1999).

58. The Regional Plan Association (RPA) has proposed a new rail network called MetroLink that includes the Second Avenue subway, as well as new rail lines in the Bronx, Brooklyn, and Queens. This network would consist of new lines and connections, as well as existing rail lines that would be incorporated into the system. In this regard, it is similar to the BRT portion of the Dual System plan, which joined old lines to new to create a new network that linked three boroughs. The MetroLink proposal is discussed in RPA's web site, www.rpa.org.

59. George McAneny, "The Responsibility of the City Administration in Regard to Subway Construction," address given at the City Club of Philadelphia, January 27, 1912, George McAneny Papers, Columbia University.

60. George McAneny, "Remarks," in *Proceedings of the Sixth National Conference on City Planning* (1914), 229.

61. According to McAneny, a planning commission would be able to halt "spasmodic, unbalanced city development." George McAneny, "Program for Comprehensive City Planning in New York City for 1917," December 21, 1916, typescript, George McAneny Papers, Princeton University.

62. Harvey Kantor, "Modern Urban Planning in New York City: Origins and Evolution, 1890–1933" (Ph.D. diss., New York University, 1971), 150.

63. *New York Times,* September 21, 1914. New York City, Board of Estimate and Apportionment, Committee on the City Plan, *Development and Present Status of City Planning in New York City* (New York, December 31, 1914), 12.

64. Committee on the City Plan, *Development and Present Status of City Planning,* 3, 37.

65. The report noted that with or without a comprehensive plan, the City would spend hundreds of millions of dollars on public improvements during the next twenty-five years. The purpose of city planning was to lay down the general lines of growth so that these expenditures would contribute in the best way possible to "the solid and permanent upbuilding of a great and even greater city—strong commercially, industrially and in the comfort and health of its people." Ibid., 12.

66. Ibid, 4. McAneny, "Program for Comprehensive City Planning."

67. Hylan opposed city planning. On February 1, 1918, Hylan and his allies on the Board of Estimate abolished the Standing Committee on the City Plan. Kantor, "Urban Planning," 232. In arguing for the abolishment

of this committee, he quipped that he had no use for "art artists." George McAneny, "Reminiscences," George McAneny Oral History Project, Oral History Collection, Columbia University, 1949, 7.

68. The reformers had hoped, for example, that the difficulty of obtaining park land in congested areas of New York would convince City officials of the necessity of reserving land for parks in outlying boroughs in advance of development. This would have been one of the functions of a city planning commission. Mayors Hylan and Walker, however, allowed private real estate interests to buy up most of the land in the outlying boroughs, thus monopolizing land that could easily have been reserved for parks. When the City later decided to build parks, it was forced to buy land from the private developers at greatly increased prices. Caro, *The Power Broker*, 337–338.

69. The reformers believed that without restrictions on the intensive use of land and related housing regulations, "physical and moral ill-health, industrial inefficiency and a long chain of preventable social maladies very costly to the community and a heavy handicap upon individual and social achievement" were likely to ensue. The problem was one "of enabling the great mass of people to live amidst decent surroundings and to bring up their children under proper conditions, and of preventing those who do not care for decent conditions . . . from inflicting a needless burden on their neighbors." George B. Ford, "The City Controlling the Development of Private Property," in Municipal Engineers of the City of New York, *Proceedings for 1915* (New York, 1916), 51.

70. Ibid., 69–70.

71. George McAneny, "Zoning for Social Welfare," address delivered to the Conference on Charities and Corrections in New York City, May 26, 1916, George McAneny Papers, Princeton University.

72. Kantor, "Urban Planning," 178, 183. S. J. Makielski, *The Politics of Zoning: The New York Experience* (New York: Columbia University Press, 1966), 115. Kevin D. Revell, "Regulating the Landscape: Real Estate Values, City Planning and the 1916 Zoning Ordinance," in David Ward and Olivier Zunz, eds., *The Landscape of Modernity* (Baltimore: Johns Hopkins University Press, 1992), 24–26, 32–40.

73. The Commission warned that "there are areas in the Bronx and Brooklyn where Lower East Side conditions of excessive congestion of population are being repeated." New York City, Board of Estimate and Apportionment, *Report of the Heights of Buildings Commission* (New York, December 23, 1913), 56.

74. Makielski, *The Politics of Zoning*, 28–36.

75. McAneny emphasized the need for regulation of private development in a speech, "Zoning for Social Welfare," delivered before the

Conference on Charities and Corrections on May 16, 1916. McAneny noted that living conditions were presently bad only within a small area of New York City. Elsewhere there were great possibilities for guided growth, since more than three-quarters of the city's land area was "yet virgin territory; farm lands and woods, not yet built upon at all." Because the lines of the Dual System already were being built into this virgin territory, zoning was an immediate necessity. Zoning and the Dual System were complementary: "The vast system of new rapid transit railways . . . will naturally redistribute the population, relieve congestion and add to the city's wealth through all its areas. The districting and building regulation plan will keep this redistribution properly directed, complementing the work of the railroad builders and laying the foundation in New York for the best and most enduring sort of city planning." McAneny, "Zoning for Social Welfare."

76. "Area districts" were created labeled A to E. "A" districts were industrial areas, largely along the waterfront. In the other districts, all new buildings, whether commercial or residential, were required to have yards, courts, and other open spaces. These ranged from the "B" districts, which allowed bulky apartment houses, to "E" districts, intended for single-family homes. Carol Willis, "A 3-D CBD: How the 1916 Zoning Law Shaped Manhattan's Central Business Districts," in Todd W. Bressi, ed., *Planning and Zoning in New York City: Yesterday, Today and Tomorrow* (New Brunswick, N.J.: Center for Urban Policy Research, 1993), 13–22, and Richard A. Plunz, "Zoning the New Horizontal City," in ibid., 35–36. Revell, "Regulating the Landscape," 20–35. Kantor, "Urban Planning," 165. Mel Scott, *American City Planning since 1890* (Berkeley and Los Angeles: University of California Press, 1969), 271. The area districts are discussed in the final report of the Commission. New York City, Board of Estimate and Apportionment, Committee on the City Plan, *Commission on Building Districts and Restrictions Final Report* (New York, June 2, 1916), 38–41.

77. Plunz, "Zoning the New Horizontal City," 36–37. Revell, "Regulating the Landscape," 41.

78. Plunz, "Zoning the New Horizontal City," 35–38. Even in the "E" districts, small apartment houses could be built among the single-family homes. George B. Ford, *New York City Building Zone Resolution* (New York: New York Title and Mortgage Co., 1920).

79. Kenneth T. Jackson notes that the entire population of the United States in 1945 could have been legally housed in New York City if all property had been developed to its maximum allowable use. Jackson, "The Capital of Capitalism: The New York Metropolitan Region, 1890–1940," in Anthony Sutcliffe, ed., *Metropolis 1890–1940* (Chicago: University of Chicago Press, 1984), 338.

80. Ford, *New York City Building Zone Resolutions*, 9.

81. Plunz also notes that the new rapid transit system was itself part of the reason why the zoning law had been weakened in terms of limiting housing densities in the outer boroughs. New subways offered hope that working families could disperse to better homes. But the subways also had to generate enough passenger traffic to cover all of their operating and capital costs, at a five-cent fare. For this to happen, higher densities were necessary than the planners had hoped. According to Plunz, this was "a reality that the 1916 commission could not afford to overlook." Plunz, "Zoning the Horizontal City," 27, 31. In the end, only part of what the reformers had wanted was achieved. The subway suburbs ended up with more people living in apartment houses than had been hoped, but at much lower population densities than the old tenement districts, and much better living conditions.

82. Plunz's article is based on a presentation he gave at a conference on zoning in New York. In a discussion following Plunz's talk, Frances Halsband argued that "the emerging mass transit systems" were more influential in "channeling development" that either the building code or the zoning code. Frances Halsband, "Commentary," in Bressi, ed., *Planning and Zoning in New York*, 105. Plunz also had said: "The question that arises, of course, is how and by whom the transit plan [the Dual System] was implemented. The most one can say here is that it was a geopolitical evolution of considerable complexity and intrigue: from the old-money families and their large estates in the Bronx, the value of which would be enhanced by the public investment in transit; to the various entrepreneurs along the way, such as Edward A. MacDougall at Jackson Heights in Queens; to simple engineering and topographical constraints." Plunz, "Zoning and the New Horizontal City," 33. Halsband's comment on this was: "Plunz asked us, 'Who planned mass transit?'; it certainly was not the City Planning Commission, which did not exist until years after the 1916 zoning ordinance was passed and much of the transit system had been built." Halsband, "Commentary," 105. In fact, as has been shown, the development of the Dual System plan was highly complex, but not in the way many people have supposed. Moreover, to the public officials who worked on the zoning resolution, it and the subway expansion plan were all part of the same broad program of city planning they hoped to implement.

83. Whether these areas are "city" or "suburb" depends on one's point of view. Peter Hall has observed that in Europe these areas of New York would be called suburbs, but that most Americans do not define them as such. Peter Hall, *The World Cities* (New York: McGraw-Hill, 1966), 194–195. In *Cities of Tomorrow: An Intellectual History of Urban Planning and Design in the*

Twentieth Century (New York: Basil Blackwell, 1988), 48–85, Hall calls such areas "mass transit suburbs." When residents of the Bronx or Brooklyn travel to Manhattan, they usually say they are going to "the city."

84. According to Deborah Dash Moore, although many of the Jews who moved to the Bronx and Brooklyn from congested areas in Manhattan preferred to live in apartments, they regarded their new surroundings as "suburban." Deborah Dash Moore, *At Home in America: Second Generation New York Jews* (New York: Columbia University Press, 1981), 24.

85. Thomas Adams, Harold M. Lewis, and Theodore McCrosky, *Population, Land Values and Government: Studies of the Growth and Distribution of Population and Land Values; and of Problems of Government,* vol. 2 of the Regional Survey (New York: Regional Plan of New York and Its Environs, 1929), 60. Also quoted in Moore, *At Home in America,* 24–25. In Boston, the areas to which Irish, Italians, and Jews moved to from the tenement districts have been called the "Zone of Emergence." Robert A. Woods and Albert J. Kennedy, *The Zone of Emergence* (Cambridge: Massachusetts Institute of Technology Press, 1962). For a discussion of defining "suburb," see Kenneth T. Jackson, "Urban Deconcentration in the Nineteenth Century: A Statistical Inquiry," in Leo F. Schnore, ed., *The New Urban History: Quantitative Explorations by American Historians* (Princeton: Princeton University Press, 1975), 111–113, and *Crabgrass Frontier: The Suburbanization of the United States* (New York: Oxford University Press, 1985), 4–6.

86. Calculations of the population in the subway suburbs from Plant, *Population Growth of New York City,* 4.

87. Calculations from statistics in Plant, *Population Growth of New York City,* 4.

88. The four districts, as defined by Plant, were the Lower East Side, the East Side between Houston Street and 48th Street, the Lower West Side to 36th Street, and Williamsburg in Brooklyn. Plant, *Population Growth of New York City,* 4. Plant's boundary for the Lower East Side was different than that used by Edward Ewing Pratt in *Industrial Causes of Congestion of Population in New York City,* Columbia University Studies in History, Economics and Public Law 43, no. 1, Whole Number 109 (New York: Columbia University Press, 1911), 34. Pratt's definition included the area between Houston Street and 14th Street.

89. Walter Laidlaw, *Population of the City of New York, 1890–1930* (New York: Cities Census Committee, 1932), 202.

90. Statistics from ibid., 212.

91. Ibid., 202.

92. The communities of the subway suburbs were the West Bronx, the East Bronx; Long Island City (including Astoria), Jackson Heights, and

South Queens in Queens; and Bay Ridge, Flatbush, and Coney Island (including much of southern Brooklyn north of Coney Island) in Brooklyn. These are the district names used in Plant, *Population Growth of New York City*, 4, 17.

93. Ibid., 4.

94. The Flatbush area of Brooklyn, served by the BRT's Brighton line and the IRT's Nostrand Avenue subway, for example, grew from a population of 79,846 in 1910 to 394,215 in 1940. Jackson Heights in Queens, served by the Flushing line, increased in population from 32,932 to 199,987. Ibid.

95. Laidlaw, *Population of the City of New York, 1890–1930*, 202, 233. For the impact of the new subways on the growth of the Bronx, see Robert A. Olmsted, "Transportation Made The Bronx," *The Bronx County Historical Society Journal* 35, no. 2 (Fall 1998): 169–173.

96. Plant, *Population Growth of New York City*, 17. In 1940, the most crowded section of the city was Central Harlem, which had 243 people per acre, compared to 201 in 1910. In contrast, Plant's District 1, the Lower East Side, had 354 people per acre in 1910, and 131 in 1940.

97. New rapid transit lines had a "profound effect on the distribution of population in the city, for the growth of various sections and the decline of others is intimately associated with the expansion of elevated and subway lines." Ibid., 9.

98. Queens Chamber of Commerce, *Queens Borough* (New York: Queens Chamber of Commerce, 1926), 11.

99. "Time Zone Map of New York City Giving Time of Travel on Completion of the Dual System from 14th Street, Manhattan, by Subway, Elevated, and Surface Lines, to All Places Reached by a 5 Cent Fare," in *Commission on Building Districts and Restrictions, Final Report*, following page 48.

100. The increases in real estate values are documented in Edward M. Law, "Real Estate Values and Population Growth along Rapid Transit Lines in the City of New York," *Municipal Engineers Journal* 21 (1936): 67–88. Law said: "When we consider that since the year 1900 over twelve billion dollars have been added to the real estate values of this city following the construction of these additional transit facilities, we may realize the tremendous returns in taxable values which have thus been created." In the late 1920s, the Regional Survey of New York stated that "all land values in the New York region have been . . . created by its transportation facilities," and that the most important influence on recent increases in land values in the outer boroughs had been the new rapid transit lines. Adams, *Population and Land Values*, 151.

101. Edwin H. Spengler, *Land Values in New York in Relation to Transit*

Facilities, Columbia University Studies in History, Economics and Public Law, Whole No. 333 (New York: Columbia University Press, 1930), 41, 131.

102. Clara Cardia, *Ils ont construit New York: Histoire de la métropole au XIX*[e] *siècle* (Geneva: Georg Editeur, 1987), 167–169, 213–214. See also John Tauranac, *Elegant New York: The Builders and the Buildings, 1885–1915* (New York: Abbeville Press, 1985).

103. Adams, *Population and Land Values*, 151–155. Spengler, *Land Values in New York*, 51–65. With respect to the growth of Midtown as a business center, Spengler argued that the new subways had not "caused" the growth of Midtown, but had accelerated growth that was already underway. Spengler, *Land Values in New York*, 65.

104. Adams, *Population and Land Values*, 164–166. Carl W. Condit, *The Port of New York: A History of the Rail and Terminal System from the Grand Central Electrification to the Present* (Chicago: University of Chicago Press, 1981), 89–100. Peter Hall, *Cities in Civilization* (New York: Pantheon Books, 1998), 763–764.

105. In comparison to the number of people coming into the CBD by subway on an average business day, the number of rail commuters has always been relatively small. On an average business day in 1948, for example, more than 2.2 million people entered the CBD by the New York subway for all purposes, whereas only 283,000 did so by commuter rail. In 1994, the figures were 1,661,941 subway and 232,053 commuter rail riders. New York Metropolitan Transportation Council, *Hub-Bound Travel 1994* (New York, February 1996), 17, 33.

106. The architecture and design of office buildings and other commercial structures in New York is discussed in Robert A. M. Stern, Gregory Gilmartin, and Thomas Mellins, *New York 1930: Architecture and Urbanism between the Two World Wars* (New York: Rizzoli, 1987), 504–621.

107. Nancy L. Green, "Sweatshop Migrations: The Garment Industry between Home and Shop," in Ward and Zunz, eds., *The Landscape of Modernity*, 217–219.

108. In 1994, Midtown had about 195 million square feet, and Lower Manhattan about 118 million. Data from Urbanomics, *The Future of the Extended Core*, 18. In 1994, the Manhattan CBD had a total of about 360 million square feet of office space; the next largest center in America was Chicago, with 115 million square feet. The balance of the office space in the CBD was in the area between Midtown and Lower Manhattan. Ibid., 5.

109. Ibid., 16.

110. Leiper, "Analyze Transit Travel Trends." New York Metropolitan Transportation Council, *Hub-Bound Travel 1994*, 17.

111. This is based on calculations of the percentage of total subway rid-

ership in 1950 boarding at stations on the Dual System lines. The balance of ridership used services of the Independent System. Board of Transportation, *Transit Record* 31, no. 3 (March 1951): 7–10.

112. Richard Plunz, A *History of Housing in New York City: Dwelling Type and Social Change in the American Metropolis* (New York: Columbia University Press, 1990), 121–122, 128–130.

113. Ibid., 150. Evelyn Gonzalez, "From Suburb to City: The Development of the Bronx, 1890–1940," in *Building a Borough: Architecture and Planning in the Bronx, 1890–1940* (The Bronx: The Bronx Museum of the Arts, 1986), 21–23.

114. Plunz, *History of Housing,* 122.

115. In the mid-1930s, Edwin H. Spengler debated the issue of causation with Edward M. Law at a meeting of the Municipal Engineers of the City of New York. In a talk to the engineers, Law had argued that by means of the extension of the subway system "into the outer open spaces of the city, the population in congested centers has been spread out to take up residence in these hitherto undeveloped areas." In his talk, Law also documented the large increases in land values in these communities. Following Law's talk, he and Spengler went back and forth over the issue of causation. Spengler said that he agreed with Law that land values had gone up along the Dual System lines, but saw the new subways as "instruments" whereby the land value increases had been made possible, rather that causes. Law, "Real Estate Values and Population Growth along Rapid Transit Lines," 67–88. Discussion following Law's talk, *The Municipal Engineers Journal* 21 (1936): 91–96. In his book, Spengler asserted that rather than being a "cause of land value changes, a transit facility should more properly be regarded as a construction which permits or facilitates, under certain circumstances, an emergence of land values." Spengler, *Land Values in New York in Relation to Transit Facilities,* 133.

116. Adams, *Population and Land Values,* 62.

117. Moore, *At Home in America,* 35–39.

118. Marion Casey, "'From the East Side to the Seaside': Irish Americans on the Move in New York City," in Ronald H. Bayor and Timothy J. Meagher, eds., *The New York Irish* (Baltimore: Johns Hopkins University Press, 1996), 396.

119. Ibid., 401.

120. Ibid., 397. A 1945 Con Ed market survey documents the fact that apartments in the outer boroughs were larger than those in Manhattan and had fewer people per room. Consolidated Edison, *Survey of the New York City Market,* 25, 43, 67, 95.

121. Casey, "From the East Side to the Sea Side," 397. Peter Hall has

analyzed the development of the "mass transit suburb" in New York, London, Paris, and Berlin from 1900 to 1940 as a reaction to the terrible housing conditions of the period up to 1900–1910 and the threats to the wider society that resulted. According to Hall, the early leaders of the planning movement were "obsessed with the evils of the congested Victorian slum city. . . . But all the time, the giant city was changing, partly through the reaction of legislators and social reformers to these evils, partly through market forces." Hall also notes that new transportation technologies "allowed this suburbanization process to occur." Hall, *Cities of Tomorrow*, 44, 48.

122. Plunz, *History of Housing*, 123–124. For more on the development of the garden apartment see Stern, Gilmartin, and Mellins, *New York 1930*, 478–520.

123. Cleveland Rodgers and Rebecca Rankin, *New York, the World's Capital City: Its Development and Contribution to Progress* (New York: Harper and Bros., 1948), 289. Peter Hall has commented that in Europe around 1900, one of the reactions to congested slum conditions was the start of public housing. He contrasts this situation to New York, where the concept of public housing was decisively rejected at this time. Regarding this rejection, Hall notes that "Peter Marcuse's explanation is that of the three reasons why housing emerged as an issue—externalities like fire and disease dangers, concern for social order, and the protection of real estate values—the first two faded after 1910, as public health and fire control improved and the immigrants were assimilated." Hall, *Cities of Tomorrow*, 40. Hall cites Peter Marcuse, "Housing Policy and City Planning: The Puzzling Split in the United States, 1893–1911," in Gordon E. Cherry, ed., *Shaping an Urban World* (London: Mansell, 1980), 23–58. To Marcuse's explanation should be added the successful implementation of the Dual System of Rapid Transit, which provided the means by which the population was able to escape to better housing, constructed by the private sector, in the subway suburbs.

124. The mix of housing types in every neighborhood of New York in the early 1940s is documented in News Syndicate, *New York City Market Analysis.* This survey divided all of the boroughs into districts and provided statistical information for each district. There were twenty-four districts for Manhattan, twenty for the Bronx, twenty-eight for Brooklyn, thirty-five for Queens, and eight for Staten Island. The one district where less than 50 percent of the buildings were single- and two-family houses was in the southwest Bronx along the Grand Concourse, where only about 40 percent were small homes.

125. The rows of solid masonry along the streets of Manhattan south of 155th Street can be seen in real estate atlases. See, for example, George W. Bromley and Walter S. Bromley, *Atlas of the City of New York, Borough of Man-*

hattan (Philadelphia: G. W. Bromley and Co., 1911), and *Manhattan Land Book of the City of New York* (New York: G. W. Bromley, 1955).

126. Most of the subway suburbs are still largely in place today. The best way to get the feel of the neighborhoods is to walk through them. There are excellent photographs and descriptions of the neighborhoods of the Bronx in Lloyd Ultan, *The Beautiful Bronx, 1920–1950* (Westport, Conn.: Arlington House, 1979), and Lloyd Ultan and Gary Hermalyn, *The Bronx: It Was Only Yesterday, 1935–1965* (The Bronx: The Bronx County Historical Society, 1992). For Brooklyn, see Citizens Committee for New York City, *The Neighborhoods of Brooklyn* (New Haven: Yale University Press, 1998). The 1943 Market Analysis also has one page of neighborhood photographs for each of its districts. News Syndicate, *New York City Market Analysis.*

127. Plunz, "Zoning and the New Horizontal City," 40.

128. Ibid.

129. The number of single- and two-family homes in these neighborhoods in the early 1940s is provided in the district summaries in News Syndicate, *New York City Market Analysis,* and in maps in Consolidated Edison, *Survey of the New York City Market.* For a look at block after block of single- and two-family homes along the Brighton and Culver lines in southern Brooklyn, see Sanborn Map Company, *Borough of Brooklyn, City of New York,* vol. 13 (1906, updated to 1930).

130. New construction figure from Plunz, *History of Housing,* 131. Even in the Bronx, however, the single-family home was the ideal. Richard Plunz, "Reading Bronx Housing, 1890–1940," in *Building a Borough: Architecture and Planning in the Bronx, 1890–1940* (The Bronx: The Bronx Museum of the Arts, 1986), 38–39.

131. Analysis of the Bedford Park neighborhood in the Northwest Bronx, for example, shows that it had many one- and two-family homes in 1911. In 1938, almost all of these homes were still there. The vacant land surrounding them, however, had been largely built up with five- and six-story apartment houses. As of 1945, 366 of the 635 residential structures in the neighborhood were one- and two-family houses. George W. Bromley and Walter S. Bromley, *Atlas of the City of New York, Borough of the Bronx, Sections 11, 12, 13* (Philadelphia: G. W. Bromley and Co., 1911), and *Atlas of the City of New York, Borough of the Bronx North of 172nd Street* (Philadelphia: G. W. Bromley and Co., 1938). Statistics from Consolidated Edison, *New York City Market Survey,* 44–45.

132. News Syndicate, *New York City Market Analysis,* pages on each neighborhood (pages not numbered). Part of this area is called Wakefield. On February 20, 1999, the *New York Times* Real Estate section cited Wakefield as a "solidly middle-class neighborhood . . . filled primarily

with one- and two-family homes, with a sprinkling of three- and four-family homes as well as some apartment houses along the main roads." In the same article, the Bronx Borough Historian Lloyd Ultan said: "The area has a sort of inner suburban air about it. . . . It's rather quiet, and the density of population is low."

133. News Syndicate, *New York City Market Analysis.*

134. In 1940, 92 percent of the dwelling units in the Bronx were rented, rather than owned. in Brooklyn, the figure was 81 percent, and in Queens, 63 percent. In Manhattan, 99 percent of the units were rentals. Consolidated Edison, *Survey of the New York City Market,* 22, 40, 64, 71.

135. The News Syndicate market analysis lists the population in 1940 for each of its district as follows: "Native White," "Foreign-Born White," "Negro," and "Other Races." In the great majority of subway suburb districts, more than 98 percent of the population was in the first two categories. African-Americans were concentrated in a small number of the outlying districts, with the greatest numbers in South Jamaica. Most African-Americans at the time lived in Harlem and the older neighborhoods of central Brooklyn. For the city as a whole, in 1940 there were 7,454,995 residents. Of these, according to the market analysis, 4,897,481 were Native Whites, 2,080,020 Foreign-Born Whites, 458,444 Negroes, and 19,050 Other Races. News Syndicate, *New York City Market Analysis.* In 1940, there were 61,000 Puerto Ricans living in New York City. Virginia Sanchez-Korrol, "Puerto Ricans," in Jackson, ed., *The Encyclopedia of New York City,* 963.

136. Frederick M. Binder and David M. Reimers, *All the Nations under Heaven: An Ethnic and Racial History of New York City* (New York: Columbia University Press, 1995), 154. Moore, *At Home in America,* 64–66. David Ment, *The Shaping of a City: A Brief History of Brooklyn* (Brooklyn, N.Y.: Brooklyn Rediscovery and Brooklyn Educational and Cultural Alliance, 1977), 70–72.

137. Ronald H. Bayor, *Neighbors in Conflict: The Irish, Germans, Jews and Italians of New York City, 1929–1941* (Baltimore: Johns Hopkins University Press, 1978), 154.

138. According to Deborah Dash Moore, the new subway lines opened between 1914 and 1921 preceded the residential boom and "unlocked the door to urban expansion," allowing the dispersal of people "to new homes in less congested neighborhoods." Moore, *At Home in America,* 33, 66.

139. Ibid., 35–39.

140. Ibid., 4.

141. Ruth Gay, *Unfinished People: Eastern European Jews Encounter America* (New York: W. W. Norton, 1996), jacket copy.

142. Casey, "From the East Side to the Sea Side," 401–402.

143. Donna R. Gabaccia, "Little Italy's Decline: Immigrant Renters and

Investors in a Changing City," in Ward and Zunz, *The Landscape of Modernity*, 235–237, 246–248. See also Gabaccia, *From Sicily to Elizabeth Street: Housing and Social Change among Italian Immigrants, 1880–1930* (Albany: State University of New York Press, 1984), 107–108.

144. The number of immigrants from different countries in New York in 1930 is listed in Laidlaw, *Population of the City of New York, 1890–1930*, 247. Countries with more than 10,000 immigrants were Ireland, Germany, Russia, Poland, Lithuania, Czechoslovakia, Hungary, Romania, Greece, Turkey, Spain, England, Scotland, France, Sweden, Norway, Denmark, Finland, and Canada. In 1930, the total number of New Yorkers born overseas was 2,358,686, of whom 2,186,182 were from Europe.

145. Ultan, *The Beautiful Bronx*, 11–18, 37–42. Ultan and Hermalyn, *The Bronx: It Was Only Yesterday*, 1–19. See also Lloyd Ultan and Gary Hermalyn, *The Bronx in the Innocent Years, 1890–1925*, 2d ed. (The Bronx: The Bronx County Historical Society, 1991); and Lloyd Ultan and Barbara Unger, *Bronx Accent: A Literary and Pictorial History of the Borough* (New Brunswick, N.J.: Rutgers University Press, 2000), chap. 4. Daily life in Brooklyn is described in David W. McCullogh, *Brooklyn . . . and How It Got That Way* (New York: Dial Press, 1983), 184–202. Life in Queens is described in various sections of Janet E. Lieberman and Richard K. Lieberman, *City Limits: A Social History of Queens* (Dubuque, Iowa: Kendall/Hunt, 1983). See also Moore, *At Home in America*, 60–87.

146. The median annual household income in these communities was $2,935, ranging from $2,609 to $3,696. In contrast, by the 1940s, most tenement districts in the older parts of the city, including the South Bronx, had median household incomes of under $2,000. In Manhattan, median household income in wealthy neighborhoods ranged from just over $5,000 to a high of $7,634 on the East Side between Fifth and Third Avenues, from 63rd to 98th Streets. The areas beyond the Dual System lines in the outlying boroughs had a wide range of incomes, from very poor to wealthy railroad suburbs such as Riverdale in the Bronx and Forest Hills in Queens. Statistics compiled from News Syndicate, *New York City Market Analysis*. The monthly rents paid by residents of the subway suburbs are another indication of their relative economic status. In the areas along the Dual System lines, most of the rents were in the range of forty to fifty-nine dollars per month, although in the best neighborhoods, such as Jackson Heights and areas in southern Brooklyn, they ranged from fifty to seventy dollars and more. In the old tenement areas, due to decreasing demand, the rents were almost all below forty dollars, and in many neighborhoods below thirty dollars. In Manhattan, the variations in rent were dramatic. In the wealthy areas on the East Side west of

Third Avenue, along Central Park South, and in much of the West Side between 66th and 96th streets, rents were all over seventy dollars a month, and some were much higher. Data from maps in Consolidated Edison, *Survey of the New York City Market.* The maps in the 1945 market survey indicate average rents by census tracts for the entire city. Rents in neighborhoods far off the subway lines showed a wide variation.

147. In 1940, auto registrations totaled only 36 percent of the households in the Bronx. The figure in Brooklyn was 42 percent, 64 percent in Queens, and only 25 percent in Manhattan. Data from borough summaries in News Syndicate, *New York City Market Analysis.*

148. Leiper, "Analyze Transit Travel Trends."

149. In 1948, 500,000 people still lived in pre-1901 tenement buildings in New York City. Rodgers and Rankin, *New York: The World's Capital City,* 287. Maps in Consolidated Edison, *Survey of the New York City Market,* show the rents paid in each area of the city.

150. The highest population densities in New York in 1940 were in Central Harlem, with 243 people per acre. The next highest areas were in West Harlem and East Harlem. Plant, *Population Growth of New York City,* 17. See also Hall, *The World Cities,* 192–196, and Joseph A. Spencer, "New York City Tenant Organizations and the Post–World War I Housing Crisis," in Ronald Lawson and Mark Naison, eds., *The Tenant Movement in New York City, 1904–1984* (New Brunswick, N.J.: Rutgers University Press, 1986), 51–93.

151. Real Estate Analysts, Inc., *Real Estate Trends in New York City with Special Emphasis on the Island of Manhattan,* Report prepared for the Committee on Real Estate Trends of the Joint Committee of the Savings Banks Association of the State of New York (St. Louis, 1942), 1.

152. The report commented that, as the African-American population had increased, conditions in Harlem had become "in many respects similar to the problem of the Lower East Side of thirty years ago. . . . In the case of the Lower East Side . . . the lack of rapid transit facilities was the 'wall' which concentrated residential use." In Harlem, it was "the unwillingness of white owners and tenants of properties surrounding this district to accept colored tenants. This has resulted in a demand for properties which can be occupied by Negroes exceeding the supply." Ibid., 10.

153. According to the savings banks report, the reason for this was that "the economic capacity of the inhabitants is so low that they cannot afford to pay an adequate return on the cost of adequate housing." In these districts, built up along the old elevated lines and the first subway, "blighted areas have developed due to the age and obsolescence of the properties and to the low income families in them. In some sections, deterioration has reached an advanced stage." Ibid., 21. Many of these areas began to have

"burn outs" (houses being destroyed by fire) from the 1950s on, reaching a crescendo during the 1970s.

154. Plunz, *History of Housing,* 209.

155. From 1940 on, the City Planning Commission, which was finally created in 1939, prepared citywide master plans of "sections containing areas for clearance, redevelopment, and low-rent housing." These areas were the ones with the highest floor to area ratios—that is, the ratio of total amount of floor space per structure to the land area—in New York. Almost none of these areas were in the subway suburbs. See New York City, City Planning Commission, *Master Plan of Sections Containing Areas for Clearance Redevelopment and Low-Rent Housing* (November 2, 1949).

156. Between 1937 and 1957, the New York City Housing Authority constructed 87,742 apartments under various government programs. By 1975, 165,892 apartments were being operated by the Housing Authority. Plunz, *History of Housing,* 234. For the negative impact of the housing policies of Robert Moses, see Joel Schwartz, *The New York Approach: Robert Moses, Urban Liberals and Redevelopment of the Inner City* (Columbus: Ohio State University Press, 1993).

157. The transformation of New York's economy is discussed in Savitch, *Post-Industrial Cities,* and Saskia Sassen, *The Global City: New York, London, Tokyo* (Princeton: Princeton University Press, 1991). See also MTA, *Regional Trends and Forecasts: Implications for Strategic Transit Planning* (New York, March 1983), and Matthew Drennan, "Economy," in Charles Brecher and Raymond D. Horton, eds., *Setting Municipal Priorities, 1982* (New York: Russell Sage Foundation, 1981), 55–88.

158. Urbanomics, *The Future of the Region's Core,* 16–18. For 1950, Leiper, "Analyze Transit Travel Trends," estimated that there were 2,271,000 jobs in Manhattan. In 1990, there were 2,010,400 people residing in the New York region and working in Manhattan. Memorandum, Journey-to-Work Tabulations, Juliette Bergman, New York Metropolitan Transportation Council, July 11, 1997.

159. Urbanomics, *The Future of the Region's Core,* 16–18.

160. Savitch, *Post-Industrial Cities,* 8. The recent revival of the Bronx, to give one specific example, is due in large part to the strength of the Manhattan economy. Emanuel Tobier, "The Bronx in the Twentieth Century: Dynamics of Population and Economic Change," *The Bronx County Historical Society Journal* 35, no. 2 (Fall 1998): 93–95.

161. These include Pelham Bay in the Bronx; Midwood, Brighton Beach, Borough Park, Bensonhurst, and Bay Ridge in Brooklyn; and Astoria in Queens. Statistics for New York neighborhoods in the 1990s are provided in The City Project and Community Studies of New York, Inc./

Infoseek, *City of Contrasts: 51 New York City Council Districts* (New York, February 1998). The subway suburbs of Brooklyn in the 1990s are described in Citizens Committee for New York City, *The Neighborhoods of Brooklyn.*

162. These were the areas where population grew rapidly from 1950 to 1970, while the total number of people living in New York City held stable. MTA, *Regional Trends and Forecasts,* 26.

163. For a discussion of the impact of government policy on northern Manhattan, see Ira Katznelson, *City Trenches: Urban Politics and the Pattern of Class in the United States* (Chicago: University of Chicago Press, 1981), 94–107.

164. As one author has noted, "the five boroughs did not feel like the culmination of the American dream. People did not want apartment houses. They wanted houses with land, a town with an actual Main Street." Susan Isaacs, "A Stew of Dreams for a Better Life," *New York Times* (Long Island Section), August 30, 1998. Jackson, *Crabgrass Frontier,* also notes the attraction of the single-family home for Americans.

165. Raymond Vernon, "From Tenement to Split Level," chapter 9 of *Metropolis 1985: An Interpretation of the Findings of the New York Metropolitan Regional Survey* (Cambridge: Harvard University Press, 1960). Some factors are easy to explain, such as the building of superhighways through urban neighborhoods, although there is still much debate going on as to relative importance. The various factors are discussed in Ray Bromley, "Not So Simple! Caro, Moses, and the Impact of the Cross-Bronx Expressway," *The Bronx County Historical Society Journal* 35, no. 1 (Spring 1998): 25–26.

166. Richard Harris, "The Geography of Employment and Residence in New York Since 1950," in John Hull Mollenkopf and Manuel Castells, eds., *Dual City: Restructuring New York* (New York: Russell Sage Foundation, 1991), 129–152. Binder and Reimers, *All the Nations,* 204–215, 243–250. Moore, *At Home in America,* 233–236. In the Bronx, for example, 98 percent of the total population was classified as white in 1940. News Syndicate, "Bronx Composite" fact sheet in *New York City Market Analysis.* In 1970, non-Hispanic whites made up 47 percent of a population of 1,472,000; 23 percent were black, 28 percent Hispanic, and 2 percent Asian/Other. (The Census itself divides the population into "non-Hispanic white" and "Hispanic." Hispanics may be of any race.) In 1997, the U.S. Census estimated that there were 1,188,000 residents of the Bronx, 19 percent white, 28 percent black, 48 percent Latino, and 5 percent Asian/Other. Tobier, "The Bronx in the Twentieth Century," 83.

167. From the 1950s on, many of the communities that had been built up along the elevated lines and the first subway, and where mainly minorities lived, went into a cycle of decline. The poorest areas of New York, in-

cluding East Harlem, Harlem, Williamsburg, Bushwick, Brownsville, East New York, and the South Bronx experienced massive "burn outs," and tens of thousands of apartments were destroyed. The housing deterioration was due in part to the city's rent control laws, but was also influenced by the difficulties landlords and owners had in obtaining mortgage financing and funding for normal repairs. Sandor Evan Schick found that the only factor explaining the decline of the South Bronx that could be quantified was a reduction in mortgage lending. Sandor Evan Schick, "Neighborhood Change in the Bronx, 1905–1960" (Ph.D. diss., Harvard University, 1982), 191–193. The process of decline in many older neighborhoods was finally halted as a result of the efforts of many local community groups. Government assistance was also important as a means of providing funds and loan guarantees for rehabilitation of older housing and the construction of new homes. Tobier, "The Bronx in the Twentieth Century," 83–93. One of the best accounts of the overall process of neighborhood change is Jill Jonnes, *We're Still Here: The Rise, Fall and Resurrection of the South Bronx* (Boston: Atlantic Monthly Press, 1986). See also Charles Orlebeke, *New Life at Ground Zero: New York, Homeownership and the Future of American Cities* (Albany: Rockefeller Institute Press, 1997), and Lee Stuart, "'Come Let Us Rebuild the Walls of Jerusalem': Broad-Based Organizing in the South Bronx," in Robert D. Carle and Louis DeCaro, Jr., eds., *Signs of Hope in the City: Ministries of Community Renewal* (Valley Forge, Pa.: Judson Press, 1997), 129–139.

168. In 1999, it was reported that about 113,000 immigrants were arriving in New York City to live each year. City planners were predicting that in the year 2000, 35 percent of New York's population would be non-Hispanic whites, 29 percent Hispanic, 26 percent black, and 10 percent Asian. *New York Times*, November 8, 1999. Maps in this article show that most of the newcomers in 1995 and 1996 had moved into the subway suburbs. See also Rosemary Scanlon, "The Changing Demographics of New York," *Liveable City* 13, no. 2 (October 1989): 2–5.

169. Richard P. Nathan, Julian Chow, and Mildred L. Owens cite a Rockefeller Institute study of zones of emergence, applying the concept to working- and middle-class neighborhoods of African-Americans and Hispanics in large American cities. These neighborhoods fight hard to stave off the ills of the inner city and are said to be the "hidden good news" for these cities. "The Flip Side of the Underclass: Working and Middle Class Minority Neighborhoods," *Rockefeller Institute Bulletin*, special issue on "Two Views of Urban America" (1995): 14–22.

170. The exception is the corridor in the West Bronx south of Fordham Road, where many apartment buildings were burned out and abandoned. There are many reasons why this particular area, which had hundreds of

high-quality apartment houses, declined from the 1970s on. One contributing factor may have been that the area had been overbuilt with too many large apartment houses, making it unattractive to middle-income residents who had other housing choices. The construction of dense walls of apartment houses may have been due in part to a new subway that opened to the area in 1933. Although planners had warned against building additional rapid transit lines close to existing ones, under the Independent System plan, a subway was built three blocks away from the Jerome Avenue elevated line under the Concourse. This set off a new wave of residential construction in the West Bronx, even in the midst of the Depression, that made the area the densest in the city outside of Manhattan. The planner's warning is in Adams, *Population and Land Values,* 62. The new apartment houses, and rising population, in the area along the Grand Concourse is in News Syndicate, *New York City Market Survey,* page on Bronx district 3.

171. Stephen Koepp, "Selling a Dream of Elegance and the Good Life," *Time,* September 1, 1986, cover story on Ralph Lauren, 54–61. Ira Hellman, "Calvin Klein," Biography (December 1997), reproduced on the web site of the *Encyclopedia Britannica,* britannica.com. The experience of growing up in this neighborhood is discussed in Leonard Kriegel, "Last Stop on the D Train," *American Scholar* 39, no. 2 (Spring 1970): 272–288.

172. *New York Times,* September 5, 1999.

173. According to the 1990 Census, 858,081 people who lived in the Bronx, Brooklyn, and Queens worked in Manhattan. Of these, 610,395, or 71 percent, took the subway to work. For travel to all workplaces in the region, 54 percent of the trips from these three boroughs were made by some form of public transit. Data compiled from tables provided by Juliette Bergman of the New York Metropolitan Transportation Council. In terms of total trips, work and nonwork, on an average business day in 1994, just under half of the 3.4 million people who came into the Manhattan CBD did so by the New York subway. New York Metropolitan Transportation Council, *Hub-bound Travel,* 1994, 33.

174. The "two cities" concept is the premise of John H. Mollenkopf and Manuel Castells, eds., *Dual City: Restructuring New York* (New York: Russell Sage Foundation, 1991), and is a theme in Robert F. Wagner, Jr., *New York Ascendent: The Report of the Commission on the Year 2000* (New York: Harper and Row, 1988), which has a section titled "A City of Rich and Poor," 51–54.

175. The City Project, *City of Contrasts,* 17–19.

176. Ibid., 18–19.

177. Data from pages for each Council District in Ibid.

178. This show aired on WNET, the main public television station for

New York City, on April 18, 1999. The comments were by Janice Perlman, of the Mega-Cities project.

179. Ximena de la Barra, "Fear of Epidemics: The Engine of Urban Planning," talk delivered at the conference "Meeting the Urban Health Challenge," New York, September 18, 1999. (De la Barra's talk was subsequently published as an article with the same title in *Planning Practice and Research* 15, nos. 1 and 2 [February/May 2000]: 7–16.) For urban areas outside the United States, see David R. Vining, Jr., "The Growth of Core Regions in the Third World," *Scientific American* 252, no. 4 (April 1988): 42–49. Living conditions in such cities are vividly described in Peter Wilsher and Rosemary Righter, *The Exploding Cities* (New York: Quadrangle/The New York Times Book Co., 1975), 17–29.

180. Hall, "The City of By-Pass Variegated; The Mass Transit Suburb: London, Paris, Berlin, New York, 1900–1940," chap. 3 of *Cities of Tomorrow.* Hall also notes that elite planners and architects "universally derided and condemned" the new neighborhoods, as they diverged from their standards of good taste. Ibid. Similar attitudes have been expressed by some residents of Manhattan about districts in the "outer boroughs."

181. Hall, *Cities in Civilization,* 768, 933. The quote is from page 933, where Hall himself is paraphrasing remarks by Colin Clark.

NOTES TO THE CONCLUSION

1. In 1998, Andrew Heiskel wrote an article in the *New York Times* about how hard it is to accomplish public works in New York. Heiskel, the former publisher of *Life* magazine and former chairman of Time, Inc., became chairman of the New York Public Library in 1981. He soon realized that Bryant Park, which occupies the same city block as the main research branch of the library, needed to be greatly improved. According to Heiskel: "Saving Bryant Park was the hardest job in my long life." The tedious public approval process involved many groups and individuals and dragged on for years. Andrew Heiskel, with Ralph Graves, "Struggling to Save Bryant Park," *New York Times,* September 13, 1998. The Dual System, a far larger project, went through a similar process and was almost destroyed by it.

2. See Chapters 4, 5, and 6 for the attacks on the public officials. According to Comptroller William A. Prendergast, William Randolph Hearst never relented in his attacks on George McAneny and Prendergast because they had backed the Dual System contracts. Prendergast believed that after the contracts were signed, Hearst "was determined that something must be done to inflict political harm" upon him and McAneny; he also blamed Hearst for instigating the two legislative investigations of the Public Service

Commission, known as the Thompson Committee investigations, which had the aim of discrediting the Dual System contracts. William A. Prendergast Oral History Project, Oral History Collection, Columbia University, 790–792. The two Thompson Committee investigations were never able to prove that anything underhanded had taken place during the negotiations leading to the Dual System contracts, although many such insinuations appear in the transcript of the committees' hearings. The report of the Second Thompson Committee could say only that "the Dual System contracts were bad for the City and State of New York," without making any specific charges. New York State, Joint Legislative Committee to Investigate the Public Service Commissions, *Complete Report* (1917), 24. During the administration of Mayor John F. Hylan (1918–1925), who gained office largely because of Hearst's support, criticism of the Dual System contracts continued. Peter Derrick, "The New York City Transit Crisis of 1918 to 1925" (Master's thesis, Columbia University, 1967). Harry A. Gordon, a special counsel to Hylan, alleged that the Dual System contracts put the city in bondage to the IRT and the BRT, calling the contracts "The Fruits of Greed." Harry A. Gordon, *Subway Nickels: A Survey of New York City's Transit Problem* (New York: M. B. Brown, 1925), chap. 5. Another of Hylan's special counsels, Henry H. Klein, criticized McAneny and the PSC for devising the contracts, claiming that these public officials were controlled by the "traction interests" and the "banks." Letter by Klein to the *Evening World*, July 5, 1917, reprinted in Henry H. Klein, *Politics, Government and the Public Utilities in New York City* (New York: Isaac Goldmann, 1933). More recently, Robert Fitch has alleged that McAneny actually represented the "transportation interests," rather than the public, in his activities. By these he means "the Morgan-Belmont Interborough Rapid Transit Co." and the "Brooklyn Rapid Transit Company . . . [which] overlapped with the Pennsylvania." Fitch also says: "Jacob Schiff served as investment banker for both lines." McAneny, in this argument, served "as power broker" for the private transit companies, who were also "the city's two biggest holders and developers." Robert Fitch, *The Assassination of New York* (New York: Verso, 1993), 63.

3. Numerous notes in Chapters 3 to 5 indicate this. Many years later Prendergast said, with regard to the planning of the Dual System, "In my observation of the course of municipal progress over a long period of time, I do not believe that any greater contribution has ever been made to the interests of city government than the accomplishments of the Honorable George McAneny in this great work." William A. Prendergast Oral History Project, Oral History Collection, Columbia University, 1951, 457.

4. Printed speech by Mayor William J. Gaynor in *Municipal Reference Library: Opening Exercises* (New York, March 31, 1913).

5. Brian J. Cudahy, *Under the Sidewalks of New York: The Story of the World's Greatest Subway System,* rev. ed. (Lexington, Mass.: Stephen Greene Press, 1988), 54.

6. This is the title of a recent book on the ethnic and racial history of New York City. Frederick M. Binder and David M. Reimers, *All the Nations under Heaven: An Ethnic and Racial History of New York City* (New York: Columbia University Press, 1995).

7. McAneny quoted in Cyrus Adler, *Jacob H. Schiff: His Life and Letters* (New York: Doubleday Doran, 1928), 1:334.

NOTES TO APPENDIX 1

1. *City of New York, by the Public Service Commission for the First District with Interborough Rapid Transit Company, Contract No. 3: Contract for Additional Rapid Transit Railroads,* March 19, 1913. In State of New York, Public Service Commission for the First District, *Annual Report, 1913,* 4:13–96. *City of New York, by the Public Service Commission for the First District with New York Municipal Railway Corporation, Contract No. 4: Contract for New Rapid Transit Railroads,* March 19, 1913. In PSC, *Annual Report, 1913,* 4:175–249. (These were the Dual System Contracts.) *Public Service Commission for the First District to Manhattan Railway Company, Certificate: Second Avenue, Third Avenue and Ninth Avenue Additional Tracks,* March 19, 1913. In PSC, *Annual Report, 1913,* 4:133–161. *Public Service Commission for the First District to Interborough Rapid Transit Company, Certificate: Webster Avenue Line, Eighth Avenue and 162nd Street Connection, Queensboro Bridge Line, West Farms Subway Connection,* March 19, 1913. In PSC, *Annual Report, 1913,* 4:97–132. (These were certificates for improvements to the elevated lines of the Manhattan Railway Company.) *Public Service Commission for the First District to New York Municipal Railway Corporation, Certificate: Jamaica Avenue Line, Liberty Avenue Line,* March 19, 1913. In PSC, *Annual Report, 1913,* 4:251–288. *Public Service Commission for the First District to New York Municipal Railway Corporation, Certificate: Broadway, Fulton Street and Myrtle Avenue Additional Tracks,* March 19, 1913. In PSC, *Annual Report, 1913,* 4:289–329. (These were the certificates for improvements on the existing BRT lines.) *City of New York, by the Public Service Commission for the First District, Supplementary Agreement: Trackage Rights, Seventh Avenue–Lexington Avenue Line, White Plains Road Line, Steinway Tunnel Line,* March 19, 1913. In PSC, *Annual Report, 1913,* 4:163–173. *City of New York by the Public Service Commission for the First District, Interborough Rapid Transit Company and New York Municipal Railway Corporation, Supplementary Agreement: Trackage Rights over Steinway Tunnel Line,* March 19, 1913. In PSC, *Annual Report, 1913,* 4:331–341. (These were the agreements for trackage rights for the

Manhattan Railway Company's elevated trains on the Jerome Avenue line, the White Plains Road line, and the IRT's lines in Queens and for trackage rights by New York Municipal Railway Corporation [BRT] trains on the IRT lines in Queens to Astoria and Woodside-Corona.)

2. When the Dual System contracts were signed, there were discussions going on regarding extension of the Corona line farther out into Queens. *New York Times,* May 25, 1913. By December 1913, the City of New York and the IRT had agreed to extend the line to Main Street, Flushing. PSC, *Annual Report, 1913,* 1:48-49. Although this was technically the first extension under the contracts, the addition to Flushing is best regarded as an integral part of the original Dual System plan.

3. Contract No. 3 specified that the City had the right to permit the New York Municipal Railway Corporation, or any other operator, to use the tracks of the Astoria and Woodside-Corona lines for up to half of their capacity. A supplemental agreement also allowed for trackage rights by New York Municipal Railway Corporation trains on the IRT lines in Queens to Astoria and Woodside-Corona. *City of New York by the Public Service Commission for the First District, Interborough Rapid Transit Company and New York Municipal Railway Corporation, Supplementary Agreement: Trackage Rights over Steinway Tunnel Line,* March 19, 1913.

4. *City of New York, by the Public Service Commission for the First District to Manhattan Railway Company, Certificate: Second Avenue, Third Avenue and Ninth Avenue Additional Tracks,* March 19, 1913. *City of New York, by the Public Service Commission for the First District to Interborough Rapid Transit Company, Certificate: Webster Avenue Line, Eighth Avenue and 162nd Street Connection, Queensboro Bridge Line, West Farms Subway Connection,* March 19, 1913. A supplemental agreement also covered trackage rights on the expanded IRT system to trains operating on the elevated lines. *City of New York, by the Public Service Commission for the First District, Supplementary Agreement: Trackage Rights, Seventh Avenue-Lexington Avenue Line, White Plains Road Line, Steinway Tunnel Line,* March 19, 1913.

5. If the cost of equipment was less than $22 million, the contract provided that the difference would go toward the cost of any construction above $116 million.

6. These were all provisions of Contract No. 3 and the related certificates.

7. According to Brian J. Cudahy, this was done "when concern developed over whether the bridge could bear up under the weight of all-steel subway trains." Brian J. Cudahy, *Under the Sidewalks of New York: The Story of the World's Greatest Subway System,* rev. ed. (Lexington, Mass.: Stephen Greene Press, 1988), 62.

8. The Fourth Avenue subway to Bay Ridge was extended to 95th Street in 1925. Robert A. Hall, Jr., *New York City Rapid Transit Chronology* (Ann Arbor, Mich.: privately printed, 1945), 7.

9. Walter Laidlaw, *Population of the City of New York, 1890–1930* (New York: Cities Census Committee, 1932), 234.

10. There was a controversy after the contracts were signed as to how much of the line should be elevated and how much subway. In part because of this controversy, this was the last of the Contract No. 4 lines to be constructed and opened for operation. The line opened to Broadway Junction in 1928, more than a decade after many of the other BRT lines. The line was connected directly to the Canarsie line. Hall, *New York City Rapid Transit Chronology*, 7.

11. *Public Service Commission for the First District to New York Municipal Railway Corporation, Certificate: Jamaica Avenue Line, Liberty Avenue Line,* March 19, 1913. *Public Service Commission for the First District to New York Municipal Railway Corporation, Certificate: Broadway, Fulton Street and Myrtle Avenue Additional Tracks,* March 19, 1913.

12. The estimated cost to the City was estimated at $101,501,991 in March 1913. *New York Times,* March 19, 1913.

13. These lines included all of the existing elevated lines that would have third tracks added and/or would be extended. Also included was the Sea Beach line and the Brighton line. The estimated cost of this work in March 1913 was $26 million. *New York Times,* March 19, 1913.

14. In March 1913, the estimated cost of the new subway and elevated railroad cars of the New York Municipal Railway was $21 million. *New York Times,* March 19, 1913.

15. Item 7 also specified that the New York Municipal Railway Corporation was to reduce the cost of construction borne by it for both the Railroad and the Existing Railroad by $1.33 million. This reduction was to bear interest from and after the beginning of initial operation, and the amount of such interest was to be paid into the revenue. The company was to accomplish this reduction, together with the interest, by applying the first sums coming to it once there was a divisible profit between the company and the City of New York over and above the itemized deductions. This clause had been included in Contract No. 4 as a result of the agreement reached between the conferees and the BRT on December 23, 1912, whereby the BRT had agreed to pay some of the interest charges on $24 million of the $40 million it had borrowed on October 1, 1912, out of future profits accruing to the company.

16. These were all provisions of Contract No. 4 and the related certificates.

Bibliography

MANUSCRIPT COLLECTIONS

City Club of New York Papers. New-York Historical Society, New York City.

City Club of New York Papers. New York Public Library, New York City.

Clippings and Correspondence from the Office of the Mayor of the City of New York, 1904–1916. Newspaper Division, New York Public Library, New York City.

Collection of Material Relating to the Congestion Exhibit. New York Public Library, New York City.

Seth Low Papers. Columbia University, New York City.

Henry MacCracken Papers. New York University Archives, New York City.

George McAneny Papers. Columbia University, New York City.

George McAneny Papers. Seeley G. Mudd Manuscript Library, Princeton University, Princeton, N.J.

John Purroy Mitchel Papers. Library of Congress, Washington, D.C.

William Prendergast Papers. Columbia University, New York City.

SPECIAL COLLECTIONS

Columbia University Oral History Collection. Columbia University Library, New York City.

John T. Hettrick, 1949.

George McAneny, 1949.

William A. Prendergast, 1951.

Lawson Purdy, 1951.

Lawrence Veiller, 1950.

New York Municipal Reference Library

New York Transit Museum Archives, Brooklyn, N.Y.

THE DUAL SYSTEM CONTRACTS, RELATED CERTIFICATES, AND SUPPLEMENTAL AGREEMENTS

City of New York, by the Public Service Commission for the First District with Interborough Rapid Transit Company, Contract No. 3: Contract for Additional Rapid Transit Railroads. New York, March 19, 1913.

City of New York, by the Public Service Commission for the First District with New York Municipal Railway Corporation, Contract No. 4: Contract for New Rapid Transit Railroads. New York, March 19, 1913.

City of New York, by the Public Service Commission for the First District to Manhat-

tan Railway Company, Certificate: Second Avenue, Third Avenue and Ninth Avenue Additional Tracks. New York, March 19, 1913.
City of New York, by the Public Service Commission for the First District to Interborough Rapid Transit Company, Certificate: Webster Avenue Line, Eighth Avenue and 162nd Street Connection, Queensboro Bridge Line, West Farms Subway Connection. New York, March 19, 1913.
City of New York, by the Public Service Commission for the First District to New York Municipal Railway Corporation, Certificate: Jamaica Avenue Line, Liberty Avenue Line. New York, March 19, 1913.
City of New York, by the Public Service Commission for the First District to New York Municipal Railway Corporation, Certificate: Broadway, Fulton Street and Myrtle Avenue Additional Tracks. New York, March 19, 1913.
City of New York, by the Public Service Commission for the First District Supplementary Agreement: Trackage Rights, Seventh Avenue–Lexington Avenue Line, White Plains Road Line, Steinway Tunnel Line. New York, March 19, 1913.
City of New York, by the Public Service Commission for the First District, Interborough Rapid Transit Company and New York Municipal Railway Corporation, Supplementary Agreement: Trackage Rights over Steinway Tunnel Line. New York, March 19, 1913.

REPORTS BY OR FOR GOVERNMENT AGENCIES

Admiral Realty Company v. City of New York. 206 *New York Reports*: 110–162. New York, 1912.
Arnold, Bion J. *The Capacity of the Subway of the Interborough Rapid Transit Company.* New York, May 22, 1908.
———. *The Return on the Investment of the Subway of the Interborough Rapid Transit Company.* New York, February 21, 1909.
———. *The Traffic of the Subway of the Interborough Rapid Transit Company.* New York, December 31, 1908.
Board of Rapid Transit Railroad Commissioners for and in the City of New York. *Annual Report,* 1901 to 1906.
Leiper, Joseph M. "Analyze Transit Travel Trends," *Interim Technical Report, Preliminary Summary Tables,* of the Transit Service Demand and Supply Evaluation Study. New York, May 1, 1984.
Metropolitan Transportation Authority. *Capital Program, 2000–2004.* New York, October 1999.
———. *MTA Capital Needs and Opportunities, 1992–2011.* New York, May 25, 1990.
———. *Regional Trends and Forecasts: Implications for Strategic Transit Planning.* New York, March 1983.

———. *Staff Report of Capital Revitalization for the 1980's and Beyond.* New York, November 25, 1980.

New York City, Board of Estimate and Apportionment. *Minutes.* Various dates.

New York City, Board of Estimate and Apportionment, Committee on the City Plan. *Commission on Building Districts and Restrictions Final Report.* New York, June 2, 1916.

———. *Development and Present Status of City Planning in New York City.* New York, 1914.

New York City, Board of Estimate and Apportionment, Special Committee on Pending Transit Proposals. *Supplementary Report of a Committee of the Board of Estimate and Apportionment with Relation to Pending Proposals for the Construction Equipment and Operation of Rapid Transit Lines in the City of New York.* New York, May 22, 1912.

New York City, Board of Estimate and Apportionment, and New York State, Public Service Commission, First District. *Rapid Transit System: Report of Conferees to Board of Estimate and Apportionment.* New York, July 20, 1911.

———. *Report of a Committee with Relation to Pending Proposals for Construction, Equipment and Operation of Rapid Transit Lines, and upon the General Transit Situation in the City of New York.* New York, June 5, 1911.

New York City, City Planning Commission, *Master Plan of Sections Containing Areas for Clearance Redevelopment and Low-Rent Housing* New York, November 2, 1949.

New York City, Commission on Congestion of Population. *Report of the New York City Commission on Congestion of Population.* New York, February 28, 1911.

New York Metropolitan Transportation Council. *Hub-Bound Travel 1994.* New York, February 1996.

New York State, Joint Legislative Committee to Investigate the Public Service Commission. *Complete Report.* Albany, 1917. (This is the report of the Second Thompson Committee.)

———. *Final Report.* 2 vols. Albany, 1915. (This is the report of the First Thompson Committee.)

———. *Minutes and Testimony.* 6 vols. Albany, 1917. (These are the minutes and testimony of the Second Thompson Committee.)

New York State, Public Service Commission for the First District. *Annual Report,* 1907 to 1914.

———. *Combination Map of the Rapid Transit Routes in Greater New York.* New York, December 31, 1909.

———. *New Subways for New York: The Dual System of Rapid Transit.* New York, June 1913; updated edition, December 1913.

New York State, Public Service Commission for the First District. *Proceedings*, vols. 1–7, 1907 to 1913.

New York State, Transit Commission. *Twelfth Annual Report.* 1932.

Parsons Brinckerhoff Quade and Douglas, Inc., Historical Perspectives, Inc., and Robert A. Olmsted, P.E. *Phase I: Reconnaissance Level Historical Survey of Transit Authority Properties. Task 1 Report: The New York City Transit System—Historical Context and Evaluation Parameters.* Report to the New York City Transit Authority, June 1991.

Prendergast, William A. "Statement of William A. Prendergast, Comptroller of the City of New York, in regard to the negotiations leading up to the signing of the Rapid Transit Contracts Nos. 3 and 4 by the Board of Estimate and Apportionment. Read into the Record of the Legislative Investigating Committee known as the Thompson Committee, June 19, 1916." New York, 1916.

Roth, Louis. "History of Rapid Transit in New York City." Memorandum for Commissioner Travis H. Whitney. New York: Public Service Commission, April 3, 1917.

United States, Department of Commerce and Labor, Bureau of the Census. *Street and Electric Railways, 1902.* Washington, D.C., 1905.

Urbanomics. *The Future of the Extended Core in the Global Economy.* New York: Draft report to the Access to the Region's Core Study, June 16, 1995.

NEWSPAPERS

The bulk of the newspaper citations are from two collections of newspaper clippings in scrapbooks, one in the George McAneny Papers at Princeton University, the other at the Newspaper Division of the New York Public Library. During his tenure as borough president of Manhattan from 1910 to 1913 and as president of the Board of Aldermen from 1914 to 1916, McAneny had his staff clip articles mentioning his name from New York City newspapers. These articles were placed in chronological order in scrapbooks that are now in the George McAneny Papers at Princeton University. Similarly, Mayors George McClellan, William J. Gaynor, and John Purroy Mitchel had their staffs clip relevant newspaper articles regarding their administrations. These scrapbooks were arranged both topically and chronologically and are now in the Newspaper Division of the New York Public Library under the title "Clippings and Correspondence from the Office of the Mayor of the City of New York, 1904–1916." The newspapers cited all had "New York" in their name, unless otherwise noted. The newspapers are: *American, Citizen, Brooklyn Eagle, Brooklyn Times, Evening Journal, Evening Mail, Evening World, Globe, Herald, Journal, Post, Press, Standard Union, Sun, Times, Tribune, World.*

BOOKS, REPORTS, AND PAMPHLETS

Adams, Thomas, Harold M. Lewis, and Theodore McCrosky. *Population, Land Values and Government: Studies of the Growth and Distribution of Population and Land Values; and of Problems of Government.* Volume 2 of the Regional Survey. New York: Regional Plan of New York and Its Environs, 1929.

Adler, Cyrus. *Jacob H. Schiff: His Life and Letters.* 2 vols. New York: Doubleday Doran, 1928.

Albion, Robert Greenhalgh. *The Rise of New York Port (1815–1860).* New York: Charles Scribner's Sons, 1939.

Bannard Fusion Campaign. *New York's Opportunity.* New York, 1909.

Bassett, Edward M. *Autobiography of Edward M. Bassett.* New York: Harbor Press, 1939.

Bayor, Ronald H. *Neighbors in Conflict: The Irish, Germans, Jews and Italians of New York City, 1929–1941.* Baltimore: Johns Hopkins University Press, 1978.

Beard, Charles A. *American City Government: A Survey of Newer Tendencies.* New York: Century Co., 1912.

Bernstein, Iver. *The New York Draft Riots: Their Significance for American Society and Politics in the Age of the Civil War.* New York: Oxford University Press, 1990.

Berrol, Selma. *East Side/East End: Eastern European Jews in London and New York, 1870–1920.* Westport, Conn.: Praeger, 1994.

Binder, Frederick M., and David M. Reimers. *All the Nations under Heaven: An Ethnic and Racial History of New York City.* New York: Columbia University Press, 1995.

Birmingham, Stephen. *"Our Crowd": The Great Jewish Families of New York.* New York: Harper and Row, 1967.

Blackmar, Elizabeth. *Manhattan for Rent, 1785–1850.* Ithaca, N.Y.: Cornell University Press, 1989.

Bobrick, Benson. *Labyrinths of Iron: A History of the World's Subways.* New York: Newsweek Books, 1982.

Bottles, Scott. *Los Angeles and the Automobile: The Making of the Modern City.* Berkeley and Los Angeles: University of California Press, 1987.

Bressi, Todd W., ed. *Planning and Zoning in New York City: Yesterday, Today and Tomorrow.* New Brunswick, N.J.: Center for Urban Policy Research, 1993.

Briggs, Asa. *Victorian Cities.* New York: Harper and Row, 1963.

Bromley, George W., and Walter S. Bromley. *Atlas of the City of New York, Borough of Manhattan.* Philadelphia: G. W. Bromley and Co., 1911.

Bromley, George W., and Walter S. Bromley. *Atlas of the City of New York, Borough of the Bronx, Sections 11, 12, 13.* Philadelphia: G. W. Bromley and Co., 1911.

———. *Atlas of the City of New York, Borough of the Bronx North of 172nd Street.* Philadelphia: G. W. Bromley and Co., 1938.

Brooks, Michael W. *Subway City: Riding the Trains, Reading New York.* New Brunswick, N.J.: Rutgers University Press, 1997.

Burrows, Edwin G., and Mike Wallace, *Gotham: A History of New York City to 1898.* New York: Oxford University Press, 1999.

Cahan, Abraham. *The Rise of David Levinsky.* New York: Harper and Bros., 1917.

Callow, Alexander B., Jr. *The Tweed Ring.* New York: Oxford University Press, 1965.

Cardia, Clara. *Ils ont construit New York: Histoire de la métropole au XIXe siècle.* Geneva: Georg Editeur, 1987.

Caro, Robert A. *The Power Broker: Robert Moses and the Fall of Mew York.* New York: Alfred A. Knopf, 1974.

Carosso, Vincent P. *Investment Banking in America.* Cambridge: Harvard University Press, 1970.

———. *The Morgans: Private International Bankers, 1854–1917.* Cambridge: Harvard University Press, 1987.

Chamber of Commerce of the Borough of Queens. *Queens Borough, New York City, 1910–1920.* New York, 1920.

Chamber of Commerce of the State of New York. *Additional Transit Facilities for the City of New York.* New York, 1894.

———. *Rapid Transit: Report on the "Tri-Borough Route."* New York, 1910.

———. *Rapid Transit in New York City and in Other Great Cities.* New York, 1905.

Chamber of Commerce of the State of New York and Merchants' Association of New York. *The Rapid Transit Problem of New York.* New York, 1910.

Cheape, Charles W. *Moving the Masses: Urban Public Transit in New York, Boston, and Philadelphia, 1880–1912.* Cambridge: Harvard University Press, 1980.

Chernow, Ron. *The House of Morgan: An American Banking Dynasty and the Rise of Modern Finance.* New York: Atlantic Monthly Press, 1990.

Citizens Budget Commission. *Studies on Transit Unification in the City of New York.* New York, September 1936.

Citizens Committee for New York City. *The Neighborhoods of Brooklyn.* Introduction by Kenneth T. Jackson. John B. Manbeck, Consulting Editor. New Haven: Yale University Press, 1998.

City Club of New York, *Building of Rapid Transit Lines in New York by Assessment upon Property Benefitted.* New York, 1908.

———. "New York City Transit: A Memorandum to the Public Service Commission of the First District." New York, 1907.

Committee on Congestion of Population in New York. *Catalogue of the Exhibit of Congestion of Population in New York.* New York, 1908.

———. *Program of the Conference Held at the Exhibit on Congestion of Population in New York.* New York, 1908.

City Project and Community Studies of New York, Inc./Infoseek. *City of Contrasts: Fifty-one New York City Council Districts.* New York, February 1998.

Cohen, Paul E., and Robert T. Augustyn. *Manhattan in Maps, 1527–1995.* New York: Rizzoli, 1997.

Condit, Carl W. *The Port of New York: A History of the Rail and Terminal System from the Grand Central Electrification to the Present.* Chicago: University of Chicago Press, 1981.

Consolidated Edison Company of New York. *Survey of the New York City Market: Manhattan, Bronx, Brooklyn, Queens.* New York: Consolidated Edison, 1945.

Council of Hygiene and Public Health of the Citizens Association of New York. *Sanitary Condition of the City.* New York, 1865.

Cromley, Elizabeth Collins. *Alone Together: A History of New York's Early Apartments.* Ithaca, N.Y.: Cornell University Press, 1990.

Cudahy, Brian J. *Cash, Tokens, and Transfers: A History of Urban Mass Transit in North America.* New York: Fordham University Press, 1990.

———. *Over and Back: The History of Ferryboats in New York Harbor.* New York: Fordham University Press, 1990.

———. *Under the Sidewalks of New York: The Story of the World's Greatest Subway System.* Rev. ed. Lexington, Mass.: Stephen Greene Press, 1988.

Cunningham, Joseph, and Leonard O. DeHart. *A History of the New York City Subway System.* Part I, *The Manhattan Els and the I.R.T.* Privately printed, 1976.

———. *A History of the New York City Subway System.* Part II, *Rapid Transit in Brooklyn.* Privately printed, 1977.

Dahl, Gerhard M. *Transit Truths.* New York: Era Publications, 1924.

Daniel, Thomas M. *Captain of Death: The Story of Tuberculosis.* Rochester, N.Y.: University of Rochester Press, 1997.

Davis, Allen F. *Spearheads for Reform: The Social Settlements and the Progressive Movement.* New York: Oxford University Press, 1967.

Day, Jared N. *Urban Castles: Tenement Housing and Landlord Activism in New York City, 1890–1943.* New York: Columbia University Press, 1999.

Day, John R. *The Story of London's Underground.* London: London Transport, 1963.

DeForest, Robert W., and Lawrence Veiller, eds. *The Tenement House Problem.* 2 vols. New York: Macmillan, 1903.

Dougherty, Peter. *Tracks of the New York City Subway.* Privately printed, 1997.

Dubos, Réne, and Jean Dubos. *The White Plague: Tuberculosis, Man and Society.* Rev. ed. New Brunswick, N.J.: Rutgers University Press, 1996.

Fischler, Stan. *Next Stop Grand Central: A Trip through Time on New York's Metropolitan Area Commuter Railroads.* Erin, Ontario: Boston Mills Press, 1986.

———. *Uptown, Downtown: A Trip through Time on New York's Subways.* New York: Hawthorn Books, 1976.

Fitch, Robert. *The Assassination of New York.* New York: Verso, 1993.

Foglesong, Richard E. *Planning the Capitalist City: The Colonial Era to the 1920s.* Princeton: Princeton University Press, 1986.

Ford, George B. *New York City Building Zone Resolution.* New York: New York Title and Mortgage Co., 1920.

Freeman, Joshua B. *In Transit: The Transport Workers Union in New York City, 1933–1966.* New York: Oxford University Press, 1989.

Freeman, Michael J., and Derek H. Aldcroft, eds. *Transport in Victorian Britain.* Manchester and New York: Manchester University Press, 1989.

Gabaccia, Donna. *From Sicily to Elizabeth Street: Housing and Social Change among Italian Immigrants, 1880–1930.* Albany: State University of New York Press, 1984.

Galambos, Louis, and Joseph Pratt, *The Rise of the Corporate Commonwealth: United States Business and Public Policy in the 20th Century.* New York: Basic Books, 1988.

Gay, Ruth. *Unfinished People: Eastern European Jews Encounter America.* New York: W. W. Norton, 1996.

Gilmartin, Gregory F. *Shaping the City: New York and the Municipal Art Society.* New York: Clarkson Potter, 1995.

Gordon, Harry A. *Subway Nickles: A Survey of New York City's Transit Problem.* New York: M. B. Brown, 1925.

Gronowicz, Anthony. *Race and Class Politics in New York City before the Civil War.* Boston: Northeastern University Press, 1998.

Grow, Lawrence. *On the 8:02: An Informal History of Commuting by Rail in America.* New York: Mayflower Books, 1979.

Hall, Peter. *Cities in Civilization.* New York: Pantheon Books, 1998.

———. *Cities of Tomorrow: An Intellectual History of Planning and Design in the Twentieth Century.* New York: Basil Blackwell, 1988.

———. *The World Cities.* New York: McGraw-Hill, 1966,

Hall, Robert A. *New York City Rapid Transit Chronology*. Ann Arbor, Mich.: privately printed, 1945.

Hammack, David C. *Power and Society: Greater New York at the Turn of the Century*. New York: Russell Sage Foundation, 1982.

Hawes, Elizabeth. *New York, New York: How the Apartment House Transformed the Life of a City (1869–1930)*. New York: Alfred A. Knopf, 1993.

Hermalyn, Gary. *Morris High School and the Creation of the New York City Public School System*. The Bronx, N.Y.: The Bronx County Historical Society, 1995.

Hirsch, Mark David. *William C. Whitney: Modern Warwick*. New York: Dodd, Mead, 1948.

Homberger, Eric. *The Historical Atlas of New York City: A Visual Celebration of Nearly 400 Years of New York City's History*. New York: Henry Holt, 1994.

Hood, Clifton. *722 Miles: The Building of the Subways and How They Transformed New York*. New York: Simon and Schuster, 1993.

Howe, Frederic C. *The City: The Hope of Democracy*. New York: Charles Scribner's Sons, 1906.

Howe, Irving. *World of Our Fathers*. New York: Harcourt Brace Jovanovich, 1976.

Huthmacher, J. Joseph. *Senator Robert F. Wagner and the Rise of Urban Liberalism*. New York: Atheneum, 1971.

Interborough Rapid Transit Company. *The New York Subway: Its Construction and Equipment*. New York, 1904.

Jackson, Kenneth T. *Crabgrass Frontier: The Suburbanization of the United States*. New York: Oxford University Press, 1985.

———, ed. *The Encyclopedia of New York City*. New Haven: Yale University Press, 1995.

Johnson, James Weldon *Black Manhattan*. New York: Alfred A. Knopf, 1930.

Jonnes, Jill. *We're Still Here: The Rise, Fall and Resurrection of the South Bronx*. Boston: Atlantic Monthly Press, 1986.

Joselit, Jenna Weissman. *Our Gang: Jewish Crime and the New York Jewish Community, 1900–1940*. Bloomington: Indiana University Press, 1983.

Kahn, Paul, and Jack May. *The Tracks of New York Number 2: Brooklyn Elevated Railroads*. New York: n.p., 1975.

Katznelson, Ira. *City Trenches: Urban Politics and the Pattern of Class in the United States*. Chicago: University of Chicago Press, 1981.

Kessner, Thomas. *The Golden Door: Italian and Jewish Immigrant Mobility in New York City, 1880–1915*. New York: Oxford University Press, 1977.

Kirkland, Edward C. *Industry Comes of Age: Business, Labor and Public Policy, 1860–1897*. New York: Holt, Rinehart, and Winston, 1961.

Klein, Henry H. *Politics, Government and the Public Utilities in New York City.* New York: Isaac Goldmann, 1933.

Kouwenhoven, John A. *The Columbia Historical Portrait of New York: An Essay in Graphic History.* New York: Columbia University Press, 1953.

Kramer, Frederick A. *Building the Independent Subway.* New York: Quadrant Press, 1990.

Kraut, Alan M. *Silent Travelers: Germs, Genes, and the "Immigrant Menace."* Baltimore: Johns Hopkins University Press, 1994.

Laidlaw, Walter. *Population of the City of New York, 1890–1930.* New York: Cities Census Committee, 1932.

Landau, Sarah Bradford, and Carl W. Condit. *Rise of the New York Skyscraper, 1865–1913.* New Haven: Yale University Press, 1996.

Landesman, Alter F. *Brownsville: The Birth, Development and Passing of a Jewish Community in New York.* New York: Bloch Publishing, 1969.

Lankevich, George J. *American Metropolis: A History of New York City.* New York: New York University Press, 1998.

Lavis, Fred. *Building the New Rapid Transit System of New York City.* A collection of articles from Engineering News printed in book form in 1915. Reprint, Belleville, N.J.: Xplorer Press, 1996.

Lewinson, Edwin R. *John Purroy Mitchel: The Boy Mayor of New York.* New York: Astra Books, 1965.

Lewis, Nelson P. *The Planning of the Modern City: A Review of the Principles Governing City Planning.* New York: John Wiley and Sons, 1916.

Lieberman, Janet E., and Richard K. Lieberman. *City Limits: A Social History of Queens.* Dubuque, Iowa: Kendall/Hunt, 1983.

Lockwood, Charles. *Bricks and Brownstone: The New York Row House, 1783–1929: An Architectural and Social History.* New York: McGraw-Hill, 1972.

———. *Manhattan Moves Uptown: An Illustrated History.* New York: Barnes and Noble Books, 1995.

Low, Seth. *Report to the Citizens' Committee on Rapid Transit.* New York, 1910.

Lubove, Roy. *The Progressives and the Slums: Tenement House Reform ln New York City, 1890–1917.* Pittsburgh: University of Pittsburgh Press, 1962.

Makielski, S. J. *The Politics of Zoning: The New York Experience.* New York: Columbia University Press, 1966.

Mandelbaum, Seymour J. *Boss Tweed's New York.* New York: John Wiley and Sons, 1965.

Markel, Howard. *Quarantine! East European Jewish Immigrants and the New York City Epidemics of 1892.* Baltimore: Johns Hopkins University Press, 1997.

Marsh, Benjamin C. *An Introduction to City Planning: Democracy's Challenge to the American City.* New York, 1909.

———. *Lobbyist for the People: A Record of Fifty Years.* Washington, D.C.: Public Affairs Press, 1953.

Martin, Albro. *Railroads Triumphant: The Growth, Rejection and Rebirth of a Vital American Force.* New York: Oxford University Press, 1992.

Martin, John. *Rapid Transit: Its Effects on Rents and Living Conditions, and How to Get It.* New York: Committee on Congestion of Population, 1909.

McClellan, George B., Jr. *The Gentleman and the Tiger: The Autobiography of George B. Clellan, Jr.*, ed. Harold C. Syrett. Philadelphia: Lippincott, 1956.

McCullogh, David W. *Brooklyn . . . and How It Got That Way.* New York: Dial Press, 1983.

McShane, Clay. *Down the Asphalt Path: The Automobile and the American City.* New York: Columbia University Press, 1994.

Ment, David. *The Shaping of a City: A Brief History of Brooklyn.* Brooklyn, N.Y.: Brooklyn Rediscovery and Brooklyn Educational and Cultural Alliance, 1979.

Meyer, John R., and José A. Gómez-Ibáñez. *Autos, Transit and Cities.* Cambridge: Harvard University Press, 1981.

Meyer, Michael D., and Eric. J. Miller. *Urban Transportation Planning: A Decision-Oriented Approach.* New York: McGraw-Hill, 1984.

Miller, Donald L. *City of the Century: The Epic of Chicago and the Making of America.* New York: Simon and Schuster, 1996.

Miller, John A. *Fares, Please! A Popular History of Trolleys, Horsecars, Streetcars, Buses, Elevateds, and Subways.* New York: Dover Publications, 1960.

Mitgang, Herbert. *The Man Who Rode the Tiger: The Life of Judge Samuel Seabury and the Story of the Greatest Investigation of City Corruption in This Century.* New York: Viking Press, 1963.

Mollenkopf, John H., and Manuel Castells, eds. *Dual City: Restructuring New York.* New York: Russell Sage Foundation, 1991.

Moore, Deborah Dash. *At Home in America: Second Generation New York Jews.* New York: Columbia University Press, 1981.

Municipal Art Society. *Report on Rapid Transit in New York City.* Bulletin No. 14. New York, 1904.

Myers, Gustavus. *The History of Tammany Hall.* New York: Boni and Liveright, 1917.

Nellison, Tom. *Commuter Trains to Grand Central Terminal.* New York: Quadrant Books, 1986.

News Syndicate Co., the New York Times, Daily Mirror, and Hearst Consolidated Publications. *New York City Market Analysis.* New York: printed by the newspaper group, 1943.

Orlebeke, Charles. *New Life at Ground Zero: New York, Homeownership and the Future of American Cities.* Albany: Rockefeller Institute Press, 1997.

Osofsky, Gilbert. *Harlem: The Making of a Ghetto, Negro New York 1890–1930.* New York: Harper and Row, 1968.

Ott, Katherine. *Fevered Lives: Tuberculosis in American Culture since 1870.* Cambridge: Harvard University Press, 1996.

Plant, Irving M. *Population Growth of New York City by Districts, 1910–1948.* New York: Report for Consolidated Edison Company, 1948.

Plunz, Richard. A *History of Housing in New York City: Dwelling Type and Social Change in the American Metropolis.* New York: Columbia University Press, 1990.

Pratt, Edward Ewing. *Industrial Causes of Congestion in New York City.* Columbia University Studies in History, Economics and Public Law 43, no. 1, Whole Number 109. New York: Columbia University Press, 1911.

Proctor, Ben. *William Randolph Hearst: The Early Years, 1863–1910.* New York: Oxford University Press, 1998.

Pushkarev, Boris, Jeffrey M. Zupan, and Robert S. Cumella. *Urban Rail in America: An Exploration of Criteria for Fixed-Guideway Transit.* Bloomington: Indiana University Press, 1982.

Queens Chamber of Commerce. *Queens Borough.* New York: Queens Chamber of Commerce, 1926.

Real Estate Analysts, Inc. *Real Estate Trends in New York City with Special Emphasis on the Island of Manhattan.* Report prepared for the Committee on Real Estate Trends of the Joint Committee of the Savings Banks Association of the State of New York. St. Louis, 1942.

Reed, Robert C. *The New York Elevated.* South Brunswick and New York: A. S. Barnes, 1978.

Reeves, William Fullerton. *The First Elevated Railroads in Manhattan and the Bronx of the City of New York.* New York: The New-York Historical Society, 1936.

Riis, Jacob A. *How the Other Half Lives: Studies among the Tenements of New York.* Originally published in 1890. Reprint, New York: Penguin Books, 1997.

Rischin, Moses. *The Promised City: New York's Jews, 1870–1914.* New York: Harper and Row, 1970.

Robinson, A. P. *Report upon the Contemplated Metropolitan Railroad of the City of New York.* New York, 1865.

Rodgers, Cleveland. *New York Plans for the Future.* New York: Harper and Bros., 1943.

Rodgers, Cleveland, and Rebecca Rankin. *New York, the World's Capital City: Its Development and Contribution to Progress.* New York: Harper and Bros., 1948.

Rodgers, Daniel T. *Atlantic Crossings: Social Politics in a Progressive Age.* Cambridge: Harvard University Press, 1998.

Rosenwaike, Ira. *Population History of New York City.* Syracuse, N.Y.: Syracuse University Press, 1972.
Rosner, David, ed. *Hives of Sickness: Public Health and Epidemics in New York City.* New Brunswick, N.J.: Rutgers University Press, 1995.
Sante, Luc. *Low Life: Lures and Snares of Old New York.* New York: Vintage Books, 1992.
Sassen, Saskia. *The Global City: New York, London, Tokyo.* Princeton: Princeton University Press, 1991.
Savitch, H. V. *Post-Industrial Cities: Politics and Planning in New York, Paris, and London.* Princeton: Princeton University Press, 1988.
Sayre, Wallace S., and Herbert Kaufman. *Governing New York City: Politics in the Metropolis.* New York: W. W. Norton, 1960.
Schwartz, Joel. *The New York Approach: Robert Moses, Urban Liberals and Redevelopment of the Inner City.* Columbus: Ohio State University Press, 1993.
Scott, Mel. *American City Planning since 1890.* Berkeley and Los Angeles: University of California Press, 1969.
Spann, Edward K. *The New Metropolis: New York City, 1840–1857.* New York: Columbia University Press, 1981.
Spengler, Edwin H. *Land Values in New York in Relation to Transit Facilities.* Columbia University Studies in History, Economics and Public Law no. 333. New York: Columbia University Press, 1930.
Stansell, Christine. *City of Women: Sex and Class in New York, 1789–1860.* New York: Alfred A. Knopf, 1986.
Stern, Robert A. M., Gregory Gilmartin, and Thomas Mellins. *New York 1930: Architecture and Urbanism between the Two World Wars.* New York: Rizzoli, 1987.
Stern, Robert A. M., Gregory Gilmartin, and John Montague Massengale. *New York 1900: Metropolitan Architecture and Urbanism, 1890–1915.* New York: Rizzoli, 1983.
Still, Bayrd. *Urban America: A History with Documents.* Boston: Little, Brown, 1974.
Strouse, Jean. *Morgan: American Financier.* New York: Random House, 1999.
Sutcliffe, Anthony, ed. *Metropolis 1890–1940.* Chicago: University of Chicago Press, 1984.
———. *Toward the Planned City: Germany, Britain, the United States and France, 1780–1914.* New York: St Martin's Press, 1981.
Tauranac, John. *Elegant New York: The Builders and the Buildings, 1885–1915.* New York: Abbeville Press, 1985.
Thomas, Lately. *The Mayor Who Mastered New York: The Life and Opinions of William J. Gaynor.* New York: William Morrow, 1969.
Truax, Rhoda. *The Doctors Jacobi.* Boston: Little, Brown, 1952.

Veiller, Lawrence, and Robert W. DeForest. *The Tenement House Problem.* New York: Macmillan. 1903.

Ultan, Lloyd. *The Beautiful Bronx, 1920–1950.* Westport, Conn.: Arlington House, 1979.

Ultan, Lloyd, and Gary Hermalyn. *The Bronx: It Was Only Yesterday, 1935–1965.* The Bronx, N.Y.: The Bronx County Historical Society, 1992.

———. *The Bronx in the Innocent Years, 1890–1925.* 2d ed. The Bronx, N.Y.: The Bronx County Historical Society, 1991.

Ultan, Lloyd, and Barbara Unger. *Bronx Accent: A Literary and Pictorial History of the Borough.* New Brunswick, N.J.: Rutgers University Press, 2000.

Vernon, Raymond. *Metropolis 1985: An Interpretation of the Findings of the New York Metropolitan Regional Survey.* Cambridge: Harvard University Press, 1960.

Wagner, Robert F., Jr. *New York Ascendent: The Report of the Commission on the Year 2000.* New York: Harper and Row, 1988.

Walker, James Blaine. *Fifty Years of Rapid Transit, 1864–1917.* New York: Law Printing Co., 1917.

Wallace, Deborah, and Rodrick Wallace. *A Plague on Your Houses: How New York Was Burned Down and National Public Health Crumbled.* New York: Verso, 1998.

Ward, David, and Olivier Zunz, eds. *The Landscape of Modernity: New York City, 1900–1940.* Baltimore: Johns Hopkins University Press, 1992.

Warner, Sam B., Jr. *Streetcar Suburbs: The Process of Growth in Boston 1870–1900.* Cambridge: Harvard University Press, 1962.

Weber, Adna Ferrin. *The Growth of Cities in the Nineteenth Century: A Study in Statistics.* New York, 1899. Reprint, Ithaca, N.Y.: Cornell University Press, 1963.

Wesser, Robert F. *A Response to Progressivism: The Democratic Party and New York Politics, 1902–1918.* New York: New York University Press, 1986.

———. *Charles Evans Hughes and Reform in New York, 1905–1910.* Ithaca, N.Y.: Cornell University Press, 1967.

White, Norval. *New York: A Physical History.* New York: Atheneum, 1987.

Wiebe, Robert H. *The Search for Order, 1877–1920.* New York: Hill and Wang, 1967.

Willis, Carol. *Form Follows Finance: Skyscrapers and Skylines in New York and Chicago.* New York: Princeton Architectural Press, 1995.

Wilsher, Peter, and Rosemary Righter. *The Exploding Cities.* New York: Quadrangle/The New York Times Book Co., 1975.

Winslow, C. E. A. *The Life of Hermann M. Biggs.* Philadelphia: Lea and Febiger, 1929.

Wolfe, Roy I. *Transportation and Politics.* New York: W. W. Norton, 1963.

Woods, Robert A., and Albert J. Kennedy. *The Zone of Emergence.* Cambridge: MIT Press, 1962.

Yellowitz, Irwin. *Labor and the Progressive Movement in New York State, 1896–1916.* Ithaca, N.Y.: Cornell University Press, 1965.

ARTICLES AND BOOK CHAPTERS

Adams, Thomas. "The Peculiar Social and Economic Conditions of New York and the Need for a City Plan." *Town Planning Review* 2, no. 3 (October 1911): 183–196.

Arnold, Bion J. "The Urban Transportation Problem: A General Discussion." *Annals of the American Academy of Political and Social Science* 48 (January 1911): 3–13.

Arnovici, Carol. "Housing and the Housing Problem." *Annals of the American Academy of Political and Social Science* 51 (January 1914): 1–7.

———. "Suburban Development." *Annals of the American Academy of Political and Social Science* 51 (January 1914): 235–244.

Baker, Ray Stannard. "The Subway 'Deal': How New York City Built Its New Underground Railroad." *McClure's Magazine* 24 (March 1905): 450–469.

Bayor, Ronald. "The Dependent Center: The First Decade of the AIDS Epidemic in New York City." In David Rosner, ed., *Hives of Sickness: Public Health and Epidemics in New York City,* 131–154. New Brunswick, N.J.: Rutgers University Press, 1995.

Blackmar, Elizabeth. "Accountability for Public Health: Regulating the Housing Market in Nineteenth-Century New York City." In David Rosner, ed., *Hives of Sickness: Public Health and Epidemics in New York City,* 42–64. New Brunswick, N.J.: Rutgers University Press, 1995.

Bromley, Ray. "Not So Simple! Caro, Moses, and the Impact of the Cross-Bronx Expressway." *The Bronx County Historical Society Journal* 35, no. 1 (Spring 1998): 4–29.

Casey, Marion R. "'From the East Side to the Seaside': Irish Americans on the Move in New York City." In Ronald H. Bayor and Timothy J. Meagher, eds., *The New York Irish,* 395–415. Baltimore: Johns Hopkins University Press, 1996.

Cohen, James K. "Capital Investment and the Decline of Mass Transit in New York City, 1945–1981." *Urban Affairs Quarterly* 23, no. 3 (March 1988): 369–388.

Condran, Gretchen A. "Changing Patterns of Epidemic Disease in New York City." In David Rosner, ed., *Hives of Sickness: Public Health and Epidemics in New York City,* 27–41. New Brunswick, N.J.: Rutgers University Press, 1995.

"Congestion in Great Cities." *Cassier's Magazine* 31 (March 1907): 456–457.

Cooley, Charles. "The Social Significance of Street Railways." *Publications of the American Economic Association* 6, no. 1 (January 1891): 65–79.

———. "The Theory of Transportation." *Publications of the American Economic Association* 9, no. 3 (May 1894): 1–148.

Cutting, R. Fulton. "A Calm View of the Rapid Transit Situation." *Outlook* 74 (April 15, 1905): 29–35.

Davies, John Vipond. "Provision for Future Rapid Transit: Subway, Elevated or Open Cut, and Their Influence on the City Plan." In *Proceedings of the Sixth National Conference on City Planning* (1914), 195–211.

De la Barra, Ximena. "Fear of Epidemics: The Engine of Urban Planning." *Planning Practice and Research* 15, nos. 1 and 2 (February/May 2000): 7–16.

Demoro, Harre. "Frank Julian Sprague: A Transit Genius." *Mass Transit* 5, no. 9 (September 1978): 60–61.

Derrick, Peter. "The N.Y.C. Mess: Legacy of the Five-Cent Fare." *Mass Transit* 8, no. 7 (July 1981): 12–13, 26.

Ford, George B. "The City Controlling the Development of Private Property." In Municipal Engineers of the City of New York, *Proceedings for 1915* (1916), 48–90.

Fox, John P. "Transit and Congestion." *Survey* 25 (March 25, 1911): 1065–1066.

Gabaccia, Donna. "Little Italy's Decline: Immigrant Renters and Investors in a Changing City." In David Ward and Olivier Zunz, eds., *The Landscape of Modernity: New York City, 1900–1940*, 235–251. Baltimore: Johns Hopkins University Press, 1992.

Gaynor, William J. "The Looting of New York." *Pearson's Magazine* 21 (May 1, 1909): 461–473.

———. "The New York Subway Situation." *Outlook* 95 (July 30, 1910): 713–726.

———. "New York's Subway Policy." *Municipal Affairs* 5 (1901): 433–438.

———. "Remarks." *Municipal Reference Library, Opening Exercises.* New York, 1913, 15–20.

Gonzalez, Evelyn. "From Suburb to City: The Development of the Bronx, 1890–1940." In *Building a Borough: Architecture and Planning in the Bronx, 1890–1940.* The Bronx: The Bronx Museum of the Arts, 1986.

Goodnow, Frank J. "Reasons for a Commission on Congestion." *Survey* 24 (April 9, 1910): 77–78.

Green, Nancy L. "Sweatshop Migrations: The Garment Industry Between Home and Shop." In David Ward and Olivier Zunz, eds., *The Landscape of Modernity: New York City, 1900–1940,* 213–232. Baltimore: Johns Hopkins University Press, 1992.

Groh, Karl. "Above the Streets of Brooklyn." *Headlights* 37 (September–November 1975): 2–20.

Harkness, LeRoy T. "The Dual System Contracts in Their Relation to the Rapid Transit History of New York City." In Municipal Engineers of the City of New York, *Proceedings for 1913* (1914), 220–280.

Harris, Richard. "The Geography of Employment and Residence in New York Since 1950." In John Hull Mollenkopf and Manuel Castells, eds., *Dual City: Restructuring New York,* 129–152. New York: Russell Sage Foundation, 1991.

Hays, Samuel P. "The Politics of Reform in Municipal Government in the Progressive Era." In Alexander B. Callow, Jr., ed., *American Urban History: An Interpretive Reader with Commentaries,* 421–439. New York: Oxford University Press, 1969.

Hendrick, Burton J. "Great American Fortunes and Their Making: Street-Railway Financiers." *McClure's Magazine* 30 (November–December 1907): 30–48, 236–250, 323, 338.

Jackson, Kenneth T. "The Capital of Capitalism: The New York Metropolitan Region, 1890–1840." In Anthony Sutcliffe, ed., *Metropolis 1890–1940,* 319–353. New York: St Martin's Press, 1981.

———. "Urban Deconcentration in the Nineteenth Century: A Statistical Inquiry." In Leo F. Schnore, ed., *The New Urban History: Quantitative Explorations by American Historians,* 110–142. Princeton: Princeton University Press, 1975.

Kantor, Harvey A. "Benjamin C. Marsh and the Fight over Population Congestion." *Journal of the American Institute of Planners* 40 (November 1974): 422–429.

Koepp, Stephen. "Selling a Dream of Elegance and the Good Life," *Time,* September 1, 1986, 54–61.

Kraut, Alan M. "Plagues and Prejudice: Nativism's Construction of Disease in Nineteenth- and Twentieth-Century New York City." In David Rosner, ed., *Hives of Sickness: Public Health and Epidemics in New York City,* 65–90. New Brunswick, N.J.: Rutgers University Press, 1995.

Kriegel, Leonard. "Last Stop on the D Train." *American Scholar* 39, no. 2 (Spring 1970), 272–288.

Lamb, Frederick S. "New York City of the Future." *House and Garden* 3 (June 1903): 295–310.

Lardner, James. "Painting the Elephant." *The New Yorker,* June 25, 1984, 41–72.

Law, Edward M. "Real Estate Values and Population Growth along Rapid Transit Lines in the City of New York." *Municipal Engineers Journal* 21 (1935): 67–88.

Lewis, Nelson P. "The Planning of Undeveloped City Areas." In *Proceedings of the Second National Conference on City Planning and the Problems of Congestion* (1910), 120–128.

Lubove, Roy. "The Twentieth Century City: The Progressive as Municipal Reformer." *Mid-America* 41 (October 1959): 191–206.

Maltbie, Milo R. "The Fruits of Public Regulation in New York." *Annals of the American Academy of Political and Social Science* 48 (January 1911): 170–190.

———. "A Rapid Transit Policy for Greater New York." In Clyde Lyndon King, ed., *The Regulation of Municipal Utilities*, 125–127. New York: D. Appleton, 1909.

———. "Rapid Transit Subways in Metropolitan Cities." *Municipal Affairs* 4 (1900): 458–480.

Martin, John. "The Exhibit of Congestion Interpreted." *Charities and the Commons* 20 (April 1909): 31–34.

Marsh, Benjamin C. "City Planning in Justice to the Working Population." *Charities and the Commons* 19 (February 1908): 1514–1518.

———. "The Public Health as Affected by Congestion of Population." In *Proceedings of the Tenth New York State Conference on Charities and Corrections* (1909), 253–258.

McAneny, George. "From Cow Path to Subway: How New York Has Solved Many Problems of Rapid Growth." *Current Affairs in New England* 15 (November 14, 1924): 13, 32.

———. "What I Am Trying to Do: Helping to Make New York a Cleaner, More Healthful, More Beautiful, and Greater City." *World's Work* 26 (June 1913): 172–181.

Miller, Claude H. "The Menace of Crowded Cities." *World's Work* 16 (May 1906): 10268–10272.

Moehring, Eugene P. "Space, Economic Growth, and the Public Works Revolution in New York." In Public Works Historical Society, *Infrastructure and Urban Growth in the Nineteenth Century*, 29-59. Essays in Public Works History no. 14. Chicago: Public Works Historical Society, 1985.

Mullin, John R. "American Perceptions of German City Planning at the Turn of the Century." *Urbanism Past and Present* 3 (Winter 1976–1977): 5–15.

Myers, Gustavus. "The Gold Mines of the New York Subway." *New York World*, March 13, 1905.

Nathan, Richard P., Julian Chow, and Mildred L. Owens. "The Flip Side of the Underclass: Working and Middle Class Minority Neighborhoods." *Rockefeller Institute Bulletin*, special issue on "Two Views of Urban America" (1995): 14–22.

Nelson, N. O. "The Remedy for City Congestion." *The Independent* 65 (September 24, 1908): 703–706.

Olmsted, Frederick Law. "Rapid Transit Relief for Mew York City." *Outlook* 92 (May 1, 1909): 6–7.

Olmsted, Robert A. "Transportation Made The Bronx." *The Bronx County Historical Society Journal* 35, no. 2 (Fall 1998): 166–186.

Plunz, Richard A. "Reading Bronx Housing, 1890–1940." In *Building a Borough: Architecture and Planning in the Bronx, 1890–1940*, 30–77. The Bronx. The Bronx Museum of the Arts.

———. "Zoning the New Horizontal City." In Todd W. Bressi, ed., *Planning and Zoning in New York City: Yesterday, Today and Tomorrow*, 27–47. New Brunswick, N.J.: Center for Urban Policy Research, 1993.

Revell, Kevin D. "Regulating the Landscape: Real Estate Values, City Planning and the 1916 Zoning Ordinance." In David Ward and Olivier Zunz, eds., *The Landscape of Modernity*, 19–45. Baltimore: Johns Hopkins University Press, 1992.

Skolnick, Richard S. "Civic Group Progressives in New York City." *New-York History* 51, no. 4 (July 1970): 409–432.

Spann, Edward K. "The Greatest Grid: The New York Plan of 1811." In David Schaffer, ed., *Two Centuries of American Planning*, 11–39. Baltimore: Johns Hopkins University Press, 1988.

Spencer, Joseph A. "New York City Tenant Organizations and the Post–World War I Housing Crisis." In Ronald Lawson and Mark Naison, eds., *The Tenant Movement in New York City, 1904–1984*, 51–93. New Brunswick, N.J.: Rutgers University Press, 1986.

Stuart, Lee. "'Come Let Us Rebuild the Walls of Jerusalem': Broad-Based Organizing in the South Bronx." In Robert D. Carle and Louis DeCaro, Jr., eds. *Signs of Hope in the City: Ministries of Community Renewal*, 129–139. Valley Forge, Pa.: Judson Press, 1997.

Sturm, Robert C. "The Sunrise Trail: A Brief History of the Long Island Rail Road." *National Railway Bulletin* 60, no. 4 (1995): 4–7.

Tarr, Joel Arthur. "From City to Suburb: The 'Moral' Influence of Transportation Technology." In Alexander E. Callow, Jr., ed., *American Urban History: An Interpretive Reader with Commentaries*, 2d ed., 202–212. New York: Oxford University Press, 1973.

Taylor, George Rogers. "Building an Intra-Urban Transportation System."

In Allan M. Wakstein, ed., *The Urbanization of America: An Historical Anthology*, 128–150. Boston: Houghton Mifflin, 1970.

Tobier, Emanuel. "The Bronx in the Twentieth Century: Dynamics of Population and Economic Change." *The Bronx County Historical Society Journal* 35, no. 2 (Fall 1998): 69–102.

———. "Manhattan's Business District in the Industrial Age." In John Hull Mollenkopf, ed., *Power, Culture and Place: Essays on New York City*, 77–105. New York: Russell Sage Foundation, 1988.

Tomkins, Calvin. "The Desirability of Comprehensive Municipal Planning in Advance of Development." In Municipal Engineers of the City of New York, *Proceedings for 1905* (1906), 226–237.

Turner, Daniel L. "Municipal Transportation in Its Relation to the City Plan." In *Proceedings of the Fourth Annual Conference of Mayors and Other City Officials of the State of New York* (1913), 240–243.

———. "The New Municipal Transportation System for New York City, and Its Relation to the City Plan." *Landscape Architecture* 3, no. 4 (July 1913): 176–196.

Twining, William S. "The Investigation of the Traffic Possibilities of Proposed Subway Lines." *Annals of the American Academy of Political and Social Science* 47 (January 1911): 56–67.

Van Norman, Louis. "A New Transportation Era for New York." *Review of Reviews* 42 (October 1910): 433–444.

Vining, David R., Jr. "The Growth of Core Regions in the Third World." *Scientific American* 252, no. 4 (April 1988): 42–49.

Weber, Adna F. "Growth of Cities in the United States: 1890–1900." *Municipal Affairs* 5 (1901): 367–375.

———. "Rapid Transit and the Housing Problem." *Municipal Affairs* 6 (1902): 409–417.

Weiner, Joseph L. "Rapid Transit." Chapter 8 of *New York City Government: Functions and Problems.* Prepared for the New York State Constitutional Convention Committee. New York, 1938.

Wilcox, Delos F. "The New York Subway Contracts." *National Municipal Review* 2, no. 3 (July 1913): 375–391.

Willcox, William R. "The Transportation Problem in New York City." *Harper's Weekly* 54, no. 13 (March 5, 1910): 11–17.

Willis, Carol. "A 3-D CBD: How the 1916 Zoning Law Shaped Manhattan's Central Business Districts." In Todd W. Bressi, ed., *Planning and Zoning in New York City: Yesterday, Today and Tomorrow*, 3–26. New Brunswick, N.J.: Center for Urban Policy Research, 1993.

Wirka, Susan Marie. "The City Social Movement: Progressive Women Reformers and Early Social Planning." In Mary Corbin Sies and Christopher Silver, eds., *Planning the Twentieth-Century City*, 55–75. Baltimore: Johns Hopkins University Press, 1996.

Wright, Henry C. "Development of Transit Control in New York City." *Annals of the American Academy of Political and Social Science* 31 (May 1908): 555–569.

———. "Rapid Transit in Relation to the Housing Problem." In *Proceedings of the Second National Conference on City Planning and the Problems of Congestion* (1910), 125–135.

———. "Transit and Congestion." *Survey* 25 (March 10, 1911): 1067.

DOCTORAL DISSERTATIONS AND MASTER'S THESES

Aronson, David I. "The City Club of New York, 1892–1912." Ph.D. diss., New York University, 1975.

Brooks, Robert C. "History of the Street and Rapid Transit Railways of New York City." Ph.D. diss., Cornell University, 1903.

Cerillo, Augustus, Jr. "Reform in New York City: A Study of Urban Progressivism." Ph.D. diss., Northwestern University, 1969.

Derrick, Peter. "The New York City Transit Crisis of 1918–1925." Master's thesis, Columbia University, 1967.

Fischer, Joel. "Urban Transportation: Home Rule and the Independent Subway System in New York City, 1917–1925." Ph.D. diss., St. John's University, 1978.

Gabel, Jack. "Edward Morse Shepard, Militant Reformer." Ph.D. diss., New York University, 1967.

Gonzalez, Evelyn Diaz. "City Neighborhoods: Formation, Growth and Change in the South Bronx, 1840–1940." Ph.D. diss., Columbia University, 1993.

Hochman, William Russell. "William J. Gaynor: The Years of Fruition." Ph.D. diss., Columbia University, 1955.

Kantor, Harvey. "Modern Urban Planning in New York City: Origins and Evolution, 1890–1933." Ph.D. diss., New York University, 1971.

Latta, Cynthia Morse. "The Return on the Investment in the Interborough Rapid Transit Company." Ph.D. diss., Columbia University, 1975.

Myatt, James Allen. "William Randolph Hearst and the Progressive Era, 1900–1912." Ph.D. diss., University of Florida, 1960.

Schick, Sandor Evan. "Neighborhood Change in the Bronx, 1905–1960." Ph.D. diss., Harvard University, 1982.

Schoenebaum, Eleanora W., "Emerging Neighborhoods: The Development of Brooklyn's Fringe Areas, 1850–1930." Ph.D. diss., Columbia Univsersity, 1977.

Skolnick, Richard Stephen. "The Crystallization of Reform in New York City, 1890–1917." Ph.D. diss., Yale University, 1964.
Waterman, Arthur J., Jr. "Integration of Rapid Transit Facilities of the City of New York." Ph.D. diss., New York University, 1940.

Index

Note: Because this book is about rapid transit in New York City, most of the index references for New York City are under their own main subject headings. Thus, population in New York City is under "Population." The exception is that there is a separate main subject heading, "New York City government," for references to the government of New York City (referred to as "City" in the text). Most of the index references to the subway and elevated railroads in New York City are under the main subject headings "Rapid transit" and "Dual System of Rapid Transit" and the names of individual lines of the rapid transit network. There are also main subject headings for "Elevated railroads" and "Subways" and for the private transit operating companies, such as the "Interborough Rapid Transit Company (IRT)" and the "Brooklyn Rapid Transit Company (BRT)." The main subject heading "Rapid transit and city development" covers all references to the paradigm about saving New York through the construction of many new rapid transit lines within the context of an overall effort to control city development.

Adler, Felix, 121
Admiral Realty Co. vs. City of New York, 208–209
African-Americans, 315n, 325n, 393n; in Harlem, 45, 390n; and housing segregation, 257; in subway suburbs, 259–260, 261, 268, 388n
AIDS, 104, 325n
Alcoholism, 9
Allied Board of Trade of the Eastern District, 214
"All the nations under Heaven" (Binder and Reimer), 268
American City, 172
American Lung Association, 324n
American Medical Association, 121
American Museum of Natural History, 112
American Newspaper Publishers Association, 136
Amsterdam, 110
Apartment houses, 242; in subway suburbs, 231–232, 243–244, 250–254, 255, 259, 260, 347n, 348n, 381n, 387n, 392n, 394n; as term for tenements in subway suburbs, 252. *See also* Housing
Archer Avenue line, 366n
Arson: in tenement districts, 3, 99
Asians: in subway suburbs, 260, 261
Asiatic cholera, 104
Assessment plan, 78, 129–130, 310n
Associated Press, 136
Astor, John Jacob, 28
Astoria: as subway suburb, 382n
Astoria line, 167, 168, 169, 171, 178, 180, 204, 225, 227, 272, 278; opening date, 284, 285
Automobile registrations, 390n
Automobiles: impact on public transit, 238; and subway suburbs, 256

Baker, Ray Stannard, 61
Banking, 93
Bannard, Otto T., 85, 86, 313n
Barney, Charles T., 346n
Bassett, Edward M., 118, 142, 192, 242, 309n, 328n; appointed to PSC, 71; and conferees report, 174, 346n; and Congestion Committee, 328n, 329n; and financing the Triborough System, 74–75; and rapid transit and city development, 105, 115, 124–125, 153–154, 264–265, 334n, 348n, 356n
Bay Ridge, 55, 56, 279; as subway suburb, 248, 251, 256, 383n
Beach, Alfred Ely, 27, 28
Beard, Charles A., 102
The Beautiful Bronx (Ultan), 256
Bedford Park: mix of housing, 253, 387n; as subway suburb, 253
Bedford Park Taxpayers Association, 339n
Bedford-Stuyvesant, 257
Belmont, August, 67–68, 311n; and financing first IRT subway, 41, 202; and

Belmont, August *(continued)*
IRT, 43, 170, 356n, 396n; and IRT merger with Metropolitan Street Railway Company, 57–58
Belmont, August (Senior), 28
Bensonhurst, 65, 74; as subway suburb, 253, 254
Bergman, Juliette, 394n
Berlin, 33, 262, 326n
Biggs, Hermann, 106, 120
Blackmar, Abel E., 208–209
Blacks, *see* African-Americans
BMT, *see* Brooklyn Manhattan Transit Corporation. *See also* Brooklyn Rapid Transit Company
Board, *see* Rapid Transit Board
Board of Aldermen, 36, 52
Board of Estimate, 52, 80, 88, 123, 129–130, 148–150, 155, 209–210, 243, 264, 333n, 344n; and city planning, 5, 241, 242, 247; as committee of the whole, 148, 150; and Dual System, 186, 191, 193–194, 195–200, 209–210, 212, 220–221; and IRT, 140, 146–152; membership and votes, 303n, 332–333n; policy, 126–127, 139–140, 149–152, 155–158; powers of, 52, 333n; and progressive reformers, 4, 91–92; and PSC, 123, 140, 153–154, 159, 264; and Triborough System, 126, 127, 129, 130, 133, 140, 146–147, 158; Transit Committee, 6, 126, 127, 128, 136, 148–150, 155–160, 174, 192
Board of Estimate and Apportionment, *see* Board of Estimate
Board of Rapid Transit Commissioners, 34, 35
Board of Rapid Transit Railroad Commissioners, *see* Rapid Transit Board
Board of Transportation of the City of New York, 236, 375n
Bombay, 318n
Borough Park: as subway suburb, 253, 255
Borough presidents: responsibilities of, 333n; *and names of individual borough presidents*
Boston, 221
Bradley-Gaffney-Steers Company, 82, 83, 85, 88
Brighton Beach: as subway suburb, 255
Brighton line, 163, 178, 179, 226, 276, 279, 345n, 383n, 387n, 399n; opening date, 285
Broadway: first subway proposed for, 25
Broadway (Brooklyn) elevated line, 32, 151, 178, 227, 276, 279, 303n. *See also* Jamaica line
Broadway BRT line, 161, 163, 167, 168, 171, 225–227, 249, 278; and IRT, 188, 350n; profitability of, 189
Broadway-Lexington Avenue line, 65, 73, 79, 80, 133, 138, 140
Broadway-Lafayette Avenue subsystem, 73–74, 82
Broadway-Lexington Avenue subsystem, 73–74
Broadway ultimatum, 166–169
Bronx, the, 1, 2, 50, 54, 73, 163, 167, 168, 250, 295n, 319n, 320n 391n; "the Beautiful Bronx," 256; congestion of population, 101, 114–115, 203, 317n, 318n; Dual System lines, 170, 179–181, 185, 222–224, 270–271, 273, 366n; first IRT lines, 38; impact of Dual System, 245–248, 250–256, 258–262, 268, 383n; impact of Third Avenue elevated and first subway, 45–46; in IRT plans, 143, 145, 150, maps 3 and 4, 128, 141; mix of housing, 253; population, 1790–1997, table 1, 10; Rapid Transit Board plans for, 50, 55; Third Avenue elevated, 30, 50, 145, 224, 238, 271, 377; *and names of individual communities and lines*
Brooklyn, 1, 2, 16, 49, 72, 95, 97, 157, 160, 250, 295n, 319n; BRT plans for, 160–161, 163–166, map 5, 162; community opposition to Dual System, 213–214; congestion of population, 95, 317n; Dual System lines, 174–176, 178–180, 185, 222, 224–227, 271–272, 277–280; elevated lines, 11, 30, 32, map 1, 31; first IRT subway, 42; impact of Dual System, 245–248, 250–256, 258–262, 268; impact of elevated lines, 45–46; in IRT plans, 143, 150; mix of housing, 252, 253; population, 1790–1997, table 1, 10; Rapid Transit

Board plans for, 51–52, 55–56; *and names of individual communities and lines*
Brooklyn and Queens: rapid transit needs compared to Manhattan and the Bronx, 115, 150, 157, 160, 170
Brooklyn Board of Real Estate Brokers, 339n
Brooklyn Bridge, 8, 12, 51; elevated lines on, 32, 50, 72, 303n
Brooklyn Democratic organization, 195
Brooklyn Eagle, 166
Brooklyn Heights, 15, 97
Brooklyn Institute, 112
Brooklyn-Manhattan loop line, 55, 65, 73–74
Brooklyn Manhattan Transit Corporation (BMT): bought out by New York City, 237; successor to BRT, 236. *See also* Brooklyn Rapid Transit Company
Brooklyn-Queens crosstown line, 56, 164, 178, 210, 367n
Brooklyn Rapid Transit Company (BRT), 32, 42, 50, 139, 158, 159, 163, 164, 173, 232; certificates for elevated improvements, 221, 280; and conferees, 166–169; Contract No. 4, 221, 225–230, 276–283; cost to of Dual System, 180, 227–228, 281, 367n, 368n, 373n, 375n; and Dual System, 6, 174–175, 178–187, 189–191, 194–195, 197, 199–200, 204–206, 208, 210–212, 219, 221–223, 225–230, 265, 276–283, 285, 371n, maps 6b and 6c, 176, 177; elevated improvements, 164, 227, 280, 371n; financing of Dual System, 180–183, 211–212, 232, 234–236, 276, 282, 360n, 372n, 373n, 374n, 375n; vs. IRT, 166–169, 171–173; IRT/BRT joint use of Queens lines, 178, 180, 204–205, 225, 272, 378n; mileage in Dual System, 365; opening dates of Dual System lines, 285; policy, 160–166; and preferentials, 165, 182–183, 186–190, 193, 204, 229–230, 282, 349n, 374n, 375n; proposals for expansion, 151–152, 160–161, 163–165, 168, map 5, 162; in Rapid Transit Board plans, 50–51, 53; reorganized as BMT, 236; ridership, 32, 45, 233; ridership estimates for Dual System, 199, 210. *See also* Brooklyn Manhattan Transit Corporation and New York Municipal Railway Corporation
Brooklyn's Needs in Transportation (Bassett), 115
Brooks, Michael W., 306n
Brownsville, 32, 75, 143, 157, 318n, 320n
BRT, *see* Brooklyn Rapid Transit Company
Bruère, Henry, 354n
Bryant Park, 395n
Budapest, 221
Building height restrictions, 154, 232, 240–243
Business community: and Congestion Committee, 111
Business services, 93
Bushwick, 2, 95, 213

Canal Street line, 56, 65
Canarsie line, 32, 276; connection to 14th Street line, 367n, 399n. *See also* Fourteenth Street–northern Brooklyn line
Caribbeans: in subway suburbs, 260
Casey, Marion, 251–252
Central Park, 293n
Central Trust Company, 211, 360n
Centre Street loop line, 51, 72, 74, 141, 151, 164, 178–179, 226–227, 276, 278–279, 303n, 342n; approval of construction, 67; opening dates, 285
Century Club, 198
Chamber of Commerce of the State of New York, 35–36, 63, 139, 141
Charity Organization Society, 112
Cheap Trains Act of 1883 (England), 109
Cherry Street: residence of George Washington, 17
Chicago, 33, 221; housing compared to New York, 326n; office space in, 287n, 384n
Child labor reform, 112
Children: in sweatshops, 100; in tenement districts, 101, 104–105, 113
Cholera, 3, 18, 102, 262
Citizens Association of Bay Ridge and Ft. Hamilton, 339n
Citizen's Association of New York: report on living conditions in Manhattan, 19–20

Citizens Union, 61, 207
The City: The Hope of Democracy (Howe), 102
City Charter: and Gaynor, 193, 195; and zoning, 242–243
City Club of New York, 120, 308–309n, 310n; and Congestion Show, 113; and planning of Dual System, 159, 174; and
City Club of New York *(continued)* PSC, 71–72, 307n; and transportation planning, 72–73, 113
City planning, 4–5, 91, 107, 110, 113, 115–119, 122, 174, 202–204, 222, 232, 240–244, 264–265, 330n, 331n, 380n
City planning commission, 232, 240–241, 391n
Civic Alliance, 86–87, 312n
Civil Service Reform Association, 119
Civil War, 18, 22
Claflin, John, 300n
"Cold water flats," 98
Coler, Bird S., 39; and Fourth Avenue line, 55; and Triborough System plan, 65
Colored Orphan Asylum, 18
Commission, *see* Public Service Commission
Commission on Building Districts and Restrictions, 243
Commission on Building Heights, 242–243
Commission on Congestion of Population, 242, 343n; and rapid transit and city development, 154
Committee on Congestion of Population in New York, *see* Congestion Committee
Committee on the City Plan (Board of Estimate), 241, 343n
Commutation: time and cost constraints, 96
Commuter railroads, 20–21, 296n, 384n; and development of Midtown Manhattan, 249; *and names of individual railroads*
Commuters, 16; defined, 296n
Comptroller: responsibility of, 333n
Concourse line, 248, 394n
Coney Island, 65, 151, 157, 279; as subway suburb, 248, 383n
Conferees, 158–173; and BRT, 160–169; defined, 159; and IRT, 160, 166–168, 171–172; and rapid-transit planning, 159; report on Dual System plan, 173–185, 186, 189; policy, 159, 166–169, 170–171
Congestion, 2, 9; at turn of twentieth century, 90, 92–106
Congestion and Preventable Diseases (Jacobi), 120
Congestion and Transportation (McCarroll), 115
Congestion Committee, 110–118, 153; Congestion Show, 112–115, 331n; creation of, 111–112, 328n; and Hughes, 113–114; members of, 328n; and PSC, 114–115; and tuberculosis, 112
The Congestion of Our People (Silverman), 101
Congestion of population, 3, 9, 21–22, 91, 94–98, 101, 109, 140, 173; causes of, 20, 107, 116–117; and Dual System, 2, 4, 199, 202–203, 207, 210, 216, 231, 246, 248, 264–265, 267–268, 350n; increase to 1910, 11, 90, 317n; and Jews, 326n; Low and, 216, 218; McAneny and, 4, 7, 118–119, 122–124, 202–205, 216, 240, 263–265, 267–268, 331n, 380n; and rapid transit and city development, 4, 5, 21–22, 107, 110, 89, 91, 116–118, 122–124, 202–205, 216, 218, 240, 263, 264–265, 267–268, 296–297n, 331n; and poverty, 95; spread to Brooklyn and the Bronx, 90, 203, 379n
Congestion Show, *see* Congestion Committee
Consolidated Edison Company, 248
Consumption, 323n
Contract No. 1, 41, 49, 60–61, 301n
Contract No. 2, 42–43, 49, 301n
Contract No. 3, 221, 223–225, 227–229, 234–235, 269–275, 373n
Contract No. 4, 221, 225–230, 234, 276–283, 373n, 399n; the "Existing Railroad," 276, 281; the "Railroad," 276, 281
Cooley, Charles, 107–110
Corning, Erastus, 28, 298n
Corona: as subway suburb, 253
Corona line, 272, 278. *See also* Corona-

Flushing line, Flushing line, and Woodside-Corona line
Corona-Flushing line, 223, 225, 227. *See also* Corona line, Flushing line, and Woodside-Corona line
County, A. J., 195
Court of Appeals, 88; and Dual System, 209
Cram, J. Sergeant, 207, 353n; vs. Dual System, 213, 214, 220, 358n; and IRT preferentials, 192–193, 206, 352n, 355n
Crime: and Italians, 105; and Jews, 105–106, 326n; in tenement districts, 3, 19, 99–101, 104–106
Croker, Richard, 39, 40, 41
Cromwell, George, 87, 157, 158, 192, 193, 333n, 339n
Cudahy, Brian J.: and BRT line on Queensboro Bridge, 367n, 398n; and Dual System contracts, 267; and Dual System lines in existing rapid transit network, 365n
Culver line, 163, 178, 226, 276, 279, 345n, 387n; opening date, 285

Davison, Henry P., 336n, 355n
"Deaf, Dumb and Blind to All Evil," cartoon 1, 201
Death rate: in tenement districts, 101
DeForest, Robert W., 106
DeKalb Avenue station, 163–164, 176, 179, 226, 278–279
De la Barra, Ximena, 262
Delaney, John: and revenues from Dual System operations, 371n
Democratic Party, *see* Tammany Hall
Democrats: independents in Fusion movement, 312n
Development routes, 79
Diphtheria, 103, 105, 121, 332n
Disease, 262, 322n; in tenement districts, 3–4, 9, 99–105; and *names of individual diseases*
Dix, John A., 193, 195, 207–208, 353n
Downtown Brooklyn, 43, 50, 55, 164, 165; and Dual System lines 176, 179, 226, 270–272
Draft riots, 18–19
Drier, Mary E., 328n
Dual System of Rapid Transit, 1, 4, 6–7, 169–185, 220–230, 263, 269–285, 364n, 365n, 366n; amount of land opened for development, 231, 370n; breaking the deadlock, 189–194, 196–200; Bronx lines, 179, 180–181, 185, 222–224, 270–271, 273; Brooklyn lines, 175–176, 178–180, 185, 206, 210, 222, 224–227, 271–272, 277–280; and BRT, 6, 174–176, 178–179, 186–187, 189–191, 194–195, 197, 199–200, 204–206, 208, 210–212, 219, 221–223, 225–230, 276–282; capacity of, 222, 360n; certificates for elevated line improvements, 221, 224, 272–273, 280; and city planning, 174, 203, 222, 232, 240–244, 264–265; and conferees report, 173–185; and congestion of population, 2, 4, 7, 199, 202–203, 207, 210, 216, 231, 246, 248, 264–265, 267–268, 350n; contracts, 7, 220–221, 223–230, 269–283; cost, 1, 6, 180–181, 227–229, 234–235, 269, 276–277, 281, 287n, 367n, 368n, 369n, 372n, 373n, 374n, 375n; court approval of, 208–209, 220; and dispersal of population, 231, 245–249, table 3, 247; distribution of revenues, 181–183, 229–230, 274–275, 282–283; engineering and construction, 221, 233, 273, 277, 281, 284–285, 368n, 369n, 371n; express services, 175, 222, 224, 270, 271, 272, 273, 277, 278, 279, 280; financial results, 232–237, 240, 267, 269, 273, 276, 281, 371n, 372n, 373n, 374n, 375n; financing, 180–183, 185–194, 196–200, 203–206, 210–212, 227–230, 232–237, 360n, 367n, 368n; five-cent fare, 179–181, 192, 221, 232, 235–236, 267, 269, 274, 281, 364–365n; and geography of New York City, 231–232, 370n; history of, 266–267; and housing, 250–254, 259–262, 263, 267–268; impact of, 1, 7, 231–262, 263, 267–268; importance of, 8, 221, 227, 230, 263, 267–268; and Independent System, 237; and IRT, 5, 6, 174–175, 179–185, 186–200, 203–206, 208, 210, 218–219, 221–225, 227–229, 265, 269–273, 234–235, 237, 349n, 364n,

Dual System of Rapid Transit *(continued)* 372n, 373n, 374n, 375n; IRT/BRT joint use of Queens lines, 178, 180, 204–205, 225, 272, 378n; lines, 174–181, 210, 213, 223–227, 269–273, 276–280; and Manhattan CBD, 8, 232, 249–250, 370n, 371n; Manhattan lines, 174–176, 178–179, 181, 185, 222–227, 269–273, 276–280; and Manhattan Railway Company elevated lines, 180–181, 205, 221, 224–225, 227, 237, 271, 272, 273, 357n, 365n, 371n; maps 6a–6c, 175–177; mileage of, 7, 221, 365n, 366n, 376n; as "monumental act of insanity," 195; New York City financing, 6, 181–183, 187–194, 196, 198–199, 203–205, 227–230, 234, 269, 273, 276–277, 367n, 368n, 371n, 373n; and New York State Legislature, 206–207, 219; opening dates of lines, 1, 7, 231, 371n, 372n, appendix 2, 284–285; operating terms, 181–183, 273–275, 281–283; opposition to, 6, 185–186, 188–189, 192–195, 200–201, 207–209, 213–216, 219, 266–267, 289n; ownership of, 181, 228, 273, 281, 287n; preferentials, 165, 180–183, 186–194, 197–200, 204–205, 208–209, 229–230, 267, 274–275, 282, 349n, 351n, 352n, 374n, 375n; and price of land, 253; Queens lines, 175, 178–180, 185, 222–223, 225–227, 272–273, 277–278, 280; ridership on, 7, 233, 234, 250, 290n, 370n, 371n, 372n, table 2, 44; ridership and revenue estimates, 183, 198–199, 204, 210, 233–234; and saving New York, 1, 8, 91, 231, 263, 268; scope of, 1, 8, 221, 222, 227, 230, 231, 365n, 370n; stations by borough, 366n; and subway suburbs, 7–8, 245–262; "Supplementary Report," 209–210; and Thompson Committee investigations, 308n, 396n; and unification, 237; use of elevated lines, 183–184; and World War I, 235
Dumbbell tenements, 98
Dutch: and New Amsterdam, 12
Dyre Avenue line, 238, 365n

East Bronx, 50, 224, 271; as subway suburb, 246, 248, 382n
Eastern Parkway line, 51–52, 133, 143, 150, 157, 164, 167, 169, 180, 224, 271, 338n; opening dates, 284
East Flatbush Taxpayers Association, 339n
East Harlem, 2, 32, 95, 97
East New York, 2, 167, 180, 184, 224, 271
East Side, 37, 38, 49–50, 96, 377n; and Dual System, 223, 238, 270, 377n
Economy (of New York), 238; growth of, 9, 14, 93; manufacturing, 90, 94, 100, 112, 113, 258–259, 316n, 317n, 391n; at turn of twentieth century, 90, 93–94
Eighth Avenue line, 55
Elections, 6, 235–236; 1897, 38–39; 1905, 63–64; 1906, 68–70; 1909, 85–89, 312n; 1913, 200, 215, 369n, 370n; rapid transit as key issue, 302n
Elevated railroads, 90–91, 297n, 348n; elimination of, 377n; first lines, 11, 24–32; impact of, 2, 32; map 1, 35; *and names of individual companies and lines. See also* Dual System of Rapid Transit and Rapid transit
Elevateds, *see* Elevated railroads
Elkins, Stephen, 40
Els, *see* Elevated railroads
Elsberg Act, 63–65, 76
Elsberg, Nathaniel, 61, 64, 306n
English: name New York, 12
Equipping: defined, 338n
Equitable Life Assurance Society, 57
Erie Canal, 14, 369n
Exhibition of Congestion of Population, *see* Congestion Committee
Eustis, John E., 71, 206, 220, 341n, 355n

Fares, 15, 16; as issue in rapid-transit expansion, 23–24; need for low fares, 108–109, 374n; in U.S. cities, 235, 374n. *See also* Five-cent fare
Federal government: and highway construction, 237; mortgage policy, 237–238; and public housing, 257
Federal Immigration Act of 1924, 325n
Fenton, Reuben, 25
Ferries, 14–16
Fifth Avenue: as upper-class residential district, 15, 96
Fifth Avenue Association, 242

Fifth Avenue (Brooklyn) elevated line, 32, 276, 345n
Fifth Avenue line, 55
Fifty-ninth–Sixtieth Street line, 164, 178, 226, 227, 249; and tunnel to Queens, 367n, 398n
Financial district, *see* Lower Manhattan
Financing, *see* Dual System of Rapid Transit, New York City government, *and names of individual companies and banks*
Finley, John H., 328n
First Avenue line, 55
First National Bank, 340n
First subways, 33–43, 45–46; impact of, 41–43, 301n, map 1, 35
Fishberg, Maurice, 324n
Fitch, Robert, 396n
Five-cent fare, 83, 165, 172; and Dual System, 179–181, 192, 221, 232, 235–236, 267, 269, 274, 281, 364–365n; and economy and society of New York, 374n, on first subways, 37, 43; on horsecar lines, 16; impact on rapid transit expansion, 24, 33–34, 75, 142, 335n; on Manhattan Railway Company lines, 181, 274; as political issue, 235, 374n; set by New York State Legislature, 24; in U.S., 109. *See also* Fares
Flatbush: as subway suburb, 248, 256, 383n
Flatbush Avenue line, 163, 180, 224, 271, 277
Flushing line, 272, 278, 383n; in original Dual System, 225, 367n, 398n; opening dates, 284. *See also* Forty-second Street–Steinway Tunnel line and Woodside-Corona line
Fogleson, Richard E., 329n
Folks, Homer, 174, 328n, 342n, 343n
Ford, John, 63
Fordham: as subway suburb, 251, 256
Fordham Club of the Borough of the Bronx, 339n
Fortune 500 companies, 257
Forty-second Street elevated line, 30
Forty-second Street shuttle, 49, 223, 270
Forty-second Street–Steinway Tunnel line, 83, 133, 145, 150, 170, 171, 180, 223, 225, 249, 270, 272, 338n, 341n. *See also* Flushing line
Fourteenth Street–northern Brooklyn line, 56, 151, 157, 167, 168, 169, 171, 176, 179, 226, 276, 277; connection to Canarsie line, 399n; extension to Eighth Avenue, 367n; opening dates, 285. *See also* Canarsie line
Fourth Avenue (Brooklyn) line, 55, 56, 65, 72, 74, 80, 126–127, 138, 142, 143, 145, 150, 163, 178, 179, 184, 226, 276, 277, 342n; and BRT railroads in southern Brooklyn, 151; extension to 95th Street, 399n; opening dates, 285; and Staten Island, 157, 367n
Fourth Avenue subsystem, 74, 82
Freedman, Andrew, 170, 195, 340n, 346n
Freeman, Joshua B., 374n
"French Flats," 96
Fulton Street (Brooklyn) elevated line, 30, 279, 277, 279, 285, 303n; opening date of extension, 285; replaced by IND subway line, 376n
Fusion movement: defined, 86; majority on Board of Estimate, 123, 313n; McAneny as leader of, 86, 126; and 1909 election, 86–88, 312n; and 1913 election, 355n, 356n, 370n
Fusionists, *see* Fusion movement

Garment center, 249
Gay, Ruth, 255
Gaynor, William J., 61, 88, 124, 126, 130, 147, 219; and assassination attempt, 137, 140; and BRT, 173, 193, 195, 197; and City Charter revision, 193, 195, 354n; death of, 369n; and Dual System, 219, 230, 266; and Hearst, 88, 135–136, 290n; and Hearst press, 216, 266–267, cartoons, 201, 217; and history of Dual System, 266–267; and IRT, 87, 124–125, 131–136, 140–141, 147, 170, 173, 193, 196–197, 200, 341n, 353n; and Morgan bank, 201, 202, 219; and 1909 election, 86–88, 313n; and 1913 election, 369n; and Prendergast, 196–197; and "subway sanity," 196; and Triborough System, 133–136, 139, 140–141, 337n, 339n
Genoa, 110
German city planning, 330n
Germans, 18, 92, 255, 315n

Germ theory, 102
Gettysburg: troops from, crush draft riots, 18
Gilbert, Rufus, 22
Gilder, Richard Watson, 328n
Gilmartin, Gregory, 119
Giuliani, Rudolph W., 344n
The Gold Mines of the New York Subway (Myers), 61
Gordon, Harry A., 396n
Gould, E. R. L., 328n
Gould, George, 39
Gould, Jay, 34
Grand Central Terminal, 249
Grand Concourse: community as subway suburb, 255
Grant, Arthur H., 172
Greater New York, 2, 38, 110, 210; creation of, 1, 92, 291n; geographic area of, 92; and rapid-transit proposals, 34, 54–55
Greenwich House, 328n
Greenwich Street: first elevated line on, 26
Greenwich Village, 95; street grid, 13, 270
Gresser, Lawrence, 95, 148, 193, 333n
Grout, Edward M., 52, 189, 190, 305n, 351n

Hall, Peter, 326n; and definition of suburbs, 381n, 382n; and Dual System, 262; and mass transit suburbs, 262, 386n, 395n; and public housing, 386n
Halsband, Frances, 381n
Hamburg, 221
Harlem, 13; and African-Americans, 45, 257; and congestion of population, 95, 383n, 390n; housing in, 45
Harvey, Charles T., 26, 28
Hearst, William Randolph, 61–62, 306n, 308n, 333n, 338n, 356n; and Dual System, 194–195, 200–202, 207–208, 213–216, 217, 219, 289n; and Gaynor, 88, 135–136, 266; and McAneny, 266, 395n; and Mitchel, 124, 194; motives of, 62, 306n; and municipal ownership and operation, 48, 62; 1905 election, 63–64; 1906 election, 68–70; 1909 election, 86, 88, 313n; and Prendergast, 124, 194, 266, 395n; and "Traction Trust," 62; and Triborough System, 124, 136
Hearstism, 62
Hearstites, 86
Hearst press: and Dual System 6, 201, 209, 216–217, cartoons, 201, 217, 266–267; and Gaynor, 136; and "plunderbund," 306n
Heiskel, Andrew, 395n
Hell Gate Bridge, 120
Hell's Kitchen, 2, 95, 97
Hendrick, Burton J., 56
Henry Street Settlement House, 111, 328n
Hewitt, Abram S., 29; and municipal financing and ownership of subways, 35–36
Highbridge, 224; as subway suburb, 256
Highways: impact on rapid transit, 237; and decline of urban neighborhoods, 392n
Hillquit, Morris, 328n
Hispanics, *see* Latinos
Hoboken, 16
Hoffman, John, 28
Hood, Clifton, 22, 374n
Horsecars, 9, 16–17, 20, 295n, 299n; companies oppose rapid transit, 25–27
"Horizontal city" (Plunz), 244
Housing, 16, 95–98, 238, 241, 265, 388n; ideals of reformers, 173, 202, 347n, 348n; luxury apartment houses, 45, 96; public housing, 257–258; reform of, 91, 106–107, 112; row houses, 16, 96; segregation of, 257, 294n; single- and two-family houses, 173, 231–232, 242–243, 245, 250, 252–254, 259, 260, 347n, 348n, 386n, 387n, 392n; in subway suburbs, 231, 250–254; units built in 1920s, 250, 290n. *See also* Apartment houses, New Law Tenement House Act, and Tenements
House of Morgan, *see* J. P. Morgan and Company
Howe, Frederic C., 102
Howe, Irving, 99
How the Other Half Lives (Riis), 97, 106
Hudson and Manhattan Railroad Company, 141

Hughes, Charles Evans, 60, 63; career of, 305n, 306n, 353n; and creation of PSC, 4, 70–71; and 1906 election, 68–70; and rapid transit and city development, 114; speech at Congestion Show, 113–114; and tuberculosis, 324n
Hull House, 111
Hylan, John F.: and city planning, 241, 378n, 379n; and Dual System, 214, 233, 361n, 396n; and five-cent fare, 235; and Independent Subway System, 236

Immigrants, 4, 18, 92, 93, 95, 104, 294n; ethnicity of, 92, 246, 315n, 389n; in subway suburbs, 254–256, 259–261, 268, 388n, 393n; in tenement districts, 2, 3, 9, 18, 91; *and names of individual groups*
IND, *see* Independent Subway System
Independence League, 68
Independent Subway System (IND), 236, 365n, 375n, 376n; and Dual System, 237, 376n; impact on development, 236–237
Independent subway systems, 48, 146
Indeterminate franchise plan, 78, 84, 127, 138, 335n
Industrial Causes of Congestion of Population in New York City (Pratt), 115–117
Infant mortality: in tenement districts, 101, 104–105
Insurance companies, 93
Interborough-Metropolitan Company, 58
Interborough-Metropolitan merger, 56–59
Interborough-Metropolitan Securities Company, 135
Interborough Rapid Transit Company (IRT), 5–6, 41–46, 61, 75, 79–81, 131–132, 135, 160–161, 163, 166, 188–189, 200, 205–206, 208, 232, 346n, 347n; board of directors, 130, 131, 168, 191, 208; and Board of Estimate, 140, 146–152, 158–159; bought out by New York City, 237; and "Broadway ultimatum," 166–169; vs. BRT, 167–168, 171–173, 188, 204, 229–230; certificates of Manhattan Railway Company elevated improvements, 221, 224, 272–273; and conferees, 160, 166–168, 171–172; Contract No. 3, 220–221, 223–225, 269–275; and Dual System, 5, 6, 174–175, 179–185, 186–200, 203–206, 208, 210, 218–219, 221–225, 227–229, 265, 269–273, 234–235, 237, 349n, 364n, 372n, 373n, 374n, 375n, maps 6a and 6c, 175, 177; and financing of subways, 5, 42–43, 125–127, 130–135, 137–138, 143, 145–147, 151, 167, 171–172; financing of Dual System, 180–183, 205, 227–230, 234–237, 269, 273, 367n, 368n, 372n, 373n, 374n, 375n; first subways, 41–43, 81, 126; and Gaynor, 87, 124–125, 131–136, 140–141, 147, 170, 173, 193, 196–197, 200, 341n, 353n; IRT/BRT joint use of Queens lines, 178, 180, 204–205, 225, 272, 378n; and Manhattan Railway Company lines, 43, 221, 224, 272–273, 357n; and Metropolitan Street Railway Company, 56–58; mileage of system, 45, 365n; and Mitchel, 124, 147–149; opening dates of Dual System lines, 284; and preferentials, 186–188, 190–194, 197–200, 204–205, 229, 274–275, 351n, 352n; profitability of first subways, 5, 43, 80–81, 311n, 350n; proposals for expansion, 73, 82–85, 127, 131, 133–135, 143–146, 157, 170–172, maps 3 and 4, 128, 144; and Prendergast, 147–149; and PSC in 1910, 125–126, 130–131, 136–137, 140, 143, 146–147; and Rapid Transit Board plans, 48–53, 55, 59; ridership, 81, 233; ridership estimates for Dual System, 198–199, 210; and Triborough System, 81, 84, 125, 131–134, 139, 143, 146
An Introduction to City Planning (Marsh), 115–116
Irish, 17, 18, 92, 95, 315n; and subway suburbs 255–256
IRT "H" lines, 49–50, 59, 65, 67–68, 72, 76, 79, 82, 127, 134, 143, 145, 146, 170, 223–224, 249, 269–270; opening dates, 284
Italian-American Improvement League of New Utrecht, 339n
Italians, 3, 93, 95, 104–105; and infant

Italians *(continued)*
mortality, 101, 105, 315n, 325n; and subway suburbs, 254, 256
Ivins, William M., 63–64

Jackson, Kenneth T., 244, 380n
Jackson Heights: as subway suburb, 248, 254, 382n, 383n
Jacobi, Abraham, 120–121, 323n, 332n
Jacobi, Ernst, 121
Jacobi, Marjorie, *see* McAneny, Marjorie Jacobi
Jacobi, Mary Putnam, 120–121
Jamaica line, 56, 178, 227, 279, 303n; opening date, 285
Jerome Avenue line, 50, 55, 65, 73, 84, 133, 138, 143, 163, 168, 170, 179, 183, 184, 223–224, 246, 260, 270, 271, 338n, 365n, 394n; and Ninth Avenue elevated line, 224; opening date, 284
Jersey City, 15
Jessup, Morris K., 52
Jews, 3, 95, 101, 106, 315n, 326n; and congestion of population, 101, 326n; and crime, 105; and disease, 101, 104; and Lower East Side, 98–99; migration from tenement districts, 255, 320n; in subway suburbs, 254–256, 382n
J. P. Morgan and Company, 93; and Dual System, 187, 201–202, 205–206, 208, 216, 218–219, cartoon, 217; and IRT, 130–131, 137, 143, 167, 198, 218–219, 336n, 337n, 340n, 355n, 358n, 359n, 362n, 396n
"Journey to Planet Earth," 261

Kelley, Florence, 121; and Congestion Committee, 111–112, 328n; and congestion of population, 112
Kidder, Peabody, and Company, 211
Klein, Calvin, 260
Klein, Henry M., 396n
Kobrin, Leon, 98
Kuhn, Loeb, and Company, 33, 93, 211, 219

Lafayette Avenue line, 138, 140, 141, 143, 150, 188, 213
Laidlaw, Walter, 246, 328n
Land use regulations, 113, 117, 154, 242–244
Latinos, 257, 325n, 388n, 392n, 393n; in subway suburbs, 259–261, 268
Latta, Cynthia Morse, 235, 373n, 374n, 375n
Lauren, Ralph, 260
Law, Edward M., 385n
Legislature, *see* New York State Legislature
Leiper, Joseph M., 391n
Lenox Avenue line, 224, 271
Lexington Avenue (Brooklyn) elevated line, 30, 276
Lexington Avenue line, 50, 54, 82, 83, 135, 168, 179, 195, 223, 224, 270, 338n, 354n, 377n; opening date, 284
Lewis, Nelson P., 357n
Lifshitz, Ralph, *see* Lauren, Ralph
Liverpool, 221
Lofts, 90, 94, 317n
London, 33, 92, 109, 221, 287n, 318n, 326n; first subway in, 23, 24–25; "mass transit suburbs" in, 262, 386n
Long Island, 110, 295n
Long Island City, 145, 170, 178; as subway suburb, 248, 382n
Long Island Rail Road, 30, 42, 43, 271, 303n, 376n
The Looting of New York (Gaynor), 87
Loud, Ruth McAneny, 331n
Low, Seth, 52, 119, 300n; and congestion of population, 216, 218; and Dual System, 184–185, 189, 191, 210, 216, 218, 240, 266, 350n, 351n, 362n; and "real designers of Greater New York," 210
Lower East Side, 106, 115, 178, 288n, 320n, 321n, 323n; congestion of population, 3, 13, 17, 95, 288n, 318n; ethnic groups in, 18, 95, 99; population dispersal from, 45, 246, 255, 268, 320n; as tenement district, 2, 3, 17, 97–99
Lower Manhattan, 2, 15–16, 90, 163–165; as business center, 12, 15, 93–94, 249, 384n; and Dual System, 196, 222, 226, 270–272, 277–279
Lower Manhattan BRT line, 163, 176, 179; opening date, 285
Lower Manhattan IRT line, 179, 223, 270; opening date, 284

MacInness, Duncan, 198–199, 210
Madison Avenue line, 84, 135
Maltbie, Milo R., 118, 216, 308n; appointed to PSC, 71; and Dual System, 213, 214, 220, 358n, 363n; and IRT preferential, 193, 206, 207, 355n; and rapid transit and city development, 124–125, 334n
Manhattan, 51, 96, 252, 253, 319n; in BRT proposal, 161, 163–166; as business center, 90, 93–94; congestion of population, 20, 154, 317n; Dual System lines, 174–176, 178–179, 181, 185, 222–227, 269–273, 276–280; elevated railroads, 30, 32, 45–46; employment, 90, 94, 249, 391n; first public transit, 15–17; first subways, 38, 41–43; geography of, 12, 92; population, 2, 95; 1790–1997, table 1, 10; *and names of individual communities and lines*
Manhattan Bridge, 51
Manhattan Bridge line, 163, 164, 176, 178, 226, 277, 278
Manhattan Central Business District (CBD), 145, 258–259, 287n, 384; commutation to, 7, 248, 250, 256, 290n, 315n, 370n, 371n, 384n, 394n; and Dual System, 115, 222, 225, 249–250. *See also* Lower Manhattan, Manhattan, and Midtown Manhattan
"Manhattan dispersion effect" (Wallace and Wallace), 324n
Manhattan Railway Company, 25, 30, 34, 39, 41, 50, 126, 131, 146; in Dual System, 180–181, 205, 221, 224–225, 227, 233, 271–273, 357n, 365n; leased by IRT, 43; ridership, 32, 43
Manufacturing, 90, 94, 100, 112, 113, 258–259, 316n, 317n, 391n
Marcuse, Peter, 386n
Markel, Howard, 324n
Martin, John, 115–116, 328n
Martin, Kingsley, 173
Marsh, Benjamin C., 115–116, 330n
"Mass transit suburbs," 262, 382n, 386n, 395n
McAdoo, William G., 141–143
McAneny, George, 150, 152, 157–158, 166, 188, 194, 207, 212, 220, 332n, 355n, 356n, 357n, 369–370n; and assessment plan, 129, 336n; background, 118–122; and Board of Estimate Transit Committee, 6, 137, 157–158; and City Club, 71–72, 120, 153; city planning, 232, 240–244, 343n, 378n; and conferees report, 169, 173–174, 184–185; and Congestion Committee, 115, 153, 328n; and Congestion Commission, 154, 343n; creator of Dual System, 6, 169, 174; defends Dual System, 6–7, 202–204, 216, 220, 265; and Dual System, 173–174, 184–185, 187–188, 190–194, 203–204, 207, 213, 216, 220, 266–268, 357n, 366n; elected borough president of Manhattan, 87–88; and Fusion movement, 86, 126, 312n; and Hearst, 152, 265, 290n, 395n, cartoons, 201, 217; and Low, 119, 184–185; and IRT, 154, 156, 169–170, 202, 355n; as leader in subway decisions, 6, 125, 140, 148–149, 152, 153, 155–159, 170, 216, 232, 240–241, 264–265; and Morgan bank, 396n, cartoon, 217; policy on rapid transit, 155–157, 202–204, 342n; and PSC, 71–73, 118, 122, 123–124, 153–155, 159; and rapid transit and city development, 4, 7, 118–119, 122, 123–124, 202–204, 216, 240, 263–265, 331n, 380n; "Supplementary Report," 209–210; and transportation planning, 140, 148, 155–156, 159, 173–174; and Triborough System, 140, 154, 339n; and zoning, 240–244
McAneny, Marjorie Jacobi, 120–121
The McAneny Report, 174
"The McAneny Subway Plan," 169
McCall, Edward E., 219, 220, 363n, 369n
McCall, John A., 219
McCarroll, William, 115, 172, 206, 355n; appointed to PSC, 71
McClellan, George B., 63–64, 67, 76–77, 88, 310n
McClure's, 61
McDonald, John B., 40–43
McKinley, William, 69
"A menace to our civilization" (Beard), 102
Merchants Association, 207

Merrill, Bradford, 194
MetroLink, 378n
"The metropolis of the world" (Tomkins), 110
Metropolitan Street Railway Company, 34, 53–54, 87, 135; merger with IRT, 56–58
Metropolitan Securities Company, 57–58
Metropolitan Transportation Authority (MTA), 237, 376n; agencies of, 299n, 376n; capital plans, 239–240, 366n
Metz, Herman, 67–68, 76–77, 80, 88
Midtown Manhattan, 1, 249, 384n; in BRT plans, 163–165; and Dual System, 7–8, 222, 249, 263, 267, 271, 277, 277–279
Miller, Cyrus L., 87, 157, 158, 192, 193, 195, 333n, 339n
Mitchel, John Purroy, 126, 332n, 334n, 353n; and assessment plan, 129, 313n; and Dual System, 210, 213, 215–216, 219–221, 359n, 363n; elected mayor, 355n, 356n, 370n; elected president of the Board of Aldermen, 87–88; and Hearst, 124, 194, 356n; and IRT, 147–149, 193; mayoral ambitions, 124, 194; and Triborough System, 124, 132, 136, 148–149, 339n
Montefiore Hospital, 323n
Montgomery, Alabama, 299n
Moore, Deborah Dash, 382n, 388n
Morgan, J. P. (Junior) (Jack), 131, 137, 354n, 355n
Morgan, J.P. (Senior), 202, 216, 289n, 336n, cartoon, 217
Morgan bank, *see* J. P. Morgan and Company
Morgenthau, Henry, 111, 328n
Moses, Robert, 8, 237
Mosholu Preservation Corporation, 260
Mt. Vernon, 84
MTA Bridges and Tunnels, 376n
MTA Long Island Rail Road, 299n, 376n
MTA Metro-North Railroad, 299n, 376n
MTA New York City Transit, 221, 299n, 376n. *See also* New York City Transit Authority
Municipal ownership, 36, 78, 147
Municipal Ownership League, 62, 68, 312n
Municipal Reference Library, 266–267
Murphy, Charles Francis, 152, 204, 215, 353n; and Gaynor, 87, 124, 136, 369n; and 1905 election, 63–64; and 1906 election, 68
Myers, Gustavus, 61, 306n
Myrtle Avenue elevated line, 30, 178, 227, 276, 279, 285

Nassau Street line, *see* Centre Street loop line
National City Bank, 340n
National Consumers League, 111, 121
New Amsterdam, 12
New immigrants, 3, 92–93
New Jersey, 110, 295n
New Law Tenement House Act (1901), 97, 106–107, 250, 301n, 319n, 327n
New Law tenements: rendered obsolete, 253
New Lots line, 180, 224, 272, 372n. *See also* Eastern Parkway line
New Metropolis (Spann), 9
New Utrecht Avenue line, 65, 72, 74, 142, 143, 145, 150, 151, 157, 163. *See also* West End line
New York American, 62, 137, 152, 194, 201
New York Central Railroad, 298n
New York City: as "City of Living Death," 3; development to 1860, 12–19; development, 1860–1910, 90–106; development, 1910–1940, 231–232, 245–256; development since 1940s, 256–262; geographic area of, 92; as world city, 110; *and names of individual subjects*
New York City Charter, *see* City Charter
New York City government, 335n; borrowing capacity, 5, 36–37, 52, 76–78, 127, 129, 139, 148, 158, 166, 289n, 303n, 305n, 317n, 336n, 342n, 344n, 345n, 348n; buys out BRT and IRT, 237; Department of Finance, 210; Department of Health, 20; and Dual System financing, 6, 181–183, 187–194, 196, 198–199, 203–205, 227–230, 234–235, 269, 273, 275, 357n, 367n, 386n, 373n; and financing pre–Dual System rapid transit, 24, 34–37, 41–43, 125–127, 128–130, 132, 135, 137–138, 141, 145–149, 156–158, 161–162, 166, 168, 171–172,

342n; investment in Dual System, 227, 234–235, 269, 273, 275, 367n, 368n, 373n; ownership of rapid transit lines, 36, 78, 147, 181, 228, 237, 273, 281n, 287n; subsidy of rapid transit, 232, 371n. *See also* Board of Estimate
New York City Railway Company, 58, 135
New York City Underground Railroad Company, 27, 28
New York City Transit Authority, 237, 376n. *See also* MTA New York City Transit
New York Civil Service Commission, 119
New York Elevated Railroad Company, 26
New York Evening Journal, 201–202, 214, 217
New York Journal, 62
New York Life Insurance Company, 219
New York Municipal Railway Corporation, 211, 221, 225, 229, 276, 360n, 364n. See also Brooklyn Rapid Transit Company
New York Post, 59, 156, 184
New York Press, 86
New York Standard Union, 169–170
New York State Constitution, 205–206
New York State Legislature, 24, 51–52, 239, 250, 297n; approves PSC legislation, 77–78; and City Charter, 193, 195–196, 243; creates PSC, 70; and Dual System, 200, 206–207, 209, 219; and rapid-transit proposals, 24–29; tenement house legislation, 20, 97–98, 106–107, 301n, 319n, 320n
New York State Public Service Commission for the First District, *see* Public Service Commission
New York State Public Service Commission for the Second District, 70
New York State Transit Commission, 234
New York Stock Exchange, 14
New York Times, 25, 59, 64, 76, 156, 172, 184, 215, 218–219, 260, 344n, 362, 363n; and Morgan bank letter, 218–219, 362n; and "philanthropic subways," 132, 337n
New York World, 61, 119, 312, 361n
Ninth Avenue elevated line, 26, 28, 30, 45, 224; Bronx extension, 83, 145, 224, 271, 365n; eliminated, 375–376n; first rapid transit line in New York, 26
NoHo, 317n
North Central Bronx, 224, 254, 271
Norwood: as subway suburb, 260
Nostrand Avenue line, 180, 224, 272, 284, 348n, 383n
Nurses Settlement House, 328n

Old Guard Republicans, 70
"Old immigrants," 92
Old Law Tenement House Act (1879), 97–98
Olmsted, Frederick Law, 293n
Omnibuses, 9, 15, 16
Onderdonk, Andrew, 41
Open land, *see* Undeveloped land
Orr, Alexander E., 300n
Outer boroughs, 395n, *and names of individual boroughs*

Page-Merritt bill, 307n
Paris, 221, 262, 287n, 318n, 326n
Park Slope, 97
Parks, 98, 241, 320n
Parsons, William Barclay, 328n; plans for rapid transit, 49–52, 59
PATH, 340n
Pelham Bay Park neighborhood: as subway suburb, 254
Pelham line, 50, 65, 73, 84, 138, 139, 143, 154, 163, 168, 170, 179, 183, 224, 246, 255, 270, 271, 338n, 354n; opening date, 284
Pennsylvania Railroad, 19, 120, 195, 196, 198, 355n
Pennsylvania Station, 120, 170, 196, 249, 303n
Perlman, Janice, 395n
Philadelphia, 13, 221
"Philanthropic subways" (*New York Times*), 132, 337n
Phthisis, 323n
Plant, Irving M., 370n, 382n
Platt, Thomas, 54
"Plunderbund," 306n
Plunz, Richard H., 250, 253, 381n; "horizontal city," 244
Pneumonia, 322n

Polio, 105; and Italians, 104
Population, 46, 90, 92, 95, 246; by borough, 1790–1997, table 1, 10; change by district, 1910–1949, table 3, 247; ethnicity of, 3, 17, 18, 31, 45, 92–93, 95, 101, 254–262, 268, 315n, 388n, 390n, 393n; growth of, 1–2, 9, 13, 46, 92, 231, 245–246, 248, 263; in subway suburbs, 231, 245–248, 251, 254–257, 259–262. *See also* Congestion of population
Population of the City of New York, 1890–1930 (Laidlaw), 246
Prague, 318n
Pratt, Edward Ewing, 101–102, 115–117
Preferentials, *see* Brooklyn Rapid Transit Company, Dual System of Rapid Transit, and Interborough Rapid Transit Company
Prendergast, William A., 126, 198, 332n, 345n, 349n, 350n, 355n, 396n; and Dual System, 193–194, 196–197, 216, 220, 227, 299, 368n; elected comptroller, 87–88, 313n, 355n, 370n; and Gaynor, 196–197; and Hearst, 124, 194, 201, 216, 290n, 395n, cartoons, 201, 217; and IRT, 136, 145, 147–148, 193–194, 197, 355n, 356n; and rapid transit and city development, 124, 333n; and Triborough System, 132, 136, 148–149, 339n
Pre–Old Law tenements, 320n
President of the Board of Aldermen: responsibilities of, 333n
Private transit companies: promotion of congestion, 5, 11–12, 24. *See also* Interborough Rapid Transit Company
Progressive reformers, 4, 5, 48, 63, 68, 69, 347n; efforts in tenement districts, 91, 106–107, 111–112; and political power, 88, 91–92, 122, 123–125; and rapid transit and city development, 5, 91, 107, 109–110, 240, 264–265; *and names of individual reformers*
Prostitution, 106
PSC, *see* Public Service Commission
Public bathhouses, 100
Public education, 91, 106–107, 326n
Public health, 19–20, 91, 106–107, 261–262. *See also* Disease *and names of individual diseases*
Public housing, 257–258, 326n, 391n
Public Service Commission (PSC), 5, 49, 68, 75, 91, 114–115, 153–155, 195, 214, 269, 344n; and Board of Estimate, 123, 140, 153–154, 159, 264; and BRT, 211–212, 360n, 364n; and City Club, 71–73; creation of, 4, 68, 70–71; and Dual System, 174, 186, 192, 198, 200, 206–207, 209, 211–212, 220–221, 233, 269, 276, 355n, 364n, 368–369n, 371n; engineering and construction of Dual System, 221, 233, 273, 277, 281, 284–285, 368n, 369n, 371n; and IRT, 73, 125–126, 127, 130–131, 135–137, 140, 143, 146–147, 172, 198, 206, 355n, 364n; legislative proposals, 77–78; and McAdoo proposal, 142–143, 146; and McClellan administration, 76–77, 310n; original members, 71; policy, 73–82, 84–85, 126, 139–140; powers of, 70–71; and rapid-transit financing studies, 74–76, 292n; succeeds RTB, 68–73; and Triborough System, 73–75, 83, 125–127, 129–132, 138–142, 146, 341n
Public transit: first lines, 14–17; as government responsibility, 12, 108–109. *See also* Commuter railroads, Elevated railroads, Horsecars, Omnibuses, Rapid transit, Street railways, Subways
Public utilities: politics of, 60–65
Puerto Ricans, 257, 268, 388n
Pulitzer, Joseph, 213
Putnam, George P., 121
Putnam, Mary, *see* Jacobi, Mary Putnam

Quackenbush, James L., 350n
Queens, 1–2, 239, 295n, 370n; BRT plans for, 161, 164–165, 167–168; and Dual System, 175, 178–180, 185, 222–223, 225–227, 272–273, 277–278, 280, 366n; IRT plans for, 145, 150, 171; population, 1790–1997, table 1, 10; RTB plans for, 51, 56; rapid-transit needs of, 157, 160, 170; and subway suburbs, 240, 245–248, 250–256, 258–262, 268; *and names of individual communities and lines*

Queensboro Bridge, 51, 83; and Dual System lines, 225, 272, 278, 367n, 398n
Queensboro Plaza station, 171, 178, 225, 226, 227, 272
Queens Borough Real Estate Exchange, 67
Queens Boulevard line, 236
Queens Chamber of Commerce, 248
Quigg, Lemuel C., 54, 57, 305n

Railroads, 93, 108. *See also names of individual railroads*
Randel, John, 292n
Rapid transit, 20–22, 45, 48, 54, 72, 108–109, 232, 238–239, 302n, 371n, 376n; defined, 21, 291n; financing as obstacle, 23–24; first lines, 24–32; first proposals, 9, 24–25, 297n; first subways, 33–43; as government responsibility, 23, 91, 107–110, 116–117, 154, 209, 342n; impact of first elevateds and subways, 32, 45–46; inadequacy of, 2, 11, 22, 44–46, 94, 154; Independent Subway System, 236–237; issue in municipal elections, 6, 302n; Manhattan Railway Company proposals, 34, 39; Metropolitan Street Railway Company plans, 54; MTA plans, 239–240; network in 1910, map 1, 31; obstacles to, 23–24; politics as obstacle, 23–24; ridership, 43–44, 237, 250, 372n, table 2, 1901–1998, 44; and saving New York, 1, 90–122, 231, 263, 268; technology, 23, 26–28, 33, 43, 48, 110, 299n; unification, 237. *See also* Dual System of Rapid Transit, Elevated railroads, Rapid transit and city development, Subways, *and names of individual companies, lines, and proposals*
Rapid Transit Act of 1875, 29–30
Rapid Transit Act of 1891, 34
Rapid Transit Act of 1894, 36; amendments, 42, 59, 64, 83, 206, 357–358n
Rapid transit and city development, 1, 4–5, 11, 19–22, 89, 91, 94, 107–110, 113–114, 116–118, 122, 123–125, 153–154, 202–204, 218, 232, 240–241, 263–265, 268, 297n, 331n, 342–343n, 356n, 374n, 380n
Rapid Transit Association, 29
Rapid Transit Board (RTB), 36, 52, 54, 59, 61–65; approves nineteen new routes, 47, 55–56; Committee on Plans, 55; and Contracts Nos. 1 and 2, 41–43, 49; and financing, 36–38, 52, 65–66; first subways, 37–38, 41–43; and Metropolitan Street Railway Company, 53–54; plans for new subways, 37–38, 47, 49–56, 59, 65–68; policy, 53–56; powers of, 36–37, 42
Rapid Transit: Its Effects on Rents and Living Conditions, and How to Get It (Martin), 115–116
Rapid Transit Subway Construction Company, 41
Ravitch, Richard, 377n
Rea, Samuel, 198
Real estate developer: and subway suburbs, 252, 255
Real estate values, 383n, 385n
Regional Plan Association (RPA), 378n
Regional Survey of New York, 245, 383n
Rents: and rapid transit, 115–116; in subway suburbs, 251, 380–381n, 389–390n; in tenement districts, 99
Republican Party, 60, 312n, 313n
The Responsibility of the City Administration in Regard to Subway Construction (McAneny), 202
Richmond Hill, 303n
Richmond, Virginia, 299n
Riis, Jacob, 97, 106, 328n
Robinson, A. P., 25
Robinson, Charles Mulford, 328n
Robinson, Herman, 328n
Rockaway line, 238, 365n
Rome, 110
Roosevelt, Theodore, 106, 294n; and 1906 election, 69–70; and PSC, 70
Root, Elihu: and 1906 election, 69–70
Route mile: defined, 365n
Ryan, Thomas Fortune, 40, 57–58

Sage-Gould interests, 41
Sage, Russell, 34
Savings banks report, 257
Saving New York, 1, 8, 91, 231, 263, 268

Schick, Sandor Evan, 393n
Schieffelin, William Jay, 312n
Schiff, Jacob H., 33, 219, 309n, 323n, 328n, 396n
Schurz, Carl, 119
Sea Beach line, 163, 178, 226, 276, 279, 345n, 399n
Seats: on Dual System lines, 222, 366n
Second Avenue elevated line, 30, 224; elimination of, 238, 377n; extension to Queens, 51, 83, 225, 272
Second Avenue subway line, 238–239, 377n, 378n
Segregation, 15, 17, 96, 294n; and African-Americans, 257
Seligman, Isaac N., 309n, 328n
Settlement houses, 91, 116; and Congestion Committee, 111–112; *and names of individual settlement houses*
Seventh Avenue line, 50, 82, 133, 137, 170, 179, 196, 223, 270, 284
Shearn, Clarence J., 207, 215
Shepard, Edward M., 119–120
Shonts, Theodore P., 130–131, 157–158, 170, 337n; and Dual System, 188–190, 205, 208, 351n; and Gaynor, 132–135; and Morgan bank, 137, 336n, 340n
Silverman, Joseph, 101, 104
Simkhovitch, Mary, 111, 289n, 328n
Sixth Avenue elevated line, 30, 298n; replaced by IND subway, 375n
Sixty-third Street line, 366n
Skyscrapers, 90, 93
Slums, *see* Tenement districts
Smallpox, 103, 105
Smith, Charles Sprague, 328n
Spengler, Edwin H., 384n, 385n
Sprague, Frank J., 33, 299n
SoHo, 317n
South Bronx, 32, 179, 253, 258, 393n; as tenement district, 2, 5, 45, 90, 114–115, 203, 252, 257, 379n
South Bronx Property Owners Association, 339n
South Queens: as subway suburb, 248, 383n
Standing Committee on the City Plan, 241, 378–379n
Starin, John H., 300n
Staten Island, 1, 295n, 319n, 370n; and Fourth Avenue line, 157, 367n; population of, 1790–1997, table 1, 10
State Gas and Electric Commission, 70
State Legislature, *see* New York State Legislature
State Railroad Commission, 70
Steers, Alfred, 87, 193, 332n, 337n
Steinway, William, 300n
Stella, Antonio, 325n, 328n
Stewart, A. T., 28
Stimson, Henry L., 353n
Streetcars, 256
Street railways: ridership, 299n, 301n
Street system, 2, 9, 90; grid plans, 13–14
Suburban Development (McAneny), 115
Suburban Rapid Transit Company, 30
Suburbs, 238, 259; definition of, 245, 381n, 382n
The Subway Deal (Baker), 61
Subways, 302n; costs, compared to elevateds, 348n; cost of first lines, 41–42, 55, 126, 342n; first lines, 2, 11, 33–43, 45, 54–55, 91; history of, 266–267; and saving New York, 1, 90–122, 231, 263, 268; as term for New York's rapid transit network, 291n. *See also* Dual System of Rapid Transit, Elevated railroads, Rapid transit, *and names of individual companies, lines, and proposals*
Subway suburbs, 1, 222, 231–232, 245–262, 267–268, 370n, 389n, 390n; automobile use in, 256; commutation, 248, 250, 256, 260–261, 290n, 370–371n, 382–383n; and Dual System, 7, 231, 244, 246, 248, 250–253, 256, 259, 260–262, 263, 267–268, 290n, 370–371n; daily life in, 232, 251, 254; ethnicity in, 254–256, 259–261, 268, 388n, 392n; geographic area of, 231, 245–246, 370n; health in, 261; and "horizontal city," 244; housing in, 231, 250–254, 260, 381n, 386n, 387n; and "mass transit suburbs," 262, 382n, 386n, 395n; mix of housing, 252–254; and New York economy, 250–251, 258–259; population growth, 1910–1940, table 3, 247; rents in, 251, 380–381n, 389–390n

Sulzer, William G., 214–216, 218–219, 361n, 362n
Sunnyside: as subway suburb, 256
"Supplementary Report" (McAneny), 209–210
Supreme Court: and Dual System, 208–209
Supreme Court, Appellate Division: and Dual System, 209
Swanstrom, J. Edward, 147
Sweatshops, 99, 100, 103, 112

Tammany Hall, 38–40, 60–61, 63–64, 119, 195, 207, 306n
Taxpayers Association of the Thirty-second Ward, 339n
Temple Emanu-El, 101
Tenement districts, 2, 4–5, 9, 11, 37, 97, 99, 101, 257, 288n; arson in, 3, 99; "bestial overcrowding," 3; congestion of population, 2, 9, 91, 94–98, 101; and crime, 3, 9, 19, 99–101, 114; development along elevated lines, 32; disease in, 3, 18–19, 99–105, 114; dispersal from, 231, 246, 257; ethnicity of, 18, 92–93, 251, 256–257, 259; and immigrants, 9, 18, 92–94, 100, 104–106, 246, 319n; problems in mid twentieth century, 256–258; rents, 99, 115–116, 251; morality in, 11, 101; population of, 19, 95, 246, table 3, 247; sanitation in, 18–19, 99–101; as threat, 3, 17–19, 100–106
Tenement House Department, 3
Tenement Houses, *see* Tenements
"Tenement Houses and Tuberculosis," 112
Tenement Museum, 320n
"Tenement to split level," 259
Tenements, 2, 14, 17, 252, 258, 321n; and children, 101, 104–105; and Congestion Committee, 112; daily life in, 9, 17–19, 97–106; definition of, 97, 319n; invention of, 17; New Law, 106–107, 253, 319n; New York State legislation, 20, 97–98, 106–107, 301n, 319n, 320n; number of, 3, 19, 319n; Old Law, 97–98, 319n; population in, 97; pre–Old Law, 17–18, 320n; sweatshops in, 99, 100, 103, 112; and tuberculosis, 103–104; and zoning, 242–244
The Theory of Transportation (Cooley), 107–109, 327n
Third Avenue elevated line, 30, 83, 224; in Bronx, 30; connection to first subway, 224; elimination of, 238, 377n; Webster Avenue extension to White Plains Road line, 50, 145, 224, 271
Third Avenue (Brooklyn) elevated line, 32, 167
Third Avenue subway line, 55, 82
Thirty-fourth Street crosstown line, 55
Thirty-fourth Street elevated line, 30
Thompson, George F.: and investigation of Dual System, 308n
Thompson Committees, 308n, 333n, 396n
Times Square station, 179
Tobier, Emanuel, 98
Tomkins, Calvin, 110, 328n
Tomkins Square Park, 320n
Towns, Mirabeau, 132
Track mile: defined, 365n
"Traction Trust" (Hearst), 62, 152, 306n
Transit Committee of the Board of Estimate, 6, 126, 127, 128, 136, 148–150, 155–160, 174, 192
Transportation: as government responsibility, 91, 107–110, 116–117, 154, 209, 342n; in pre-automobile age New York, 315n; social function of, 107–109
Transportation planning, 72–73, 108–110; and Dual System, 146, 155–156, 159, 173–174, 309n
TriBeCa, 317n
Triborough Bridge and Tunnel Authority, 376n
Triborough System, 6, 79–80, 139, 141, 158, 181, 195, 279, 339n; and Board of Estimate, 126–127, 129–130, 133, 140, 146–147, 339n; cost of, 126, 139–140, 312n; demise of, 138–142, 158, 160; financing of, 74–76, 125, 127, 129–130, 133, 311n; and Gaynor, 133–136, 337n; and IRT, 84, 125, 131–134; map 2, 66; and McAdoo, 141–142; McAneny and, 140, 154, 339n; and Mitchel, 124, 132, 136, 148–149, 339n; and Prendergast, 132, 136, 148–149, 339n; and PSC,

Triborough System *(continued)* 73–75, 83–84, 125–127, 129–132, 138–142, 146, 341n; and RTB, 65; and Willcox, 80, 140
Tuberculosis, 102–105, 112, 322n, 323n, 324–325n; and Congestion Committee, 112; and Hughes, 324n; as Jewish disease, 104, 324–325n
Tuberculosis League, 324n
Tweed, William Marcy, 27–29, 216
Typhoid fever, 3, 102–103
Typhus, 3, 18, 103

Ultan, Lloyd, 388n
Undeveloped land, 2, 20, 95–96, 173, 238, 295n
Unification, 237
Union Square station, 176, 226
University Heights: as subway suburb, 254, 256
Upper-class housing, 96–97

Veiller, Lawrence, 106, 304n, 314n, 328n; and "typical New York tenement," 98
Venice, 110
Von Siemens, Werner, 33

Wagner bill, 207
Wagner, Robert F., 207, 215
Wakefield: as subway suburb, 387–388n
Wald, Lillian, 328n
Walker, James J., 241, 379n
"Walking city," 14–15
Wall Street: as defensive barrier, 12. *See also* Lower Manhattan
Wall Street banks, 188. *See also names of individual banks*
Wall Street district, *see* Lower Manhattan
Wallace, Deborah, and Roderick, 324n
Warburg, Felix M., 309n
Warburg, Paul M., 309n, 328n
Washington, George: residence on Cherry Street, 13, 17
Washington Square, 15
Weber, Adna Ferrin, 109–110
Webster Avenue extension of Third Avenue elevated line, 50, 145, 224, 271
Weiner, Joseph L., 235
West Bronx, 50, 143, 223, 224; as subway suburb, 246, 248, 382n, 393–394n
Westchester, 110, 224, 295n
West End line, 163, 226, 279, 345n; opening date, 282. *See also* New Utrecht Avenue line
West Farms, 38
Westphal, Dart, 260
West Side, 33, 38, 45, 49–50, 96, 143; and Dual System, 223, 224, 270, 271
West Side and Yonkers Patent Railway Company, 26
White, Gaylord S., 328n
White Plains Road line, 50, 84, 133, 145, 163, 170, 179, 224, 270–271; opening date, 284
Whitney, William C., 40, 57–58
Whitney-Ryan group, 40–41
Widener, P. A. B., 40
Willcox, William R., 135, 159, 353n; appointed to PSC, 71; and BRT, 79–80, 140; and Dual System, 187–188, 190–192, 207, 212–216, 266, 352n, 355n, 361n; and Hearst, 290n, cartoon, 217; and IRT, 79–82, 85, 131, 205–206; and McAdoo offer, 142–143; and McAneny, 118; and rapid transit and city development, 124–125, 153–154, 240, 264–265, 334n; and Triborough System, 80, 140
Williams, George V. S.: appointed to PSC, 207–208; and Dual System, 220, 358n
Williams, Timothy S., 161; and BRT proposal, 161, 163–166, 168–169; and IRT, 173
Williamsburg, 2, 32, 95, 150, 213
Williamsburg Bridge, 51
Williamsburg Bridge line, 51, 226, 226–227
Willson, Hugh B., 24–26
Winter, E. W., 151–152, 161
Woodlawn Cemetery, 76
Woodside: as subway suburb, 251, 256
Woodside-Corona line, 178, 180, 184, 204–205. *See also* Corona-Flushing line, Flushing line, and Woodside line
Woodside line, 167, 168, 169, 171. See also *See also* Corona-Flushing line, Flushing line, and Woodside-Corona line

Woolworth Building, 90
Working class families, 21–22; and subway suburbs, 251, 262; and tenement districts, 94, 96–98
World War I: impact on Dual System finances, 232, 235
Wright, Henry, 14, 174

Yellow Fever, 18
Yorkville, 32

"Zone of Emergence," 382n
Zoning, 232, 241–244; and congestion of population, 113, 117, 154; 1916 zoning resolution, 243, 250, 380n

About the Author

Dr. Peter Derrick works as the Archivist for The Bronx County Historical Society, where he also edits the Society's semi-annual *Journal*. He earned his Ph.D. from New York University in 1979. His research has focused on major political decisions regarding the expansion and capital improvement of New York's subway system. He has also had practical experience working for the Metropolitan Transportation Authority and the New York State Legislature, holding several positions dealing with the capital renewal and expansion of the transit network in the New York region.

CPSIA information can be obtained
at www.ICGtesting.com
Printed in the USA
JSHW021923030821
17532JS00001B/19

9 780814 719541